THE RHETORIC OF FREE SPEECH IN LATE ANTIQUITY AND THE EARLY MIDDLE AGES

The early Middle Ages is not a period traditionally associated with free speech. It is still widely held that free speech declined towards the end of Antiquity, disappearing completely at the beginning of the Middle Ages, and only re-emerging in the Renaissance, when people finally learned to think and speak for themselves again. Challenging this tenacious image, Irene van Renswoude reveals that there was room for political criticism and dissent in this period, as long as critics employed the right rhetoric and adhered to scripted roles. This study of the rhetoric of free speech from c. 200 to c. 900 AD explores the cultural rules and rhetorical performances that shaped practices of delivering criticism from Antiquity to the Middle Ages, examining the rhetorical strategies in the letters and narratives of the late antique and early medieval men, and a few women, who ventured to speak the truth to the powerful.

IRENE VAN RENSWOUDE is Professor of Medieval Manuscripts and Cultural History at the University of Amsterdam, and researcher at Huygens ING, a research institute of the Royal Netherlands Academy of Arts and Sciences. She was awarded the Heineken Young Scientist Award for History for her research on free speech and censorship, and is the co-editor of several volumes, including *Strategies of Writing: Studies on Texts and Trust in the Middle Ages* (2008) and *The Annotated Book in the Early Middle Ages* (2017).

Cambridge Studies in Medieval Life and Thought
Fourth Series

General Editor
ROSAMOND MCKITTERICK
Emeritus Professor of Medieval History, University of Cambridge, and Fellow of Sidney Sussex College

Advisory Editors
CHRISTOPHER BRIGGS
Lecturer in Medieval British Social and Economic History, University of Cambridge

ADAM J. KOSTO
Professor of History, Columbia University

ALICE RIO
Professor of Medieval History, King's College London

MAGNUS RYAN
University Lecturer in History, University of Cambridge, and Fellow of Peterhouse

The series *Cambridge Studies in Medieval Life and Thought* was inaugurated by G.G. Coulton in 1921; Professor Rosamond McKitterick now acts as General Editor of the Fourth Series, with Dr Christopher Briggs, Professor Adam J. Kosto, Professor Alice Rio and Dr Magnus Ryan as Advisory Editors. The series brings together outstanding work by medieval scholars over a wide range of human endeavour extending from political economy to the history of ideas.

This is book 115 in the series, and a full list of titles in the series can be found at:
www.cambridge.org/medievallifeandthought

THE RHETORIC OF FREE SPEECH IN LATE ANTIQUITY AND THE EARLY MIDDLE AGES

IRENE VAN RENSWOUDE
University of Amsterdam and Huygens ING, The Netherlands

CAMBRIDGE
UNIVERSITY PRESS

University Printing House, Cambridge CB2 8BS, United Kingdom

One Liberty Plaza, 20th Floor, New York, NY 10006, USA

477 Williamstown Road, Port Melbourne, VIC 3207, Australia

314–321, 3rd Floor, Plot 3, Splendor Forum, Jasola District Centre,
New Delhi – 110025, India

79 Anson Road, #06–04/06, Singapore 079906

Cambridge University Press is part of the University of Cambridge.

It furthers the University's mission by disseminating knowledge in the pursuit of education, learning, and research at the highest international levels of excellence.

www.cambridge.org
Information on this title: www.cambridge.org/9781107038134
DOI: 10.1017/9781139811941

© Irene van Renswoude 2019

This publication is in copyright. Subject to statutory exception
and to the provisions of relevant collective licensing agreements,
no reproduction of any part may take place without the written
permission of Cambridge University Press.

First published 2019

Printed in the United Kingdom by TJ International Ltd, Padstow Cornwall

A catalogue record for this publication is available from the British Library.

Library of Congress Cataloging-in-Publication Data
NAMES: Renswoude, Irene van, author.
TITLE: The rhetoric of free speech in late antiquity and the early Middle Ages /
Irene van Renswoude.
OTHER TITLES: Cambridge studies in medieval life and thought ; 4th ser., 115.
DESCRIPTION: Cambridge, United Kingdom : Cambridge University Press, 2019. |
Series: Cambridge studies in medieval life and thought ; fourth series, 115
IDENTIFIERS: LCCN 2019014541 | ISBN 9781107038134
SUBJECTS: LCSH: Latin literature, Medieval and modern – History and criticism. | Christian literature, Early – Latin authors. | Freedom of speech – Europe, Western – History – To 1500. | Freedom of speech – Religious aspects – Christianity. | Rhetoric – Political aspects. | Rhetoric – Social aspects. | Criticism, Personal, in literature.
CLASSIFICATION: LCC PA8035 .R46 2019 | DDC 870.8/003–dc23
LC record available at https://lccn.loc.gov/2019014541

ISBN 978-1-107-03813-4 Hardback

Cambridge University Press has no responsibility for the persistence or accuracy of URLs for external or third-party internet websites referred to in this publication and does not guarantee that any content on such websites is, or will remain, accurate or appropriate.

For Janneke

CONTENTS

Acknowledgements	*page* viii
List of Abbreviations	ix
INTRODUCTION	1
Part I	19
1 THE STEADFAST MARTYR	21
2 HILARY OF POITIERS	41
3 THE DETACHED PHILOSOPHER	63
4 AMBROSE OF MILAN	87
5 THE SILENT ASCETIC	109
EPILOGUE PART I	127
Part II	131
6 THE FRANK HOLY MAN	133
7 GREGORY OF TOURS	161
8 THE WISE ADVISER	180
9 AGOBARD OF LYON	206
10 POPE GREGORY	230
EPILOGUE PART II	243
Bibliography	250
Index	274

ACKNOWLEDGEMENTS

This book grew from my doctoral thesis on late antique and early medieval truth-tellers entitled *Licence to Speak*, which I completed in 2011 at the Research Institute for History and Culture of Utrecht University. Throughout the process of turning this dissertation into a book, I had help from my own truth-tellers who sharpened my thinking, read chapters or commented on drafts and papers that served as preliminary studies. I would like to thank Mariken Teeuwen, Carine van Rhijn, Rutger Kramer, Walter Pohl, Els Rose, Irene O'Daly, Henry Mayr-Harting, Jinty Nelson, Stuart Airlie, Peter Raedts, Courtney Booker and Conrad Leyser for their advice and encouragements. I am very grateful to the anonymous CUP reviewer, whose report greatly helped me to clarify my arguments. Now that I have discovered the identity of this reviewer, I am pleased to be able to thank Richard Flower by name.

Among the colleagues and friends who supported me over the years, my gratitude goes to four people in particular, without whom I could not have written or completed this book. Mary Garrison put me on the track of free speech many years ago. She gave me a copy of Foucault's *Fearless Speech*, after which I was hooked on the topic. Her research on early medieval *parrhesia* has been a source of inspiration, and I have profited immensely from her advice. Special thanks go to Mayke de Jong, my former supervisor, for her unwavering support over the years. While I wrote this book, she completed her *Epitaph for an Era*. It was a great pleasure to share the joys, and the occasional burdens, of writing with her. Rosamond McKitterick carefully read the entire manuscript and offered invaluable advice and suggestions for improvement. I cannot thank Rosamond and Mayke enough for prodding me to finalise the manuscript, when other obligations and projects got in the way. Lastly, I want to thank my long-time friend and inspiring colleague Janneke Raaijmakers. Janneke has read every version of every chapter of this book, until the very last footnote, and has been a true critic in the best sense of the word. This book is dedicated to her.

ABBREVIATIONS

ACM	*The Acts of the Christian Martyrs*, ed. and trans. H. Musurillo, Oxford Early Christian Texts (Oxford, 1972)
Atti e passioni	A. A. R. Bastiaensen, A. Hilhorst, G. A. A. Kortekaas, A. P. Orbán, M. M. van Assendelft (eds.), *Atti e passioni dei martiri*, Scrittori greci e latini (Milan, 1987)
BAV	[Vatican,] Biblioteca Apostolica Vaticana
BnF	[Paris,] Bibliothèque nationale de France
CCCM	*Corpus Christianorum, Continuatio Mediaevalis* (Turnhout, 1966–)
CCSL	*Corpus Christianorum, Series Latina* (Turnhout, 1952–)
CSEL	*Corpus Scriptorum Ecclesiasticorum Latinorum* (Vienna, 1866–)
GCS	*Die griechischen christlichen Schriftsteller* (Leipzig, 1897; NS Berlin, 1995–)
LCL	*Loeb Classical Library* (Cambridge, MA; London, 1912–)
MGH	*Monumenta Germaniae Historica*

	AA	*Auctores antiquissimi*, 15 vols (Berlin, 1877–1919)
	Conc.	*Concilia, Legum sectio* III, *Concilia* II, ed. A. Werminghoff (Hanover, 1906–8)
	Epp.	Epistulae III-VII (*Epistulae merovingici et karolini aevi*) (Hanover, 1892–1939)
	SRG	*Scriptores rerum Germanicarum in usum scholarum separatim editi* (Hanover, 1871–1987)

List of Abbreviations

SRM	*Scriptores rerum Merovingicarum*, ed. B. Krusch and W. Levison, 7 vols (Hanover, 1885–1951)
SS	*Scriptores* in folio, 30 vols (Hanover, 1826–1924)
NPNF-2	*Nicene and Post-Nicene Fathers*, second series, ed. P. Schaff and H. Wace (Peabody, 1890–)
PG	*Patrologiae Cursus Completus, Series Graeca*, ed. J. P. Migne (Paris, 1857–1866)
PL	*Patrologiae Cursus Completus, Series Latina*, ed. J. P. Migne (Paris, 1841–1864)
RLM	*Rhetores latini minores*, ed. C. Halm (Leipzig, 1863)
SC	*Sources Chrétiennes* (Paris, 1941–)

INTRODUCTION

It was the time of the sacred festival in honour of Jupiter Capitolinus. Emperor Commodus (r. 177–92 AD) had just taken his seat in the imperial chair to watch the performance of a group of famous actors. An orderly crowd filled the theatre and quietly occupied their assigned seats. Suddenly a half-naked philosopher, carrying a staff in his hand and a leather bag on his shoulder, jumped onto the stage. Before anyone could say anything to stop him, he silenced the audience with a sweep of his hand and said: 'Commodus, this is no time to celebrate festivals and devote yourself to shows! The sword of Prefect Perennis is at your throat. Unless you take precautions, you shall be destroyed before you realise it.'[1] According to the Greek historian Herodian of Antioch (d. 240 AD), who recounts this story in his *History of the Empire*, the emperor was thunderstruck. Although everyone suspected the words were true, Herodian says, they pretended not to believe them. The man was dragged from the stage, and executed as a punishment for his insane lies. Although it later turned out the philosopher was right and the emperor was indeed in danger, Herodian shows no moral indignation when he described the philosopher's death. He judges the man to have 'paid the penalty for his ill-timed free speech (*parrhesia*)'.[2]

Throughout Antiquity, free speech (*parrhesia* in Greek, *libertas* in Latin) was a highly valued political and social virtue. Individuals who had the courage to speak truth to power were much admired by their contemporaries, at least in theory. Speaking freely before authorities was not without danger, as Herodian's philosopher found out to his cost. Not only did he incur the wrath of the emperor, he also suffered Herodian's criticism for speaking out at the wrong time and in the wrong place. Rhetoricians were keenly aware of the risks of speaking one's mind to

---

[1] Herodian, *History of the Empire* 1, 9, 4, ed. and trans. Whittaker, LCL 454, pp. 54–5.
[2] Ibid. 1, 9, 5, ed. and trans. Whittaker, LCL 454, pp. 56–7.

Introduction

those in power, and showed a pragmatic approach to the ideal of free speech. From the first century BC onwards, recommendations on how to criticise the powerful in a way that was both effective *and* safe were incorporated into handbooks on rhetoric.[3] Nowadays, rhetoric, the art of persuasion, has become almost synonymous with insincerity. 'That's just rhetoric' is a proverbial expression used to dismiss a political speech as empty verbiage. In Antiquity, however, rhetoric and truth were intricately related, although their relationship was culturally strained. One strand of rhetoric was considered to have a special relation to the truth, namely, the rhetoric of free speech. Teachers of rhetoric offered practical suggestions about what to say and what not to say in conversation with someone of superior rank. Some rhetoricians advocated indirect and veiled language, while others discussed more direct strategies to deliver the truth to a ruler's face.

As rhetoricians in Antiquity recognised, free speech is an idealistic construction. It is a culturally significant rhetorical performance that adheres to a social script. The Roman rhetorician Quintilian (first century AD) devoted much attention to the rhetorical figure of free speech in his *Institutes of Oratory*.[4] He advised his students on how to offer criticism or unwelcome opinions to authorities. He strongly recommended always to heed time, place and circumstances, as well as status difference and decorum. What was appropriate for one person to say was inappropriate for another.[5] Surely there was such a thing as honourable frankness, he said, but frank words were not tolerated from everyone and were certainly not appropriate on every occasion.[6] In his opinion, free speech was only rarely free. Surely some people truly spoke freely, but as soon as persuasion came into play, he argued, 'free speech' was no longer free, but belonged to the realm of rhetoric.[7]

What we can learn from the rhetorical handbooks of Quintilian and other ancient rhetoricians is that free speech is the result of intricate negotiations within any given society concerning who is allowed to speak, for how long and under what circumstances. Rhetoricians

---

[3] See for example *Rhetorica ad Herennium* (first century BC) IV, 36–7 (*licentia*), ed. Caplan, LCL 403, pp. 349–55; Rutilius Lupus, *De figuris sententiarum et elocutionis* (first century AD) II, 18 (*parrhesia*) ed. Halm, *RLM* pp. 20, 21; Quintilian, *Institutio oratoria* (first century AD) IX, 2, 26–9 (*licentia, parrhesia*) and XI, I, 37 (*libertas*), ed. Russell, LCL 127, pp. 46–8 and LCL 494, p. 28; Julius Rufinianus, *De figuris sententiarum et elocutionis* (fourth century AD) 33 (*parresia, oratio libera, licentia*), ed. Halm, *RLM*, p. 46; *Carmen de figuris vel schematibus* (fourth or fifth century AD), vv. 130–3 (*parrhesia*), ed. Halm, *RLM*, p. 68.
[4] Quintilian, *Institutio oratoria* IX, 2, 26–9, ed. Russell, LCL 127, p.46–9.
[5] Ibid. III, 8, 48, ed. Russell, LCL 125, p. 138 and XI, 1, 36–8, 43–59, ed. Russell, LCL 494, pp. 26–8, 30–8.
[6] Ibid. XI, 1, 37, ed. Russell, LCL 494, p. 28.
[7] Ibid. IX, 2, 26–7, ed. Russell, LCL 127, pp. 46–8.

Introduction

acknowledged that there are unspoken rules and social codes that determine what we can and cannot say — that is, if we want to get our message across to an audience. Even within cultures that we tend to regard as tolerant and liberal, as the literary theorist Stanley Fish states in his book *There's No Such Thing as Free Speech: And It's a Good Thing, Too*, there are certain taboos that cannot be broken and social boundaries that cannot be crossed. He observes that free speech is possible only against the silent background of what cannot be said.[8]

Free speech is not a natural given; it is a cultural construction, governed by social norms, legal rules, rhetorical conventions and scripted roles. This book is about the history of that cultural construction. It deals with the rhetoric of free speech from c. 200 to c. 900 AD and studies the cultural rules and rhetorical performances that shaped practices of delivering criticism from Antiquity to the Middle Ages. In this book, I explore the processes of transformation by which the classical tradition of free speech was transmitted to the Middle Ages. I examine the continuities and changes in rhetorical strategies for expressing criticism in letters and narratives of late antique and early medieval authors, who ventured to speak the truth to the powerful. The authors whose speeches and letters are discussed in this book were outspoken figures in their own day; some of them could even be called political dissidents. The martyr Perpetua (d. 202), Bishop Hilary (d. 368), the missionary monk Columban (d. 615) and Bishop Agobard (d. 840), to name but a few, employed a rhetoric of free speech to communicate what they considered to be the truth to the rulers of their day. To what extent, if at all, was their rhetoric related to the classical tradition of free speech? And can we detect in their writings the same traditional values that were once connected to the ancient practice of truth-telling?

The early Middle Ages is not a period one readily associates with free speech. Studies on the history of free speech tend to pass over the early Middle Ages and go straight from Antiquity to the early modern period.[9] Only recently, the editors of *The Art of Veiled Speech* characterised texts from fifth-century Athens and Republican Rome as 'famous for setting the benchmark for free speech', and texts from the medieval period as equally famous for setting the standard for censorship.[10] It is still widely held that free speech declined towards the end of Antiquity, disappeared completely with the beginning of the Middle Ages, and only re-emerged in the Renaissance, when people finally learned to think and speak for

---

[8] Fish, *There's No Such Thing as Free Speech*, p. 104.
[9] A case in point is Smit, van Urk (eds.), *Parrhesia: Ancient and Modern Perspectives*.
[10] See the blurb of Baltussen, Davis (eds.), *The Art of Veiled Speech*.

Introduction

themselves again.[11] This tenacious image is based on the preconception that free expression was unthinkable in a period in which 'the Church' was dominant and religious diversity was suppressed. And yet, as we shall see in the following chapters, the ancient tradition of free speech did not so much become extinct, as take on different cultural shapes. Dissident speakers of late Antiquity and the early Middle Ages often styled themselves, for example, as outcasts and as marginal speakers. Yet their message could find an audience only with the support of people who were connected to the 'centre' that they wished to criticise. Free speech rarely reaches an audience without any relation to structures of power and authority. The essence of creating a 'licence to speak' is that it is a *licence*, and a licence has to be granted by an institution. Regardless of whether this institution is a political assembly, a community, a jury or a ruler, someone who is in charge of the forum and decides its rules has to grant the speaker permission to speak. As Pierre Bourdieu argues in *Language and Symbolic Power*, no speech can be effective if the speaker holds no authority whatsoever to speak.[12] The mechanism of this relation between effective speech and authority, he suggests, can best be exemplified by the Greek ritual of the passing of the *skeptron*. In the *Iliad*, Homer describes the custom at assemblies of passing a staff, belonging to the ruler or whoever was in charge of the meeting, to a person who wished to take the floor, to indicate that he was allowed to let his opinion become known.[13] No matter how boldly or audaciously the speaker subsequently expressed his opinion, the *skeptron* showed that he could do so, because he had been granted permission. Now as much as then, free speech is the result of careful construction, negotiation and ritual setting. Its effectiveness depends on the willingness of others to listen.

A BRIEF HISTORY OF FREE SPEECH IN ANTIQUITY

Most scholars are of the opinion that free speech originated in the Greek world and was intrinsically connected to the rise of democracy.[14] Others, however, argue that the need for free speech is a universal phenomenon that exists in most societies and ages, at least in the form of improvised expressions of opinion, such as heckling and shouting.[15] Whatever its

---

[11] Hargreaves, *The First Freedom*; Davis, *The Origins of Modern Freedom in the West*, p. 1; More nuanced are Tierney, 'Freedom and the medieval church', p. 65, and Bouwsma, 'Liberty in the Renaissance', p. 203.
[12] Bourdieu, *Language and Symbolic Power*, pp. 107–16.   [13] Homer, *Iliad* II, 275–85.
[14] For a background of (and nuance on) this idea, see the introduction of Sluiter and Rosen in *Freedom of Speech*, pp. 1–19.
[15] Momigliano, 'Freedom of speech in Antiquity'.

Introduction

precise origin, the Greeks turned free speech into a political and communal value. They developed the concept and gave it a specific name.[16] The notion of *parrhesia,* to be translated as 'free speech', 'frank speech' or 'frankness in speaking the truth', emerged in Greek literature from about the fifth century BC, the time when citizens of the city-state of Athens obtained the political and civic privilege (*isegoria* or *parrhesia*) to speak freely in political forums. The privilege was, however, granted only to free male citizens and did not extend to women, foreigners, immigrants or slaves.[17] The privilege to speak freely, moreover, held no guarantees for the personal safety of the speaker.[18] As Frederick Ahl noted, Greek writers of fifth- and fourth-century Athens were keenly aware that expressing unpopular opinions about religious, moral or political issues was dangerous, even in a democracy.[19]

By the third century BC, when democracy in Athens had given way to oligarchy and eventually to autocracy, *parrhesia* had changed from an institutional privilege to speak freely in public meetings to a personal, ethical practice of speaking the truth.[20] Under the influence of Epicurean, Cynic and Stoic philosophy, *parrhesia* entered the field of moral philosophy. Ethical notions of truth-telling checked the limits of what could, or should, be said. A genuine *parrhesiast* (truth-teller) did not say anything he pleased, but only what he knew to be true. *Parrhesia* came to be seen as the virtue par excellence of a select group of philosophers, whose opinion was considered valuable on the grounds that they led a virtuous life, and therefore had access to the truth. Stoics further elaborated the ethical definition of *parrhesia* in connection to self-knowledge and self-control. They held that only those who were free from passions, such as anger and jealousy, could truly speak freely. The Epicureans appreciated *parrhesia* above all as a quality of friendship and an instrument of moral correction. For them, moral correction was a means of improving oneself, provided the admonition was offered by a well-meaning friend. Just as a physician cures a physical disease by applying the right dose of medication, so, they believed, friends should cure each other's spiritual ailments by speaking the truth frankly.[21]

In the Roman world, *parrhesia* was adopted as a Greek loanword,[22] but free speech also went by its own Latin name: *libertas*. This word was used

---

[16] Raaflaub, 'Aristocracy and freedom of speech', p. 42.
[17] Balot, 'Free speech, courage and democratic deliberation', p. 233.
[18] Momigliano, 'Freedom of speech in Antiquity', p. 258.
[19] Ahl, 'The art of safe criticism', p. 174.
[20] Bartelink, *Quelques observations sur* παρρησία, p. 10.
[21] Glad, 'Philodemus on friendship and frank speech'.
[22] See the Latin rhetorical treatises listed in note 3.

Introduction

to denote the free status of the citizen as well as his freedom of speech. The fact that *libertas* could mean both free speech and free status shows how much the two values were linked in Roman thought, and underlines the fact that citizenship and a free status were a prerequisite for freedom of speech.[23] *Libertas* was a key concept in Roman thought. It was connected to the ideals of the Roman Republic, long after that republic was gone. When Roman historiographers praised the freedom of speech of certain individuals, who offered frank or honest counsel, or who courageously stood up to a ruler, the ideals of the Republic kept resounding in their use of the term *libertas*.[24] While in Greek literature such outspoken individuals were usually philosophers and outsiders, in Roman historiography they were members of the Roman establishment, such as senators, orators, generals or the emperor's ministers. Yet the free-speaking outsider continued to feature in Roman histories, notably as the embodiment of political opposition. Suetonius recounted in his *Lives of the Caesars* (c. 121 AD) how Emperor Vespasian (r. 69–79 AD) 'tolerated the outspokenness of his friends and the impudence of philosophers',[25] while Tacitus (d. 117) tended to attribute freedom of speech to men outside the senate, such as Cicero's friend Atticus, who shied away from politics and refused to express allegiance to one particular party, but whose opinion was valued by everyone.[26]

In Antiquity, *parrhesia* stood in an uneasy relation to rhetoric. *Parrhesia* was seen as a type of speech that was open, straightforward and sincere, without ornamentation or cover: the precise opposite of speaking with rhetorical flavour. Yet when the notion of free speech became embedded in Roman oratory, *parrhesia* was included among the rhetorical figures. Antique and late antique Latin rhetoricians incorporated the Greek notion of *parrhesia* into their system of rhetoric and translated it as *libertas*, *licentia* or *oratio libera*.[27] In Latin there was not one specific term to translate the Greek *parrhesia*, and each choice of translation implied a different interpretation or evaluation. When *parrhesia* was translated as *licentia*, an element of criticism or reservation was often implied, while the term *libertas* usually expressed a positive evaluation of freedom of speech.[28] In the Roman world, the rhetoric of free speech moved in a different social and political setting from that of the ancient Greeks. In

---

[23] Raaflaub, 'Aristocracy and freedom of speech', pp. 43, 46, Baltussen, Davis, 'Parrhesia, free speech and self-censorship', p. 1–2.
[24] Vielberg, *Untertanentopik*, p. 35.
[25] Suetonius, *De vita Caesarum* 8, 13: 'Amicorum libertatem, causidicorum figuras ac philosophorum contumaciam lenissime tulit.'
[26] Vielberg, *Untertanentopik*, p. 34.   [27] See note 3.
[28] Wirszubski, *Libertas*, p. 7, Braund, 'Libertas or licentia?', p. 409; compare Quintilian, *Institutio oratoria* XI, 1, 37, ed. Russell, LCL 494, p. 28: 'vox honestissimae libertatis'.

Introduction

the Athenian democracy, *parrhesia* had been a civic privilege, in the Hellenistic period, it became a moral duty, and in Rome, frank speech became connected with the art of persuasion in law courts. The Roman rhetorician Rutilius Lupus (fl. 49 BC) explained how the rhetorical figure *parrhesia* could be used in a courtroom situation. 'With *parrhesia* it is possible to discuss matters with a judge in a vehement manner', he wrote, 'and to reproach him face to face for a fault or error in an audacious manner.'[29] Rutilius warned, however, against frequent and careless use of free speech, to avoid annoying the judge. It was better, he said, to pretend to speak out of sadness, or better still, out of necessity. A good strategy, for example, was to claim one could no longer remain silent, but had to speak out for the common good.[30]

A decade or two earlier, another rhetorician had offered advice on how to employ frank speech in a tactful manner. This was the anonymous author of the *Rhetorica ad Herennium,* a handbook written in the second decade of the first century BC. From the time of Jerome, its author was believed to be Cicero, which added to the popularity of the treatise in late Antiquity and the early Middle Ages. As James Murphy has noted, the description of rhetorical figures in the *Rhetorica ad Herennium* influenced almost every medieval rhetorical theorist.[31] The anonymous author of the *Rhetorica ad Herennium* defines free speech, here called *licentia,* in the following manner: 'It is Frankness of Speech when, talking before those to whom we owe reverence or fear, we yet exercise our right to speak out, because we seem justified in reprehending them, or persons dear to them, for some fault.'[32] After providing this definition, the author adds advice, tips and warnings on how best to employ frank speech. He cites examples from famous political speeches to illustrate his point and suggests some helpful lines from everyday discourse to use in conversation. He recommends the addition of a few words of kindness after proffering criticism, to mitigate offence. The recipient of the admonitions will then realise that the critic only has his best interests at heart, and that he is not speaking out of malice or from a spirit of insubordination. As the author observes, such a strategy works well in friendship too.[33] Kind words

---

[29] Rutilius Lupus, *De figuris sententiarum et elocutionis* II, 18 (*parrhesia*), ed. Halm, *RLM*, p. 20: 'Parresia. [...] Nam in hoc vehementer cum iudice agendum est, et vitium aut erratum eius audacter coram eo reprehendendum.' Note that Rutilius Lupus does not provide a Latin synonym for *parrhesia*.

[30] Ibid., ed. Halm, *RLM*, p. 21, quoting a speech of Demosthenes.

[31] Murphy, *Medieval Rhetoric*, p. 11.

[32] *Rhetorica ad Herennium* IV, 36, ed. and trans. Caplan, LCL 403, pp. 348, 349: 'Licentia est cum apud eos quos aut vereri aut metuere debemus tamen aliquid pro iure nostro dicimus, quod eos aut quos ii diligunt aliquo in errato vere reprehendere videamur.'

[33] *Rhetorica ad Herennium* IV, 37, ed. Caplan, LCL 403, pp. 350, 351.

Introduction

smooth ruffled feathers. The speaker should convince the person he is criticising that his words, however harsh, are spoken out of love and respect. The author recognises that criticism can disturb perfectly good relationships, and this undesirable side-effect should be avoided, especially if the person who is being criticised holds some power or authority over the critic.

Although free speech became part of a stock repertoire of rhetorical figures, its inclusion in rhetorical handbooks did not imply that unlimited and unguarded use of it was promoted. In fact, most rhetoricians warned against over-extensive and incautious use of the rhetoric of free speech.[34] Quintilian holds that sometimes it is better not to put matters too bluntly and to use figured speech instead.[35] A friendly tone of advice can be more effective than raging invective, for it involves a lesser chance of offending the addressee.[36] Quintilian knew the importance of cloaking political criticism, for he practised and taught rhetoric in a period of political upheaval.[37] He lived through the civil wars of the late 60s of the first century AD and witnessed the rule of Galba, Otho and Vitellius and the Flavian emperors, Vespasian, Titus and Domitian. Although today Domitian is no longer considered the harsh and cruel emperor that contemporary historians, notably Tacitus and Suetonius, make him out to be, the political situation was nevertheless such that one had to mind one's tongue. Quintilian recommends a resort to figurative speech in dangerous situations, and suggests that one should make sure one's words are ambiguous.[38] If a speech does not go down well with the addressee, one can always claim to have intended something different.

Rhetoricians not only gave advice on how to increase the effectiveness of free speech, they also offered ethical guidelines. As the author of the *Rhetorica ad Herennium* argues, free speech should be informed by a concern for the well-being of the addressee, or at least create that illusion.[39] Its purpose is to offer correction for improvement, not to give free rein to annoyance with someone else's faults. Authors such as Cicero and Seneca, whose ideas were influential in the formation of Christian ethical thought, connected the Roman ideal of *oratio libera* or *libertas* to the Stoic ideal of restraining one's passions. The ideal orator and philosopher, according to Cicero, had his passions under control and spoke with *constantia* (stability of mind, or self-possession).[40] *Constantia*

---

[34] See for example Rutilius Lupus, *De figuris sententiarum et elocutionis* (first century AD) II, 18 (*parrhesia*), ed. Halm, *RLM*, p. 20.
[35] Quintilian, *Institutio oratoria* IX, 2, 67, ed. Russell, LCL 127, p. 74.
[36] Ibid. XI, 1, 67–72, ed. Russell, LCL 494, pp. 42–6. [37] Ahl, 'The art of safe criticism', p. 190.
[38] Quintilian, *Institutio oratoria* IX, 2, 67, and IX, 2, 75, ed. Russell, LCL 127, pp. 74, 78.
[39] *Rhetorica ad Herennium* IV, 37, ed. Caplan, LCL 403, pp. 350–2.
[40] Graver, *Cicero on the Emotions*, p. 169; Scarpat, *Parrhesia*, p. 8.

Introduction

became an important notion in the Christian vocabulary of free speech, as we shall see below. It was one of the terms by which *parrhesia* in the Greek New Testament was translated into Latin.

The word *parrhesia* occurs frequently in the books of the Greek New Testament, in particular in the Gospel of John, the Acts of the Apostles and the Pauline epistles. The New Testament meaning of *parrhesia* was influenced by Hellenic culture and Judeo-Hellenic literature.[41] The word is used, among other things, to describe Jesus' way of speaking with his disciples, the later apostles.[42] The apostles, in their turn, spoke and acted with *parrhesia* when they defended their faith in Christ being the son of God before religious and secular tribunals.[43] If one looks at the way in which the term *parrhesia* is used in the New Testament, for instance in the Acts of the Apostles, it becomes clear *parrhesia* does not exclusively denote speech acts, but also refers to a person's behaviour. To act with *parrhesia* meant to act boldly and courageously. Just as speech could be unveiled, transparent and frank, without taking recourse to the cover of figured speech, so too a person's actions could be open, bold and clear. This meaning of *parrhesia* did not emerge for the first time, or exclusively, in the New Testament, but was part of a widespread trend in *parrhesia*'s semantic development. New meanings of *parrhesia* can be found in the writings of the Judeo-Hellenic authors Flavius Josephus (d. c. 100 AD) and Philo of Alexandria (d. c. 50 AD), who used the term *parrhesia* to refer to the religious privilege of free access to God.[44] The complex of Greek texts that formed the corpus of the New Testament showed that *parrhesia*'s field of reference was differentiated, ranging from freedom to say everything to familiarity, courage, frankness and openness. When Jesus speaks openly to his disciples, he uses a different type of speech from that used by his disciples when they proclaim Christ's message to the world, although in both cases the word *parrhesia* is used. In the first example, Jesus' *parrhesia* refers to an open and clear mode of speaking, as opposed to speaking metaphorically or in parables,[45] while in the second example the disciples' *parrhesia* refers to their ability to preach with confidence and courage.[46]

When the Greek books of the Bible were first translated into Latin in the second century AD, the translators were faced with the problem of how to translate the highly charged term *parrhesia*. The word had different meanings, which sometimes overlapped and intersected, and there was not one equivalent in Latin that captured all senses of *parrhesia*. Different

---

[41] Peterson, 'Zur Bedeutungsgeschichte', p. 292. [42] John 16:29. [43] Acts 4:13; Acts 26:24.
[44] Momigliano, 'Freedom of speech in Antiquity', p. 262. [45] John 11:14; John 16:25
[46] For example, Acts 4:29–31; Eph. 6:1 and 1 Thess. 2:2.

Introduction

Latin words and expressions were used in the Vetus Latina and later in the Vulgate translation of the Bible to transmit the term *parrhesia*. The translators chose words like *audenter, audere, palam, manifeste, libertas (libere agere), constantia (constanter)* and *fiducia (fiducialiter)*, depending on the context in which *parrhesia* occurred.[47] The way in which Jesus addresses his disciples is translated as *(in) palam* or *manifeste (dicere)*,[48] whereas the boldness of those who preach the gospel without fear of repercussions is most often translated as speaking with *fiducia* or *constantia*, to emphasise the courage that was needed to spread the Christian faith.[49] Likewise, the verb *audere* and the adverbs *constanter* and *audenter* brought the courageous aspects of speaking with *parrhesia* to the fore.[50] These same expressions – to speak or act with *fiducia* and *constantia* – are employed to refer to the confidence of Christ's apostles when they are defending their faith before secular or religious authorities. The terms *fiducia* and *constantia* were borrowed from the vocabulary of Cicero and Seneca, and carried Stoic meaning.[51] *Constantia* referred to stability of mind, tranquillity and self-assurance: the exemplary virtues of the Stoic philosopher.[52] Likewise, *fiducia* referred to stability and tranquillity, and, flowing on from that undisturbed state of mind, to the ability to speak with courage and self-confidence.[53]

Parrhesia thus never meant any one thing at any one time in Antiquity. Free speech took on many different shapes and forms, and over the course of the centuries it spread from the political and the judicial to the moral and the religious sphere, while retaining its importance as a tool of political criticism. From the second century AD, a Christian rhetoric of free speech came into being, which took its inspiration from this varied and multi-layered classical tradition. In this book, I investigate which aspects of the rich cultural cluster of free speech late antique Christians adopted and adapted when they made the tradition of truth-telling their own. This book offers a study of the changes and continuities in the rhetoric of free speech from late Antiquity to the early Middle Ages, with special attention to both rhetorical performances and the vocabulary of speaking truth to power.

---

[47] Scarpat, *Parrhesia*, pp. 117, 118; Engels, *Fiducia dans la Vulgate*, p. 101.
[48] John 11:14 and 16:25.
[49] For example, Acts 4:13 (Vetus Latina: *constantia*, 'Itala': *fiducia*); Acts 4:31 and Acts 4:29 (*cum fiducia omni loqui* (in all Vetus Latina versions); Acts 13:46 (*constanter dicere* (all Vetus Latina versions, except 'Itala'); Acts 26:26 (*parrhesia* of the apostle Paul before king Agrippa: Vetus Latina 'Itala', *constanter loqui, fiducialiter loqui*); for other instances of *constantia* and *fiducia* in translation of Greek *parrhesia* see also Acts 26:26, Eph. 6:18; 4:13; 4:29; 9:27; 13:46; 14:3; 26:26; 28:30; 1 Thess. 2:2.
[50] Engels, *Fiducia dans la Vulgate*, p. 130. [51] Scarpat, *Parrhesia*, pp. 118–34.
[52] Scarpat, *Parrhesia*, 'Il termine *constantia*', pp. 118–22.
[53] Scarpat, *Parrhesia*, 'Il termine *fiducia*', pp. 122–34; Engels, *Fiducia dans la Vulgate*, p. 106.

Introduction

THE OUTLINE AND STRUCTURE OF THIS BOOK

Thanks to the seminal work of Peter Brown, the afterlife of classical free speech is placed firmly on the map of late antique research. Brown's study *Power and Persuasion in Late Antiquity* (1988) in particular has made scholars of late Antiquity aware of the continuing influence of the classical ideal of *parrhesia* and its accompanying public expectations. Since then, Claudia Rapp, Andrea Sterk and Richard Flower, amongst others, have shown that free speech retained its prominence in the public sphere.[54] Late antique bishops made use of the ancient rhetoric of free speech when they spoke before Roman emperors or discussed religion at episcopal synods. Although it remains to be seen which of the many available strands of *parrhesia* bishops took up and how they transformed the tradition to suit their own rhetorical purposes, as the first part of this book sets out to investigate, it no longer needs to be argued that the classical tradition of free speech lived on in the late antique Mediterranean world.

Practices and traditions of free speech in the early Middle Ages, by contrast, are less well explored. As Rita Copeland observes in the introduction to her volume *Criticism and Dissent in the Middle Ages* (1996): 'The history of medieval critical discourse as ideological form and cultural practice has yet to be written.'[55] In the last ten or fifteen years, scholars of the early Middle Ages have started to address what has long been a blind spot in modern research, and have shown that critical discourse was alive and well in the early Middle Ages.[56] Recent research on debate and disputation, for example, has revealed that there was room for discussion at early medieval councils, even on topics that were considered heretical.[57] The system of ecclesiastical censorship, moreover, allowed some leeway for letting the opinions of deviant thinkers be heard and read.[58] The studies of Mayke de Jong and Jinty Nelson have been especially instrumental in creating awareness of the fact that, at the courts of Louis the Pious and Charles the Bald, criticism of the ruler was tolerated, provided it was presented according to established and accepted practices of delivering criticism.[59] De Jong looks at biblical models, in particular the figure of the Old Testament prophet, to understand the

---

[54] Rapp, *Holy Bishops in Late Antiquity;* Sterk, *Renouncing the World;* Flower, *Emperors and Bishops.*
[55] Copeland, introduction to Copeland (ed.), *Criticism and Dissent,* p. 1.
[56] See especially the publications of Garrison, De Jong, Booker and Nelson in the bibliography.
[57] See for example the articles collected in the special issue on Carolingian cultures of dialogue and debate in *Early Medieval Europe* 25/1 (2017); Dartmann, Pietsch, Steckel (eds.), *Ecclesia disputans*; Noble, 'Kings, clergy and dogma'; Kramer, *Rethinking Authority.*
[58] Pezé, *Le virus de l'erreur;* Renswoude, Steinová, 'The annotated Gottschalk'.
[59] Nelson, *Opposition to Charlemagne;* Nelson, 'History-writing at the courts of Louis the Pious and Charles the Bald'; Nelson, 'The *libera vox* of Theodulf of Orléans'; De Jong, 'Becoming Jeremiah'; De Jong, *The Penitential State;* De Jong, '*Admonitio* and criticism of the ruler'; De Jong, *Epitaph for*

Introduction

origins and vocabulary of such accepted modes of criticism.[60] The prophet was indeed a classical exemplar for those who wanted to style themselves and others as free speakers in the early Middle Ages, but the Old Testament prophet was not the only role model, as will be seen in the following chapters.

Mary Garrison was the first to point to the continuing influence of the classical tradition of free speech in her 2004 article on the epistolary network of the scholar and court adviser Alcuin of York (d. 804).[61] In 2008 and 2009, she and I organised two strands at the International Medieval Congress in Leeds, inviting colleagues from theology, patristics, language studies and history to reflect on the transmission of classical free speech in early medieval texts and authors.[62] Our prime concern at the time was the question of methodology: how does one study traces of a 'forgotten' tradition, and what are the best tools for analysing continuity and discontinuity? I was fortunate to be part of these exploratory investigations and discussions, which inspired my dissertation on the rhetoric of free speech in late Antiquity and the early Middle Ages. This book grew from that dissertation.

The principal sources for this book are the letters of authors such as Hilary of Poitiers (d. 368), Ambrose of Milan (d. 397) and Agobard of Lyon (d. 840) who had a reputation for being outspoken. A study of their letters reveals how these authors went about their task of telling the truth and how they composed and delivered their written admonitions of rulers. On occasion I compare the selected authors' literary strategies of delivering criticism to the advice given in classical handbooks. Such a comparison is, however, fraught with difficulties, as is shown in Mathew Kempshall's book on rhetoric and historiography in the Middle Ages.[63] We know little about how knowledge of classical rhetorical strategies and figures was transmitted to the early Middle Ages, nor how rhetoric was taught in this period.[64] No medieval manuscript of Rutilius Lupus' handbook, for example, has survived, while the oldest complete manuscript of Quintilian's *Institutes of Oratory* dates to the tenth century.[65] Earlier manuscripts from the ninth century are incomplete. In

---

an Era. But see also, earlier, Brunner, *Oppositionelle Gruppen* and Ganz, 'The *Epitaphium Arsenii* and opposition to Louis the Pious'.

[60] See the references to De Jong in the previous footnote, especially De Jong, *The Penitential State*.
[61] Garrison, 'Les correspondents d'Alcuin', and later also 'An aspect of Alcuin'.
[62] Participants were Augustine Casiday, Hildegund Müller, Christine Phillips, Mayke de Jong, Sumi Shihamara, Stuart Airlie, Michael Clanchy, Mariken Teeuwen, Kaarina Hollo, Paul Dutton and Courtney Booker.
[63] Kempshall, *Rhetoric and the Writing of History*.
[64] But see for the high and late Middle Ages Murphy, *Latin Rhetoric and Education*.
[65] Halm, *RLM*, p. 3; Winterbottom, 'Quintilian', in Reynolds, *Texts and Transmission*, pp. 332–4.

Introduction

comparison, the number of early medieval manuscripts of the *Rhetorica ad Herennium,* especially of its fourth book, on rhetorical figures, is more substantial, but the number is still not overwhelming.[66] Evidently, rhetorical expertise travelled via routes other than rhetorical handbooks alone, for example via oral instruction, or model letters and speeches. However, one should take care not to presuppose any knowledge of classical rhetoric where there is no internal evidence and no manuscripts to support it.

Another factor that complicates the analysis of early medieval letters against the background of classical rhetoric is that the advice of rhetorical handbooks was directed at an oral, and not a written practice of free speech. The art of letter-writing and the art of public speechmaking were, however, closely related. For one, the rhetorical rules that applied to composing a speech were also applied to writing letters.[67] Letters, moreover, were delivered orally, just like speeches; they were read aloud to their recipients, often by the messenger who delivered the letter. Frequently, a messenger was instructed to deliver a message orally in addition to the letter, the content of which the sender did not want to include in the written text, because the message was too dangerous or too sensitive to put into writing.[68] Letters were written with the intent that they should resemble a speech. Some letters imitate the setting and circumstances of oral delivery so closely that they give the impression that the writer is standing face to face with the person they are addressing, as if they were delivering the speech in person.[69]

The other texts that I have selected for this study, besides letters, are narratives that portray truth-tellers, describing, for example, the speech a free speaker delivered, the circumstances in which he or she spoke or wrote, the effects of the speech or letter on the addressee, or the impact their actions had on a wider audience. For each author whose letters are discussed in this book, I have included, where possible, contemporary or near-contemporary accounts that describe the truth-teller's actions, portray their bodily posture and gestures, offer a (semi-)verbatim account or paraphrase of their speech, or discuss the reception of their words. A close reading of letters and narratives taken together allows a study of free speech as a rhetorical performance, with close attention to the scripted

---

[66] Hafner, *Untersuchungen zur Überlieferungsgeschichte der Rhetorik ad Herennium;* Winterbottom, 'Ad Herennium', in Reynolds, *Texts and Transmission,* p. 99. On the medieval manuscripts of these rhetorical treatises, see Van Renswoude, *Licence to Speak,* pp. 364–8.
[67] Murphy, 'Quintilian's influence'.
[68] Constable, *Letters and Letter-Collections,* p. 53; Hoffmann, 'Mittelalterlichen Brieftechnik', pp. 145–7.
[69] See for example Hilary of Poitiers' letter to Emperor Constantius II, *Ad Constantium,* discussed in chapter 2.

Introduction

roles of acclaimed or self-proclaimed truth-tellers, and the effects their words and acts had on their social world.

The term 'truth-teller' is currently a popular term in modern parlance; it occurs frequently in moral–political essays on the value of free speech in politics and society. 'Truth-teller' is, however, also the translation of the Greek word *parrhesiastes*: 'the one who speaks the truth', or 'he who speaks freely'. Although the term *parrhesiastes* was rarely used in classical Greek, it became more prominent in the Greco-Roman period.[70] In classical thought, the 'truth' involved in the speech act of truth-telling was related to the convictions and moral standards of the speaker. It had nothing to do with our modern notion of evidence-based argumentation. Truth was simply what the truth-teller believed to be true.[71] He did not say anything he pleased, but expressed the truth as he perceived it.[72] I therefore consider the terms truth-teller and truth-telling apt to describe the self-perception and activities of the authors and protagonists who hold centre stage in this book.

I have often found it difficult to decide how best to translate the terms *parrhesia*, *licentia* and *libertas*. Sometimes I have considered 'free speech' the most appropriate translation, while at other times 'frank speech' seemed to be a more fitting English equivalent. In the present day, 'free speech' is commonly understood as a universal human right – a notion which does not apply to premodern society. While acknowledging the conceptual difference between ancient and modern conceptions of freedom of speech, I employ the term 'free speech' to refer to a political privilege or a civic attribute, and 'frank speech' to denote a specific way of speaking and the ability to say what one thinks.[73] Frank speech can take place in a political setting, but it can also be used in a social and moral context. When a friend speaks frankly to a friend and tells them the truth to their face, this is not 'free speech' in a political sense. Yet when someone exercises his or her right to speak freely in the political arena, that person will often use frank speech. In other words, free speech is nearly always frank speech, but frank speech is not always free speech.

The critics discussed in this study are nearly all ecclesiastics, and nearly all are men. Famous examples of truth-telling women in classical and early Christian literature are the prophetess Cassandra in Aeschylus' tragedy *Agamemnon* and the African noblewoman Perpetua (d. 202), whom we shall meet in chapter 1. In late Antiquity and the early Middle Ages, speaking truth to power was not a quality generally ascribed

---

[70] Foucault, *Fearless Speech*, p. 11.   [71] Foucault, *Fearless Speech*, pp. 14, 15.
[72] Parkin-Speer, 'Freedom of speech', p. 65.
[73] See the terminological reflections in Baltussen, Davis, 'Parrhesia, free speech and self-censorship' and Carter, 'Citizen attribute, negative right'.

Introduction

to women. In early medieval narratives, we occasionally come across women who speak the truth, either because they are possessed by a demon, or because they are transmitting moral warnings that have come to them in a dream or vision.[74] Being a passive conduit of truth, however, is not the same as being an active truth-teller. The holy virgin Genovefa (d. c. 520), whose biography will be discussed in chapter 6, is a notable exception, in that she is presented as a truth-teller who possesses the same qualities of courage, constancy and *virilitas* as her male colleagues. The absence of evidence of truth-telling women in this period, and consequently in this book, has to do not only with their social position and limited access to literacy, but also with the fact that, as we shall see in the following chapters, the practice of truth-telling became connected to the priestly office. Since women were excluded from the priesthood, they were automatically disqualified from becoming truth-tellers. Moreover, as Mary Beard has pointed out, rhetorical theory taught that the voices of women were not to be credited with authority. The classical rhetorical tradition, which has had a long and rich afterlife in the Middle Ages up until the present age, sprang from a classical culture that systematically excluded the female voice from public speech.[75]

In this book, I study the transmission of the classical tradition of free speech from three different angles. First, I examine the practice of free speech by analysing rhetorical forms of expression and codes of behaviour in letters and narratives, in which an author expresses criticism of authorities. Second, I analyse conceptual thinking about free speech that can be found in prescriptive texts such as rhetorical treatises or in advisory literature such as mirrors for princes (see chapter 8). The third approach lies in the domain of historical semantics. By focussing on semantic developments in their particular historical contexts, I aim to chart changes in the meaning and use of words that were traditionally employed to describe the practice as well as the concept of free speech, such as *parrhesia* and *libertas*. By paying close attention to contrasting words, synonyms, rival terms and qualitative adjectives (for example: *honourable* free speech or *disgraceful* licence), it is possible to get a better grip on how a word or term is evaluated in its specific semantic context, and chart shifts of meaning over time.[76]

The method I employ to study the letters and narratives of late antique and early medieval critics owes much to socio-rhetorical interpretation,

---

[74] See for example the *Vision of the Poor Woman of Laon*, discussed in Dutton, *The Politics of Dreaming*, pp. 67, 68.
[75] Beard, 'The public voice of women'.
[76] An exemplary study that makes use of this method is Vielberg, *Untertanentopik*, and see now Jussen, Rohmann, 'Historical semantics in medieval studies'.

Introduction

which views texts as performances of language in particular historical and cultural situations.[77] This means that I not only analyse how speeches and letters are composed, which rhetorical strategies are used, or how the semantic field of 'free speech' is structured, but that I also take the social dynamics of texts, authors and readers into account. The socio-rhetorical method, as employed in particular in the field of biblical criticism, builds on interpretative strategies developed in sociology, anthropology and socio-linguistics. Its aim is to study rhetorical strategies and structures not as a goal in itself, but as a means of discovering the cultural and moral values of the author and the time in which he or she lived. In other words, socio-rhetorical interpretation is not only about texts, it is also about the people who composed, delivered, read, quoted, censured and ignored these texts.

Special attention is paid to the roles that the authors assumed within and outside their texts. Studying an author's self-styling and rhetorical performance is relevant to our understanding of the mechanisms of free speech in writings from the past. Free speech is a means of persuasion that, just like other forms of rhetoric, aims to effect change in the social and political world. How did late antique and early medieval authors fashion themselves and their words to get the best results? Speaking truth to power was, and is, not only an art: it is also an act, which needed to be performed according to specific rules and codes of conduct. Some of the authors who are central to this book present themselves in their texts as outsiders, who speak the truth from a marginal position or a place of exclusion. They advise and criticise the centre of power from its margins. Outside their texts, however, in the reality of their own lives, many of them were men (and occasionally women) of social and political importance. One of the issues this book addresses is the question of whether it was a matter of coincidence that these authors styled themselves as marginal truth-tellers, or whether the role of outcast was part and parcel of a cultural performance of free speech. This book is thus also a study of the social roles, performances and personas that truth-tellers adopted and developed to present themselves as free-speaking critics, with the intention to change and steer the political agenda of rulers effectively. It does not seek to uncover historical facts, but studies representations, in order to examine the social ideals and rhetorical practices connected to the art of speaking freely.

This study consists of two parts, one dealing with the rhetoric of free speech in late Antiquity and one with the early Middle Ages. Part I consists of five chapters. It starts with a chapter on the free speech of

---

[77] Robbins, 'Socio-rhetorical interpretation'; Robbins, *Exploring the Texture of Texts*.

Introduction

martyrs, such as Polycarp (late second century), Perpetua (d. 202) and Pionius (d. third century) as represented in the accounts of their martyrdom (chapter 1). It is followed by a case study on Bishop Hilary of Poitiers (d. 368), who employed the tropes of martyrdom to style himself as a stout defender of orthodoxy against the 'Antichrist' emperor, Constantius II (chapter 2). Chapter 3 deals with the role of the pagan philosopher in late antique society. It shows how, over the course of the fourth century, Christian hermits, monks and bishops stepped into the footsteps of the pagan philosophers, and made their prerogative to speak truth to power their own. Chapter 4 is a case study of the letters of Ambrose of Milan (d. 397), the bishop who became famous for rebuking Emperor Theodosius. Part I closes with a chapter that discusses the doubts and reservations that arose in the fifth and sixth centuries in some ascetic circles regarding the tradition of speaking frankly (chapter 5). These reservations can be seen to live on, in some form, in performances of free speech in the Middle Ages. Throughout the first part of this book, special attention will be paid to semantic developments in the Greek and Latin profane and ecclesiastical vocabulary of free speech.

In Part II, we leave the late antique Mediterranean world and turn to medieval western Europe. It starts with a chapter on the role of the frank holy man, as represented in Merovingian letters and narratives (chapter 6). This chapter is dedicated to memorable truth-tellers such as Genovefa (d. 520), Nicetius (d. 561), Columban (d. 615) and Leudegar (d. c. 675). It is followed by a case study of Bishop Gregory of Tours (d. 594), who squared up against the Merovingian King Chilperic (chapter 7). Chapter 8 focusses on the role of the frank adviser and the genre of advisory literature from about 750, when this genre started to flourish, reaching its peak in the period that is often referred to as the 'Carolingian renaissance'. Chapter 9 is an analysis of the letters of Agobard of Lyon (d. 840), who drew on classical traditions to legitimise his criticism of Emperor Louis the Pious. Part II closes with a case study (chapter 10) that deals with one letter, namely the letter ascribed to Pope Gregory IV in which an unknown author urges the bishops of Francia to speak frankly to Emperor Louis and persuade him to take the right course of action.

This study aims to demonstrate that the classical tradition of free speech, and the values and social roles that were attached to it, outlived the end of Antiquity. The discourse of free speech was appropriated, transformed, Christianised and given a place in late antique and early medieval society, where it continued to be practised by individuals who spoke up to their rulers to correct the course of politics. Over the centuries, the discourse of free speech continued to be transformed; its

Introduction

practitioners made use of old elements while adapting to new social and political circumstances. In the following chapters, therefore, I shall trace this process of transformation, by looking at how the rhetoric of free speech was constructed in the letters and narratives of late antique and early medieval truth-tellers.

PART I

1
THE STEADFAST MARTYR

In the second century AD, probably during the reign of Emperor Marcus Aurelius (r. 161–80), the octogenarian bishop Polycarp was condemned to be burned at the stake. As tradition has it, Polycarp was one of the last persons to have been personally instructed by the apostles, who appointed him bishop of Smyrna.[1] According to the anonymous author who drew up the account of his martyrdom, Polycarp went to his death calmly. Before he was executed, a remarkable exchange took place. The governor who was in charge of the trial offered Polycarp a chance to escape execution, if he were willing to renounce Christ. The old bishop answered:

'For eighty-six years I have been his servant and he has done me no wrong. How can I blaspheme against my king and saviour?' But the other insisted once again, saying: 'Swear by the emperor's Genius!'
He answered: 'If you will delude yourself into thinking that I will swear by the emperor's Genius, as you say, and if you pretend not to know who I am, listen to me with *parrhesia*: I am a Christian.'[2]

Thereupon the bishop was bound with ropes to a wooden structure and, while the fire was lit, he raised his face to heaven and prayed. When the flames could not consume his holy body, the author says, one of the executioners came forward and stabbed him to death with a dagger. Witnesses saw a dove fly from the wound and disappear in the sky.

The anonymous report of the *Martyrdom of Polycarp* is taken to go back to the third quarter of the second century, and has been preserved in five manuscripts written between the ninth and the eleventh centuries.[3] The

---

[1] Irenaeus of Lyon, *Adversus haereses* III, 3, 4, ed. Harvey, vol. 2, p. 12.
[2] *Martyrium Polycarpi* 9, 3–10, 1, ed. Orbán, *Atti e passioni*, p. 16; translation (adapted) Musurillo, *ACM*, pp. 9–11. Compare Eusebius, *Historia ecclesiastica* IV, 15, ed. Schwartz, *Eusebius Werke*, p. 344, lines 11, 12.
[3] Musurillo, *ACM*, pp. xiv–xv. On the problematic dating and transmission history of pre-Constantinian martyr acts, see Barnes, *Early Christian Hagiography and Roman History*, pp. 356–9.

Part I

report was shaped as a circular letter, issued by the congregation of Smyrna to inform other Christian communities of Polycarp's fate.[4] Irenaeus of Lyon (d. 202 AD), who recounted the bishop's death in his book *Against the Heretics*, praised Polycarp as a steadfast witness to the truth, who suffered martyrdom gloriously and most nobly.[5]

In recent studies, Christian martyrs have been described as parrhesiasts par excellence, because of the boldness and fearlessness they displayed before Roman officials.[6] As pointed out in the Introduction, the classical tradition of *parrhesia* was highly valued throughout late Antiquity by Christians and non-Christians alike. Martyr narratives that were written after the Great Persecution credit their protagonists with a bold freedom of speech that was traditionally ascribed to individuals who spoke truth to those in power at great risk to their personal safety. To a certain extent this also holds true for the martyr acts of the second and third centuries, but these earlier narratives of the pre-Constantinian period also attest to a more complex relationship between traditional *parrhesia* and the fearlessness of the Christian martyr. It is this complex relationship that is the topic of this chapter. The authors of the early martyr texts present their protagonists as courageous individuals who were not afraid to profess their faith in Christ and incur the wrath of their interrogators, yet they give the martyrs' *parrhesia* a distinctive interpretation. According to the author of the *Martyrdom of Polycarp*, as we have just seen, Polycarp did not speak with *parrhesia*, but encouraged his interrogator to *listen* with *parrhesia* (*meta parrhesias akoue*); he asked him, in other words, to open his mind to the truth of his testimony.[7] This chapter investigates representations of free speech in martyrdom accounts of the pre-Constantinian period to see how and why the authors re-contextualised traditional *parrhesia*. Should their attempts to reinterpret the age-old values of free speech be seen as part of a process of acculturation, or rather as indicative of a growing reluctance among Christians to criticise those in power?

Throughout late Antiquity and the Middle Ages, stories about the deaths of the early Christian martyrs were immensely popular. Martyr literature was a widely read genre that continued to be written long after the height of the persecution of Christians, which is generally accepted to have ended in 313. The literary form, language and themes of the early

---

[4] See the *salutatio* of the *Martyrium Polycarpi*, ed. Orbán, *Atti e passioni*, p. 6.
[5] Irenaeus of Lyon, *Adversus haereses* III, 3, 4, ed. Harvey, vol. 2, p. 12.
[6] Foucault, *Le courage de la vérité*, p. 302: 'Le martyr, c'est le parrèsiaste par excellence'; Szakolczai, *Genesis of Modernity*, p. 239; Rapp, *Holy Bishops*, p. 252; Flower, *Emperors and Bishops*, pp. 2, 148; Grig, *Making Martyrs*, p. 22.
[7] Eusebius, *Historia ecclesiastica* IV, 15, ed. Schwartz, p. 344, lines 11, 12; compare Rufinus, *Historia ecclesiastica* IV, 15, ed. Mommsen, p. 345, line 23: 'cum omni libertate audi a me'.

22

The Steadfast Martyr

martyr acts served as the basis for later literature about old (and new) martyrs of the church whose faith was put to the test, and they were a major source of inspiration for hagiographers who recorded the lives of the saints.[8] Literary tropes of martyrdom, such as steadfastness in the face of death, control of emotions and the open confession of religious beliefs before persecutors, proved to be of lasting appeal for later generations, up until the early modern period.[9]

This chapter deals with martyr narratives that are generally dated to the pre-Constantinian period. In the estimation of Timothy Barnes, nineteen independent martyrdom accounts have survived from the period between the 150s and the end of the Great Persecution in 313.[10] The manuscripts in which these texts were preserved, however, often date to later periods and may well represent later redactions.[11] The complex manuscript transmission history affects the proposed analysis of representations of free speech. It is difficult to ascertain beyond doubt whether a particular term or description already occurred in an early version of the text, or should be attributed to later redactions. The martyr acts discussed in this chapter will therefore be compared, whenever possible, to other sources from this period describing the same events. Eusebius' *Ecclesiastical History* (c. 323) contains reports of the martyrs' deaths that were also recorded in the independent and often anonymous martyrdom narratives. Although the *Ecclesiastical History* was written in a period just outside the chronological scope of this chapter, it is nevertheless a valuable source of comparison, as Eusebius made use of existing written records from the pre-Constantinian period for his descriptions of the martyrs' trials and deaths.[12] In 401 or 402, Rufinus of Aquileia (d. 410) translated and edited Eusebius' *Ecclesiastical History*, and added two further books, which gained a wide currency in the West.[13]

Early Christian martyrdom narratives come in different literary shapes. Usually a distinction is made between *passiones* that record the last days and death of the martyr and *acta* that take the form of official records of court proceedings. The question of whether the *acta martyrum* go back to actual court records, or whether the authors imitated the formal structure of these records to enhance the immediacy and credibility of their accounts, is still under discussion.[14] Martyr texts had a performative

---

[8] Bowersock, *Martyrdom and Rome*, p. 24   [9] Gregory, *Salvation at Stake*.
[10] Barnes, 'Early Christian hagiography and the Roman historian', p. 17; Barnes, *Early Christian Hagiography and Roman History*, pp. 356–9.
[11] Rhee, *Early Christian Literature*, p. 4. Cooper, 'The martyr, the *matrona* and the bishop', p. 306, n. 29.
[12] Eusebius, *Historia ecclesiastica*, ed. Schwartz, Mommsen, p. 8.
[13] Humphries, 'Rufinus's Eusebius'; McKitterick, *History and Memory*, pp. 226–33.

23

function, and their resemblance to courtroom proceedings increased their dramatic efficacy. Martyr acts were read aloud on the martyr's annual festival in churches and communal gatherings, with the aim of making the martyr present in the performance of his or her story.[15] The free-spoken words and behaviour of the martyrs at their trials were thus actualised in a liturgical performance, providing a moral example for the audience to imitate.

Martyr texts addressed themes that were of importance to Christians at the time. Besides the abovementioned tropes of constancy, courage and free confession of faith, they include motifs such as chastity, the place of women in the new religion and the (un-)importance of family ties.[16] These were issues by which Christians sought to define their identity vis-à-vis the prevalent culture of Greco-Roman society. And yet, while distinguishing their own culture and religion from pagan practices, Christian authors drew upon the traditional repertoire of values and traditions that they shared with other citizens of the Roman Empire.[17] One of the issues early martyrdom narratives addressed was that of how a Christian should behave when he or she stood trial before secular authorities, and what measure of frank speech was appropriate in this situation.

PAGAN AND BIBLICAL MODELS

According to the gospels, Christians should go out into the world, proclaim the truth of Christ, and bravely face the dangers of spreading the word.[18] As the Gospel of Matthew has it, they were to hold fast to the truth when they were handed over to councils, flogged in synagogues and brought before governors and kings (Matt. 10:18). Martyr narratives further promoted the expectations of courageous and steadfast behaviour that are voiced in the New Testament: those who professed their faith in Christ and were prepared to suffer persecution, torture and martyrdom in the name of the truth merited the highest praise and lasting admiration. The glorification of heroic deaths was not exclusive to Christian circles. Courageous endurance and steadfastness in the face of execution were also qualities that were highlighted in narratives about the pagan philosopher–martyr. The term *martys or martus*, which in pre-Christian Greek

---

[14] See Barnes, 'Early Christian hagiography and the Roman historian'; Grig, *Making Martyrs*, especially pp. 23–56 and the literature cited there.
[15] Grig, *Making Martyrs*, p. 4; Gemeinhardt and Leemans, 'Christian martyrdom in Late Antiquity', p. 1.
[16] Cooper, 'The martyr, the *matrona* and the bishop', p. 298.
[17] Buc, *The Dangers of Ritual*, p. 124.   [18] Compare Matt. 10:18 and Mark 15:16.

The Steadfast Martyr

simply meant (judicial) 'witness', was in this period used to describe a person who testified to his or her religious beliefs under threat of death at the hands of persecutors.[19] Philosophers who gave their lives for their cities and remained true to their principles were also known as martyrs.[20] The *Acta Alexandrinorum,* also known as the *Acts of the Pagan Martyrs,* recorded the final moments of the lives of Alexandrian philosophers who were executed because they defied an emperor. The *Acta Alexandrinorum* are a collection of disparate texts, written between the first and third century AD, which survived in papyrus fragments found in Egypt.[21] Like the Christian martyr acts, the *Acta Alexandrinorum* follow the structure of formal protocols of interrogation and pivot around a conversation between an Alexandrian philosopher and a hostile Roman emperor, which usually ends with the philosopher's execution.[22] It has often been noted that the fearless speech of the Christian martyr before his persecutors resembles the *parrhesia* of the pagan philosopher–martyr reproving a tyrant.[23] There are indeed some striking parallels to be observed. Both the Christian martyr and the philosopher are willing to risk their lives to speak the truth.

A model, however, that may have provided a more influential template for the narrative representation of the Christian martyrs' speech and behaviour was the trial and execution of Jesus, as recorded in the gospels. In contrast to the Alexandrian martyrs, who spoke boldly during their trial, Jesus remained silent when he was tried before the council of the high priest. According to the Gospel of Matthew, Jesus chose not to defend himself against the charges that were brought against him, and kept silent or gave short, evasive answers (Matt. 26:63; 27:14).[24]

A biblical model for the Christian martyr acts that allowed more room for outspokenness were the Acts of the Apostles. The fourth chapter of the Acts recounts how the apostles Peter and John preached the word of God to the people openly, with great boldness (*meta parrhesias*), in spite of the threats they had received (Acts 4:27–31). In chapter 26, moreover, it is noted with admiration that the apostle Paul spoke with *parrhesia* when he was brought before King Agrippa to defend his faith (Acts 26:25–6). In the opening of his defence speech, Paul appealed to the king's *paideia* when he declared: 'What I am saying is sober truth. The king is well acquainted with these matters and to him I can speak freely

---

[19] Grig, *Making Martyrs.* [20] Musurillo, *Acts of the Pagan Martyrs,* p. 236.
[21] Bohak, 'Acts of the Alexandrian martyrs', p. 16. [22] Ibid.
[23] Peterson, 'Zur Bedeutungsgeschichte', p. 293; Musurillo, *Acts of the Pagan Martyrs,* pp. 218, 219; Bartelink, 'Quelques observations sur παρρησία', p. 35, nn. 1 and 2, with references to older literature.
[24] Compare Mark 14:53–62; 15:1–5; Luke 22:66–71; 23:8–10.

Part I

(*parrhesiazomenos*), for I am convinced that none of this has escaped his notice' (Acts 26:26). Magistrate Festus, who led the interrogation, declared Paul to be mad, but King Agrippa, according to the Acts, was interested in hearing what Paul had to say.

A further martyrological model was the story of the Maccabean martyrs, a group of Jews who were killed around 167 BC by the Greek king Antiochus IV. Their deeds were recorded in the second and fourth Book of Maccabees, written around 125 and 100 BC, respectively.[25] In spite of the fact that these martyrs were not Christians but Jews, who were killed for holding fast to their religious customs and not for professing their faith in Christ, Christians greatly admired their courage and boldness. In the late fourth century, the Christian cult of the Maccabean martyrs took off properly, but second-century Christians were already acquainted with their story.[26] As Lucy Grig has pointed out, it cannot be proved that the authors of the early Christian martyr acts actually read the Book of Maccabees, but they were familiar with a version of 'a shifting and highly popular story, which seems to point to a milieu and religious discourse of which Christianity was also a product'.[27] According to the fourth Book of Maccabees, the martyrs had spoken frankly, even abusively to King Antiochus and his guards, shortly before they were put to death.[28] They called the king an abominable tyrant and foretold that he would be punished for his cruelty towards them.[29] The martyrs underwent torture with remarkable composure and refused to ask for mercy, because, as the author of the Book of Maccabees has it, 'they were contemptuous of emotions and sovereign over agonies' (4 Macc. 8:28).

These four stories, or rather collections of stories, can be taken as representative of the widely divergent attitudes regarding frank speech before persecuting authorities that existed at the time, ranging from boldness and contempt for authorities (the philosopher–martyrs, the Maccabean martyrs), sophisticated defence (the apostle Paul), open and courageous preaching of the truth to the people (the apostles Peter and John), to silence and reticence (Jesus).[30] Which model, or combination of models, the authors of martyrdom accounts chose to adopt depended on their outlook and the communities for which they wrote. Although we can find different stances towards frank speech throughout the period in

---

[25] Van Henten, *The Maccabean Martyrs*, p.4.
[26] Norris, 'Apocryphal writings', p. 35; Rouwhorst, 'The emergence of the cult of the Maccabean martyrs'; Boyarin, *Dying for God*, pp. 114–30.
[27] Grig, *Making Martyrs*, p. 10.
[28] 4 Maccabees 9:14–18; 30–2; 10:9–11, 17–21; 11:21–7; 12:11–19.
[29] 4 Maccabees 9:15 and 9:32.
[30] Other models for Christian martyr narratives are discussed below, pp. 32–34.

which the genre flourished, many of the martyr narratives from the pre-Constantinian period show a preference for the silent model of Jesus. A possible explanation for this preference can be found in the earlier mentioned *Martyrdom of Polycarp*.

RESPECT FOR AUTHORITIES

The *Martyrdom of Polycarp* is regarded as the earliest known martyrdom account, going back to the third quarter of the second century.[31]. A significant portion of the narrative can be found in the fourth book of Eusebius' *Ecclesiastical History*.[32] The martyrological language and motifs of the *Martyrdom of Polycarp* bear a close resemblance to the trial and passion of Jesus, as recorded in the gospels. According to the narrative, Polycarp was invited to deliver a defence speech before the crowd that had gathered to witness his trial and execution. This opportunity was presented to him at the end of the interrogation, just after Polycarp had declared that he was a Christian. The governor, realising that it was pointless to put further pressure on Polycarp to renounce Christ, offered him a chance to speak to the people to win their sympathy. The old bishop declined the governor's offer; he considered the bloodthirsty mob unworthy to listen to a speech of defence from him. He was, however, willing to engage in discussion with the governor himself, for, as he told him, he had been taught to pay respect to authorities.[33] Polycarp, or rather the author of the account of his martyrdom, believed that God had given power to rulers and magistrates and allowed them to exercise authority over Christians. Respect was therefore due to them.

In a similar vein, the Christian apologists of the second century AD, such as Justin Martyr, Tertullian and Athenagoras, whose thought influenced the authors of the early martyr acts, held that a Christian should respect secular authority, even if that authority engaged in the persecution of Christians. They developed this position in response to the mistrust of their contemporaries, who regarded the adherents to the Christian faith as disloyal citizens of the Roman Empire.[34] The fact that Christians refused to sacrifice to the gods was interpreted as a demonstration of disobedience to the imperial edicts and disrespect of the emperor, and, perhaps more worrying, as a sign of atheism, which was regarded as a threat to the stability of the Empire. Because of their

---

[31] See note 3.   [32] Eusebius, *Historia ecclesiastica* IV, 15.
[33] *Martyrium Polycarpi* 10, 2, ed. Orbán, *Atti e passioni*, p. 16.
[34] Rhee, *Early Christian Literature*, pp. 164–8.

perceived subversive attitude, Christians were seen as a dangerous sect that undermined time-honoured Roman traditions.[35] The apologists were eager to demonstrate that Christians were in fact faithful citizens of the Roman Empire, who respected the Roman traditions, cherished the Roman virtues and held the emperor in the highest esteem.[36] The respect they owed to the emperor extended to the governors who ruled the provinces and administered justice in his name. On the one hand, the apologists aimed to show that Christians blended in and formed no threat to the safety or continuity of the Roman Empire; on the other hand, they wanted to distinguish themselves as a group to ensure their survival. The need both to blend in and to stand out were mingled in the writings of the apologetic fathers as well as in the early martyrdom accounts that followed the apologists' lead. These conflicting concerns gave rise to an ambiguous attitude amongst Christians when it came to the question of how to behave towards secular authorities, and how much frank speech was appropriate in discussions with Roman magistrates.

The genre of martyr acts is commonly described as 'opposition literature', given the fact that the acts record how Christians defied the orders of political authorities and refused to obey the imperial decrees. The martyrs resisted the command to sacrifice to the emperor, swear by the emperor's Genius, acknowledge the Roman gods, or practise any other aspect of the Roman tradition that went against their Christian beliefs. Yet their defiant stance in religious matters did not necessarily lead to contempt of the interrogating authorities, as the example of the *Martyrdom of Polycarp* shows. A fierce demonstration of contempt for rulers, such as is displayed in the *Acta Alexandrinorum* and the Book of Maccabees, cannot be found in pre-Constantinian martyr acts. This respectful stance towards authorities changed in later martyr literature. In fifth- and sixth-century martyrdom accounts, Christian martyrs speak much more boldly to their interrogators, and sometimes even use abusive language, as we shall see further on in this chapter.

In the earlier martyr acts, however, most martyrs acknowledge the authority of their interrogators and executioners and behave in a courteous and civil manner, as far as their faith allows them. Thus, they conform to the apostolic injunction, expressed in Titus 3:1, to be 'subject to rulers and authorities, to be obedient, to be ready for every good work, to speak evil of no one, to avoid quarrelling, to be gentle and to show courtesy to everyone'. But there is also another apostolic instruction, provided in Paul's letter to Timothy: 'Proclaim the message, be persistent whether the time is favourable or unfavourable; convince,

---

[35] Ibid., pp. 12–15. [36] Ibid., p. 168.

rebuke and encourage' (Tim. 4:2). Although the two directives are not necessarily incompatible, they did create a field of tension. If a Christian were interrogated, accused, perhaps even abused by authorities, should he or she 'be obedient and avoid quarrelling' or speak freely and 'convince, rebuke and encourage'?

We find traces of this ambiguous attitude towards political authority especially in martyr acts that go back to the period in which the apologists were active. In these narratives, the martyr's fearlessness went hand in hand with public signs of respect for secular authority. This ambivalent attitude is particularly evident at one specific narrative moment that often occurs towards the end of the martyr act, when the martyr takes the opportunity to speak one last time just before execution and warns the interrogators, judges and executioners of the impending judgement of God. Not all martyrs were as polite as the apologists had recommended. In the *Martyrdom of Carpus, Papylus and Agathonica*, the martyr Papylus declares from the stake that he looks forward to the true judgement of God, and despises the commands of mortal judges.[37]

Other martyrs, however, are represented as being polite to the very end. The martyr Apollonius (d. 185 AD), for example, is said to have had an utterly civil conversation with his interrogator, the prefect Perennis. According to the author, Apollonius even went so far as to thank the prefect for pronouncing the death sentence. Perennis would have preferred to release the martyr, the author says, but since that was not possible, he granted him a merciful death. The narrative ends with Apollonius expressing words of gratitude to his judge, whose sentence, he says, brought him the salvation of all those who believe in Christ.[38] The martyr Cyprian (d. 258) is reported to have expressed his thanks to his executioner by offering him twenty-five gold pieces.[39] The gesture is meant to convey Cyprian's magnanimity and good manners. He did not show hatred towards the official, who is said to have delivered his sentence with difficulty and reluctance, but rather was grateful to his executioner for allowing him to die as a martyr.[40]

The Martyrdom of Pionius mentions the Roman custom, called *parrhesia*, which allowed the accused to deliver a defence speech and persuade the crowd or the jury of his innocence.[41] Martyr acts that are modelled upon

---

[37] *Martyrium Carpi, Papyli et Agathonicae*, ed. Musurillo, *ACM*, p. 33, lines 24–7; see also the succinct reference in Eusebius, *Historia ecclesiastica* IV, 15, 48, ed. Schwartz, Mommsen, p. 354.
[38] *Martyrium Apollonii* 46, ed. Musurillo, *ACM*, p. 103, lines 18–21; Compare Eusebius, *Historia ecclesiastica* V, 21, ed. Schwartz, Mommsen, pp. 484–6. For a similar polite exchange, see *Acta Phileae* 5, ed. Kortekaas, pp. 299–303.
[39] *Acta Cypriani* 1, 4, ed. Bastiaensen, p. 228.
[40] Hunink, 'St Cyprian, a Christian and Roman gentleman', p. 32.
[41] *Martyrium Pionii* 4.9, ed. Hilhorst, *Atti e passioni*, p. 158.

Part I

the example of Christ being silent before Pilate present martyrs who willingly gave up this privilege to speak out and defend themselves. The apologist Justin (d. c. 165 AD), according to the acts of his martyrdom, did not respond to the questions of his interrogator, the prefect Rusticus, with the kind of lengthy defence speech one might have expected from an apologist. Even when the prefect came to talk to him a second time, and appealed to Justin's reputation for eloquence and great knowledge of truth, Justin was rather unforthcoming in his reply.[42] One person who was more talkative than Justin was a martyr we just encountered, Apollonius of Rome, who was executed during the reign of Emperor Commodus in 185 AD. It is difficult to establish when exactly the account of his martyrdom was written, but a condensed version of the story can be found in Eusebius' *Ecclesiastical History*.[43] Apollonius of Rome is one of the few martyrs of whom it is reported that he took the opportunity to make a defence speech when it was offered to him.[44] His speech is modelled on the speeches of the Apostle Paul as recorded in the Acts of the Apostles. Apollonius' speech of defence, moreover, contains arguments and turns of phrase that are familiar from the work of an Athenian philosopher who converted to Christianity, the apologist Athenagoras (c. 133–90 AD).[45] The similarities between Apollonius' defence speech and the work of Athenagoras illustrate how the ideas of the apologists influenced the martyr accounts and provided arguments to Christians who were exposed to persecution.

THE MARTYR'S PARRHESIA

The authors of the early martyrdom accounts credited their martyrs with *parrhesia*, but attached new meanings and connotations to the word.[46]

---

[42] *Martyrium Iustini*, recension C, 4, ed. Musurillo, *ACM*, p. 60.
[43] Eusebius, *Historia ecclesiastica* 5, 21, ed. Schwartz, Mommsen, pp. 484–6.
[44] *Martyrium Apollonii* 14–42, ed. Musurillo, *ACM*, pp. 94–102; see also the defence speech of Pionius, *Martyrium Pionii* 4, ed. Hilhorst, *Atti e passioni*, p. 156–62.
[45] Crehan, introduction to Athenagoras, *Legatio pro Christianis*, p. 3.
[46] Examples of the *parrhesia* of martyrs can be found in *Martyrium Polycarpi* 10, 1, ed. Orbán, *Atti e passioni*, p. 16, line 4 ; *Passio Perpetuae* (Greek version) 17, 1 and 18, 4, ed. Amat p. 162, line 4 and p. 166, line 14; *Martyrium Iustini* 4, recension C, ed. Musurillo, *ACM*, p. 58, line 20; *Martyrium Dasii* 6, ed. Musurillo, *ACM*, p. 276, line 5; *Martyrium Lugdunensium* 1.18, ed. Orbán, *Atti e passioni*, p. 68, line 95; 1.49, ed. Orbán, *Atti e passioni*, p. 84, line 294, 295; 2.4, ed. Orbán, *Atti e passioni*, p. 92, line 25 and in Eusebius' *Historia ecclesiastica* IV, 15, 21, ed. Schwartz, p. 344, line 11; IV, 15, 47, ed. Schwartz, p. 354, line 2; V, 1, 18, ed. Schwartz, p. 408, line 17; V, 1, 49, ed. Schwartz, p. 422, line 3; 5, 2, 4, ed. Schwartz, p. 428, line 24; 6, 3, 4, ed. Schwartz, p. 524, line 23; 8, 9, 5, ed. Schwartz, p 758, lines 4, 5. In Rufinus' Latin translation of Eusebius' *Historia ecclesiastica*, these instances of martyrs' *parrhesia* have either been translated as *libertas*, *fiducia* or *constantia*; see for

The Steadfast Martyr

Van Unnik, who observes that the authors do not use the term *parrhesia* to describe bold criticism of persecutors, wonders whether perhaps the term *parrhesia* had undergone a change.[47] I propose that, instead of the word undergoing a change of meaning, certain strands that were already present in the multifaceted concept of *parrhesia* were drawn out, emphasised and associated with new metaphors. In early Christian martyr acts, martyrs go to their death gladly, in the expectation that a better life awaits them in heaven, where their martyrdom will grant them *parrhesia* before the throne of the heavenly judge.[48] The knowledge that they will receive the privilege to speak freely before Christ's heavenly court of justice, as a reward for their willingness to suffer martyrdom at the hands of an earthly judge, gives martyrs the courage to endure the proceedings of their trials quietly, and to suffer torture and offence in silence, just as Jesus had done.[49]

According to the Gospel of John, Jesus spoke in an open and straightforward manner, although, as was discussed earlier, not during his trial. Shortly before he was arrested, however, he spoke with *parrhesia* to his disciples. His disciples had reacted with joy at the sudden clarity of Jesus' speech and exclaimed: 'Yes, now you are speaking plainly, not in any figure of speech!' (John 16:29–30). Here, *parrhesia* refers to an open and clear way of speaking, without ambiguity, that is juxtaposed with figurative speech. As we have seen in the Introduction, *parrhesia*'s field of reference had become differentiated in the books of the New Testament. Its meanings range from bold actions and confidence to openness and unreservedness in speaking. In relation to Jesus, however, the meaning of the word *parrhesia* is confined to an open and direct mode of speaking, devoid of rhetorical intricacies. When Jesus spoke with *parrhesia* his speech was comprehensible to all. In the gospels of Mark and John, Jesus' *parrhesia* denotes words as well as acts that were open and public and were aimed at revealing his identity and his privileged relation to God.[50] Shortly before his execution, according to the gospels, Jesus proclaimed a public message that was open to everyone, not just to his intimate circle.

---

example ed. Mommsen p. 345, line 11 (*libertas*); p. 429, line 429 (*fiducia*), p. 525, line 31 (*fiducia*), p. 355, line 2 (*constantia*).

[47] Van Unnik, 'The Christian's freedom of speech', p. 283.
[48] Scarpat, *Parrhesia*, pp. 82, 83; Bartelink, 'Quelques observations sur παρρησία', p. 22.
[49] See for example *Martyrium Iustini*, recension C, 4, 6, ed. Musurillo, *ACM* 59, line 20. Compare to recension B, 5, 6, ed. Musurillo, *ACM*, p. 52, line 14.
[50] Mark 8:32; John 7:26; John 10:24; John 11:54; John 16:25; John 16:29. Cf. Klassen, '*Parrhesia* in the Johannine corpus', pp. 242–3.

Part I

It is this very precise sense of *parrhesia* that we often encounter in the early Christian martyr acts. The term is employed to refer to the martyr's public proclamation of the gospel, to unreserved and unembellished words addressed to God, or to a clear statement of one's Christian identity and unwavering dedication to Christ.[51] Is this Christian interpretation of *parrhesia* so very different from the freedom of speech that was traditionally ascribed to courageous individuals who spoke truth to power? Yes and no. When, in the interrogation scene of the *Martyrdom of Polycarp*, with which I opened this chapter, Polycarp plainly declares to the governor that he is a Christian, he courageously confronts a persecuting authority with a truth that the governor does not want to hear. The fact that the author of the account of his martyrdom has Polycarp do so in a polite manner does not alter the fact that Polycarp does indeed speak the truth at great risk to his personal safety. Even though the term *parrhesia* is never used in early Christian martyr texts to denote a bold, confrontational attitude towards authorities, this does not mean the audience of the narratives did not interpret their speech and behaviour as such. It was, however, essential to the Christian understanding of a martyr's *parrhesia* that the truth was proclaimed in a plain, unadorned manner, and moreover that this was done publicly. The protagonists of early Christian martyr texts, such as Polycarp, Dasius, the martyrs of Lyon and many others, do not talk back to their interrogators in the way that the Alexandrian or Maccabean martyrs are reported to have done, nor do they make rhetorically refined defence speeches, but simply said, for everyone to hear and understand: 'I am a Christian'.[52] The emphasis on the public nature of their statement fitted the Christian rhetorical ideal of ordinary or simplified speech (*sermo humilis*), also known as the 'language of fishermen' (*sermo piscatorius*), which had as its aim the wide accessibility of Christ's truth.

RHETORIC AND TRUTH

Earlier in this chapter, I mentioned four stories or story collections that served as models for the literary shape and themes of early martyr acts.

---

[51] *Martyrium Iustini*, recension B 5, ed. Musurillo, *ACM*, p. 52, line 14 (confidence about being admitted to heaven); recension C 4.6, ed. Musurillo, *ACM*, p. 58, line 20 (freedom of speech at the tribunal of Christ); *Martyrium Polycarpi* 10, 1, ed. Orbán, *Atti e passioni*, p. 16, line 4 (statement of Christian identity); *Martyrium Dasii* 6, ed. Musurillo, *ACM* 276, line 5 (statement of Christian identity); *Martyrium Lugdunensium* 1.18, ed. Orbán, *Atti e passioni*, p. 68, line 95 (bold statement of faith); 1.49, ed. Orbán, *Atti e passioni*, p. 84, line 294 (outspokenness in spreading the gospel); 2.4, ed. Orbán, *Atti e passioni*, p. 92, line 25 (great openness). See also the clear and public statement of Christian identity in Latin martyr acts, *Acta Marcelli*, recension N, ed. Musurillo, *ACM*, p. 254: 'publice et clara voce respondi me christianum esse confessum.'

[52] See the references in the previous footnote.

There were also other narratives that provided examples, in particular for the representation of the martyr's plain speech. The Acts of the Apostles record a speech of the proto-martyr Stephen before the Council of Jerusalem (Acts 7:2–53) that the authors of martyr texts took as an example of a rhetoric of plain speech.[53] Another historical model was the story of the trial and death of Socrates. According to Plato and Xenophon, Socrates had declined the use of (studied) rhetoric during his trial in favour of an open and plain mode of speaking. In his *Apology of Socrates*, Plato quotes the words with which Socrates opened his (improvised) defence speech: 'From me you will hear the whole truth, though not, by Zeus, gentlemen, expressed in embroidered and stylised phrases like theirs [referring to his accusers]; but things spoken at random and expressed in the first words that come to mind.'[54] Socrates' plain speech was emphatically presented as anti-rhetorical, although, evidently, his speech had a rhetoric of its own. His denunciation of rhetoric was rather a statement that his words contained no tricks, and that he spoke only the plain truth.

Xenophon's Socrates does realise that a properly prepared, formal defence speech will be more effective if he wishes to escape the death penalty, and yet he refuses to defend himself in the manner of the professional rhetoricians of his day.[55] If the result of this decision is death, he is willing to accept it. According to Xenophon, Socrates was not afraid to die; he even welcomed death.[56] The trial and death of Socrates provided a source of inspiration for authors of the early Christian martyr acts. The Christian apologists, who, as I pointed out earlier, influenced the authors of the early martyr texts, regarded Socrates' death as a type for Christian martyrdom, and saw his work as a preparation for the work of Christ.[57] Justin Martyr based his entire *Apology* to Emperor Antoninus Pius on Socrates' defence at his trial.[58] The unjust accusations that were levelled at Socrates, his willingness to face the death penalty, his death in the name of truth, reminded them of Jesus' trial, and, ultimately, of Christian martyrdom.[59]

In early Christian martyr texts, we see a clear preference for plain speech over studied rhetoric. The Christian martyr did not need to be accomplished in rhetoric, for it was believed that God himself would give

---

[53] Kennedy, *Classical Rhetoric*, p. 148.
[54] Plato, *Apologia Socratis* 17 b–c, trans. Grube, p. 22; See also 24 a–b; compare Xenophon, *Apologia Socratis*, pp. 2–4.
[55] Xenophon, *Apologia Socratis* 2–4; cf. Quintilian, *Institutio oratoria* 11, 1.
[56] Xenophon, *Apologia Socratis* 7–10 and 33, 34.
[57] Benz, 'Christus und Sokrates', pp. 199ff.; Bowersock, *Martyrdom and Rome*, pp. 8–9.
[58] Barnard, Justin Martyr, *The First and Second Apologies*, p. 109.
[59] Justin Martyr, *Second Apology* 10; *Martyrium Apollonii* 41, ed. Musurillo, *ACM*, p. 100.

Part I

the martyr the words to speak. In the Gospel of Mark, Jesus had said: 'When they bring you over to trial and hand you over, do not worry beforehand about what you are to say; but say whatever is given to you at the time, for it is not you who speak, but the Holy Spirit' (Mark 13:11). The authors of martyr texts emphasise the divine origin of their martyrs' wisdom and underline the inspired nature of their words. Yet some authors apparently did feel the need to stress the supremacy of the martyr's plain speech over the classically schooled speech of pagan philosophers and rhetoricians. Perhaps especially for an audience that was well versed in classical rhetoric, they wished to demonstrate that plain speech was in no way inferior to rhetorically accomplished discourse. What better example to prove their point than the defence speech of Socrates, admired by Christian and non-Christian Romans alike? The manner in which some of the authors of early martyr narratives drew on Socrates illustrates their need to present their protagonists and their Christian identity as standing out *and* blending in vis à vis Greco-Roman culture and the norms and restrictions of *paideia*, as the following example shows.[60]

In the *Martyrdom of Pionius the Presbyter and His Companions*, written shortly before 300 AD,[61] the story of Socrates' trial serves to highlight the superiority of the martyr's anti-rhetorical speech over the sophisticated rhetoric of his opponent. The author relates how the martyr Pionius (d. second half of the third century) had an exchange with one of the bystanders present at his trial, named Rufinus, who called the martyr a fool. Pionius rebuffed Rufinus' remark with an appeal to Socrates: if he, Pionius, was a fool because he was prepared to die for the truth, then so was Socrates.[62] He compared Rufinus to Anytus and Meletus, the prosecutors at Socrates' trial.[63] The author of *The Martyrdom of Pionius* was presumably well informed about the details of the story of Socrates' trial if he even knew the names of his accusers. Just like Socrates, who was accused and slandered by rhetoricians who had no love for truth but delighted only in the cleverness of their own arguments, Pionius is pictured as being abused and challenged by Rufinus, who, according to the author, had a reputation for superiority in rhetoric.[64] Rufinus'

---

[60] Other early martyr acts that contain programmatic references to Socrates' trial and death are the *Martyrium Apollonii* and the *Acta Phileae*. See also Roskam, 'The figure of Socrates in *Acta Martyrum*'.
[61] Musurillo, *ACM*, p. xxix.
[62] *Martyrium Pionii* 17, 1–4, ed. Hilhorst, *Atti e passioni*, p. 182; compare Eusebius IV, 15, 47, ed. Schwartz, Mommsen, pp. 352–4.
[63] Ibid., 17, 2, ed. Hilhorst, *Atti e passioni*, p. 182.
[64] Ibid., 17, 1, ed. Hilhorst, *Atti e passioni*, p. 182.

rhetorical talent, however, was no match for Pionius' straightforward defence, for the martyr had him silenced in no time.

The stories about Jesus, Socrates and Stephen furnished examples for the authors of the early martyrdom accounts to represent the plain, anti-rhetorical speech of their martyrs. Some authors appear to have aimed to distinguish the speech of the Christian martyrs, and notably their *parrhesia*, from the sophisticated language of their educated contemporaries. The persuasive force of the martyr's words resided in God's wisdom, not in the style and composition prescribed by the rhetorical schools.[65] At the same time, their references to Socrates' trial and death demonstrated their intimate knowledge of Greek literary culture, and proved that neither the Christian authors nor their protagonists were the unsophisticated 'frogs' that some of their educated contemporaries took them for.[66] The same argument probably holds true for their representation of the martyrs' *parrhesia*: the authors showed that they were well aware of the importance of *parrhesia* as a cultivated virtue, but chose to give it a different interpretation. The *parrhesia* of their martyrs sprang naturally from their inner independence, their detachment from worldly desires and their disdain for rhetorical conventions. The audience of the narratives should, however, not be misled into thinking that the martyrs, or their biographers, were unaware of old-style *parrhesia* and its intimate connection to the culture of *paideia*. The authors imply that their martyrs could have jumped into that tradition with both feet had they wanted to. Instead, they chose to do it differently, just as Socrates and after him Jesus and Stephen had done.

LATIN TERMINOLOGY OF FREE SPEECH

The martyr acts that have been discussed so far were all written in Greek. Let us now turn to a Latin martyr text, the *Passio of Perpetua and Felicitas,* to see which Latin words were used to describe the speech and behaviour of a Christian martyr. By looking at the terms that were employed in Latin texts, we may gain a better understanding of how a certain type of behaviour and manner of speaking that was generally understood as *parrhesia* in Greco-Roman culture was interpreted in Latin. The *Passio of Perpetua and Felicitas* is one of the earliest surviving Latin martyrdom accounts. Tertullian (c. 155–c. 240) already referred to it, and some scholars therefore took him to be its author.[67] The narrative is of special

---

[65] Compare Origen, *Contra Celsum* 3, 39, ed. Borret, vol. 2, pp. 92–4 on the power and persuasiveness of divinely inspired speech that surpassed Greek rhetorical skill.
[66] Origen, *Contra Celsum* 4, 23, ed. Borret, vol. 2, p. 290, lines 20, 21.
[67] Van den Eynde, 'The *Passio Perpetuae*', p. 25.

interest since it has been transmitted in both a Latin and a Greek version, with the Greek version postdating the Latin.[68] The Latin *Passio* was probably written in the early third century AD.[69] The account includes part of a prison diary that was believed to have been written by the martyr Perpetua herself, which would make it one of the earliest surviving texts written by a Christian woman.

The *Passio of Perpetua and Felicitas* recounts the heroic death of two Christian women: the African noblewoman Vibia Perpetua and her slave-girl Felicitas, who were martyred in 202 AD.[70] The author of the Latin version recounts how the martyrs spoke with *constantia* to the people on the day before their execution. Their speech was of a confrontational nature: according to the author of the Latin version the martyrs' *constantia* was such that they 'beat the people about the head with their words' (*eadem constantia ad populum verba ista iactabant*).[71] They warned the crowd about God's judgement and testified to the joy they would have in their suffering. According to the author, everyone departed from the prison in amazement, and many of them began to believe.[72]

In Stoic writings, *constantia* refers to stability of mind, tranquillity and self-possession, the virtues of the philosopher who has his passions under control. In Cicero's vocabulary, *constantia* often refers to the wise person's consistency of belief and action.[73] *Constantia* is also one of the terms by which the *parrhesia* of the apostles is rendered in Latin translations of the New Testament. This choice of translation adds a Stoic interpretation to the apostles' frankness and bold behaviour.[74] I would suggest that the *constantia* of Perpetua, Felicitas and their companions should be understood in this Stoic sense. The martyrs speak to the people in a steadfast manner, with emotional poise, unafraid of the torture that is awaiting them. Perpetua herself is reported to have resisted her interrogator and torturers with *constantia* 'until the very end'.[75]

In the *Passio of Perpetua and Felicitas* we also find a more traditional Latin expression to indicate free speech, namely *libere loqui*. Interestingly, it is not Perpetua to whom this action is ascribed, but her pagan father, who delivers an emotional speech in the hope of persuading Perpetua to renounce her Christian faith. He asks his daughter to have pity on his

---

[68] Bowersock, *Martyrdom and Rome*, pp. 33, 34.
[69] Barnes, *Early Christian Hagiography and Roman History*, p. 358, suggests 204 as a probable date.
[70] Van den Eynde, 'The *Passio Perpetuae*', p. 23.
[71] *Passio Perpetuae* 17, 1, ed. Amat, p. 162, lines 3, 4.   [72] Ibid.
[73] Graver, *Cicero on the Emotions*, p. 169.   [74] See the introduction and the literature cited there.
[75] *Passio Perpetuae* 18, 4, ed. Amat, p. 166, lines 11, 12: 'generosa illa in finem usque constantia repugnavit'.

grey head and not abandon him to be the reproach of men (*ne me dederis in dedecus hominum*).[76] He begs her to think of her mother, aunt, brothers and newborn baby, who, he says, will not be able to live any more when she is gone. He closes his speech with a passionate plea: 'Give up your pride! You will destroy all of us! None of us will ever be able to speak freely again (*libere loquetur*) if anything happens to you.'[77]

Perpetua's father expresses his distress at the thought that his daughter will die as a martyr for the Christian faith, and is anxious about his own future and social position. His speech seems to imply that loss of social status compromised one's liberty to speak freely in public. The author chose the expression *libere loqui* to describe the privilege that Perpetua's father held dear, while he or she ascribed *constantia* to Perpetua when she spoke freely. The author may have considered the term *constantia*, with its specific Stoic ring, inappropriate to assign to Perpetua's father, who evidently was not in control of his emotions. Perhaps this differentiation in vocabulary is a coincidence, but it may also have been a deliberate choice on the part of the author to distinguish Christian from non-Christian free speech. Perpetua's pagan father's *libere loqui* was connected to social status and to his fear of losing it. Loss of social status was not relevant to Perpetua, and this lack of fear is embodied in her *constantia*. The Greek version of the *Passio of Perpetua and Felicitas* does not make this distinction in vocabulary, but refers to both Perpetua's free speech and that of her father as *parrhesia*.[78]

SCENES OF CONFRONTATION

Many of the martyrs who are featured in the early martyrdom accounts show respect for Roman authorities, as the New Testament had taught them to do. They submit themselves willingly to the death penalty, and go to their (often gruesome) death in a quiet and dignified manner, following the example of Socrates, Jesus and the proto-martyr Stephen. Nevertheless, it was important to the authors of the martyr acts that the martyrs' obedience, their respectful attitude towards authorities or their reticence during interrogation, should not be taken as signs of weakness. To avoid that impression, martyr acts often include one or more scenes in which the martyr is taunted or challenged by a member of the crowd.

---

[76] Ibid. 5, 2, ed. Amat, p. 118, line 7.
[77] Ibid. 5, 4, ed. Amat, p. 120, lines 9–11: 'Depone animos; ne universos nos extermines: nemo enim nostrum libere loquetur, si tu aliquid fueris passa.'
[78] *Passio Perpetuae*, Greek version, 5, 4; 17, 1 and 18, 4, ed. Amat, p. 120, line 11, p. 162, line 4 and p. 166, line 14. The Greek version postdates the Latin version, see Bowersock, *Martyrdom and Rome*, pp. 33, 34.

Part I

In these confrontational scenes, the martyr manages to silence his or her accuser with a few well-placed, smart remarks.[79] Such scenes of confrontation serve to show that the martyr did not lack courage and sharp wit and could speak boldly if he or she wished to do so.

In confrontations with the crowd, the antagonists of the martyr are usually described as self-confident rhetoricians, pagan philosophers or insolent Jews. In the view of the authors of many martyr narratives, these antagonists did not deserve the same respect as Roman authorities; they were regarded as accomplices of the devil, sent with the express purpose of taunting the martyr and breaking his or her self-control.[80] These three types of opponents – philosophers, rhetoricians, Jews – were probably selected because they represented three categories within or against which Christians needed to define their own identity: philosophy, rhetoric and religion. The martyrs' opponents stood for the cultural heritage that the Christian authors of the narratives wished both to link up to and distinguish themselves from. They selected the useful elements of this heritage and assimilated them into their own Christian culture. *Parrhesia* was part of the cultural tradition that was adopted and infused with meanings that corresponded to the values and ideals of early Christians, and that put a distinguishable stamp on their identity as free Roman citizens with a superior *libertas* in Christ.

CONCLUSION

Pre-Constantinian martyr texts attest to a process of re-evaluation of frank speech in relation to other Christian values such as modesty, obedience and self-control. The authors of the early martyrdom accounts present Christians who were courageous, steadfast, respectful to authorities, frank if they had to be, plain-spoken and poised. The authors' use of the term *parrhesia,* and in Latin martyr texts *constantia,* reflects these values, although not necessarily all of them at the same time.[81] Early Christian authors emphasise different aspects of the multifaceted and polyvalent concept of *parrhesia,* bringing out new meanings while drawing on the cultural capital of the old.

This chapter has illustrated a tendency that can be observed in early martyrdom accounts: namely, a preference for the open and anti-

---

[79] See *Martyrium Pionii* 17, ed. Hilhorst, *Atti e passioni,* p. 182; *Martyrium Apollonii* 33, 34, ed. Musurillo, *ACM,* p. 98; *Passio Perpetuae* 16, 2–4, ed. Amat, p. 158, line 6; p. 160, line 16.
[80] Bastiaensen, Introduction to *Eeuwig geluk,* pp. 21–2.
[81] For references to (speaking with) *constantia* in Latin martyr acts, besides the examples discussed above from the *Passio Perpetuae,* see the *Passio Montani et Lucii* 14, 1 and 5, ed. Musurillo, *ACM,* p. 226, lines 20, 21 and line 31, and the *Acta Phileae* 7, ed. Kortekaas, p. 306, line 4.

rhetorical *parrhesia* of Jesus and Socrates over the bold or sophisticated *parrhesia* of other truth-tellers. This tendency can be interpreted as a response to a growing criticism of or uneasiness towards unbridled free speech and (schooled) rhetoric. We should, however, keep in mind that it was one trend among many, and one that built on earlier currents. Authors of other martyr texts selected different aspects from the rich repertoire of free speech, and did not hesitate to present their martyrs as sophisticated orators who engaged in lengthy discussions with their interrogators, or as bold rebels opposing a persecuting authority. Especially post-persecution narratives tended to emphasise boldness and contempt for authority, if that authority was clearly in the wrong. The martyrs depicted in Prudentius' *Crowns of Martyrdom* (c. 400), for example, are often blatantly insolent towards Roman authorities. Prudentius recounts how the martyr Eulalia of Mérida (d. 304) spat in the eyes of her interrogator, abused the governor and destroyed the symbols of his pagan religion.[82]

The process of adaptation and transformation of free speech was thus no linear development in which *parrhesia* gradually gave way to obedience and compliance, but an oscillating process that showed fluctuations in response to contemporary interests and needs. In the first half of the fifth century, a new version of the passion of the proto-martyr Stephen was written, in which Stephen is portrayed as speaking brazenly to his interrogator, calling him an inhabitant of hell and accomplice of the devil.[83] This new *Acta Stephani* depicted Stephen's demeanour in a way that was markedly different from the rational, controlled behaviour that was ascribed to him in the Acts of the Apostles. Evidently, the old account of Acts 26 was no longer deemed sufficient to meet the circumstances and priorities of the new age.[84] Perhaps the authors of martyr narratives writing in the period after the Great Persecution, when Christianity had become an accepted religion in the Roman Empire, no longer felt the need to demonstrate that Christians were obedient, respectful citizens of the Roman Empire. They did not share the reluctance of their pre-Constantinian colleagues to ascribe bold and oppositional *parrhesia* to the martyrs of the past whose deeds and speech they glorified. Authors writing shortly after the age of persecution had to deal with a different type of oppression, caused by competition among different Christian schools of thought and the mistreatment they suffered at the hands of their Christian rivals. It would appear that an abusive, confrontational type of *parrhesia* fitted the context of that inter-confessional strife among

---

[82] Prudentius, *Peristephanon* 3, ed. Thomson, LCL 102, pp. 122–30.
[83] Quotation in Grig, *Making Martyrs*, p. 95.   [84] Ibid.

Part I

Christians better than it had suited the earlier cultural clash between 'pagan' and Christian citizens of the Roman Empire. The subject of the next chapter, Bishop Hilary of Poitiers, styled himself as a martyr of the post-persecution era. In his writings we can observe two different stances towards free speech: respect for God-given authority and bold opposition to a persecutor of the correct Christian faith.

2

HILARY OF POITIERS

It is the time for speaking, since the time for silence has now passed. Let Christ be expected, because the Antichrist has assumed power. Let the shepherds shout, because the hired men have fled. Let us lay down our lives for the sheep, because the thieves have entered and the raging lion prowls. Let us advance to martyrdom with these words, because the angel of Satan has transformed himself into an angel of light.[1]

With these words, Bishop Hilary of Poitiers (d. 367) imperiously declared his willingness to suffer martyrdom for the sake of truth, following the illustrious examples of early Christian martyrs such as Polycarp, Justin, Perpetua and many others. The 'Antichrist' he was railing against, however, was no pagan governor or tyrant such as the early Christian martyrs had been confronted with, but a Christian emperor. Hilary lived and wrote in the days after the Great Persecution, when the chances that one would be executed for standing up for the Christian faith were slim. His call to advance to martyrdom met with practical impediments, for there were no persecuting pagan rulers of the calibre of Nero and Decius anymore, as Hilary did not fail to recognise.[2] The addressee of his invective, Emperor Constantius II (r. 337–61), was in fact a promoter and protector of Christian orthodoxy. But the emperor's orthodoxy was not Hilary's orthodoxy.

At the beginning of the fourth century, after the age of persecution had come to an end, disputes broke out between several Christian factions. A theological controversy arose, known as the Arian controversy, that pitched supporters of different interpretations of Christian doctrine

---

[1] Hilary, *In Constantium* 1, ed. Rocher, p. 166: 'Tempus est loquendi, quia iam praeteriit tempus tacendi. Christus expectetur, quia obtinuit antichristus. Clament pastores, quia mercennarii fugerunt. Ponamus animas pro ovibus, quia fures introierunt, et leo saeviens circuit. Ad martyrium per has voces exeamus, quia angelus satanae transfiguravit se in angelum lucis.' Trans. Flower, *Imperial Invectives*, p. 115.
[2] Ibid. 4, ed. Rocher, p. 174.

against each other. In this highly contentious atmosphere, in which bishops vied for the emperor's support, or criticised him for backing the wrong religious party, free speech was considered of vital importance. After the dust of the Christological controversies had settled and the Nicene party emerged triumphant, three bishops were remembered with particular favour for their courage in speaking truth to power: Athanasius of Alexandria (d. 373), Lucifer of Cagliari (d. 371) and Hilary of Poitiers (d. 367). As Robert Markus has demonstrated, Hilary and other members of the Nicene opposition under 'Arian' emperors placed themselves in the tradition of the martyrs, proclaiming themselves as their true heirs.[3] In their missives to Emperor Constantius II, written from their places of exile, bishops Athanasius, Lucifer and Hilary styled themselves as stout champions of truth, who were willing to die for defending their interpretation of Christian doctrine, even though dying for Christ's truth was no longer a realistic prospect.

This chapter investigates the implications of the changed conditions in the Roman Empire for the rhetoric of Christian free speech, after Christianity had become an accepted religion and a variety of belief systems coexisted throughout the empire. Bishops such as Athanasius, Lucifer and Hilary needed to find a new stance and a 'new rhetoric of opposition' that fitted the realities of the post-persecution era.[4] Was it acceptable to inveigh against a Christian emperor, or against a fellow bishop for that matter, because he subscribed to an alternative interpretation of Christ's truth? In the eyes of Nicene bishops, Constantius had accepted a heretical confession of faith, but he was still an emperor who had embraced Christianity and supported the church. In this chapter, I shall focus on the rhetoric of Hilary of Poitiers, who came to be regarded as the head of the anti-Arian faction in the West.[5] In Hilary's letters, we find a new vocabulary and rhetoric of free speech which covered a whole range from persuasion to criticism, from polite advice to outright abuse.

In 356, three years after he became bishop of Poitiers, Hilary was deposed from his see and exiled to Phrygia.[6] The reasons for his deposition and banishment are not entirely clear. Some scholars say it was because he refused to subscribe to the banishment of Athanasius, while others maintain that he was exiled because of his political opposition to

---

[3] Markus, *End of Ancient Christianity*, p. 85; see now also Flower, *Emperors and Bishops*, especially pp. 146–63.
[4] Flower, *Emperors and Bishops*, p. 17.
[5] Hunter, 'Fourth-century Latin writers', p. 302; Heil, 'Homoians in Gaul', p. 271, and see the references in Flower, *Emperors and Bishops*, p. 7.
[6] Wickham, *Hilary of Poitiers, Conflicts of Conscience and Law*, p. xiii.

Constantius and support of the usurper Silvanus.[7] By Hilary's own account, he was banished by heretics because he defended the orthodox faith.[8] During his exile, he composed two speeches which he addressed to Emperor Constantius II. In the first speech, he pleads with the emperor to hear his case; in the second, he harshly inveighs against him. A comparison between the two speeches, which were written less than a year apart, shows how Hilary abruptly turned from respectful admonition to downright invective. Like the martyrs, Hilary presented himself as a dauntless champion of orthodox truth, who was not afraid to speak freely against those in power and, if necessary, to rail against them.

As discussed in the previous chapter, early Christian martyr acts featured persecuted Christians who stoutly defended the truth before pagan magistrates. For fourth-century bishops who were confronted with the challenge of finding new modes of persuasion to influence a Christian ruler or their own audiences, the language of the martyr acts provided a model of free speech that fitted their position as exiled defenders of truth. The discourse of martyrdom, however, could not be adopted without modification. It may have been acceptable for a martyr to attack a pagan ruler verbally, but it did not go without saying that it was considered proper for a bishop to act in a similar manner against a Christian ruler. Some early martyr texts had explicitly promoted respect for all authorities.[9] How far could one go in criticising a God-given emperor? To answer this question, we need to take a closer look at how Hilary justified his harsh attack on the Christian emperor Constantius, when he switched from admonition to invective. But first let us attend to the circumstances in which Hilary composed his first, deferential speech *to* Constantius, before turning to his later invective *against* him.

IN THE PRESENCE OF THE EMPEROR

When Hilary was exiled to Phrygia in 358, he composed his major theological work *On the Trinity* and wrote a history of councils from Nicaea to his own time, called *On the Synods* (c. 385).[10] The latter work was addressed to the bishops of Gaul in preparation for the upcoming double synod of Ariminum (Rimini) in the West and Seleucia in the East, convened by Emperor Constantius in an attempt to resolve the controversy. In his epistolary address *On the Synods*, Hilary tried to bring different schools of thought closer together, hoping, he said, to contribute

---

[7] Hunter, 'Fourth-century Latin writers', p. 302. For the first view, see Doignon, *Hilaire de Poitiers avant l'exile*, pp. 455–513; for the latter, more recent view, see Williams, 'A reassessment'.
[8] Hilary, *Ad Constantium* 2, ed. Feder, p. 198.   [9] See chapter 1, pp. 27–30.
[10] Beckwith, *Hilary of Poitiers on the Trinity*, p. 217.

Part I

to a solution of the doctrinal dispute.[11] In 359, or early in 360, he wrote an address to Constantius (*Liber ad Constantium*; hereafter, *To Constantius*), in which he pleaded with the emperor to grant him a hearing at the Council of Constantinople and offered his services to mediate in the conflict.

The status of Hilary's address to Constantius is ambiguous. While *To Constantius* is called an *epistola* in the earliest surviving manuscript, it does not take the form of a letter proper. Rather, it is shaped as a public speech, delivered, or to be delivered, in the emperor's presence. I shall therefore refer to this text as an epistolary speech. According to the heading of the text in the oldest two manuscripts, Hilary personally handed over his address to Constantius when he was in Constantinople.[12] In Jerome's catalogue *On Famous Men* (c. 392) we find an entry saying that Hilary handed his *libellus* to 'the emperor then living at Constantinople'.[13] Although it seems highly improbable that an exiled bishop would be permitted physical access to the emperor, Hilary was indeed in that city at the time. He had been present at the Council of Seleucia in 359, which ended in division, and then moved on to Constantinople for the conclusion of the assembly.[14] Apparently Hilary enjoyed relative freedom of movement during his time in exile and was even allowed to attend councils.

Hilary's *To Constantius* contains several cues that suggest an oral delivery in the emperor's presence, such as 'listen, I beg you', 'bend your ears' and 'God has presented me the opportunity of your presence'.[15] He may have deliberately shaped his address to Constantius as a public speech, delivered to the emperor in person, to make his plea more persuasive. Readers should imagine Hilary standing before the emperor, making his plea on behalf of the entire Christian church. In the setting he chose for his speech, the emperor has benevolently granted him a 'candid hearing' (*sincera audientia*) at his court.[16] In his epistolary speech, Hilary pleads with the emperor to grant him another hearing, this time at the Council of Constantinople that was taking place at that very moment. He says that he hopes for an opportunity to expound his views publicly before the emperor and the bishops present at the council. In *To Constantius*, he does not attack the 'Arian' faction directly, nor does he criticise the

---

[11] Humfress, *Orthodoxy and the Courts*, p. 239; Barnes, 'Hilary of Poitiers on his exile', p. 129.

[12] Rocher, *Hilaire de Poitiers*, p. 25, note 2.

[13] Jerome, *De viris illustribus* 100, ed. Herding, pp. 56, 57 : 'Est eius et "ad Constantium" libellus, quem viventi Constantinopoli porrexerat.'

[14] Hanson, *Search for the Christian Doctrine*, p. 464; Wickham, *Hilary of Poitiers, Conflicts of Conscience and Law*, p. xiv, Flower, *Imperial Invectives*, p. 27.

[15] Hilary, *Ad Constantium* 10, ed. Feder, p. 295: 'Audi, rogo'; 'summitte aures tuas'; ibid. 1, ed. Feder, p. 197: 'mihi a deo [de] praesentiae tuae opportunitas praestita'.

[16] Ibid. 8, ed. Feder, p. 203, line 7.

emperor for supporting them, although he does suggest cautiously that Constantius has perhaps not been listening to the (right) bishops.[17] Instead, he points out in general terms that conflict and strife such as the Church had seen since the Council of Nicaea does not benefit the Christian faith.

Hilary's denunciation of the fierce debates could be read as a complaint about the behaviour of his opponents, but he tactfully does not put the blame on the other party, at least not explicitly. He consistently speaks of 'we' and of 'our failures' when censuring the bickering and arguing in the church that, to his mind, divided the church and estranged people from Christ himself.[18] He does not divert the wrongs that were committed solely to his opponents, nor does he pit the emperor and the Arian party as 'them' (or 'you') against 'us'. Instead, he has chosen to share in the guilt by subsuming himself under an unspecified 'we'. He thus presents the controversy over the correct interpretation of the Christian faith as a problem that concerns both parties, and as a source of concern for both the emperor and himself. He praises the emperor for the fact that Constantius, just like Hilary himself, wishes to arrive at a simple apostolic creed that all parties can agree on.[19] Stressing their shared interests, Hilary aims to establish a common ground between the emperor and himself. He glosses over the theological hurdles that stand in the way of reaching consensus and presents the desire for a commonly shared creed as a devout and straightforward wish that could be fulfilled if only the opposing parties would talk to each other. Towards the end of his speech, he thanks Constantius for his willingness to listen to him, and begs for a chance to speak at the Council of Constantinople.[20]

PRIEST–BISHOP IN EXILE

The speaker position that Hilary adopts in his epistolary speech to Constantius is that of an exiled priest–bishop, who speaks words of God. Just as earthen jars sometimes contain valuable treasures, Hilary says, quoting from the Apostle Paul's letter to the Corinthians, so someone as low in status as an exile can be a spokesman of truth.[21] As Hilary reminds Constantius at the opening of his speech, allegedly spoken in the emperor's presence, even in exile he is still a bishop, holding the authority of a bishop.[22]

---

[17] Hilary, *Ad Constantium* 4, ed. Feder, p. 199, line 3.   [18] Ibid. 6, ed. Feder, pp. 201–2.
[19] Ibid. 8, ed. Feder, pp. 203, lines 1–5.   [20] Ibid. 8, ed. Feder, pp. 203, lines 7–10.
[21] Ibid. 8, ed. Feder, p. 203, lines 10–12, with a quotation from 2 Cor. 4:7.
[22] Ibid. 2, ed. Feder, p. 197, line 17–p. 198, line 2.

Part I

Hilary does not turn his remark about his exiled status into an accusation against the emperor. He briefly mentions the conflict that led to his exile, but quickly says that he realises Constantius had been deceived. Treacherous bishops had advised him badly and had put the emperor up against his faithful bishop.[23] Hilary wears this self-designation, 'exiled priest–bishop of the Lord', as a badge of honour. The role he adopts in his epistolary speech *To Constantius* is reminiscent of Old Testament prophets, such as Jeremiah and Ezekiel, who spoke words of truth from exile.[24] In his epistolary speech *To Constantius* he stresses the fact that he is still a *sacerdos* and still a mediator between God and people. By virtue of his position as a priest–bishop in exile, Hilary could speak freely to the emperor and warn him against the dangers of the present conflict in the church. He used the image of independence and detachment connected to the status of the exile to offer his services as a mediator in a controversy that, to his mind, threatened the stability of the church. Thus, he intricately connected the exilic position with the liberty to speak freely.[25]

In his epistolary speech *To Constantius*, Hilary speaks words of reconciliation in a mild voice of admonition, blaming in the first place not the emperor for the present conflict within the church, but a collective 'we' and, occasionally, an unspecified 'them'.[26] In that sense Hilary, although he emphasises his status as exiled bishop, does not present himself as an outsider, but as an insider. He volunteers his services to mediate in the conflict as a priest–bishop who belongs to the same church as the emperor, and promises him that if he will grant him a hearing at the Council of Constantinople, he will not use this opportunity to add fuel to the fire of dissent. He will take care not to offend anyone, least of all the emperor himself. 'I give a guarantee of my future speech in your presence,' he assures Constantius; 'I will not advocate anything to cause offence, nor defend anything outside the gospel.'[27] Hilary implies that the conflict between the Homoian and Nicene party could be resolved through rational discussion. It is up to the emperor to create an opportunity for such a discussion and to grant him a forum to speak.

---

[23] Ibid. 2, ed. Feder, p. 198, lines 2–10.   [24] Mein, 'Ezechiel as a priest in exile', p. 212.
[25] Hilary returned to the Old Testament prophet as a model for independent free speech in his *Commentary on the Psalms*; see below.
[26] See Hilary, *Ad Constantium* 6, ed. Feder, pp. 201–2.
[27] Hilary, *Ad Constantium* 11, ed. Feder, p. 204, lines 19–20: 'Praemitto interim pignus futuri apud te sermonis mei, non aliqua ad scandalum neque, quae extra evangelium sunt, defendam.' Trans. Wickham, p. 109.

Hilary of Poitiers

In his address *To Constantius*, Hilary addresses the emperor frankly, but respectfully. The epistolary speech is a showpiece of rhetorical refinement. Hilary had received a classical education in the liberal arts in Gaul, and was familiar with the techniques and patterns of classical rhetoric. According to Lionel Wickham, Hilary's skill in public speaking and debate owed much to the lessons of the first-century rhetorician Quintilian.[28] The rhetorical strategies that he employs in addressing Constantius correspond to the advice offered in rhetorical handbooks on how to speak frankly to a ruler.[29] He assures the emperor in the exordium of his speech, for example, that he has come to speak with him only because 'the office of his conscience' (*conscientiae meae officium*) compels him to speak out, which reminds us of Rutilius Lupus' advice to 'pretend to speak involuntarily and out of necessity' when addressing a person of superior authority.[30] Hilary says he fears God's judgement if he were to remain silent, when the hope, life and immortality of the emperor and all men are at stake.[31] This expression of concern for the well-being of the emperor and all his subjects in the Christian church is reminiscent of the advice of the author of the *Rhetorica ad Herennium* (first century BC), to address the criticised person as if one only had his best interest at heart. Hilary assures Constantius that he is not concerned about himself, but only about the emperor's well-being.

In the following section of the epistolary speech, Hilary admonishes the emperor in a rather gentle manner. His main critique is that Constantius was not able to hear the truth from (the right, that is Nicene) bishops, but this criticism is compensated for by abundant praise of Constantius' devotion to Christ and to the Church.[32] Hilary's goal was reconciliation, not putting further strain on a relationship that was already under pressure. Rather than drawing attention to the conflict that had led to his banishment, which would have placed the author of the speech in opposition to his addressee, he emphasises the zeal that he and the emperor share for the unity of the Christian Church. He preferred to cast Constantius in the role of ally, addressing him as his partner. Whether Constantius was really as interested in returning to a simple, scriptural

---

[28] Wickham, *Hilary of Poitiers, Conflicts of Conscience and Law*, p. xii, Borchart, *Hilary of Poitiers' Role*, pp. 6–8. See also Smulders, *Hilary of Poitiers' Preface to His* Opus historicum, comparing Hilary's rhetorical strategies to Quintilian's recommendations.

[29] See the rhetorical treatises and their discussion of free speech, listed in the introduction, note 3.

[30] Hilary, *Ad Constantium* 1, ed. Feder, p. 197, lines 14, 15; compare Rutilius Lupus, *De figuris sententiarum et elocutionis* II, 18, ed. Halm, *RLM*, p. 20, lines 21–2: 'ac simulandum est invitos necessario dicere'.

[31] Hilary, *Ad Constantium* 3, ed. Feder, p. 198, lines 21–4.

[32] Ibid. 4, ed. Feder, p. 199, lines 2–3 and 8, ed. Feder, p. 203, lines 1–5.

creed 'as laid down by the synod of our forebears' (i.e. the synod of Nicaea) as Hilary made him out to be, was not essential to the intended effect of the plea.[33] It was part of Hilary's strategy of persuasion to create an ideal image of the emperor in his epistolary speech.[34] By addressing Constantius as a ruler who cares for the unity of the Church and who is prepared to listen to the words of an exiled priest, Hilary presses the emperor to conform to that image and behave accordingly.

THE LIMITS OF ACCEPTABLE CRITICISM

Constantius denied Hilary's appeal and did not grant him a platform at the synod of Constantinople. The council ratified the Homoian creed to put an end to the division of the Council of Seleucia, where Hilary had been present. Shortly after, Hilary wrote a tract against Constantius, known as the *Liber in Constantium* (hereafter, *Against Constantius*) in which he vehemently attacks the emperor for his support of the 'Arian' faction. According to Timothy Barnes, the tract was written 'at white heat of fury at the outcome of the council of Constantinople'.[35] Hilary criticises Constantius for banishing bishops of the Nicene party and for neglecting to protect the orthodox faith. The polemical tone of this tract is markedly different from the polite voice of his epistolary speech *To Constantius*, even though the texts were written in the same year. In *To Constantius*, Hilary had addressed Constantius as 'most devout emperor'; in his diatribe *Against Constantius*, he blatantly calls the emperor the Antichrist.[36]

Hilary's invective *Against Constantius* is a strongly worded piece of writing, in which the emperor is depicted as a liar, a hypocrite and a cheat. It had been years now, Hilary writes in the opening of the invective, since his fellow bishops Paulinus, Eusebius, Lucifer and Dionysius were exiled, and years since he himself had been separated from communion with the bishops of Gaul.[37] Now the time had come when he could no longer hold his tongue. 'To remain silent for ever', Hilary writes, 'is just as dangerous as never to be silent at all.'[38] He returns to this theme again and again in

---

[33] Hilary, *Ad Constantium* 7 ('synodo patrum nostrorum'), ed. Feder, p. 202, line 16 and ibid. 8, ed. Feder, p. 203, lines 1–3.

[34] On letters of petition reflecting the kind of relationship the author of the letter hoped for, see Poster, 'A conversation halved', p. 26 and Creece, *Letters to the Emperor*, p. 2.

[35] Barnes, 'Hilary of Poitiers on his exile', p. 130. Against this view, see Flower, *Imperial Invectives*, p. 29, n. 137.

[36] Hilary, *Ad Constantium* 1, ed. Feder, p. 197, line 5: 'piissime imperator'; ibid. 4, ed. Feder, p. 199, lines 2–3: 'optime ac religiosissime imperator'. Hilary, *In Constantium* 5, ed. Rocher, p. 176, line 2: 'Constantium antichristum'.

[37] Hilary, *In Constantium* 2, ed. Rocher, p. 170, line 1–6.

[38] Ibid. 1, ed. Rocher, p. 168, lines 29–31: 'Ulterius enim tacere diffidentiae signum est, non modestiae ratio, quia non minus periculi est semper tacuisse quam numquam.'

the first chapters of his tract, each time slightly rephrasing its central thought, to justify both his previous reticence and his present outspokenness. He explains to his audience why he has remained silent for so long, and why it is now time to speak. Breaking the silence had already been a theme in his earlier address *To Constantius,* where he had argued that his conscience, his fear of God's judgement and concern for the well-being of the emperor and the empire forced him to speak out. Then, he had offered his unasked-for advice politely; now it is time to speak openly.

In his invective *Against Constantius,* Hilary borrows the language of martyr acts to present himself as a fearless and bold champion of truth, yet does not fail to point out that times have changed since the days of the martyrs. And yet, to his mind, the conditions nowadays for supporters of the true faith have not necessarily improved. If only, Hilary exclaims, he had lived in the age of persecution! At least back then it was crystal clear who the enemy was. He would rather have confessed his faith in those days and suffered torture, he says, than endure the present, confusing regime that does not allow him to give up his life for his testimony.[39] Had he lived then, he and other Christians faithful to the Nicene Creed would have fought 'renegades, torturers and murderers openly and courageously'.[40] Constantius flatters bishops and builds churches, and yet he is no less a persecutor than the pagan emperors had been. While they had the power to kill the body of faithful Christians, Hilary said, Constantius Antichrist threatens their souls.[41]

It is difficult to combat an enemy like Constantius, Hilary argues, because he avoids a good fight. He does not engage in discussions, out of fear of being defeated by better arguments. Perhaps here Hilary is indirectly referring to Constantius' refusal to grant him a hearing at the Council of Constantinople. Hilary presents a negative portrait of Constantius by comparing him to the pagan emperors Nero and Decius, although Constantius, in his view, is much worse than they had been. They had been straightforward enemies of the Christian faith, while Constantius is elusive and treacherous. In that sense, these notorious persecutors of the Christian faith were not even vicious enough for Hilary's purpose to serve as models of bad rulership. He needed another model of depravity to bring out the dangerous qualities of a ruler who knew Christ but opposed him. He found that model in the exact opposite of a follower of Christ: the Antichrist, whose deeds appeared to be good, but brought about death.

---

[39] Ibid. 4, ed. Rocher, p. 174, lines 1–22.   [40] Ibid. 4, ed. Rocher, p. 174, lines 18–20.
[41] Ibid. 5, ed. Rocher p. 176, lines 1–9.

Part I

Hilary was aware that others would think it highly inappropriate to call a Christian emperor Antichrist. He responds to the objections of his imagined (or real) critics by pointing out that there are plenty of examples to be found in biblical history of brave and holy men who spoke frankly and impudently to a ruler. It is the duty of bishops as 'agents of the truth' (*veritatis ministri*) to speak out and not shy away from unpleasant criticism:

> Let the rumour spread by slanderers and the suspicion of falsehood cease. For ministers of the truth should proclaim what is true. If we speak falsely, may our slanderous speech become ill-famed. If, however, we show that what we say is evidently true, then we do not go beyond the limits of apostolic freedom of speech (*apostolica libertas*) and moderation, when we express criticism after a long period of silence.[42]

There have, Hilary continues, always been people throughout biblical history, who have spoken frankly to a ruler and been willing to suffer the consequences. He refers to the example of John the Baptist rebuking King Herod for unlawfully taking his brother's wife as his own, for which John paid with his life, and to the story of the Maccabean martyrs to illustrate what he considers justified boldness towards a ruler. The Maccabean martyrs, as discussed in the previous chapter, were a group of Jewish martyrs who abused the Greek king Antiochus shortly before they were put to death.[43] By quoting these examples, Hilary aligns his own bold act of directing an invective against Constantius to the courage of John the Baptist and the heroic frankness of the Maccabean martyrs. Thus, he presents himself as a would-be martyr, who would have been happy to be tortured and killed for the truth, if only Constantius had allowed it.

Hilary further justifies his vituperation against Constantius by carefully delineating the limits of acceptable criticism. He argues that his abuse of Constantius is still within the boundaries of 'apostolic freedom of speech' (*apostolica libertas*) for the simple reason that his accusations are true, although he allows that to others it may seem inconsiderate or imprudent to say such things plainly. As Richard Flower has observed, Hilary employs the Latin term *libertas* as an analogy to the Greek term *parrhesia*, 'thus furthering his claim to be a fearless narrator of the truth in the face of oppressive authority'.[44] Hilary portrays himself, according to Flower, as

---

[42] Hilary, *In Constantium* 6, ed. Rocher, p. 176, line 1–p. 178, line 6: 'Cesset itaque maledictorum opinio et mendacii suspicio. Veritatis enim ministros decet vera proferre. Si falsa dicimus, infamis sit sermo maledicus; si vero universa haec manifesta esse ostendimus, non sumus extra apostolicam libertatem et modestiam post longum haec silentium arguentes'.

[43] 4 Maccabees 9:14–18, 30–32; 10:9–11, 17–21; 11:21–27; 12:11–19. On the Christian reception of the story of their martyrdom, see Rouwhorst, 'The emergence of the cult of the Maccabean Martyrs' and Boyarin, *Dying for God*, especially pp. 115–19.

[44] Flower, *Bishops and Emperors*, p. 151.

'freely conversing with Constantius in the manner and vocabulary of martyrs, confronting persecuting emperors', 'demonstrating the same bravery and *parrhesia*'.[45] Although I basically agree with this observation, it is worthwhile to take a closer look at what *kind* of freedom of speech Hilary lays a claim to, and whether he intentionally aims to connect it to the martyr's *parrhesia* in particular.

Hilary defines his apostolic *libertas* and its boundaries with the help of a rhetorical scheme called *paradiastole*.[46] He allows that some people will think him rash and judge his criticism of Constantius to be impudence (*petulantia*) rather than steadfastness (*constantia*),[47] but his freedom of speech is 'no rashness (*temeritas*) but trust (*fides*), no lack of consideration (*inconsideratio*), but reasonableness (*ratio*), no anger (*furor*), but courage (*fiducia*)'.[48] The words *fides*, *ratio* and *fiducia* function as the positive paradigmatic references of *libertas*, while *temeritas*, *inconsideratio* and *furor* are its opposites (or negative paradigmatic references). By carefully qualifying the nature and intentions of his apostolic *libertas*, Hilary aimed to convince his critics that his invective *Against Constantius* was not out of order, but well within the boundaries of acceptable criticism according to the standard set by the apostles. His frankness sprang from the right motives and was tempered by a balanced mind that kept undesirable emotions under control. The theme and some of the vocabulary (*constantia, fiducia*) are familiar from Latin martyrdom accounts,[49] but also from the Acts of the Apostles and the Pauline epistles, to portray the emotional poise and steadfastness of their free-speaking protagonists.[50] Hilary employs these and other terms (*constantia, fiducia, ratio, fides*) that indicate control of emotions to delineate the parameters of his *libertas*. Thus, he creates a kind of Stoic safety net that, as he assures his readers, keeps his frankness within acceptable bounds. By keeping silent for so long, Hilary says, he has learned to restrain the perturbations of the mind that could otherwise have led to impudent and immoderate speech.[51]

At long last, Hilary could bear witness to the truth with faithful freedom of speech in Christ (*fideli in Christo libertate*).[52] The reasons why he considered his diatribe against Constantius not to be improper were the following: his speech was modified by a long silence, it did not spring

---

[45] Ibid., p. 150.   [46] See for example Rutilius Lupus, *De figuris sententiarum et elocutionis* I, 4.
[47] Hilary, *In Constantium* 6, ed. Rocher, p. 178, line 8.
[48] Ibid. 6, ed. Rocher, p. 178, lines 23–5: 'Non est istud temeritas sed fides, neque inconsideratio sed ratio, neque furor sed fiducia.'
[49] *The Martyrdom of Perpetua and Felicitas* 17, 1 (*constantia*); *The Martyrdom of Montanus and Lucius* 14, 1 (*constanter dixerit*), 14,5 (*constanter militate*), 18 (*magna fiducia*); *The Acts of Phileas* 7 (*constantia*).
[50] See the references in note 49 of the introduction.
[51] Hilary, *In Constantium* 3, ed. Rocher, p. 172, lines 1–5.
[52] Ibid. 3, ed. Rocher, p. 172, lines 3–4.

from uncontrolled emotions and it was not motivated by self-interest. Yet the most important reason why he believed he was now allowed to speak out vehemently against Constantius follows at the end of the paragraph: he had come to understand that he had to break his silence for Christ. It was Christ himself who wanted him to speak out against the heretical emperor.

In his invective *Against Constantius,* Hilary uses the term *libertas* to refer to his freedom of speech in connection with the freedom he has as a Christian. As explained in the introduction, in Roman literature the term *libertas* refers to the free status of a Roman citizen as well as to his privilege of free speech, for the two were closely related in Roman law. Hilary employs the term *libertas* in a similar, connected sense but has transposed it to a Christian frame of reference. Just as a Roman citizen enjoyed the privilege of freedom of speech, resulting from his free status as citizen of the Roman Empire, so Hilary and other Christians possessed freedom of speech because they were free in Christ. Hilary redefined Roman *libertas* as apostolic *libertas*. The privilege to speak freely was a duty and prerogative of every Christian who had been freed by Christ's sacrifice on the cross, and had thus become, so to speak, a free citizen of Christ's kingdom.[53] I would therefore conclude that Hilary's interpretation of *libertas* forged a link in particular to the courageous speech and bold behaviour of the apostles, with overtones of Roman *libertas*, and not predominantly to the *parrhesia* of martyrs.

There is no doubt that the martyr acts were a source of inspiration to Hilary when he created the persona of a fearless truth-teller in the face of an oppressor in his invective *Against Constantius*. He refers explicitly to the story of the Maccabean martyrs and borrows literary themes and turns of phrase from the Christian martyr acts to justify his outspoken criticism of the emperor.[54] Qualities such as control of emotions, keeping silent before speaking out and steadfastness in the face of danger, which, Hilary says, checked his outspokenness, are prominent in martyrdom accounts. Yet Hilary also constructed and delineated his *apostolic libertas* in relation to older models and traditions in a complex and rich way. The martyr's *parrhesia* was only one string among many in this bundle of values and practices. Another string was the frank speech and fearless behaviour of the apostles, referred to in the Greek New Testament as *parrhesia*.[55] Just

---

[53] It could be surmised that Hilary ascribed apostolic *libertas* to bishops in particular; see below.
[54] See for examples Flower, *Bishops and Emperors,* p. 150.
[55] The Vetus Latina and Vulgate translations did not choose the term *libertas* to translate the apostles' *parrhesia* in the Greek New Testament, but *constantia* and *fiducia* (see introduction, note 49). Although Hilary chose *libertas* as his core term, he used *constantia* and *fiducia* as paradigmatic references, perhaps to give *libertas* a New Testament gloss, while retaining the 'Roman' ring.

like the early Christian martyrs, the apostles were not afraid to speak the truth to authorities with boldness and courage, but in a controlled and rational manner. Hilary's invective perhaps does not immediately strike a modern reader as 'controlled', but if we accept the explanation he gives of his apostolic freedom of speech ('no rashness but trust, no lack of consideration, but reasonableness, no anger, but courage'), then that is how he wanted his readers to regard it.

RHETORIC OF ABUSE

The tone of Hilary's tract *Against Constantius* gets more insolent as the text proceeds. After establishing that vituperation is justified, he calls Constantius a rapacious wolf, a deceitful flatterer and a tyrant.[56] Just two years earlier, Hilary had stressed in his *Opus historicum* that one owed reverence to an emperor, even if one did not agree with his decisions, as kingship was given by God.[57] The martyr acts had promoted a similar attitude of respect for God-given authority. So where had that reverence gone? How could such abuse as he heaped upon Constantius be reconciled with the obligation of a Christian citizen to show respect to an emperor?

It should be noted that Hilary was not the only bishop who ventured to write an invective against Constantius. Bishop Athanasius of Alexandria wrote a derogatory pamphlet against the emperor around 358, and Lucifer of Cagliari wrote no less than five provocative tracts attacking Constantius between 355 and 361. Lucifer uses strongly abusive terms to run Constantius down, such as *carnifex* (torturer, scoundrel), *leno* (brothel-keeper), *vipera* (viper), *pestis* (plague or curse) and *sentina* (scum).[58] It can be somewhat surprising from our modern perspective to see devout bishops such as Hilary, Athanasius and Lucifer using such foul language. Writing invectives was, however, an acceptable literary enterprise in the fourth century, even for Christian bishops.[59] The invective was an established genre that had a place in the system of rhetoric as a subcategory of epideictic speech.[60] The rhetorical principles that guided the encomium of a ruler also applied to the composition of an invective.

---

[56] Hilary, *In Constantium* 7, ed. Rocher, p. 180, line 5: *tyrannus*; Ibid. 11, ed. Rocher, p. 188, line 1: *lupe rapax*; Ibid. 20, ed. Rocher, p. 206, line 1: 'O fallax blandimentum tuum!'.
[57] Hilary, *Preface to the Opus historicum* 5, ed. Smulders, p. 37, lines 23–5: 'licet potissima regi sit deferenda reverentia – quia enim a deo regnum est'.
[58] Opelt, 'Formen der Polemik', pp. 216–22: 'Fortleben paganer Herrscherpolemik'.
[59] See Flower, *Emperors and Bishops*.
[60] Sulpicius Victor, *Institutiones oratoriae* 3; Priscian, *Praeexercitamina* 7: *De laude*; Quintilian, *Institutio oratoria* 3, 7, ed. Russell, LCL 125 pp. 111–13. On invectives as a genre popular among Roman exiles, see Claassen, *Displaced Persons*, chapter 5: 'Exilic invective'.

In fact, the scheme of the invective (*vituperatio*) was the inverse of the scheme of the encomium (*laus*). Quintilian considered both forms of epideictic speech as a test of character.[61] The *vituperatio* functioned as an inverted mirror in which a ruler could see character traits and vices that the author, and the social circle he represented, did not consider befitting to a ruler. Fourth-century audiences that were familiar with the literary tradition of the *vituperatio* need not necessarily have been shocked by abusive language, even if it came from the mouth of a bishop, if they recognised his choice of words as a generic convention. André Rocher, editor of Hilary's *Against Constantius,* regards Hilary's invective as a fairly conventional exercise, composed according to the rules of political invective, with abuses that are traditional, not personal. In Rocher's opinion, Hilary's invective is relatively mild, compared to the vituperations of Athanasius and Lucifer.[62] Bishop Lucifer, for example did incur criticism at the time from near-contemporaries for his choice of words. Jerome, although basically in agreement with Lucifer's views, said he did not approve of the language in which Lucifer expressed his criticism.[63] Yet Lucifer was also admired for his courage to stand up to a heretical emperor, and so were Hilary and Athanasius.[64]

Later generations regarded Hilary as a stout defender of the orthodox faith, who spoke truth to power at great risk to his episcopal career and personal safety.[65] But was Hilary's invective against Constantius really an act of *parrhesia*, with all the risks that such an act would need to involve to be acknowledged by contemporaries as such? Was he as audacious as the Maccabean martyrs whom he admired, who spoke boldly to King Antiochus shortly before they were executed? Or as courageous as John the Baptist, who was beheaded for rebuking King Herod? If we look at the historical circumstances of Hilary's exile, he did not endure extreme hardships, did not suffer torture, and enjoyed a certain freedom of movement during his exile. What is more, he faced no repercussions for writing his invective against Constantius. While his colleague Lucifer was banished to a more remote place as punishment for his scathing invective, Hilary's banishment was lifted and he was allowed to return to his see.

---

[61] Quintilian, *Institutio oratoria* 3, 7, ed. Russell, LCL 125 pp. 111–13.
[62] Rocher, *Hilaire de Poitiers,* pp. 50, 51.
[63] Hanson, *Search for the Christian Doctrine,* p. 510, with reference to Jerome, *Dialogus contra Luciferanos* 20.
[64] See Jerome's entry on Lucifer in *De viris illustribus* 95, ed. Herding, p. 55.
[65] Sulpicius Severus (d. 420), *Chronicon* II, 45, 2–7, ed. CCSL 63, p. 302; Venantius Fortunatus (d. 610), *Vita Sancti Hilarii*.

Hilary of Poitiers

INTENDED AUDIENCE

Previously, scholars explained this paradox by assuming that Hilary never sent his invective to Constantius, but only published it after the emperor's death in 361.[66] This is in accord with the account of Jerome, who explicitly says in his catalogue *On Famous Men* that Hilary wrote his invective against the emperor *post mortem eius*.[67] More recently, however, scholars have rejected this suggestion and have argued that Hilary did publish his invective while Constantius was still alive, although he never delivered it to the emperor himself.[68] I propose a middle position between the old and the new theory: I should like to suggest that Hilary initially wrote the text for a selected group of readers during Constantius' lifetime and published it for a wider audience after the emperor's death.[69] This intended audience of Hilary's text can be established by looking at the structure of the text and the strategies of persuasion employed. It boils down to the simple question: whom was Hilary trying to persuade of what, and what was the change he aimed to effect?

Let us first look at the structure of Hilary's *Against Constantius*. The core of the text (chapters 7–11 and 16–27) is the diatribe proper, in which Hilary attacks the emperor directly. In the first six chapters, however, and in four further chapters in the middle of the text (chapters 12–15), Hilary addresses his fellow bishops in Gaul and speaks about the emperor in the third person. André Rocher has proposed that the chapters in which Hilary addresses the emperor directly as 'you' (chapters 7–11 and 16–27) represent the first version of Hilary's text.[70] He proposes that Hilary wrote the core of the text shortly after the Council of Constantinople in 359 to vent his frustration over the fact that Constantius had not granted him a hearing, which to Hilary's mind could have changed the outcome of the council in favour of the Nicene party.[71] The other chapters, Rocher suggests, date to a later period, perhaps to the time of Hilary's return from exile in 360. Rocher speculates that Hilary sent a first draft to friends and supporters to hear their opinion, and revised the text later in response to their criticism, adding

---

[66] This explanation is still supported by Wickham, *Hilary of Poitiers, Conflicts of Conscience and Law*, pp. xxii–xxvi.
[67] Jerome, *Liber de viris illustribus* 100, ed. Herding, p. 57: 'alius [libellus] in Constantium quem post mortem eius scripsit'.
[68] Flower, *Imperial Invectives*, pp. 29, 30, and see the literature cited there.
[69] This is basically what André Rocher has argued. Richard Flower, however, considers Rocher's suggestion of a two-stage process of composition unnecessarily convoluted. Flower, *Imperial Invectives*, p. 30.
[70] Rocher, *Hilaire de Poitiers*, pp. 30–2.   [71] Ibid., p. 30.

some introductory chapters (1–6) and inserting a few chapters in the middle (12–15) to justify his sharp attack on the emperor.

Although I find Rocher's analysis entirely plausible, the alternating structure of the chapters, addressing now Constantius, now the bishops, does not necessarily point to a composition of the text in two stages. Rather, this structure reveals the intended audience of the text. It was a generic convention to address the audience over the head of the person one was criticising. Invectives such as Hilary's *Against Constantius* were not written primarily for the eyes of the person who was being criticised. Other fourth-century invectives such as Lucifer's *On Apostate Kings* and Athanasius' *History of the Arians* show a similar alternating address. As Jo Marie Claassen has demonstrated in her study of the literature of exile from the first century BC to the sixth century AD, it was a characteristic feature of exilic invectives to switch from second to third person address.[72] Speaking about one's antagonist in the third person was a sign of contempt and often served the same function as a comic aside.[73] The fact that Hilary switches between speaking *to* and speaking *about* Constantius, therefore, does not necessarily indicate that the text was written in two stages. It is possible that Hilary justified his vituperation of the emperor (chapters 1–6 and 12–15) not in response to but in anticipation of criticism that he expected his invective would provoke.

What would have happened if Constantius had not died that same year and Hilary *had* presented his invective to the emperor? André Rocher suggests that the emperor might have been amused had he read it, provided Constantius had any sense of humour.[74] As long as the abuse was over the top and not personal, and the rules of the genre were followed, invectives could be considered humorous, even by the person who was criticised.[75] If an emperor shrugged his shoulders or smiled in amusement at such a frenzied attack, he showed himself to be a cultivated ruler who could take criticism gracefully.[76] Nevertheless, it remained a daring enterprise to send a scathing text to the emperor, not least because the author ran the risk of losing the support of a wider audience if he hit the wrong note, as the reception of the invectives of Hilary's contemporary Lucifer shows.[77]

---

[72] Claassen, *Displaced Persons*, pp. 132–53.
[73] Ibid., p. 135. On the humorous aspects of Christian invectives, and especially of Hilary's *Against Constantius*, see Humphries, 'Savage humour'.
[74] Rocher, *Hilaire de Poitiers*, p. 51.
[75] Humphries, 'Savage humour'; Rocher, *Hilaire de Poitiers*, pp. 50, 51.
[76] See for example Suetonius, *De vita Caesarum, Vita Tiberii* 28 and *Vita Augusti* 89.
[77] See Rocher, *Hilaire de Poitiers*, pp. 50, 51.

A more important question to ask is what Hilary could have hoped to achieve had he presented his invective to the emperor. To admonish a ruler, and, if need be, rebuke him to warn him away from danger, was considered beneficial both to the ruler and the empire. Hilary's invective *Against Constantius,* however, nowhere contains what we would now call constructive criticism. Although the invective may have served as an inverted prince's mirror in which Constantius could see his sins reflected and learn how a Christian emperor should *not* rule, I do not think that this was the primary aim of the text. When we look at the intended audience of the rhetoric of the text, it becomes clear that the persuasive force of the argument is not aimed at the emperor, but at Hilary's fellow bishops; they are the ones he hopes to convince that they should rise up against the Arians and resist an imperial policy that supports them. To my mind, Hilary did not write this invective to show Constantius what an inadequate emperor he was, hoping that he would mend his ways, or to educate his audience's expectations of Christian rulership by presenting them the inverted image of a good Christian emperor; his primary goal was rather to mobilise his fellow bishops. His strong language was intended to appeal to their emotions and fire their zeal. I suggest that even the parts of the invective in which Hilary addresses Constantius directly were written for the bishops, to convince them that the emperor's ecclesiastical politics were outrageous and should be rejected. *Against Constantius* is a militant, vigorous text with humorous traits that encourages bishops to take a stand.

The opening line of the exordium summarises the central theme of the text and offers the key to its interpretation, when Hilary boldly proclaims: 'The time to be silent has passed; now it is time to speak.'[78] Hilary did not write that line for Constantius; he wrote it for bishops just like him, who had been silent and cooperative for a long time. In his *Opus historicum,* written shortly before the *Against Constantius,* he had likewise challenged the reticence of the bishops of Gaul concerning 'Arian' theology prevalent in the East.[79] It was now time to speak out in defence of true doctrine. This is probably the reason why Hilary redefined *libertas* as an apostolic, and perhaps specifically episcopal, duty to speak courageously and freely, rather than as a Roman privilege or as a tried and tested rhetorical strategy of frank speech. If Hilary indeed wrote this invective for his fellow bishops, it stands to reason that they were the ones who should lay a claim to this *libertas apostolica.*[80] He appealed to their episcopal

---

[78] See note 1.   [79] Hilary, *Preface to the Opus historicum* 3, ed. Smulders, p. 36.
[80] Elsewhere, he calls his fellow (Nicene) bishops 'apostolic men' (*viri apostolici*); see Hilary, *Preface to the Opus historicum* 3, ed. Smulders, p. 36.

Part I

sense of duty to convince them of the necessity to proclaim (Nicene) faith in Christ. The bishops of Gaul should follow the example of the apostles and start speaking out for Christ's truth. If Hilary published this text shortly before the synod of Paris in 361, he probably aimed to prepare his addressees for this meeting and put this issue high on the synod's agenda. At the synod of Paris in 361, the Gallic bishops distanced themselves from the Homoian double synod of Ariminium (Rimini) and Seleucia and accepted the wording of the Nicaean creed. In modern scholarship, this is regarded as a decisive moment in Gaul's turn to Nicene Christianity. It is still held today that this turn should be largely credited to the work and writings of Hilary.[81]

The comparison between Hilary's address *To Constantius* and his diatribe *Against Constantius* has shown how the bishop turned from respectful admonition to scathing invective. To Hilary, both forms were manifestations of free speech, with the difference that the frankness of his first address was constructed according to the polite principles of classical rhetoric, while the frankness of the second was inspired and justified by the themes and vocabulary of free speech in the New Testament and martyr narratives. Rather than assuming that Hilary changed his mind about the best type of frankness and turned away from classical models in favour of biblical models in order to promote a freedom of speech that was specifically Christian, it is more fruitful to look at the audience of the strategies of persuasion of each of the two epistolary speeches. While *To Constantius* aims to convince the emperor himself, *Against Constantius* sets out to persuade Hilary's fellow bishops to take a certain course of action. For the latter purpose, invective is a suitable means; for the first, the classical rhetorical strategies of frank speech are more appropriate. One should hope to be more persuasive by showing due respect and establishing shared interests between speaker and addressee, than by acting like a raging truth-teller who gives his oppressor the full blast.

Hilary's other writings, spanning the period from the beginning of his exile to the time after his return to Gaul, show that he did not substantially change his views on free speech or abandon his conviction that reverence was due to an emperor. He remained of the opinion that the deepest respect should be paid to the emperor since his sovereignty derived from God, but also maintained that bishops should not uncritically accept every decision taken by the emperor.[82] If their priestly integrity (*simplicitas sacerdotalis*) told them that an imperial ruling was unacceptable, they

---

[81] Heil, 'Homoians in Gaul', p. 271.
[82] Hilary, *Preface to the Opus historicum* 5, ed. Smulders, p. 37.

should not tolerate it, but speak out against it.[83] That, according to Hilary, was what *libertas* was all about. Quoting the Apostle Paul, he firmly stated that where there is *fides*, there is *libertas*.[84] As I hope to have demonstrated in this chapter, Hilary's *libertas*, which he associated with the apostles, denotes a Christian's freedom of speech that is not restrained by fear of repercussions thanks to faith and trust in Christ.

STEADFAST AND UNWAVERING

I should now like to turn briefly to Hilary's exegetical work. Although the primary focus of this book is on speeches and letters, it is worthwhile to have a look at Hilary's biblical commentaries, because it is here that he further elaborates upon the delicate balance between respect and frank speech and the limits of acceptable criticism that he touched upon in his epistolary speeches to and against Constantius.[85]

After his return from exile, Hilary wrote his *Commentaries on the Psalms*, in which he returned to the figure of the Old Testament prophet–priest as an example worthy of imitation for contemporary truth-tellers. In an exegesis of Psalm 118 he defended the right to take an emperor to task on matters of the Christian faith, with reference to the Old Testament prophets who admonished their rulers *constanter* (firmly, immovably). It is the duty of the prophet, Hilary argues, and of those who are called to follow the prophet's example in the present day, to stand up to rulers in defence of God's commands.[86] Hilary does not explicitly say who these latter-day prophets are, but does indicate that they should be experts in the law of God, i.e. well-educated bishops and exegetes like himself.[87] Just as the prophets spoke firmly (*constanter*) against the princes of the earth, he explains, so 'we' should preach Christ before kings and governors and not be afraid of the law of secular power, 'so that with an unwavering and common faith (*constans et publica fides*) that scorns all confusion, we do not disown God'.[88]

Constantia is an important notion for Hilary. In his invective *Against Constantius* he links it to apostolic freedom of speech, *apostolica libertas,* and here in his *Commentaries on the Psalms* he associates it with *publica fides,* commonly shared faith. In his biblical commentaries, he employs the

---

[83] Ibid. [84] Ibid.: 'quamvis apostolo dicente: ubi fides est, libertas est [2 Cor. 3:17]'.
[85] See for example Hilary, *Commentary on Psalm 118*, 3, 20, ed. Milhau, vol. 1, p. 172.
[86] Hilary, *Commentary on Psalm 118*, 6, 10, ed. Milhau, vol. 1, p. 238.
[87] Ibid. 6, 11, ed. Milhau, vol. 1, p. 238. On the legal training and forensic education of late antique churchmen, see Humfress, *Orthodoxy and the Courts*.
[88] Hilary, *Commentary on Psalm 118*, 6, 10, ed. Milhau, vol. 1, p. 238: 'quominus omni confusio reiecta constanti et publica fide Deum [. . .] non negemus [cf. Matt. 10:33].''

Part I

term *constantia* frequently in connection to prophetic speech and the courage of the Old Testament prophets to proclaim the word of God and speak out against sin.[89] Interestingly, the word *constantia* and its cognates do not occur in the Latin Old Testament books of the prophets. Instead, we find it in Vetus Latina and Vulgate translations of the books of the New Testament and particularly the Acts of the Apostles and the Pauline letters. There, as we have already seen, *constantia* is used, together with *fiducia*, to render into Latin the *parrhesia* of the apostles.[90] As Gerard Bartelink notes in his study of *parrhesia* in early Christian literature, Hilary's *fiducia* should be understood as a Latin equivalent of *parrhesia*.[91] In his *Commentaries on the Psalms*, Hilary connects New Testament *constantia* (speaking freely with an unshaken state of mind) to the courage of prophets to confront kings, and *fiducia* to the voice of the blessed apostle Paul.[92] They should all raise the bold voice of the apostle, Hilary says, because it is the best weapon against unruly passions and disturbance (*turbatio*).[93]

This steadfast and unwavering quality is here related to a specific content, namely *publica fides*. Traditionally, *publica fides* referred to the collective good faith of the Roman people and stood for loyalty to the Roman state. After the state became an empire, it denoted loyalty to the emperor in particular, with overtones of personal trust and faithfulness.[94] Hilary, however, employs the term to refer to a common faith in Christ. I assume that for him such a *publica fides* involved a creed that all parties could agree upon, for which he argues in his epistolary speech *To Constantius*. To achieve the desired outcome, he holds, it is not always possible to accept the emperor's decisions uncritically, if these decisions clearly do not contribute to the ideal of *publica fides*.[95]

A commonly shared faith that was governed by steadfastness presented a much-needed antidote to the confusion that, to Hilary's mind, was currently shaking the stability of the empire. In the introduction to his *Opus historicum*, transmitted in a dossier of fragments of polemical and exegetical texts, Hilary paints a vivid picture of a palace in disarray, where bishops run about, high officials hurry back and forth, the emperor is

---

[89] Hilary, *Commentary on Psalm 118*, 7, 1, ed. Milhau, vol. 1, p. 264: 'propheta constanter ait'; 8, 10, ed. Milhau, vol. 1, p. 264: 'Propheta itaque secundum apostolum non saeculo vivens constanter et libere ait'; See also 118, 8, 11, ed. Milhau, vol. 1, p. 270: 'Propheta libere loquitur.'
[90] See the introduction, pp. 8–10.
[91] Bartelink, 'Quelques observations sur παρρησία', p. 17, note 3, in reference to Hilary's commentary on Psalm 14 (*In Ps.* 14, 11).
[92] Hilary, *Commentary on Psalm 118*, 8, 12, ed. Milhau, vol. 1, p. 272; 118, 8, 13, ed. Milhau, p. 274.
[93] Ibid. 118, 8, 13, ed. Milhau, vol. 1, p.274.
[94] Morgan, *Roman Faith and Christian Faith*, p. 83.
[95] Hilary, *Commentary on Psalm 118*, 6, 10, ed. Milhau, vol. 1, p. 238.

constantly vexed and commotion is all around.[96] Given that the imperial palace, by the rule of *pars pro toto*, reflected the entire realm, the feverish confusion that presently spread through its halls was a cause for alarm. To Hilary's mind, only unwavering, commonly shared faith could restore the tranquillity of the palace and bring cohesion and unity to the empire. This 'constant' faith should be firmly preached to wavering rulers such as the present emperor who, ironically, was called *Constantius,* the steadfast one. 'If we can say [with the prophet] with freedom of speech (*libertas*): I cling to your testimonies', Hilary wrote, 'we are freed from the confusion of the scandalous faults of the past.'[97]

CONCLUSION

In his invective *Against Constantius,* Hilary created the persona of a persecuted truth-teller who heroically fought against heretics and stood up against an emperor who supported them. This self-constructed image was uncritically accepted by later biographers and chroniclers.[98] According to the chronicle of Sulpicius Severus (d. c. 420), an author born in Aquitaine, 'our regions of Gaul were set free from the crime of heresy through the benevolent efforts of Hilarius alone', to which he added that this was not just his opinion but a fact admitted by all.[99] After returning from exile, Hilary attended the synod of Paris in 361 and managed, as scholars have it, to strengthen Nicene resistance to the 'Arian' party in Gaul.[100] He became known as the 'Athanasius of the West' and 'Hammer of the Arians'. In his writings, and in the work of his colleagues Athanasius and Lucifer, the idea of martyrdom gained a new interpretation. Martyrdom was not necessarily about suffering torture and a gruesome death, but about the willingness to lose everything: status, office, respect, home, so as to gain the independence of mind (*libertas*) that was needed to speak the truth. These qualities did not apply only to the martyr, but as Hilary showed in his *Commentaries on the Psalms,* also to the apostle and the prophet.[101]

---

[96] Hilary, *Preface to the Opus historicum* 4, ed. Smulders, pp. 36, 37.
[97] Hilary, *Commentary on Psalm 118*, 4, 10, ed. Milhau, vol. 1, p. 190: 'si et nos [in imitation of the prophet] dicere cum libertate possimus: Adhaesi testimoniis tuis. His enim adhaerentes a confusione pudendorum et anteriorum criminum liberamur.'
[98] Sulpicius Severus (d. c. 420), *Chronicon* II, 45, 2–7, ed. *CCSL* 63, p. 102; Venantius Fortunatus (d. 610), *Vita Sancti Hilarii* 5, discussed in chapter 6.
[99] Sulpicius Severus, *Chronicon* II, 45, 7, ed. *CCSL* 63, p. 102: 'Illud apud omnes constitit unius Hilarii beneficio Gallias nostras piaculo haresis liberatas.'
[100] See the references in note 5.
[101] Hilary, *Commentary on Psalm 118*, 3, 20, ed. Milhau, vol. 1, p. 172.

Part I

In his speeches to and against Constantius, as well as in his exegetical work, Hilary created a new, powerful image of a Christian truth-teller that was built on the cultivated memory of martyrs, apostles and prophets, such as Jeremiah and Ezekiel, who confronted king and people with the truth from their places of exile. Hilary's interpretation of apostolic freedom of speech (*libertas apostolica*) was governed by *constantia, fiducia* and other virtues of self-control, which he infused with the symbolic capital of prophets, martyrs and apostles and put in the service of establishing orthodoxy and stability in the realm. That, to Hilary's mind, was the main responsibility of bishops in the post-persecution age. One traditional role model was not present in Hilary's constellation, at least not prominently, and that was the model of the philosopher. The figure of the outspoken philosopher, who possessed *parrhesia* by virtue of his calling, embodied norms in and expectations about truth-telling that were highly relevant to late antique society. The 'pagan' court philosopher, who in fact had much in common with Hilary's image of the Old Testament prophet, provided another classical exemplar of self-representation for Christian truth-tellers, especially for late antique bishops, as we will see in the next two chapters.

3

THE DETACHED PHILOSOPHER

From about 350 to the mid-380s, the Hellenic philosopher Themistius was a prominent figure at the court in Constantinople. Themistius (d. 390 AD) was a senator, panegyrist, philosopher and an advisor of emperors. Several Christian rulers sought the counsel of this non-Christian philosopher and welcomed his praise and advice on how to govern well. Themistius was an advocate of religious toleration. When Emperor Valens (r. 363–78) persecuted 'Nicene' Christians, it was Themistius who admonished the emperor to be more tolerant towards divergent opinions.[1] The fifth-century church historians Socrates and Sozomen remembered the philosopher favourably and ascribed Valens' change of policy to the admonitions of Themistius, who, they said, managed to mitigate the emperor's severity.[2] The two Christian historians described Themistius as the archetypical court philosopher, who was not afraid to voice a contrary opinion and helped the ruler control his passions.

Peter Brown has described how, over the course of the fourth century, monks, hermits and bishops took over the role that was traditionally the province of the court philosopher, and started offering advice and criticism to emperors.[3] When they stepped into the tradition of truth-telling, he observed, they took over some of the characteristics of their pagan predecessors. Perhaps it would be more accurate to say that Christian biographers *ascribed* these characteristics to their protagonists, but the bishops themselves can also be seen to adopt aspects of this tradition in their self-presentation, as Claudia Rapp's study *Holy Bishops in Late Antiquity* has demonstrated. Whether they did so intentionally or not, Christians appropriated the performance, language and ideals that

[1] Penella, *Private Orations*, p. 3.
[2] Socrates, *Historia ecclesiastica* IV, 32, ed. PG 67, cols. 552a–b; Sozomen, *Historia ecclesiastica* VI, 36–7, ed. PG 67, cols. 1401c–1403b.
[3] Brown, *Power and Persuasion*, pp. 35–70.

Part I

characterised the role of the free-spoken philosopher in late antique society. In this chapter, I shall discuss biographies and histories from the fourth and fifth centuries AD, and one speech delivered by the court philosopher Themistius, to bring into sharper focus the elements of a cultural tradition that was widely acknowledged as *parrhesia*, even if not all authors used that specific technical term for it. This chapter thus provides a background to the case study that follows in the next chapter, on Bishop Ambrose of Milan, who borrowed the symbolic capital of the free-spoken court philosopher to create the public persona of an independent bishop speaking truth to power.

The sources of the period show that different types of *parrhesia* were relevant to late antique society, such as religious *parrhesia*, the *parrhesia* of friendship and political *parrhesia*. As has been discussed in the introduction, *parrhesia* was never only one thing at any given time. It could take on many different shapes and meanings. Here I shall focus on the cultural construction, performance and narrative representation of two varieties of political *parrhesia* in particular – to wit, 'bold speech' and 'privileged access' – that were relevant to the pagan philosopher and later to the free-speaking bishop who followed in his footsteps. These two constructions of free speech would come to play an important role in the political discourse of the early Middle Ages.

Next to a discussion of the exemplary 'type' of the philosopher, this chapter will introduce another, connected role model that would inform the performance and language of the free-speaking bishop in the Latin West: namely, the figure of the ambassador, who was sent to court on behalf of his city to petition the ruler. According to the narrative sources, cities often chose a philosopher to represent their interest, but this should not be taken as an indication that the roles of ambassador and philosopher were interchangeable. As we shall see, late antique bishops adopted and blended the roles, characteristics and rhetoric of philosophers, holy men and ambassadors to shape their own performance as truth-tellers. Such a performance responded to existing social norms and expectations, but was at the same time flexible enough to meet the demands of a new era.[4]

FREE-SPOKEN PHILOSOPHERS

Philosophers were credited with a quality that was highly appreciated and admired by their contemporaries: namely, resolutely honest and frank speech. This quality enabled them, at least in theory, to speak freely and

---

[4] This chapter owes much to Peter Brown's *Power and Persuasion* and to Claudia Rapp's study of leadership models for late antique bishops, *Holy Bishops*.

The Detached Philosopher

openly to power. Every Greek city worthy of the name had a favourite philosopher, who enhanced the glory of the city by his teaching and who could be consulted on practical, political and moral issues.[5] Philosophers acted as the public face and spokesmen of Hellenistic communities. From the earliest days of the polis to the late Roman Empire, philosophers were sent to the court to offer a petition to the emperor on behalf of the community.[6] That, at least, is the image that comes to the fore in narrative sources; the reality may have been different.[7] The fourth-century historian Ammianus Marcellinus tells the story of how the people of Epirus, who suffered under the harsh administration of the praetorian prefect Petronius Probus, selected the philosopher Iphicles as their envoy. Iphicles went to Emperor Valentinian and, 'like a philosopher who professed himself a teacher of truth', brought the corrupt mismanagement of Probus to his attention.[8] Actually, the people of Epirus had sent the philosopher as an envoy to the prefect, but somehow Iphicles ended up having an audience with the emperor instead. Although Emperor Valentinian, according to Ammianus, had showed himself deaf to earlier complaints about his prefect, the speech of the philosopher Iphicles struck a chord, and at long last he decided to look into the matter.[9]

As Evangeline Lyon has observed, the image of the philosopher in the public imagination remained surprisingly stable across several centuries.[10] The philosopher was defined by his *parrhesia*, disregard for wealth and social conventions, equanimity and an uncompromising attitude towards political authority. He was therefore considered particularly well suited to offering political advice, possessing the knowledge as well as the moral virtues required for the task. The demands on the philosopher's performance were high: he had to combine a dedication to contemplation with political engagement and outstanding moral virtues. Contemporaries were quick to criticise the philosopher's attitude and lifestyle if they were under the impression that his performance deviated from the ideal. These public demands and expectations changed very little between classical times and late Antiquity, although there was some variety of opinion among different schools concerning the proper balance between contemplation and action, seclusion and societal engagement.[11]

Late antique biographies and histories tend to picture a philosopher's mission to the court as a resounding success. His philosophical learning,

---

[5] Hahn, *Der Philosoph und die Gesellschaft*, pp. 148–55.
[6] Lyons, *Hellenic Philosophers as Ambassadors*.   [7] Fowden, 'The pagan holy man', p. 50.
[8] Ammianus Marcellinus, *Res gestae* XXX, 5, 9, ed. Seyfarth, vol. 2, p. 146: 'ut philosophus veritatis professor'.
[9] Ibid. XXX, 5, 10, ed. Seyfarth, vol. 2, p. 146.
[10] Lyons, *Hellenic Philosophers as Ambassadors*, p. 1.   [11] Ibid.

Part I

courage and comportment were bound to make an impression on the emperor, who was, ideally, brought up with the same philosophical ideals and the same standard of learning. This shared set of ideals and learning was commonly referred to as *paideia*. Literally, the Greek word *paideia* means 'instruction' or 'education', but its field of reference was much wider. *Paideia* referred to the shaping of character, based on Greek ideals of the human personality. These ideals were passed on to young men from the upper classes through education, notably in philosophy and rhetoric. *Paideia* came with specific modes of comportment. To be a man of *paideia* meant that one adhered to strict codes of courtesy and self-control.[12] *Paideia* was, moreover, linked to the ideal of a magnanimous and merciful exercise of authority.[13] An emperor who was brought up with the ideals of *paideia* was raised to rule as a philosopher-king. He would speak, or at least recognise, the language of philosophers and would therefore be inclined to listen to the words of a philosopher who had come to speak to him.

The Athenian sophist and biographer Philostratus described in his *Lives of the Sophists* (c. 202 AD) what he considered to be good qualities in a ruler. He indicated that successful interaction between a philosopher and an emperor depended as much on the virtues of the ruler as on those of the philosopher. According to Philostratus, Emperor Hadrian (r. 117–38 AD) had learned to master his anger as a true philosopher-king. He debated on terms of equality with men he could easily put to death if he wanted to, but he was never tempted to cut off the head of any of his discussion partners.[14] Philostratus wrote this entry around the turn of the third century, shortly before the period of civil war and economic depression that has become known as the 'crisis of the third century'. He looked back at a period when emperors such as Hadrian, born into a Roman aristocratic family, could indeed be expected to have received a classical education. Emperors in the later Roman Empire, however, often had a military background and were not all raised from a young age with the ideals of *paideia*. Yet third- and fourth-century philosophers and orators continued to address these emperors as if they shared the same principles and virtues that came with a thorough education in rhetoric, philosophy and classical literature.[15]

An emperor who wished to be known as a man of *paideia* was expected to grant a philosopher the privilege of *parrhesia*. He was supposed to exercise self-control if the philosopher's frank words offended him. The

---

[12] Jaeger, *Paideia: The Ideals of Greek Culture*, vol. 1, p. ix.
[13] Brown, *Power and Persuasion* p. 4; Jaeger, *Paideia: The Ideals of Greek Culture* vol. 3, p. 87.
[14] Philostratus, *Vitae sophistarum* 489, ed. Wright, LCL 134, p. 22.
[15] Vanderspoel, *Themistius and the Imperial Court*, p. 14.

The Detached Philosopher

ideals of *paideia* and *parrhesia* thus mutually reinforced each other. The philosopher used his *parrhesia* to remind the emperor of his obligation to rule according to the principles of *paideia,* while the emperor in his turn, by granting the philosopher the privilege to speak to him frankly, could show he was a cultivated ruler.[16] That, at least, was the ideal scenario. Whether the everyday reality of diplomatic proceedings ever matched the lofty ideal that was expressed in narrative and normative texts is a matter of debate.

In the early fifth century, the sophist and historian of Greek culture Eunapius of Sardis published his *Lives of the Philosophers and Sophists* (c. 405 AD), in which he recorded the lives and deeds of the most prominent sophists and philosophers of his age, from the early fourth century up to his own time. In his biography of the philosopher Sopater, he tells the story of how Sopater first came to the court of Emperor Constantine (r. 306–37), hoping to convert the emperor's policy with his arguments.[17] Eunapius does not bother giving his readers any practical information as to how Sopater managed to get access to the emperor. Normally, the route to the emperor's ear was long, with many obstacles to overcome. One had to talk to the right people and had to pay the right tariffs to open the doors to the imperial reception hall.[18] In Eunapius' account, however, the philosopher Sopater appears to have ignored protocol; he simply barged into Constantine's court. Eunapius describes Sopater's undertaking as a quick triumph: Constantine was impressed by his courage, character and eloquence and made the philosopher his trusted adviser. Eunapius does underline, however, that Sopater exposed himself to danger when he approached the emperor in this manner. This element of danger is a recurrent theme in late antique representations of *parrhesia,* although it should be noted that Eunapius does not actually use that term.

PRIVILEGED ACCESS AND BOLD SPEECH

Not every display of frank speech entailed the same amount of risk as the philosopher Sopater, according to his biographer Eunapius, was willing to take. In late antique narratives we also encounter a low-risk type of free speech in the form of privileged access to a ruler. If an emperor granted a trusted advisor the privilege to speak freely, such a privilege would also be acknowledged as *parrhesia* in contemporary sources. In his *Ecclesiastical*

---

[16] See, for example, Suetonius on Emperor Vespasian, *De vita Caesarum* 8, 13, ed. Rolfe, LCL 38, p. 290.
[17] Eunapius, *Vita philosophorum et sophistarum* 462, ed. Wright, LCL 134, p. 380.
[18] On the highly regulated route to the emperor's ear, see Rapp, *Holy Bishops,* p. 261.

Part I

History, the fifth-century church historian Theodoret describes Theodosius' advisor Rufinus, who had privileged access to the emperor's rooms and person, as having *parrhesia* with the emperor.[19] 'Privileged access' was often contrasted to 'bold speech': the high-risk type of free speech that was not granted in advance but claimed by the speaker. These two (narrative) constructions of free speech could, however, also be presented as being connected. As we have seen in chapter 1, the martyr's trust in having a privileged access to Christ gave him or her the confidence and courage to speak boldly to persecuting authorities. Both traditions could be denoted with the term *parrhesia*.

Parrhesia in the sense of 'privileged access' was granted to people who were close to the ruler, while *parrhesia* in the sense of frank criticism or unasked-for advice was often ascribed to an outsider. The outsider–truth-teller was a popular character in narratives, where we find bold individuals who did not enjoy the emperor's familiarity and had not gained permission to speak freely, but spoke up anyway and subverted established protocol. It was, moreover, a favoured stance for orators to adopt when composing a speech for a ruler, even if they did so from a position of 'privileged access'. We see this stance, for example, in Themistius' address to Emperor Constantius II (r. 337–61 AD) and in Synesius of Cyrene's oration on imperial rule, addressed to Emperor Arcadius (r. 383–408 AD).[20] A speaker who employed this type of *parrhesia* usually stressed the fact that his speech and his behaviour were out of bounds. Stories about such truth-tellers never fail to mention an element of shock and surprise, which is one of the textual markers that draws attention to the fact that we are dealing with a dangerous and subversive instance of free speech, at least in the eyes of the author who has recorded or imagined it.[21] Eunapius tells the story of how the Gothic general Fravitta infringed court ceremonial and spoke loudly and openly to Emperor Arcadius, which aroused much commotion among those who were present.[22]

These two (narrative) constructions of *parrhesia*, 'privileged access' and 'boldness of speech' came with their own cultural rules and social evaluations. And yet, the dividing line between them was not absolute. In narratives, but also in speeches of orators delivering a ceremonial speech

---

[19] Theodoret, *Historia ecclesiastica* V, 18, 6, ed. Parmentier, Hansen, p. 406, lines 37, 38.
[20] Synesius of Cyrene, *On Imperial Rule* 1, 1–3, ed. PG 66, cols. 1053–5; Themistius' address to Emperor Constantius II will be discussed below.
[21] See for example Herodian's story about the philosopher who jumped on the stage to address a thunderstruck Emperor Commodus, with which I opened the introduction. Herodian, *History of the Empire* 1, 9, 4, ed. and trans. Whittaker, LCL 454, pp. 54–5.
[22] Eunapius, *Historia*, ed. Blockley, p. 113. The interpretation of this passage as a breach of court ceremonial is from Blockley, *The Fragmentary Classicising Historians*, p. 148.

The Detached Philosopher

to an emperor, a person could move from one type of free speech to another.[23] The philosopher Sopater, for example, who became Constantine's trusted adviser, was initially depicted as a fearless truth-teller when he went to court to change Constantine's policy.[24] His biographer Eunapius describes how, when Sopater's bold conduct pleased the emperor, he became Constantine's counsellor and moved over to the other type of *parrhesia*: privileged access. As the emperor's trusted adviser, he was seated to the right of his throne, which was a remarkable sign of familiarity and proximity to the ruler. In Eunapius' account of Sopater's career, however, an element of risk was lurking at the background. For Constantine's courtiers were, in the words of Eunapius, bursting with jealousy because of the favour the emperor bestowed on Sopater. They worried that the philosopher's influence would damage their own position at court.[25] The motive of the jealous courtiers is a topos in late antique narratives and serves to contrast a group of established insiders with a newcomer. This motive, which reflected a reality of fierce competition at the court, brings into sharp focus some structural features of free speech that were considered important at the time, such as a disregard for social hierarchy and an individualistic attitude. In the end, Constantine's courtiers turned the emperor against his trusted adviser by spreading false rumours about him. The philosopher was accused of magical malpractices and was decapitated.[26] In Eunapius' narrative, Sopater thus ended his life as a bold truth-teller again: someone who had come to court in the hope of changing the emperor's mind and paid for his audacity with his life.

BETWEEN SOLITARY LIFE AND SOCIAL DUTY

In a discussion of the role of the pagan philosopher in late antique society, Peter Brown has shown that the fourth-century image of the philosopher was double-sided. He points out that philosophers were seen as recluses who were free from society, while at the same time they were expected to represent the interests of others and speak up to authorities to defend the powerless.[27] A philosopher needed to conform to two sets of ideals and public expectations that were not easily compatible. On the one hand, he was expected to live a simple, solitary life and to devote himself entirely to philosophical contemplation. On the other hand, he should be prepared to leave his solitude to teach, advise and interfere in public matters, which

---

[23] Compare Hilary of Poitiers' switching of positions in his address *Ad Constantium*, discussed in the previous chapter.
[24] Eunapius, *Vita philosophorum et sophistarum* 462, ed. Wright, LCL 134, p. 380.   [25] Ibid.
[26] Ibid. 463, ed. Wright, LCL 134, p. 384.   [27] Brown, *Power and Persuasion*, pp. 62–4.

was precisely what he had set out to avoid. By virtue of his secluded life, a philosopher was believed to develop certain qualities, such as equanimity, strength of character and constancy, which made him, in the eyes of his contemporaries, just the person to intervene in the world around him.[28] Yet if he left his solitude to meet public demands, he was no longer free from the alluring forces of society that could disturb his philosophical equanimity.

These conflicting public demands that Brown has persuasively sketched for the fourth century were, however, not exclusive to this period. The tension between a life of contemplation and political engagement can also be seen in Plato's representation of Socrates (d. 399 BC).[29] Plato (d. 347 BC) portrays Socrates in *The Apology* as a distinctly apolitical person, who worried that political involvement would interfere with his vocation as a philosopher.[30] Yet, in spite of his reluctance, Plato's Socrates took his political duties in the Council of Athens very seriously and was always ready to defend the interests of his fellow citizens. Plato presented Socrates as an outsider, a provocative gadfly granted by God to the city to sting the Athenian people into acknowledging their duties and responsibilities.[31] This outsider status was given a civic interpretation: Socrates showed genuine care for his fellow citizens, was loyal to his city, and upheld standards of justice and civic responsibility.[32] When later philosophers were accused of too much worldly involvement, they would often draw on the cultural memory of Socrates to justify their own political activities. Socrates embodied all the virtues of the stereotypical philosopher – namely, self-control, *parrhesia* and independence – but, as these later philosophers were eager to point out, he had willingly accepted the presidential office of the Athenian Senate when it was his turn.[33]

The ambiguity in public expectations regarding the social role and duties of the philosopher is reflected in narrative representations of the truth-telling philosopher. Authors felt the need to stress the unwillingness of the philosopher to undertake an embassy to the court. By emphasising that the philosopher was persuaded by his townsmen, or was pressed by the emperor himself to come to the palace, the authors highlighted his reluctance to comply, and thus cleared the philosopher of any suspicions of ambition or desire for wealth and glory.[34] It was believed that life at

---

[28] Ibid., pp. 62–4.
[29] For this observation, see Lyons, *Hellenic Philosophers as Ambassadors*, p. 5, on which this paragraph is largely based.
[30] Ibid., p. 5, with reference to Plato, *Apology* 23b; 31d–e, 36b–c.   [31] Plato, *Apology* 30e.
[32] Lyons, *Hellenic Philosophers as Ambassadors*, p. 5, note 15.
[33] See for example Themistius, *Oratio* 34, discussed below.
[34] Ammianus Marcellinus, *Res gestae* XXX, 5, 8–10, ed. Seyfarth, vol. 2, p. 146; See Eunapius on the philosopher Chrysantius, *Vita philosophorum et sophistarum* 478, ed. Wright, LCL 134, p. 446.

The Detached Philosopher

court could corrupt even the most steadfast and constant philosopher. Eunapius tells us how the Neoplatonic philosopher Maximus of Ephesus (d. c. 372), who had been the teacher of Emperor Julian (r. 361–3), began to grow arrogant when he suddenly found himself at the centre of attention at Julian's court. The admiration and gifts that were bestowed on him went to his head and his behaviour changed. He started wearing clothes that, in the opinion of Eunapius, were too luxurious for a philosopher and he became more and more difficult to approach.[35] According to Eunapius, the change in Maximus' outer appearance reflected his inner disposition, which was no longer that of a sincere philosopher who loved only truth. Ammianus Marcellinus shared Eunapius' criticism of Maximus, although he put some of the blame on the emperor, who, in Ammianus' view, had bestowed too much honour on the philosopher. Ammianus wrote that Maximus came across as an excessive seeker of empty fame, and he reminded his readers of Cicero's warning against philosophers who only pretended to despise glory and praise.[36]

Eunapius contrasted the behaviour of Maximus with the noble attitude of the philosopher Priscus of Epirus (d. 395 AD), who was also invited by Emperor Julian to join his court. When he arrived, reluctantly, he behaved with great modesty and he was not as easily corrupted by the pleasures of court life as his colleague, the philosopher Maximus. Although many sought his favour, Eunapius said, Priscus remained unmoved and was not puffed up with pride.[37] The stories that late antique authors collected about the philosophers of their own days and the recent past showed that not everyone who called himself a philosopher was considered a wise and steadfast person whose words could be trusted without reservation.[38] One could recognise a true philosopher by his constant character and by the absence of pride, arrogance and ambition. A genuine philosopher was reluctant to leave his solitude to set a course for the imperial court; he was not interested in the material rewards and the acclaim such an undertaking might entail. When Ammianus tells the story, mentioned earlier, of how the people of Epirus chose the philosopher Iphicles as their envoy, he finds it necessary to stress the fact that the philosopher was very unwilling to undertake the commission.[39] One had to be persuaded by one's fellow citizens, by the gods or by fate to take on

---

[35] Eunapius, *Vita philosophorum et sophistarum* 478, ed. Wright, LCL 134, p. 447.
[36] Ammianus Marcellinus, *Res gestae* XXII, 7, 3–4, ed. Seyfarth, vol. 1, p. 258.
[37] Eunapius, *Vita philosophorum et sophistarum* 478, ed. Wright, LCL 134, p. 447.
[38] See for example Ammianus Marcellinus on the philosopher Epigonius, *Res gestae* XIV, 9, 5, ed. Seyfarth, vol. 1, p. 25.
[39] Ammianus Marcellinus, *Res gestae* XXX, 5, 9, ed. Seyfarth, vol. 2, p. 146.

Part I

this public role. As soon as ambition came into play it spelled the end of the philosopher's independent behaviour, equanimity, virtuous life and truly free speech: that is, of the qualities that made him, in the eyes of his contemporaries, a true philosopher in the first place.

The Court Philosopher Themistius

So far, this chapter has focussed on narratives, and on the image of the ideal philosopher that they present. Let us now turn to an actual speech, written by a philosopher and addressed to an emperor, to see if and how that philosopher responded to social expectations that we find in narrative sources. The speech concerned is a panegyric that the philosopher Themistius delivered before Emperor Constantius II. Themistius (d. 390 AD) is of special interest for the purpose of this chapter, for this philosopher was a rival for imperial favour to bishops such as Hilary of Poitiers and Ambrose of Milan. Themistius' career and ceremonial speeches illustrate how a politically active philosopher struggled with the expectations of society regarding honest, disinterested truth-telling.

Themistius was active in public life as a panegyrist, philosopher and adviser for almost thirty years. He regularly received imperial favours in reward for his services and was severely criticised for it. Themistius served under several Christian emperors as a panegyrist and adviser, although he himself was not a Christian. He was close to Constantius II, Jovian, Valens and Theodosius I. He was admitted to the Senate in 355 as a direct result of imperial favour, and became prefect of Constantinople in 384.[40] His contemporaries reproached him for accepting public office and accused the philosopher of using his rhetorical talents for material gain and for the advancement of his public career. Themistius justified his decision by stating that he had accepted the urban prefecture only to be of service to society and had never benefitted from it financially. Yet according to some, even without financial rewards the responsibilities that came with the office compromised his position as an independent and objective philosopher. Entanglement in the imperial administration, it was held, could only get in the way of offering disinterested advice. Themistius, however, held that a philosopher should not distance himself from the practical problems of society. Had the great Socrates himself not held public office in Athens, Themistius countered, without descending from philosophy?[41] In one of his later orations he proudly asserts that he elected

---

[40] Heather, Moncur, *Politics, Philosophy, and Empire*, pp. 108–14.
[41] Themistius, *Oratio* 34 ('In reply to those who found fault with him for accepting public office'), 10, trans. Heather, Moncur, p. 318.

The Detached Philosopher

the kind of philosophy that operates in the public arena.[42] Building on Aristotle's political philosophy, Themistius argued that a philosopher could not and should not retreat from society to hide in the wilderness, but should use his eloquence for the good of the whole body politic.[43]

The panegyric that Themistius addressed to Emperor Constantius II (r. 337–61) is the earliest surviving oration of Themistius. According to the rubric attached to the speech in the manuscript tradition, Themistius delivered this oration in Ancyra between 347 and 350, in Constantius' presence.[44] In the opening lines, Themistius makes his entrance as a 'truthful praise-giver':

> Now for the first time, your majesty, there comes on the scene for you both an independent speech- and a truthful praise-giver, and there is no word, however insignificant, that he would utter of his own free will for which he shall not render account to philosophy.[45]

Themistius, who had a penchant for dramatic language, pictures the setting of his speech as a theatre in which he is delivering his oration.[46] The speech itself thus becomes a theatrical performance before a courtly audience. In this first speech to Constantius, Themistius adopts the public persona of impartial adviser and objective philosopher, who can speak nothing but the truth.[47] Being a philosopher, he claims that he was able to distinguish 'the true king', while others only admired the surface of the emperor's power and qualities.[48] After declaring his intentions, Themistius, perhaps to get ahead of his critics, addresses the topical opposition between speaking the truth and giving praise. He assures the emperor and the wider audience of his speech that the praise he offers is certainly no flattery but a witness to virtue, 'for nothing is more inimical to truth than flattery.'[49] Instead of glossing over the tension between the profession of a panegyrist and the moral obligation of a philosopher to speak with *parrhesia*, he promises to do both: he will praise the emperor *and* offer him the truth.

Although panegyric is not an obvious genre for truth-telling, it was generally acknowledged that a speech of praise could be a vehicle for advice, or even for criticism.[50] In Themistius' view, the one did not preclude the other. Praise, as Themistius points out, is no flattery if it

---

[42] Penella, *Private Orations*, p. 4, with reference to Themistius, *Oratio* 31.352c.
[43] Themistius, *Oratio* 34. 6, trans. Penella, p. 213 and *Oratio* 26.325, trans. Penella, p. 156, discussed in Penella, *Private Orations*, p. 8.
[44] Heather, Moncur, *Politics, Philosophy, and Empire*, pp. 69 and 76.
[45] Themistius, *Oratio* 1.1a, trans. Heather, Moncur, p. 78.   [46] Ibid., n. 84.
[47] Heather, Moncur, *Politics, Philosophy, and Empire*, p. 73.
[48] Themistius, *Oratio* 1.1b, trans. Heather, Moncur, p. 79.
[49] Ibid. 3c, trans. Heather, Moncur, p. 90.   [50] Flower, *Emperors and Bishops*, pp. 49–55.

happens to be the truth – all the more so if it comes from the mouth of a philosopher who has looked straight into the heart of the ruler, as Themistius claims he has. He saw no reason, as he would explain in one of his later orations, why admonition should be expressed in harsh words, or criticism clothed in the language of abuse. There is no harm in sweetening one's words, Themistius argues, if it is done with the purpose of making it easier for the addressee to swallow the bitter pill of criticism. That, in Themistius' book, is no cheap flattery, but common decency.[51]

In the next section of his speech, Themistius offers his services to become the emperor's ears and the people's mouthpiece. He promises that he will bring before Constantius what people in the marketplaces, in the theatres and in the baths are saying about him. He proposes to bring all that he has heard, the rumours and the praise, to the emperor's attention.[52] The role he promises to take upon himself stands midway between that of an ambassador, bringing complaints and requests to the ruler's attention, and that of the independent truth-teller, who will tell the ruler frankly what others do not dare to say to his face.

In the remainder of his speech, Themistius touches upon all the familiar themes of a philosopher's oration before a philosopher-king, with frequent borrowings from Dio Chrysostom's orations on kingship.[53] He establishes common ground between traditional Hellenic culture and Constantius' Christian religion, by drawing on Platonic thought, attractive to Hellenes and Christians alike, and by employing metaphors that appealed to both groups, such as the metaphor of the shepherd looking after his flock.[54] Themistius went to great lengths, moreover, to compliment Constantius on his admirable self-restraint.[55] As is fitting for a philosopher-king who cares for mankind, Themistius says, Constantius is able to control his anger and soften his passions.[56] Was this flattery? It certainly was. Themistius knew that Constantius prided himself on his self-control and wished to be known as a just and merciful ruler. He told the emperor exactly what he wanted to hear in terms that the emperor himself favoured.[57] By making self-control a central theme of his panegyric, he broadcasted the quality he ascribed to the emperor to a wider audience, but at the same time he

---

[51] Themistius, *Oratio* 22, 276c–77c, trans. Penella, p. 101.
[52] Themistius, *Oratio* 1, 3d–4a, trans. Heather, Moncur, pp. 80, 81.
[53] Heather, 'Themistius: A political philosopher', p. 129.
[54] Suchan, *Mahnen und Regieren*, pp. 26–65.
[55] Themistius, *Oratio* 1, 4b–7d, trans. Heather, Moncur, pp. 81–5.
[56] Ibid. 7c, trans. Heather, Moncur, p. 84.
[57] Vanderspoel, *Themistius and the Imperial Court*, p. 79. This is reminiscent of Quintilian's observation that flattery often hides under the cover of *parrhesia*. Quintilian, *Institutio oratoria*, IX, 2, 26–9, ed. Russell, LCL 127, pp. 46–8.

imprinted on the emperor's mind the idea that he had better continue showing self-restraint in future. He told his addressee in the traditional language of the philosopher what the people for whom Themistius acted as spokesman wanted from their ruler.

As Peter Heather has pointed out, however, this conventional explanation of what a panegyric was meant to 'do' both underneath and via the surface layer of praise is not sufficient to explain the main purpose of Themistius' speech. It cannot have come as a surprise to Constantius to be told that his subjects wished their emperor to be in control of his anger, for mastery of passions was a traditional virtue of rulers in panegyrics and princely mirrors. This was probably the reason why Constantius wanted to be known as an even-tempered ruler in the first place. Rather, Themistius used the opportunity of delivering a panegyric to Constantius to demonstrate to the emperor how he could be of service as an imperial propagandist and a cultural broker between Hellenic traditions and Christian religion. At the time of his first panegyric to Constantius, Themistius was still a spokesman for his own interests. After 355, when the emperor had promoted him to the Senate, he acted as a middle man between Senate and emperor, bringing the senate's interests to the emperor's attention, and advocating imperial policy to the Senate.[58]

According to Heather, it was especially this mediating aspect of Themistius' agency that made him an attractive asset to several Christian emperors. Themistius was well cast to act as publicist of imperial policy to the Hellenistic elites, not only when he gave praise, but also, and perhaps especially, when he criticised the imperial administration. When Themistius, for example, reproached the 'Arian' emperor Valens for his harsh attitude towards 'Nicene' Christians and argued for a policy of religious toleration, this may have been exactly what this emperor wanted to be said out loud in public, to help negotiate a new direction of imperial policy with the audiences of Themistius' speeches and make that policy publicly acceptable.[59] Criticism expressed in a public speech could thus serve to test the waters. If the emperor subsequently displayed more tolerance towards religious diversity, the emperor would be praised for listening to the criticism of his adviser and the people he represented. In Themistius' ceremonial speeches, propaganda and negotiation may have been hiding underneath his criticism, while the criticism was simultaneously presented in the framework of praise. Yet it was not all smoke and mirrors. Themistius probably did exert influence on policy-making thanks to his close proximity to rulers and their dependence on his

---

[58] Heather, 'Themistius: A political philosopher', p. 145.   [59] Ibid., pp. 141–3.

Part I

rhetorical talents as 'spin doctor' of imperial administration.[60] Heather's interpretation of Themistius' agency accords well with Evangeline Lyons' observation that Hellenistic philosophers under the Roman Empire used their prestige, authority and eloquence on behalf of their cities in much the same way as they had done under the Hellenistic kingdoms, but gradually became 'advocates *for* the imperial government to their communities, rather than representatives of the polis *to* the imperial government'.[61]

Themistius would continue to deploy the persona of the parrhesiast who always spoke the truth even when he gave praise throughout his public career, in spite of, or perhaps especially because of, the criticism he faced from his contemporaries. He had no qualms about ruthlessly damning the faults of emperors, but only after they had died.[62] Time and again, he returned in his speeches to the topical tension between flattery and honesty, between public office and independence. Perhaps he needed to continue broaching this touchy subject in order to uphold and maintain his credibility as a truth-teller who did not shy away from criticising the very emperors from whom he received favours. In the mid 380s, around the time he retired from public life, Themistius looked back on the days he served Emperor Constantius and the remarkable position of 'privileged access' he enjoyed: 'He often took advice from me in council, while I was wearing my philosopher's cloak, and he often made me his dinner guest and his travelling companion. He gently endured it when I admonished him and did not take it badly when I rebuked him.'[63] As far as Themistius was concerned, a philosopher could appreciate the marks of public distinction an emperor bestowed upon him, while retaining the independence of mind to rebuke him when necessary. At least, that was how Themistius wished to remember his days with Constantius, and how he wished to be remembered by others.

INSIDERS AND OUTSIDERS

Although Themistius presented himself in his speeches as a detached philosopher, in the eyes of some of his contemporaries he was very much part of the establishment that he was supposed to advise and criticise from the outside. In late antique narratives, the philosopher–parrhesiast was often an outsider: the 'odd one out', who dared to express

---

[60] Ibid., p. 143.   [61] Lyons, *Hellenic Philosophers as Ambassadors*, p. 7.
[62] Heather, 'Themistius: A political philosopher', pp. 139–40.
[63] Themistius, *Oratio* 34 ('Reply to those who found fault with him'), 16, trans. Penella, p. 220. Themistius does not mention the name of this emperor, but it is generally accepted that it was Emperor Constantius; see Penella, *Private Orations*, p. 3.

The Detached Philosopher

a contrarian opinion against the view of the court clique. John Crook has suggested there was much room for frank speech in the emperor's council, and many opportunities to speak freely in the presence of the emperor. Crook, however, also allows that he may be giving too much credence to stories that were written with the intention to laud the patience and magnanimity of the ruler.[64] Yet it was widely held, he points out, that the opinion of an independent philosopher offered a necessary counterweight to the yes-men and flatterers of the emperor's regular entourage.[65]

Although contemporary historians and biographers tend to laud the courage of such outsider–critics, they do occasionally praise 'insiders', i.e. office-holders and members of the imperial household, for their positive effect on the ruler's mind and regime. The sophist Himerius (d. c. 386) compliments Hermogenes of Corinth (d. 361) for softening the tyrannical regime of an unnamed ruler, who may have been Emperor Licinius (r. 308–324).[66] Hermogenes later became proconsul of Greece, but at the time that he, according to Himerius, exerted his pacifying influence on the emperor, he was still a young member of the imperial household, serving as guardian of secrets: that is, a notary entrusted with taking messages from the ruler.[67] Himerius depicts young Hermogenes as a philosopher on the make, who appealed to the emperor's *paideia* and discussed ancient literature with him in order to soften his mood.[68] Once Hermogenes reached full adulthood, Himerius says, he walked away from the palace and from a position of power to follow the path of philosophy and study astronomy and geography.[69] He then went to Constantinople to offer his services to an emperor, possibly Constantius II, who recognised the usefulness of his knowledge and at once made him his adviser. The emperor trusted him in everything, Himerius says, and regarded him a helmsman of his rule.[70] 'Standing as an intermediary between the emperor and those under his rule,' Himerius writes, 'Hermogenes provided him with the needs of his subjects, and them with his commands.'[71]

Ammianus Marcellinus offers similar words of praise to Eutherius, the head chamberlain of Emperor Julian. Eutherius was, according to Ammianus, kind, loyal, clever, temperate, consistent, full of sound counsel: a man of great self-restraint who never disclosed a secret and who was never tempted to increase his wealth.[72] It is a catalogue of virtues that

---

[64] Crook, *Consilium Principis*, p. 142.   [65] Ibid.
[66] For another suggestion, see Barnes, 'Himerius and the fourth century', p. 219.
[67] Himerius, *Oratio* 48, 18–19; Penella, *Man and the Word,* p. 209; Barnes, 'Himerius and the fourth century', p. 219.
[68] Himerius, *Oratio* 48, 19, trans. Penella, pp. 265, 266.   [69] Ibid. 48, 20, trans. Penella, p. 266.
[70] Ibid. 48, 29, trans. Penella, p. 268.   [71] Ibid. 48, 30, trans. Penella, p. 269.
[72] Ammianus Marcellinus, *Res gestae* XVI, 7, 4–8, ed. Seyfarth, vol. 1, pp. 77, 78.

a Eunapius or Philostratus would have been eager to attribute to a philosopher, but Ammianus ascribes these philosophical qualities to a member of the imperial household. According to Ammianus, Eutherius was in the habit of criticising Emperor Julian for his lack of constancy, and if the Emperor Constans (r. 337–50), Ammianus adds, had only listened to this man, who urged honourable and upright conduct upon him, he would certainly have behaved much better.[73]

Himerius and Ammianus considered members of the imperial household and office-holders to be well equipped for the task of criticising, placating and counselling the ruler, as long as they were virtuous and not motivated by self-interest. Meinolf Vielberg concludes from Ammianus' favourable descriptions of ministers and officials who spoke frankly to the ruler that the ideal of frank speech (*Freimütigkeit*) had evidently turned into a *Funktionärstugend*.[74] It is, however, significant to note that when Ammianus and Himerius describe the positive influence of Eutherius and Hermogenes on their respective rulers and their regimes, they present them *as if* they were detached philosophers, uninterested in worldly advancement. Perhaps this was a necessary strategy to convince their audiences that one did not have to look far beyond the palace to find independent critics.

To sum up: being outsiders to palace hierarchy, philosophers were regarded as independent counsellors and critics. Owing allegiance to no one, they were believed to have the nerve as well as the independence of mind to stand up to the emperor and voice an opinion no one else dared to express. Emperors, in their turn, were expected to accept more frankness from a philosopher than they would normally accept from anyone. This social agreement between philosopher, ruler and society operated for a long time to everyone's satisfaction, at least as an ideal. One could doubt whether in reality a philosopher could plainly confront an emperor with an unwelcome truth and get away with it unscathed, but the public image of the relationship between an emperor and a philosopher must have had an effect on the daily reality of late antique politics, as the case of Themistius demonstrates. An emperor could not simply ignore public expectations, nor could a philosopher behave very differently from what was expected of him. If both parties heeded the social demands connected to their roles, the arrangement could be exploited to mutual advantage.

This social agreement did not dissolve the moment the Roman Empire became a Christian Empire. Under the rule of the first Christian emperors, non-Christian philosophers such as Themistius and Libanius still delivered ceremonial speeches, taught at the court, offered counsel or

---

[73] Ibid. XVI, 7, 5, ed. Seyfarth, vol. 1, p. 77.   [74] Vielberg, *Untertanentopik*, pp. 80, 82.

The Detached Philosopher

acted as Imperial Secretary. By employing old-style philosophers, Christian emperors sent an important signal to the Hellenic elites that, amidst all the changes and novelties that Christianity introduced, the emperors continued to value the good old Hellenic traditions.[75] When a philosopher praised the virtues and the *paideia* of a Christian emperor, addressing him as a philosopher-king, while the emperor showed favour to the philosopher and respected his *parrhesia*, this was a powerful affirmative sign of cultural continuity to the non-Christian elites.[76]

Themistius was the last of the non-Christian court philosophers. He retired around 384/5, after having served several Christian emperors. As Sozomen's and Socrates' ecclesiastical histories show, some fifty years after Themistius' withdrawal from public life Christian historiographers appreciated in retrospect the positive influence of a pagan philosopher on a Christian emperor's mind. The traditional task of philosophers to advise, correct and admonish a ruler thus lost none of its importance, but a new class had emerged that could do the job equally well. Christian holy men showed, in the words of Peter Brown, that they could 'sway the will of the powerful as effectively as had any philosopher'.[77]

Ascetic truth-tellers figure prominently in Christian literature. They are presented as possessing the pagan philosopher's appearance, lifestyle, virtues and, notably, his *parrhesia*. In late antique church histories, two traditions of political free speech come to the fore, and are sometimes intermingled: namely, that of the trustworthy minister who lives in proximity to the ruler and can therefore freely express his opinion, and that of the free-spoken outsider, who just passes by to give the emperor a piece of his mind. In between these two models of free speech, that of 'privileged access' and that of 'bold free speech', we find the figure of the bishop speaking up for his city, who may be seen as having the characteristics of both varieties of free speech.

A HOLY MAN GOES TO THE COURT

The sophist and biographer Eunapius witnessed the rising social prominence of Christian hermits. He was disgruntled, to put it mildly, that these dishevelled and uncultivated men rivalled the philosophers and sophists he so much admired and whose lives he recorded.[78] The monks' lack of *paideia* was appalling to him and contrasted sharply with the behaviour of

---

[75] Heather, Moncur, *Politics, Philosophy, and Empire*, p. 24.
[76] For an explanation as to why Christian emperors stopped employing non-Christian philosophers, see Heather, Moncur, *Politics, Philosophy, and Empire*, pp. 22–5.
[77] Peter Brown, *Power and Persuasion*, p. 4.
[78] Eunapius, *Vita philosophorum et sophistarum* 472, ed. Wright, LCL 134, p. 446.

Part I

his well-educated philosophers. The hermits and monks who were presented as truth-tellers in Christian narratives were, like the philosophers before them, solitary figures, devoted to a life of contemplation. The church historian Sozomen (d. 450 AD) called the holy men that he portrayed in his *Ecclesiastical History* 'philosophers of asceticism' or 'ecclesiastical philosophers', and noted that they practised philosophy in a distinguished way.[79] Perhaps this was Sozomen's attempt to depict his monks and hermits as equals to Eunapius' men of *paideia*.

In late antique Christian narratives, we encounter the topical tension that was also present in biographies of philosophers: that is, a tension between social responsibilities and a life of seclusion. Christian authors emphasise their protagonists' dedication to a life of simplicity and contemplation and stress their reluctance to leave their solitude to meet the demands of society. As Andrea Sterk has shown in her study on the monk–bishop in late Antiquity, Christian church histories and saints' lives often included an episode in which a hermit or desert father is ordained priest or bishop against his will. Thus the holy man is forced to take on social and ritual responsibilities, which he had attempted to avoid by living a life of solitude, away from society.[80] And yet, according to the Church historian Theodoret (393–466 AD), who espoused a rather flexible view of what he called the 'philosophy of solitary life', the choice between desert and town was not necessarily problematic for a Christian ascetic. After recounting how the holy monk Anthony was forced to leave the desert and came to the city of Antioch to warn its citizens of the dangers of the 'Arian' heresy, Theodoret draws the conclusion that godly men such as Anthony knew when to remain inactive and at rest, and when to leave the deserts for towns.[81] The fact, however, that Theodoret felt it necessary to stress the harmonious balance between Anthony's solitary life and his social responsibilities suggests that there remained a tension in public expectations concerning the social role of the Christian hermit, not unlike the ambivalence we have encountered with respect to the role of the philosopher.

Like the Stoic philosophers, the Christian 'philosophers of asceticism' mastered their passions through ascetic practices and cultivated those virtues that enabled them to confront power in a self-contained, courageous and tranquil manner. When holy men appropriated for themselves the role of the court philosopher, the truth-teller's task remained essentially unaltered: he should help the king control his anger and keep other

---

[79] Sozomen, *Historia ecclesiastica* VI, 27–34, especially 34, ed. *PG* 67, cols. 1393c–1397a.
[80] Sterk, *Renouncing the World*, pp. 2–6.
[81] Theodoret, *Historia ecclesiastica* IV, 28, ed. Parmentier, Hansen, p. 308.

undesirable passions in check. Like the court philosopher, the holy man was credited with the ability to detect hidden vices and point them out in a manner that was perhaps painful, but effective, as a capable doctor would treat a patient. The main difference was that the unruly passions of ancient philosophy were now being discussed in biblical terms of sin and atonement. Christian thinkers, influenced by Stoic views on virtues and passions, considered passion (in Latin often indicated by the word *perturbatio*) not solely as a threat to philosophical peace of mind, but also as a road that led to sin.[82] Holy men should warn the emperor not to let his uncontrolled passions present a danger to wise government. Gluttony, intemperance, adultery and anger were taken to exercise a negative influence on a ruler's political decisions. It was the duty of holy men to confront the emperor with his sins and persuade him to mend his ways. If a ruler were willing to atone, he could make up for the offence he had given God and, hopefully, ward off divine retribution. The stakes were high, for the ultimate consequence of a ruler's sin was cosmological disaster that destabilised the order of the entire empire. This far-reaching consequence of a ruler's misdemeanour for the stability of the cosmos, which was already present in Hellenic political thought, became an indissoluble part of the Christian discourse of admonition.[83]

The public image of a truth-telling holy man was that of an independent, free-acting agent. Late antique church histories and saints' lives contain episodes in which a holy man comes to the court, confronts an emperor briskly with the truth and leaves again to return to his solitude. Hardly ever do late antique Christian narratives present a truth-telling hermit or monk as a regular presence at the court. Most of the time, a holy man has just happened to pass by. Sometimes this was quite literally so, as in the case of the holy monk Aphraates, who came by the palace on his way to the soldiers' training ground to administer pastoral care to his flock. Emperor Valens, who was looking down from a gallery in his palace, saw the hermit passing by, walking in haste. When the emperor asked the monk where he was going, Aphraates replied that he was on his way to pray for the Empire.

'You had better stop at home,' said the emperor, 'and pray alone like a monk.' The old monk replied boldly: 'Yes, so I was bound to do and so I always did till now, as long as the Saviour's sheep were at peace. But now they are grievously disturbed and in great peril to be caught by beasts [...]. You have set fire to our

---

[82] Auerbach, *Literary Language*, p. 67.
[83] Dvornik, *Early Christian and Byzantine Political Philosophy*, vol. 1, pp. 241–77; Meens, 'Politics, mirrors of princes and the Bible'.

Father's house and we are running about in the endeavour to put it out.' So said Aphraates and the emperor threatened him and said no more.[84]

The conversation, in which the monk Aphraates tells the emperor frankly that he is not taking care of the empire in the way a Christian emperor should, confirms the social rule that a holy man should stay put and devote himself to a life of contemplation and prayer. But it also confirms the acceptable exception to that rule. The story of the monk Aphraates displays a literary trope common to many stories about truth-telling holy men. Hardly ever does one hear of a hermit who goes to court of his free will, or who stays on at the court to offer his services as counsellor to the emperor. In Sozomen's *Ecclesiastical History*, Christians who did stay at court as confidants of the emperor, who enjoyed his trust and were granted the privilege of free speech, were usually the wrong type of Christians (that is, in Sozomen's book, Arians), who used their privileged position to plot against true Christians.[85]

The role of the holy man, which he inherited from the philosopher, was defined by strict codes of behaviour that shaped his social contract with the ruler. Although there were clear norms and expectations to which he had to conform, his function at the court was rarely a formal one. The prevailing image of the philosopher, and later of the holy man, was of an independent individual who possessed courage, constancy of character, self-control, independence from social and material rewards and freedom of mind and expression. The latter two characteristics, independence and freedom, were perceived as incompatible with a formal role at the court, or with a public office that entailed certain benefits. If a philosopher were to take office, he could still be seen as an honest and wise adviser, but he would run the risk of no longer being considered an impartial and objective truth-teller. The same lesson applied to holy men and, from the fourth century onwards, also to bishops.

Freedom from social ties and lack of interest in worldly preferment were considered necessary preconditions for expressing oneself freely. Another precondition for candid counsel was *libertas* of mind. A truth-teller should not even care for the good opinion of contemporaries, or, for that matter, the good opinion of the ruler himself.[86] If the emperor

---

[84] Theodoret, *Historia ecclesiastica* IV, 26, ed. Parmentier, Hansen, p. 302, lines 23–32. Trans. Jackson, p. 127. Compare ibid. IV, 35, ed. Parmentier, Hansen, pp. 318–20 on Isaac, the monk of Constantinople who confronted Emperor Valens when he saw the emperor marching out with his troops.

[85] Sozomen, *Historia ecclesiastica* II, 22 and 27, ed. PG 67, cols. 989A and 1009B.

[86] Compare Sozomen, *Historia ecclesiastica* VI, 16, ed. PG 67, cols. 1332b–1334b, on the speech of Basil of Caesarea to Emperor Valens and his prefect.

The Detached Philosopher

were willing to listen, it was for the better; if not, no fear of losing the emperor's favour should keep the holy man from telling the truth. After all, and this was an advantage a holy man had over a court philosopher, he drew the legitimation for his frank speech from a power higher than the emperor's. His authority to confront an emperor with the truth was not based on a *familiaritas* with the ruler, but on a privileged access to God and a right to speak freely to the heavenly ruler. Privileged access to God, as we have seen in chapter 1, was also referred to as *parrhesia*.[87] This specific religious notion of *parrhesia* came to imbue the political discourse of late Antiquity and the early Middle Ages. Saints' lives and martyr acts stress how the privilege of having *parrhesia* with God gave the saint confidence and courage when confronted with hostile civic authorities, without being held back by fear of repercussions. Christian emperors valued the advice of a holy man, especially because of his *parrhesia* with God, which made him just the right person to intercede on behalf of the emperor and his realm.[88] Because of their special status, exemplary way of life and immunity to the allurements of worldly gain, Christian holy men were, like the philosophers before them, very well cast for the role of independent truth-tellers. In that respect, nothing much changed in the social mechanisms of free speech when solitary monks and hermits took over the role of truth-tellers from the philosophers. This situation shifted when bishops started to claim this position for themselves as well.

THE BEST OF BOTH WORLDS

Sozomen recounts the story of how, when the famous pagan orator Libanius (d. 394) was on his deathbed, his friends asked him who should replace him. Libanius replied that it would have been John, 'had not the Christians taken him from us'.[89] The man Libanius referred to was John Chrysostom, soon to be bishop of Constantinople (d. 407), who became famous for his eloquent orations and his denunciations of abuse of power. Over the course of the fourth century, an increasing number of bishops ventured into the domain of political oratory and offered advice and criticism to emperors. Of the two routes to the emperor's ear, the 'privileged access' route was probably more realistic, albeit available to few, than the 'bold speech' route. But it was the latter route that appealed most to the public imagination. Bold speech was the stuff of legends. It

---

[87] See also Scarpat, *Parrhesia*, pp. 82, 83; Bartelink, 'Quelques observations sur παρρησία', pp. 11, 22.
[88] Bartelink, 'Quelques observations sur παρρησία', pp. 7, 12.
[89] Sozomen, *Historia ecclesiastica* VIII, 2, ed. PG 67, col. 1513b, trans. Hartranft, p. 399.

was a popular stance of orators delivering a speech and a favourite mould in which to describe the performance and language of political advice and criticism. This also applied to the speeches of Christian orators and bishops.[90]

Late antique Christian narratives portrayed bishops, especially 'Nicene' bishops under 'Arian' emperors, as independent figures, and did not hesitate to ascribe bold *parrhesia* to them. Church histories feature free-speaking bishops who did not patiently wait to be granted an audience with the emperor, but seized the opportunity themselves. After all, it was God who told them when and how to speak, not the emperor. Sozomen tells us how Bishop Athanasius of Alexandria positioned himself before Emperor Constantine right in the middle of the highway, when Constantine was on his way back to Constantinople on horseback. Athanasius did not politely ask for an audience; he demanded one. Constantine was not inclined to grant it to him at first, but because the bishop was so bold and persistent, he decided to let him speak after all.[91] Bishops such as Athanasius of Alexandria, Ambrose of Milan and John Chrysostom of Constantinople are depicted in church histories as courageous champions of truth who were willing to disregard the risks that speaking freely posed to their position.[92] By contrast, bishops who were friendly with the emperor and who enjoyed a privileged position at court are often portrayed as suspect figures, while the bishops whose relationship with the emperor was strained, and who were deposed, exiled and killed, are presented as heroes who spoke up for truth.[93] Exile, a dramatic death or other forms of suffering were interpreted as a sign of divine favour. There was an incontrovertible logic behind this: if someone was killed or exiled for his words, he had probably spoken the truth.

The narrative strategies that represented the bishop as a cast-out truth-teller, could, however, not hide the fact that bishops held a position of authority in a Christian society and were, by dint of their function as community leaders, no solitary 'outsiders'. They were important pillars of society and assumed the role of ambassador for the city in which their

---

[90] See the exordium of Bishop Synesius of Cyrene's oration to Emperor Arcadius *On Imperial Rule* 1, ed. *PG* 66, cols. 1053–1056.
[91] Sozomen, *Historia ecclesiastica* II, 28, ed. *PG* 67, cols. 1013d–1016a.
[92] Athanasius, *History of the Arians* 33, ed. *PG* 25, col. 732 (on Dionysius of Milan, Eusebius of Vercelli and Lucifer of Cagliari); Sozomen, *Historia ecclesiastica* II, 28, ed. *PG* 67, cols. 1013d–1016a (on Athanasius), VI, 16, ed. *PG* 67, cols. 1332b–1334b (on Basil of Caesarea), VIII, 24, ed. *PG* 67, col. 1524 (on John Chrysostom).
[93] Sozomen, *Historia ecclesiastica* II, 22 and 27, ed. *PG* 67, col. 989 and col. 1009; on negative parrhesia attributed to heretics, in particular to Arians, see Bartelink, 'Quelques observations sur παρρησία', p. 12 and Athanasius, *Historia Arianorum,* ed. *PG* 25, col. 721B.

church was located, to represent the city's concerns.[94] Because of their social and political responsibilities, which made them far from disinterested counsellors in the eyes of the general public, they could not step into the scripted roles of the court philosophers as easily as the hermits before them had done.

This is not to say that they did not try. When approaching an emperor, a bishop could present himself not (only) as a person of high social standing, but as a man of God, who possessed the same qualities as holy hermits and philosophers, and who could therefore lay a claim to the same amount of *parrhesia* as they did. Bishop Gregory Nazianzen (d. 390 AD), known for his outspokenness, stressed his ascetic authority rather than any authority that derived from his episcopal status and role in society when he delivered a dramatic speech to Emperor Theodosius I in 381, at the Council of Constantinople.[95] In an autobiographical poem, Gregory looks back on his meeting with the emperor, and describes his behaviour towards Theodosius in terms that would have befitted a philosopher of old. Gregory profiles himself as a man of God, who came to the emperor 'just as he was', that is, as a holy man of God, not a bishop who boasted of his intellectual training and social status, although he let his readers know that he could have done so, had he wanted to. In his poem, Gregory creates the persona of a bishop who is torn between the responsibilities of the office and the spiritual benefits of a life of contemplation.[96] He wanted his readers to remember him as a man who had mixed the serenity of the ascetic life and the practical responsibilities of the episcopal office.[97] In that sense, Gregory's self-representation bears a resemblance to that of Themistius, who wished to be known as a man who was perfectly capable of combining the duties and rigid self-control of the philosopher with the responsibilities and renown of public office.

CONCLUSION

In late Antiquity a process of 'ascetization' of the episcopal office took place. The ideal bishop was the monk–bishop, in whom the wisdom and tranquillity that could only be gained from a life of contemplation came together with the social and spiritual responsibilities of the episcopal

---

[94] Rapp, *Holy Bishops*, p. 262; see Synesius of Cyrene, who introduces himself in his oration to Emperor Arcadius as the representative of his city, Cyrene, *On Imperial Rule* 2, 1, ed. *PG* 66, col. 1056.
[95] On Gregory's reputation for outspokenness, see Sterk, *Renouncing the World*, p. 119.
[96] Gregory Nazianzen, *De vita sua* (*Carmen* 2.1.11) vv. 1871–9, trans. White, p. 149. In the discussion of this passage I follow the interpretation of Rapp, *Holy Bishops*, p. 272.
[97] Gregory Nazianzen, *De vita sua*, vv. 310–11, trans. White, p. 33.

office. Care for one's own soul met with pastoral care for others. What Andrea Sterk has termed the 'near institutionalisation of asceticism in the ascendance of the monk–bishop' was an attempt to preserve and contain the charisma of the holy man in the episcopacy.[98] Status and charisma were highly appreciated in late antique society. A bishop who could bring the advantages of both his social status and the ascetic charisma of the holy man into play was a person to be reckoned with. As the previous case study on Hilary of Poitiers has illustrated, Hilary increased the authority and appeal of his invective by presenting himself as a martyr and an exile, tapping into the reservoir of authority and prestige that was connected to a particular type of sanctity that came with martyrdom and exile. As the studies of Andrea Sterk and Claudia Rapp have demonstrated, the ideal of the monk–bishop made use of the old models of sanctity within a pragmatic setting for the sake of the administrative, social and pastoral responsibilities of the episcopal office. Free speech was part and parcel of the capital of institutionalised charisma.

Not all bishops, however, could plausibly present themselves as ascetics, martyrs or exiles. But there were other ways to lay a claim to the authority of the independent truth-teller, without having to go to the desert, get exiled or arrested, or otherwise spend time in isolation from the rest of society.[99] The position of the free-speaking outsider and the language of the detached philosopher–parrhesiast could be appropriated in more than one way, as the next case study, on Bishop Ambrose of Milan, shows. Ambrose (d. 397) was never exiled, nor was he much inclined towards asceticism or martyrdom. And yet, he managed to present himself as an outsider, who spoke boldly to Emperor Theodosius.

---

[98] Sterk, *Renouncing the World*, p. 7. See also Diem, 'Monks, kings and the transformation of sanctity'.
[99] Cain, 'Vox clamantis in deserto'.

4

AMBROSE OF MILAN

In the late summer of 390, so the story goes, a bishop squared up against an emperor in front of his church in Milan. The bishop was Ambrose of Milan (d. 397), and the emperor Theodosius I (r. 379–95), also known as Theodosius the Great. The cause of their confrontation was a dramatic incident for which Ambrose called the emperor to account. Theodosius had ordered a certain number of citizens of Thessalonica to be put to death, in response to a riot that had taken place in that city, during which one of Theodosius' generals had been killed.[1] His order led to wider bloodshed, and many civilians lost their lives. When Ambrose heard the news of the Thessalonica massacre, he rebuked the emperor and told him that he was not allowed to enter the church until he had atoned for the death of so many innocent people. According to the Greek church historian Sozomen (d. 450 AD), Ambrose stopped Theodosius in the porch of the church and told him the truth in no uncertain terms. He called out to the emperor: 'Stand back! A man defiled by sin, and with hands imbued in blood unjustly shed, is not worthy, without repentance, to enter within these sacred precincts, or partake of the holy mysteries.' The emperor did not get angry at Ambrose's bold conduct, but, in the words of Sozomen, 'he was struck with admiration at the *parrhesia* of the bishop'.[2] He realised that Ambrose had spoken the truth, and retraced his steps. Some time later, the emperor publicly confessed his sins in church and willingly accepted the penance that Ambrose imposed on him. Sozomen recounts this story about the confrontation between the emperor and the bishop for a specific reason, as he explains at the end of his

---

[1] This is the version of the massacre of Thessalonica as presented by the church historian Sozomen in his *Historia ecclesiastica* VII, 25, ed. Bidez, Hansen, GCS 50, pp. 338–40.
[2] Sozomen, *Historia ecclesiastica* VII, 25, ed. Bidez, Hansen, GCS 50, p. 399, lines 1–3, trans. Hartranft, *NPNF*-2, p. 394.

account. He wished to show 'with what *parrhesia* [Ambrose] addressed those in power when the service of God was in question'.[3]

Sozomen was not the only author to recount the Thessalonica incident. Other authors presented their own version of the altercation between Ambrose and Theodosius, and, by extension, offered an interpretation of what they considered to be the ideal relationship between a bishop and an emperor.[4] The source that is closest to the date of the event is a letter that Ambrose wrote to Theodosius upon the occasion. In this letter, Ambrose berates Theodosius for his rash decision to punish the citizens of Thessalonica and strongly recommends that the emperor do penance for his sins.[5] The letter suggests that Ambrose did not address the emperor publicly in the porch of the church of Milan, as Sozomen has it, but that he rebuked the emperor 'privately', by letter.[6] In this letter, as Peter Brown observes, Ambrose adopted the traditional role of the philosopher–parrhesiast, and fearlessly told the emperor the truth.[7]

The language that Ambrose employed to berate the emperor and the role he took upon himself differed, however, from that of the traditional court philosopher, and even of the earlier Christian truth-tellers. By the time Ambrose wrote his letter, there were several paradigms of free speech available; there was more than one way to speak truth to power, and more than one way to legitimise it to a wider audience. As we have seen, Christian martyrs and holy men spoke freely to Roman officials and emperors, confident of their *parrhesia* before God. Bishop Hilary of Poitiers admonished Emperor Constantius II in the role of an exiled prophet–priest, and later abused him under appeal to his apostolic freedom of speech (*libertas apostolica*). The new-style court philosopher and imperial propagandist Themistius made full use of the old philosopher's prerogative of *parrhesia* to achieve the desired effect in his ceremonial speeches. Ambrose combined all these roles to create something new.

In 390, when Ambrose confronted Emperor Theodosius, circumstances were already very different from those under which Hilary, thirty years earlier, had admonished Constantius II. Theodosius was not an 'Arian' emperor, but belonged to the same 'Nicene' party as Ambrose. In 380, the emperors Theodosius, Gratian and Valentinian II had issued a decree that declared Nicene Christianity to be the legitimate imperial

---

[3] Ibid. VII, 25, ed. Bidez, Hansen, *GCS* 50, p. 340, lines 27, 28, trans. Hartranft, *NPNF*-2, p. 394.
[4] These other sources are the *Vita Ambrosii*, written shortly after Ambrose's death by his former secretary Paulinus of Milan (around 422), the chronicle of Rufinus (a Latin translation and continuation of Eusebius' *Historia ecclesiastica* written before 410) and Augustine's *De civitate Dei* (early fifth century).
[5] Ambrose, *Ep. extra collectionem* 11, ed. Zelzer, *CSEL* 82.3, pp. 212–18.
[6] The extent to which this private letter was 'private' is an issue to which I shall return below.
[7] Brown, *Power and Persuasion*, pp. 111–12.

religion. This was also the decade that saw the end of the 'pagan' court philosopher. Around 388, a few years before Ambrose wrote his letter to Theodosius, Themistius retired from public life. The philosopher had been a favourite of Emperor Theodosius, serving as his imperial secretary and guardian of his son Arcadius. Themistius had advocated tolerance for religious plurality to several Christian emperors, apparently with some success, but under Theodosius' administration state support for polytheist religion ended. In 392, Theodosius would prohibit pagan worship full stop. These changes in imperial policy were welcomed by bishops such as Ambrose, who had little patience for the coexistence of religions, but that did not mean that there were no more subjects on which a bishop and an emperor would disagree, as the Thessalonica incident shows.

Ambrose was a man of *paideia*. He came from a senatorial family and was educated in the liberal arts in Rome, according to his biographer (previously his secretary) Paulinus.[8] He began his career as an advocate at the court of a praetorian prefect and received the thorough rhetorical training required for that profession. The strategies and vocabulary of Ambrose's letters reveal that he was well versed in the classical rhetorical tradition of *parrhesia* and familiar with the conventions that determined who was allowed to tell the truth to whom, when and in which manner.[9] What is new about Ambrose's *parrhesia*, however, is that when he confronts Theodosius with the truth, he does so as a bishop and a priest who is responsible for the emperor's soul. Hilary of Poitiers had employed that same priestly stance when he addressed Emperor Constantius II, but Ambrose connects the duty of the priest to warn rulers from sin to the Roman idea of *libertas*. Where Hilary's freedom of speech had only carried overtones of Roman *libertas,* Ambrose makes the association between Christian and 'classical' free speech explicit.

This chapter is about the rhetoric of Ambrose's letters to Theodosius and the public image of their confrontation in the porch of the church of Milan, as transmitted by later narratives. I analyse the rhetorical strategies that Ambrose employs in his letters to Theodosius to see how these strategies relate to the classical rhetorical tradition of free speech, and to determine which specifically Christian elements have been added to the traditional repertoire.[10] The Thessalonica letter will be discussed in relation to another letter that Ambrose wrote to the emperor two years earlier, in 388. This earlier letter, commonly known as the Callinicium

---

[8] On Ambrose's family background and education, see McLynn, *Ambrose of Milan* pp. 31–5; Vocino, 'Bishops in the mirror.'
[9] See also the opinon of Hürten, '*Libertas* in der Patristik', p. 7.
[10] Roger Rees' article 'Authorizing freedom of speech under Theodosius', which appeared in 2018, came to my attention too late to be fully acknowledged in this chapter.

Part I

letter, is relevant to the present investigation, for Ambrose here laid down the foundation for a claim to the priestly privilege of free speech to which he would later return.[11] The purpose of this chapter is not to discover 'what really happened'. As Neil McLynn and others have pointed out, it is highly unlikely that Ambrose publicly rebuked the emperor in front of the church, as the fifth-century historians Sozomen and Theodoret would have it.[12] Instead, I am interested in the process of image-making that produced a powerful public image of Ambrose as a courageous truth-teller and provided a source of inspiration and legitimisation for future generations of truth-tellers.[13]

SHUT OUT FROM DELIBERATIONS

Ambrose was not the person to eschew a direct confrontation. Before his dealings with Theodosius, he had engaged in head-to-head encounters with Emperor Gratian, Emperor Valentinian II and Empress Justina. When, in 388, Emperor Theodosius, who previously had resided in Constantinople, took up residence in Milan, Ambrose had high hopes of being included in the intimate circle of Theodosius' counsellors, as he suggests in his letters. Initially, however, he did not manage to establish the same privileged mode of communication with Theodosius as he had developed with the courts of the emperors Gratian and Valentinian.[14] Theodosius had brought his own advisers from Constantinople along with him to Milan and, apparently, was reluctant to grant Ambrose privileged access.[15] However, we have only Ambrose's testimony that Theodosius excluded him from deliberations.[16] There are no other sources that corroborate this.

Ambrose considered himself well suited to offer sound advice to the emperor and have a voice in his decisions. After all, who could be a better ambassador to represent the interests of the city of Milan than its bishop?

---

[11] The Callinicium letter is *Ep.* 74, the Thessalonica letter *Ep. extra collectionem* 11. I follow the numbering of the letters according to the edition of Zelzer, *Epistularum liber decimus*. In the old Benedictine/Maurist edition, the letters are numbered 40 and 51. More information on Ambrose's letter collection will follow later in this chapter.

[12] McLynn, *Ambrose of Milan*, p. 291; Palanque, *Saint Ambroise*, p. 423; Canivet, *Théodoret de Cyr*, p. 406, n. 1; Dvornik, *Early Christian and Byzantine Political Philosophy*, p. 785. Theodosius' penance is also recounted in Rufinus, *Historia ecclesiastica* II, 18 and Augustine, *De civitate Dei* V, 26, but without reference to Ambrose. According to Rufinus, Theodosius was admonished by 'the priests of Italy' and unnamed 'bishops'. The only other source to refer to Ambrose's admonitions (albeit not in the porch of the church) is Paulinus, *Vita Ambrosii* 24.

[13] See especially chapter 8. See also Vocino, 'Bishops in the mirror'.

[14] McLynn, *Ambrose of Milan*, p. 298.

[15] Ibid. p. 297, on the advisers that Theodosius brought from Constantinople.

[16] Ambrose, *Ep. extra collectionem* 11, 1–2.

Ambrose of Milan

In the two years between Theodosius' arrival in Milan (388) and the Thessalonica incident (390), Ambrose put several petitions before the emperor, some of which Theodosius granted, Ambrose says, albeit reluctantly. As Ambrose writes to his sister Marcellina, it had taken strong means of persuasion to make the emperor listen to his advice.[17] By the time Ambrose wrote the famous Thessalonica letter, his relationship with the emperor had reached a low point. At least, that is how Ambrose presents the situation. In the exordium of his letter, Ambrose complains that, when the riot at Thessalonica was discussed in the palace and the emperor and his advisors were considering what measures to take, he was shut out from their consultations. What is more, he says, he was not even allowed to hear news from the consistory, because the emperor did not want him meddling in his affairs. Ambrose indicates that he presented many petitions in an attempt to prevent this atrocity, but that no one paid heed to his warnings.[18]

Ambrose opens the letter with a proper *captatio benevolentiae*, thanking the emperor profusely for previous favours and acts of kindness, and thereby suggesting that there had been a time when the emperor still listened to Ambrose's petitions on behalf of others. The present situation was different, much to Ambrose's regret. Apparently, Theodosius was annoyed because Ambrose had obtained knowledge of a number of decisions taken in the consistory, and had made sure that no report relating to imperial decisions reached him any more. 'It seemed to me', Ambrose complains, 'that I alone at all of your court have been stripped of the natural right to receive a hearing, with the result that I have also been deprived of the office of speaking.'[19] Therefore, he wants the emperor to know, he cannot be held to account for what happened subsequently. Evidently, Ambrose is hinting here at the Thessalonica incident, but he does not refer to it explicitly. No one had told him anything, he had not been included in the decision-making process and he was not permitted to speak. He allows that he should have protested more, but his hands had been tied. Theodosius had shut him out from deliberations and Ambrose had conformed to his imperial wish, out of respect for the emperor and fear of his anger.

---

[17] Ambrose, *Ep. extra collectionem* 1. In *Ep. extra collectionem* 11, 2, Ambrose mentions acts of intercession to which Theodosius had favourably responded.
[18] Ambrose, *Ep. extra collectionem* 11, 6, ed. Zelzer, p. 214.
[19] Ibid. 11, 2, ed. Zelzer, p. 212, rr. 9, 10: 'Soli mihi in tuo comitatu ius naturae ereptum videbam audiendi, ut et loquendi privare munere.' Trans. Liebeschutz, p. 263.

Part I
A Careful Opening

In the first five chapters of the letter (following the modern subdivision), Ambrose does not state his reason for writing his letter. Only in the sixth chapter does he bring up the massacre. This careful style of opening is called *insinuatio,* and was usually employed in judicial speeches when the case was considered disreputable, and it took all manner of subtlety and tact to address the crime without showing the accused in an unfavourable light.[20] There is also another reason why Ambrose waits so long to broach the subject: he first needs to establish the importance of free speech and negotiate the terms of engagement, before he can launch his criticism at Theodosius.

It was not unusual in late antique speeches to point out the significance of free speech and to announce that one was going to speak freely *before* offering advice or criticism, as can for instance be seen in Synesius of Cyrene's speech *On Kingship* addressed to Emperor Arcadius (r. 383–402). In the exordium of his speech, Synesius announces that he is going to speak with *parrhesia*: 'Now, in as much as I perceive that some of you are already disconcerted and take in dudgeon my freedom of speech, let such remember that I announced this as my intention beforehand'.[21] Thus Synesius gives his hearers, the emperor and his entourage, fair warning, so that they can brace themselves for the criticism that is about to follow.

Like Synesius, Ambrose announces that he is about to speak freely, but he does so by means of a string of questions. 'What in the circumstances was I to do? Hear nothing? Disclose nothing? Was I to hold my tongue?'.[22] He underlines the predicament he found himself in. Should he have remained obedient to the emperor and keep his mouth and ears shut, or should he rather have listened to the voice of his conscience and speak out? Of course he knew the right answer: he should not have remained silent, for it is the duty of the priest to speak out and admonish a wrongdoer.[23] Here, Ambrose quotes from the Book of Ezekiel, where God gives the prophet–priest Ezekiel the task of warning the righteous against sin (Ezek. 3:17–18). Ambrose transfers this biblical passage to his present situation, thus implying that he, Ambrose, has been equally to blame for the massacre of Thessalonica, since he neglected to warn the emperor sufficiently.

---

[20] See *Rhetorica ad Herennium* I, 4–6, ed. Caplan, LCL 403, pp. 10-20.
[21] Synesius of Cyrene, *De regno* 3, trans. Fitzgerald, pp. 110-11.
[22] Ambrose, *Ep. extra collectionem* 11, 3, ed. Zelzer, p. 212, line 22–p. 213, line 25: 'Quid igitur facerem? Non audirem? [...] Proderem? Tacerem?'.
[23] Ambrose, *Ep. extra collectionem* 11, 3, ed. Zelzer, p. 213, lines 27-9.

Ambrose of Milan

Once Ambrose has established that he and Theodosius are in this together, he begins to reprimand the emperor. Signalling a shared guilt and a shared responsibility to make amends to God, he has prepared the ground for speaking freely to the emperor, confronting him with his sins and offering him the solace of penance. Near the conclusion of his letter (ch. 15), Ambrose thematises his self-accusation as a prelude to his criticism of Theodosius, with a reference to Proverbs 18:17: 'At the beginning of his speech, the just man accuses himself'.[24] Although Ambrose is convincing Theodosius of the importance of confession in this paragraph, this particular sentence is clearly about himself. As we have seen, Ambrose accuses himself at the end of the exordium of the letter. His exordium thus sets the stage for what is about to follow: he accuses himself first of neglecting his duties, before reprimanding Theodosius for *his* sins. Proverbs 18:17 is one of Ambrose's favourite biblical quotations, and supports an important theme in his work: namely, the need to search one's own conscience before uncovering the faults of others.[25]

Ambrose's exordium combines traditional handbook rhetoric with a biblical–ethical programme of prophetic admonition. Once he has announced that he is going to speak freely and established the shared guilt of the accuser and the accused, he can finally start reprimanding the emperor:

Listen to this, august emperor. That you are zealous for the faith, I cannot deny. That you fear God, I do not dispute. But you have been born with a passionate nature. When there is somebody around to calm you, you quickly channel it to pity, but if somebody inflames it, you let your passion grow to such a pitch that you can scarcely control it. May nobody ever be there to inflame your passion, unless there is also somebody to allay it![26]

It is a familiar classical theme that Ambrose addresses here: a ruler needs a wise counsellor, preferably a philosopher, to help him control his anger. Is Ambrose here offering his services to Theodosius, to become his personal anger-manager? It seems so, but then he takes a step back: 'Rather than risk arousing your passionate nature by any public act of

---

[24] Ibid. 11, 15, ed. Zelzer, p. 218, line 53, trans. Liebeschuetz, p. 269.
[25] See for example Ambrose, *Apologia David* 47, 47. Pierre Hadot, *Apologie de David*, p. 136, n. 53, lists fifteen quotations of Proverbs 18:17 in Ambrose's work.
[26] Ambrose, *Ep. extra collectionem* 11, 4, ed. Zelzer, p. 213, lines 30–5: 'Accipe illud, imperator auguste. Quod habeas fidei studium non possum negare, quod dei timorem non diffiteor; sed habes naturae impetum, quem si quis lenire velit cito vertes ad misericordiam, si quis stimulet in maius exsuscitas ut eum revocare vix possis. Utinam si nemo mitiget, nullus accendat.' Trans. Liebeschuetz, p. 264.

Part I

mine, I preferred to leave it to you to deal with it in private.'[27] Ambrose grants Theodosius his autonomy as a Christian ruler who is guided by piety, and therefore well capable of controlling his passionate nature himself. Like a true panegyrist, he compliments the emperor on a quality that every ruler likes to have ascribed to him. Why does Ambrose take back what he has just said? His rhetoric reveals a complex choreography, taking two steps forward and one step back. He keeps returning to areas already trodden, only to tread them again in a different manner. In this part of the letter (chh. 4–5) he turns once more to the reasons why he has neglected his episcopal duty to speak out. This time, however, he stresses not his position as an outsider to Theodosius' court, but the issue of private versus public admonition. He indicates that he had been worried that any public protest from his side could be interpreted as lack of love and respect for the emperor. This was the reason, he explains, that he used illness as an excuse not to be present at Theodosius' *adventus* into Milan, to avoid having to confront the emperor in public.[28]

PROPHETIC WARNING

Ambrose continues on this note, until he has reached the core of the *argumentatio* of his letter (chh. 7–9), where he persuades the emperor to reconcile himself with God and do penance. He holds up the biblical example of King David's repentance to Theodosius as a model to follow. If it was not humiliating for King David to confess his sins, so Ambrose argues, then it is not degrading for Theodosius to humble himself before God and do penance. Here, Ambrose takes on the role of the prophet Nathan, accepting the prophetic duty that, he says, he initially shied away from when he let himself be silenced. Just as Nathan was sent by God to confront David with his sins, so it was Ambrose's duty to point out to Theodosius his wrongdoings. Yet, where David could offer sacrifices to show his remorse and be reconciled with God, Theodosius can only atone for his sins by doing penance: 'For in those days there were sacrifices for sin, but these have now become sacrifices of penance.'[29] To emphasise further the importance of penance as a more up-to-date alternative, Ambrose wrote the *Apologia David* and dedicated it to

---

[27] Ibid. 5, ed. Zelzer, p. 213, lines 37, 38: 'Hunc ego impetum malui cogitationibus tuis secreto committere quam meis factis publice fortassis movere.' Trans. Liebeschuetz, p. 265.

[28] Ibid. 5. For an interpretation of this passage, see Liebeschuetz, *Ambrose of Milan: Political Letters and Speeches,* p. 265, n. 1. On Ambrose's absence from the *adventus* ceremony in Milan, see McLynn, *Ambrose of Milan,* p. 326.

[29] Ambrose, *Ep. extra collectionem* 11, 9, ed. Zelzer, p. 215, lines 87, 88: 'erant enim tunc sacrificia pro delictis, haec nunc sunt sacrificia poenitentiae.' Trans. Liebeschuetz, p. 267.

Ambrose of Milan

Theodosius.[30] Peter Brown surmises that Ambrose attached the *Apologia* to his letter to Theodosius as a further means of persuasion.[31] The *Apologia*, an exposition on the penitential Psalm 50(51), which David was believed to have composed after Nathan rebuked him, provides further arguments to convince Theodosius that penance now offers the only way out of this crisis.[32]

Ambrose speaks with the voice of the prophet Nathan to confront the emperor with his sins,[33] yet, like Hilary of Poitiers, he does not employ the Old Testament vocabulary of reproach and rebuke for his own prophet-style warnings. In the Latin versions of the Old Testament, verbs such as *corripere* or *increpare* are commonly used to describe a prophet's moral rebuke.[34] Ambrose, by contrast, employs verbs from the classical vocabulary of exhortation to describe his mode of addressing the emperor: 'I persuade', 'request', 'encourage', 'admonish' (*suadeo, rogo, hortor, admoneo*), familiar from Roman historiography and speeches.[35] These verbs suggest a mode of admonition that is milder than the fierce scolding of the Old Testament prophets. But Ambrose's final instrument of persuasion, which he puts forward as if hesitantly, is rather forceful. Ambrose confesses that he did not dare to offer the sacrifice in the presence of the emperor.[36] He presents his excommunication not as a punishment or ultimatum to force Theodosius to do penance, but as a predicament in which he found himself. And yet, excommunication is what it was, in spite of the polite wording.[37] God told him in a dream, Ambrose says, that he was not allowed to offer the Mass if Theodosius came to the church. Ambrose hastens to assure the emperor that his decision not to celebrate the Eucharist in his presence was not inspired by any impudence towards the emperor (*contumacia*, a word that is often used as a negative paradigmatic reference for freedom of speech), but by obedience to God.[38] Moreover, it was

---

[30] Hadot, *Apologie de David*, pp. 37–40.   [31] Brown, *Power and Persuasion*, p. 111.

[32] The *Apologia David* has many themes in common with the Thessalonica letter. For correspondences between the two texts on the subject of penitence, see Hadot, *Apologie de David*, p. 41.

[33] Ambrose, *Ep. extra collectionem* 11, 16, ed. Zelzer, p. 218, lines 161–2: 'This I share with the prophets'; 'Istud mihi commune est cum prophetis.'

[34] De Jong, '*Admonitio* and criticism', pp. 320–1.

[35] On later connotations of *admonitio* in relation to the Old Testament prophet, see chapter 8 and De Jong, '*Admonitio* and criticism'. Seneca classifies *admonere* as a subgenre of advisory speech: Seneca, *Ep.* 94, 25: 'admonere genus adhortandi est'. On exhortation, admonition, *paraenesis* and advisory discourse in patristic literature, see Starr, Engberg-Pedersen (eds.), *Early Christian Paraenesis in Context*.

[36] Ambrose, *Ep. extra collectionem* 11, 13, ed. Zelzer, p. 216, line 123.

[37] Neil McLynn points out that Ambrose's excommunication of Theodosius is not a general excommunication that banned the emperor from *all* Italian churches. McLynn, *Ambrose of Milan*, p. 326.

[38] Ambrose, *Ep. extra collectionem* 11, 13, ed. Zelzer, p. 216, line 122. For *contumacia* as negative paradigmatic reference of freedom of speech, see for example Suetonius, *De vita Caesarum* 8, 13, discussed in the introduction.

Part I

guided by honourable motives: fear for the emperor's salvation, love for his person and grief over his sins.[39] In the conclusion of the letter, Ambrose implores the emperor to understand his actions and to acknowledge that he is speaking the truth.[40]

PRIVATE LETTER, PUBLIC PENANCE

Shortly before concluding the letter, Ambrose returns to the issue of private versus public admonition. He assures the emperor that he has written this letter 'with my own hand, for you alone to read'.[41] Theodosius should know that this is not a public rebuke but a private admonition. Writing a letter in one's own hand was considered a sign of friendship and a mark of politeness.[42] Sending and receiving a letter was, however, hardly a private affair. Even if we accept that Ambrose wrote the letter with his own hand instead of dictating it to a scribe, he still needed a messenger to deliver the letter to the palace, where established practice dictated that its contents be read aloud in the presence of Theodosius' courtiers. The confidential nature of the communication was therefore limited. The emperor's subsequent penance, moreover, was very much a public act. According to the (later) descriptions of the event, Theodosius went to the church of Milan without his imperial regalia and tearfully professed his responsibility for all to witness.[43] If a formal rebuke was part of the procedure, then all those who were present in church will have heard the bishop's admonition and will have seen the emperor accepting the penalty imposed on him.[44] Penance was public by nature, for it was not only a means of reconciling the sinner with God, but also a way of restoring relations with the community of Christians. In this particular case, the emperor's public penance, which was a novelty at the time, was also a political act. It was a symbolic act of communication which was intended to restore his damaged public image after the massacre of Thessalonica.[45]

There is no reason to doubt that the penance took place in reality and proceeded more or less as described in the sources. Instead of looking at

---

[39] Ambrose, *Ep. extra collectionem* 11, 12, ed. Zelzer, p. 216, line 110 (*dolor*); ibid. 11, 13, ed. Zelzer, p. 216, line 122 (*timor*); ibid. 11, 17, ed. Zelzer, p. 218, line 165 (*amor*).
[40] Ibid. 11, 17, ed. Zelzer, p. 218.
[41] Ibid. 11, 14, ed. Zelzer, p.217, line 126: 'scribo manu mea quod solus legas'.
[42] Julius Victor, *Ars rhetorica* 27, ed. Halm, *RLM*, pp. 447–8; Murphy, *Rhetoric*, p. 198.
[43] For this description of Theodosius' penance, see Ambrose, *De obitu Theodosii* 34, ed. Faller, p. 388 and Rufinus, *Historia ecclesiastica* 12, 18, *PL* 21, p. 525.
[44] Mc Lynn, *Ambrose of Milan*, p. 327.
[45] On the unprecedented character of Theodosius' penance, see Schieffer, 'Von Mailand nach Canossa', p. 341 and McLynn, *Ambrose of Milan*, pp. 327–30.

Ambrose of Milan

the public event, though, which must have made quite an impression at the time, I wish to focus on Ambrose's letter and address the problem of its reception and impact. Although Ambrose's words of warning and advice were offered in a private letter, presumably 'for your eyes only', it nonetheless became publicly known that Ambrose had rebuked the emperor. Word got out, with the result that, by about fifty years later, Ambrose's private admonitions had grown into the legend of his public rebuke in the porch of the church of Milan in the account of Sozomen and others.

Ambrose may have had no illusions about keeping his letter a secret, but apparently it was important to him to evoke a sense of confidentiality. Perhaps he was mindful of the pastoral advice of Jesus, who had said, according to the Gospel of Matthew, that one should point out the fault of a brother or sister in private ('just between the two of you', Matt. 18:15). Yet if we look at *parrhesia* as a cultural performance – and we need to bear in mind that Ambrose's rebuke was perceived in those terms – any privacy was necessarily a semi-privacy.[46] *Parrhesia* needed a public to witness its effect and bring out its full potential. A witness or an audience needed to evaluate the act, confirm that the critic's motives and words were right and honourable and observe how they were taken by the recipient, before it could be acknowledged as *parrhesia*. It was in fact essential to the effectiveness of *parrhesia* that it be recognised as such by others.

OUTSIDE THE COLLECTION

Ambrose probably had a hand in spreading the news that he had fearlessly admonished Theodosius, but not by distributing his Thessalonica letter. On the contrary, he took care that his letter should not become publicly known, at least not during Theodosius' lifetime or his own. After the emperor's death in 395, Ambrose published a tenth book in addition to his nine books of collected correspondence.[47] Whereas the first nine books contained letters on practical and religious issues, addressed to friends and colleagues, the tenth book was concerned with his dealings with Roman emperors. Ambrose probably borrowed this idea from the collection of Pliny, who had also published his letters in ten books, the last

---

[46] See the beginning of this chapter: Sozomen, *Historia ecclesiastica* VII, 25; Theodoret, *Historia ecclesiastica* V, 18, 23.

[47] Zelzer, *Epistolarum liber decimus, Prolegomena* pp. xx–xxv and Liebeschuetz, *Ambrose of Milan: Political Letters and Speeches*, introduction II, pp. 27–46. Liebeschuetz (p. 27) is more cautious, saying that it cannot be proven that Ambrose published the letters of the tenth book himself, but that it certainly looks as if he did.

of which is devoted to his correspondence with Emperor Trajan.[48] In the tenth book of his collection (hereafter, Book Ten), Ambrose published a selection of letters he had written to emperors in the course of his episcopal career, as well as sermons and speeches he (presumably or actually) delivered before these emperors.[49] Ambrose did not, however, include the Thessalonica letter in Book Ten.

After the death of Ambrose in 397, his secretary Paulinus published some of the remaining letters that Ambrose had not incorporated into his collection.[50] The remaining seventeen letters, which were transmitted in two series, have been edited in the *CSEL* as the *Epistolae extra collectionem*.[51] Among the letters that were transmitted outside the collection were letters that Ambrose wrote to the emperors Gratian, Valentinian, Theodosius and Eugenius, but also one that he wrote to his sister, Marcellina, in which he recounts how he fearlessly told Emperor Theodosius the truth.[52] The Thessalonica letter was again not included in this collection of remaining letters published by Paulinus. Perhaps Ambrose's secretary did not even know the letter existed.[53] Michaela Zelzer suggests that Ambrose hid it because he did not want Paulinus to find it. Paulinus had clearly not seen this letter when he wrote his biography of Ambrose.[54] One may wonder why Ambrose did not simply destroy the evidence, if he really did wish to keep this letter out of circulation. Eventually, the Thessalonica letter was discovered and published among a group of letters that now form the second series of *Epistolae extra collectionem*. The identity of the individual who found the letter is unknown, but we do know that a codex containing this particular letter was copied in the scriptorium of S. Tecla Cathedral in Milan, that is, Ambrose's *basilica nova*, where he delivered many of his sermons.[55]

Book Ten of the letter collection may have been intended to provide examples of how to write letters of admonition to rulers. Although the

---

[48] Zelzer, '*Plinius Christianus*', pp. 205–6.
[49] For an overview of the letters, speeches and documents contained in Book Ten of the collection, see Zelzer, *Epistolarum liber decimus, Prolegomena* pp. xix–xx.
[50] As convincingly argued by Klein, 'Kaiserbriefe', pp. 367–70.
[51] For a list of the first group of letters *extra collectionem* see Zelzer, *Epistolarum liber decimus, Prolegomena* p. lxxxv, and for the second group, ibid. p. civ. The first group was transmitted in six manuscripts dating from the twelfth to the sixteenth century (ibid. pp. xcvii–ci), while the second group survived in five manuscripts dating from the tenth to the fifteenth century (ibid. pp. cxxix–cxxx).
[52] Ambrose, *Ep. extra collectionem* 1, to his sister Marcellina.
[53] Zelzer, *Epistolarum liber decimus, Prolegomena*, p. cx, against Klein, 'Kaiserbriefe', pp. 366–7, arguing against Palanque, *Saint Ambroise*, p. 235.
[54] Zelzer, *Epistolarum liber decimus, Prolegomena*, p. lix.
[55] Milan, Biblioteca Ambrosiana, Ms. J. 71 sup., Zelzer, *Epistolarum liber decimus, Prolegomena*, pp. xli, xlii.

Thessalonica letter, in which Ambrose confronts the emperor with his sins, was not included in Book Ten, another letter of admonition, which he wrote to Theodosius two years before the massacre of Thessalonica, was. This letter (*Ep.* 74), written after an incident that took place in Callinicium in 388, may have been considered more suitable for authors looking for a model letter of admonition than the now much more famous Thessalonica letter. In the words of Wolfgang Liebeschuetz, the letter is a 'set piece rhetorical argument'.[56] The Callinicium letter, which was Ambrose's first letter to Theodosius, circulated widely in the Middle Ages.[57] Against three manuscripts containing the Thessalonica letter, about a hundred manuscripts of Book Ten have survived, many of which include the Callinicium letter.[58] In the Callinicium letter, to which I will now turn, Ambrose lays the groundwork for a priestly privilege of free speech and establishes the rules of engagement between a truth-telling bishop and a Christian emperor.

EMPERORS CHERISH FREEDOM OF SPEECH

In 388, Christians in Callinicium burned a Jewish synagogue to the ground. Rumour had it that the bishop of Callinicium had instigated the fire. Theodosius ordered the bishop to finance the rebuilding of the synagogue in compensation, and to punish those Christians who had been involved in burning it down. The bishop was also to punish those responsible for the destruction of a meeting place of the Valentinian sect.[59] With this order, the emperor aimed to protect the rights and coexistence of different religious groups within the empire, just as Themistius had been advising Christian emperors to do for years. As mentioned, Themistius retired from public life and imperial service in or shortly after 388.[60] Therefore, when Ambrose wrote his first letter of

---

[56] Liebeschuetz, *Ambrose of Milan: Political Letters*, p. 96.
[57] Ambrose had addressed letters to Theodosius before, on behalf of a synod of bishops, or on the request of Emperor Gratian, but this was the first letter he wrote to Theodosius under a personal title.
[58] Klein, 'Kaiserbriefe', p. 345. The three (rather late) manuscripts that contain the Thessalonica letter are: Bamberg, Staatsbibliothek Msc. Patr. 7, olim montis S. Michaelis (s. X^{ex}), Milan, Biblioteca Ambrosiana Ms. J. 71 sup. (s. XI^{med}) and Copenhagen, Ms. fol. 22 (s. XV); see Zelzer, *Epistolarum liber decimus, Prolegomena*, pp. cxxix, cxxx. Medieval manuscripts that include the 'Callinicium letter' are listed in ibid., pp. xxxix–xliv.
[59] Ambrose, *Ep.* 74, 16, ed. Zelzer, pp. 63, 64. According to Neil McLynn, Ambrose conflates two unrelated incidents. The destruction of a Valentinian chapel in Antioch took place on a different date. McLynn, *Ambrose of Milan*, p. 301.
[60] The last surviving oration of Themistius addressed to Theodosius dates to 385, but in 387 or 388 he still acted as the guardian of Theodosius' son Arcadius. Vanderspoel, *Themistius and the Imperial Court*, p. 214.

Part I

admonition to Theodosius in 388, he may have had the ambition to fill the vacant, or soon to be vacant, slot of imperial adviser and critic.

Ambrose objected to the punitive measures of Theodosius, which to his mind were too severe, and exhorts the emperor to repeal his sentence. He argues that Theodosius' decision to make the bishop of Callinicium rebuild the synagogue shows undue favour to Jews and sends the wrong message to Christians. Christians should abhor the 'perfidious practices of the Jews', Ambrose says, 'not assist in constructing their synagogues!'[61] But before setting out his main arguments as to why the emperor should repeal his order, Ambrose begins his letter by begging him to listen to his pleas:

I beg you listen patiently to what I have to say. For if I am unworthy to be heard by you, I am also unworthy to offer sacrifice for you, to be trusted with your vows and prayers. So will you really not listen to the man whom you would want to be heard praying on your behalf? [...] As it is not the part of an emperor to deny freedom of speech (*libertas dicendi*), so it is not that of a priest to refrain from saying what he thinks. For no quality is so popular and loveable in you who are emperors as your cherishing of freedom even in the case of those who are your subordinates in the imperial service. In fact this is the difference between good and bad princes, that the good love freedom, the bad slavery. But in a priest nothing is so dangerous before God or so disgraceful among men as not to state freely what he thinks.[62]

Ambrose artfully switches between a classical and a Christian register of free speech. He reminds the emperor that he, as bishop of Milan, which was currently Theodosius's residence, is his intercessor with God. He prays and sacrifices for him, and for this reason alone the emperor should listen to him. Just as God hears Ambrose when he intercedes on behalf of Theodosius, the emperor should hear his bishop, who is speaking up for the Christians of Callinicium. After this opening, Ambrose changes gear and turns to the language of panegyrics. By saying that no emperor can deny freedom of speech, he appeals to values connected to the office of the Roman emperor. He calls to mind the principle that respect for freedom (*libertas*) is what has always distinguished a good from a bad

---

[61] Ambrose, *Ep.* 74, 10, ed. Zelzer, pp. 60, 61.
[62] Ambrose, *Ep.* 74, 1–2, ed. Zelzer, p. 54, line 7–p. 55, line 22: 'Itaque peto ut patienter sermonem meum audias; nam si indignus sum qui a te audiar, indignus sum qui pro te offeram, cui tua vota, cui tuas committas preces. Ipse ergo non audies eum quem pro te audiri velis? [...] *Sed neque imperiale est libertatem dicendi negare neque sacerdotale quod sentiat non dicere.* Nihil enim in vobis imperatoribus tam populare et tam amabile est quam libertatem etiam in his diligere qui obsequio militiae vobis subditi sunt. Siquidem hoc interest inter bonos et malos principes quod boni libertatem amant, servitutem improbi. *Nihil etiam in sacerdote tam periculosum apud deum, tam turpe apud homines, quam quod sentiat non libere denuntiare* [emphasis mine].' Trans. Liebeschuetz, pp. 96–7.

100

Ambrose of Milan

Roman ruler. This was a familiar theme in panegyrics.[63] Thus Ambrose emphasises that the freedom of speech that he claims for himself is in fact a good old Roman tradition. As explained in the introduction, *libertas* was one of the most important cultural and political values in the Roman world; it was considered a right as well as a duty of every free Roman citizen.[64] The high ideals of the old days of the Roman Republic resounded through the word *libertas*.[65] In his letter, Ambrose strategically invokes the image of an ideal Roman emperor who grants freedom of speech to petitioners in order to persuade Theodosius to listen to his pleas and admonitions. His pagan contemporary Symmachus does exactly same thing in a letter to Emperor Valentinian II, as many orators and philosophers had done before him.[66] They praised the emperor's love of freedom of speech, and by doing so induced the emperor to grant it to them. In his letter, Ambrose constructs an ideal image of the emperor and persuades him to adopt that image and behave accordingly.[67] Symmachus fashions himself in his letters to Valentinian II as a polite senator who defers to the emperor. Ambrose constructs a different ideal image of himself. The sender of the Callinicium letter is a bishop–priest who has the prophetic duty to speak out and warn against sin.

After having established the traditional, Roman nature of the privilege of free speech, Ambrose returns to a biblical register and stresses that in his case, as he is a bishop, God expects him to speak out. A *sacerdos* has to state freely what he thinks. If he remains silent, he puts himself in danger. 'In a priest nothing is so dangerous before God or so disgraceful among men as not to state freely what he thinks', Ambrose writes.[68] This is an indirect reference to the aforementioned 'watchman passage' of Ezekiel 3:18.[69] Ambrose would draw on the exact same passage from the Book of Ezekiel two years later in the Thessalonica letter, but here he links the two traditions much more strongly. Roman freedom of speech is firmly attached to the duty of the prophet–priest to speak out against injustice. The emperor has to listen to him, Ambrose argues, because his bishop is both a free Roman, who can make a claim to

---

[63] Creece, *Letters to the Emperor*, p. 183.   [64] Wirszubski, *Libertas as a Political Idea*, especially p. 8.
[65] Vielberg, *Untertanentopik*, p. 35. Roger Rees has maintained that *libertas dicendi* was not a standard term for freedom of speech. Rees, 'Authorizing freedom of speech', p. 298. Based on the evidence of instances of *libertas* as a translation of *parrhesia* that we have encountered in late antique Latin sources so far, I should like to argue that *libertas* was a standard term, although not necessarily in combination with the verb *dicere*.
[66] Creece, *Letters to the Emperor*, p. 183.
[67] Compare Hilary's epistolary speech to Emperor Constantius II, discussed in the previous chapter, in which he adopts a similar strategy.
[68] For the Latin, see note 62.
[69] The text, here referred to indirectly, is quoted verbatim two lines further on in the letter, Ambrose, *Ep.* 74, 2, ed. Zelzer, p. 55, lines 23–8.

Part I

freedom of speech, and a priest, who cannot be silenced because God has commanded him to speak. In Ambrose's skilful entwining of Greco-Roman and biblical tradition, Roman *libertas* meets the Old Testament prophet–priest.

God's commission to Ezekiel, Ambrose suggests, applies to him as well, not only because he is *a* priest, but because he is *Theodosius'* priest, who makes offerings for the emperor at his request. I have therefore translated the word *sacerdos*, which in this period can mean either 'bishop' or 'priest', with 'priest', although most modern translators choose 'bishop'. In the opening of his letter, Ambrose had already invoked the liturgical arrangement between an emperor and his *sacerdos*: 'For if I be unworthy to be heard by you, I be also unworthy to offer sacrifice for you, to be trusted with your vows and prayers.'[70] At first glance, this is a polite enough sentiment, but if one removes the courteous polish of the subjunctive mood, what is left verges on sacramental blackmail. If Theodosius does not grant Ambrose a hearing, he will not sacrifice and pray for him. Is this an indirect threat to excommunicate the emperor, two years before Ambrose would actually do so in response to the Thessalonica massacre? Ambrose invokes his priestly powers of intercession that made him responsible for the emperor's soul. The bishop's privileged access to God, via the liturgy, on which Theodosius depended for the salvation of his own soul as well as for the well-being of the empire, form the basis of Ambrose's claim to freedom of speech. As we have seen in the previous chapters, Christian emperors relied (or were expected to rely) on the intercession of holy men who were credited with privileged access to God. Their *parrhesia* towards God granted them *parrhesia* towards the emperor. Ambrose calls on a similar arrangement, but does not fail to notice that freedom of speech was not just a privilege that the emperor could or could not bestow on a person who interceded on his behalf, but also a priestly duty for which Ambrose did not need the emperor's permission. Ambrose implies he had no choice but to speak out. If he failed to warn Theodosius that his order to rebuild the synagogue of the Jews was wrong, and that he was about to commit a grave sin if he did not repeal his sentence, God would require Theodosius' blood from Ambrose's hand. If, however, Ambrose did speak out and the emperor listened, they would both be saved. Thus, Ambrose connects his own fate to that of the emperor, and in doing so he establishes a shared responsibility for a correct handling of the Callinicium affair. 'For you will be implicated in the danger of my silence, while you will benefit from the

---

[70] For the Latin, see note 62.

Ambrose of Milan

good of my outspokenness.'[71] A priest's freedom of speech, Ambrose maintains, should therefore be more pleasing to Theodosius than his silence.[72]

Towards the end of the letter, after enumerating many examples and quotations from the bible to harness his case, Ambrose once again assures the emperor of his good intentions towards him. He trusts that Theodosius will not withdraw his favour from him, because he has after all addressed him with such frankness only because he loves the emperor sincerely.[73] 'I need not therefore fear', he says, 'to lose in one moment the favour, which every priest must have and which I have enjoyed for many years.'[74] Apparently, Ambrose considered it to be of the utmost importance to impress on the emperor's mind that, although his words might strike Theodosius as presumptuous, they sprang from love and devotion (*amore et studio*).[75]

To sum up, in this letter to Theodosius concerning the restoration of the Jewish synagogue in Callinicium, Ambrose alternates between a classical and a Christian register. He addresses Theodosius as a powerful Roman emperor, who has the power either to grant or to dismiss an appeal, and as a Christian ruler who dependes on the intercession of a bishop–priest, and who has to be warned and admonished just like any other member of the Christian community entrusted to the bishop's care. In the Callinicium letter, Ambrose searches for the right balance between criticism and flattery, between the prophetic voice of warning to which his episcopal office compels him and the tone of respect due to a Roman emperor.

The Callinicium letter cannot be taken at face value, and not just because of its artful rhetoric. The letter has been transmitted in two versions: one was published by Ambrose in Book Ten of his letter collection (*Ep.* 74), the other by his secretary Paulinus in the *Epistulae extra collectionem*, which Ambrose did *not* select for publication. The letter that, in Zelzer's edition, is numbered *extra collectionem* 1a was transmitted as an attachment to a letter that Ambrose sent to his sister Marcellina.[76] The latter version of the Callinicium letter (*Ep. extra collectionem 1a*),

---

[71] Ambrose, *Ep.* 74, 3, ed. Zelzer, p. 54, line 33: 'Nam silentii mei periculo involveris, libertatis bono iuvaris.'
[72] Ibid., ed. Zelzer, p. 54, lines 32, 33: 'clementiae tuae displicere debet sacerdotis silentium, libertas placere'.
[73] Ibid. *Ep.* 74, 25, ed. Zelzer, p.70, lines 291, 292: 'nemo maiore fiducia utitur quam qui ex affectu diligat'.
[74] Ibid., ed. Zelzer, p. 70, lines 291–4: 'non timere [...] ne tot annorum conceptam cuiuscumque sacerdotis gratiam uno momento amittam.' Trans. Liebeschuetz, p. 108.
[75] Ibid., ed. Zelzer, p. 70, line 287.
[76] Ambrose's letter to Marcellina is edited in the *CSEL* as *Ep. extra collectionem* 1, the attachment as *Ep. extra collectionem* 1a.

Part I

differs in several places from the letter that Ambrose published himself after Theodosius' death (*Ep.* 74). When one compares the two versions, it becomes apparent that the letter Ambrose incorporated into Book Ten (*Ep.* 74) was substantially altered before it was put into circulation. Editing a letter was not uncommon; it was a regular procedure to make the text ready for publication. A letter was not so much regarded as an authentic piece of communication, but rather as a work of art. A published letter was a demonstration of the author's rhetorical and diplomatic skills. It was not considered to be a piece of historical 'evidence' that should not be tampered with. And yet, Ambrose rewrote the Callinicium letter more substantially than other letters in Book Ten.[77] For example, he added an extra paragraph at the end of the letter, which ends with the portentous words: 'I for my part have done all that I could, while showing due respect, to get you to hear me in the palace, so that it might not become necessary for you to hear me in church.'[78] In other words, for now Ambrose chose to address the emperor in the most respectful manner available to him. He did not lecture him in public, but instead wrote a letter that Theodosius could read in semi-private surroundings and discuss with his counsellors in the palace. Should the emperor not be willing to listen to his bishop under these conditions, then, runs the almost explicit warning, Ambrose has no other option but to confront Theodosius again, and this time publicly, in church.

BEHIND THE SCENES?

The ominous last sentence of the added paragraph refers to an incident that appears to have taken place shortly afterwards. In a letter Ambrose wrote to his sister Marcellina in 388/9, he recounts what happened when, not long after he had made his plea on behalf of the bishop and Christians of Callinicium, the emperor attended Ambrose's church. As he explains to Marcellina, he and Theodosius had some unfinished business to attend to.[79] For although Theodosius had revoked the edict that ordered the bishop of Callinicium to rebuild the synagogue, he had not responded to the second part of Ambrose's petition, in which Ambrose pleaded with the emperor not to punish the monks who had destroyed a meeting place of the Valentinians. When his petitions met with little success, Ambrose

---

[77] Michaela Zelzer has shown ten significant differences between the version published in Book Ten of the collection and the *extra collectionem* version of the 'Callinicium letter'. Zelzer, *Epistularum liber decimus, Prolegomena*, pp. xx–xxiii.

[78] Ambrose, *Ep.* 74, 33, ed. Zelzer, p. 73: 'Ego certe quod honorificentius fieri potuit feci, ut me magis audires in regia, ne si necesse esset audires in ecclesia.' Trans. Liebeschuetz, p. 111.

[79] Ambrose, *Ep. extra collectionem* 1, 1, ed. Zelzer, p. 145.

says, he felt he needed to bring the matter to the emperor's attention once more.[80] And so, when Theodosius visited the church, as Ambrose tells his sister, he delivered a sermon on the prophet Jeremiah which he brought to bear on the unresolved situation between himself and the emperor. He interpreted the verse 'take to yourself the rod of an almond tree' (Jer. 1:11) as a metaphor for the benefits of frank speech. Ambrose connected the almond rod of the prophet Jeremiah to the priest Aaron's rod that started to sprout and even blossomed after a while (Num. 17:8), a comparison that led him to the following exegesis:

> It seems to mean that the counsel of a prophet or a priest ought to be forthright, so that it urges what is useful, rather than what is pleasing. The reason why the prophet is ordered to take up a rod of almond is that the fruit of that tree is bitter in the rind, hard in the shell, juicy within, so that in like manner the prophet should display a bitter and hard exterior and not be afraid to proclaim harsh truths. Similarly the priest: although his advice for a time seems bitter to some, and like the rod of Aaron is laid up for a long time in the ears of people who pretend not to have heard, nevertheless sometimes, when it is thought to have withered, it bursts into bud.[81]

In the next part of the sermon, Ambrose proceeded from Jesus' forgiveness of sins to health-bringing tears of penance, and ended with a reference to the prophet Nathan's reproach of King David. Ambrose tells Marcellina that Theodosius understood the sermon was about him: 'You have been preaching about me', Ambrose reports the emperor to have said; to this, Ambrose replied, 'I treated a topic relevant to your welfare.'[82]

Once Ambrose had finished his sermon, he left the altar and came over to Theodosius to present his petition once more. This time, however, he was more persistent with his request. Ambrose refused to proceed to celebrate the Eucharist until Theodosius had given him his word that he would spare the monks. After some protest, Theodosius gave in. He promised Ambrose that he would revoke his order. When Ambrose received Theodosius' promise that he would show mercy to the

---

[80] Ibid., lines 10, 11.
[81] Ambrose, *Ep. extra collectionem* 1, 2–3, ed. Zelzer, p. 146, lines 19–29: 'Nam videtur significare quod directa esse debeat prophetica vel sacerdotalis auctoritas ut non tam dilectabilia quam utilia persuadeat. Ideoque nucinum baculum sumere iubetur propheta, quia memoratae pomum arboris amarum in cortice, durum in testa, intus est fructuosum, ut ad eius similitudinem propheta quoque amara et dura praetendat et denuntiare tristia non reformidet. Similiter etiam sacerdos quia praeceptio eius etsi ad tempus aliquibus amara videatur et tamquam virga Aaron reposita diu in auribus dissimulantium, tamen aliquando cum aestimatur aruisse floruerit.' Trans. Liebeschuetz, pp. 112–13.
[82] Ibid. 1, 27, ed. Zelzer, p. 160, line 243–p. 161, line 351: 'ait mihi: "De nobis proposuisti." Respondi: "Hoc tractavi quod ad utilitatem tuam pertineret."'

Part I

monks, he went back to the altar and continued with the liturgy. 'All was done as I wished' is the conclusion of his report to Marcellina.[83]

In his letter to Marcellina, Ambrose presents himself as being fully in charge of the situation, putting pressure on the emperor in such a way that Theodosius cannot but grant Ambrose's petition. However, the confrontation, if it took place in the way Ambrose describes it, need not have been publicly humiliating for the emperor. All that the congregation in the Church would have seen was a bishop who humbly pleaded with the emperor to show *clementia*, the virtue that characterised a good Roman emperor. The scene, as it was stage-directed by Ambrose, made both the emperor and the bishop look good. Both acted according to the ideals that contemporaries ascribed to their office. The bishop played the role of supplicant on behalf of his fellow Christians, while the emperor was allowed to play the role of merciful ruler.

The Callinicium letter was probably never sent to Theodosius, at least not in the form that was included in Book Ten of the letter collection.[84] Although it is very possible that Ambrose brought several petitions before the emperor to plead for clemency for the bishop of Callinicium and for the monks of Antioch,[85] the published Callinicium letter was written *after* Theodosius had already revoked the order.[86] It appears that Ambrose composed this letter not so much to persuade the emperor, as to convince a wider audience of his powers of persuasion. Ambrose wanted his readers to know that Theodosius' change of heart should be credited to the force of the bishop's arguments. This is probably why he published the Callinicium letter as part of his collection, wishing to document his (oral) petition and the success of his intervention for posterity.

The same applies to Ambrose's letter to his sister. It was no private letter in our sense of the word, but intended for a wider audience. The letter publicised Ambrose's interpretation and view of events, and advertised a picture of a courageous bishop who was not afraid to speak his mind to emperors. The image of Ambrose the fearless truth-teller and defender of the Church that we later encounter in fifth-century Church histories was very much a creation of Ambrose himself. Through Book Ten of his public letter collection and the private letters to his sister, he communicated to posterity a view of how a bishop should behave towards an emperor, and how an emperor should, ideally, respond.

---

[83] Ibid. 1, 28, ed. Zelzer, p. 161, line 363: 'Omnia itaque gesta sunt ex sententia.'
[84] Liebeschuetz, *Ambrose of Milan: Political Letters and Speeches*, p. 96.
[85] See *Ep.* 74, 9 and *Ep. extra collectionem* 1, 1.
[86] As Ambrose already indicated in the letter itself: *Ep.* 74, 9, ed. Zelzer, p. 60, line 112: 'licet ipse hoc revocatum'.

Ambrose's letter to his sister Marcellina does not allow us a glimpse behind the scenes; it is itself a scene, and a carefully scripted one at that.

CONCLUSION

As described above, Ambrose spread knowledge of his admonitions of the emperor after the Thessalonica massacre. Although he did not include the Thessalonica letter in Book Ten of his letter collection, he made sure others knew that he was the person who persuaded the emperor to accept the medicine of penance. For the penance of Theodosius not only remedied the emperor's damaged image; it would also greatly enhance Ambrose's own, if people realised that it was he who had persuaded the emperor. In his funeral oration for Theodosius, delivered in the presence of Theodosius' sons, Arcadius and Honorius, and the congregation of his church, Ambrose praises the emperor for his humble but glorious penance. Although he does not say explicitly that he, Ambrose, had brought the emperor to perform this devout act, he implicitly points to his own role in the proceedings. 'I have loved the man', Ambrose says in his funeral oration, 'because he appreciated a critic more than a flatterer.'[87] Theodosius' willingness to listen to criticism was the quality that made him, in Ambrose's mind, a good emperor, worthy of the love of the citizens of Milan and its bishop. The audience of the oration was probably meant to understand that Ambrose was that critic to whom Theodosius had listened. Towards the end of Theodosius' life, Ambrose implies in his oration, he who had been shut out from deliberations had gained privileged access to the emperor. Theodosius had even asked for him on his deathbed.[88] Thus Ambrose writes himself into the account of Theodosius' penance, without saying in so many words that he was the person who persuaded Theodosius to atone for his sins. Although Ambrose left the Thessalonica letter out of Book Ten of his letter collection, he did include his funeral oration for Theodosius. Perhaps he preferred this version of the event over the version presented in the Thessalonica letter.

Ambrose probably published his letters to provide other bishops with models for letter-writing, as noted above.[89] His letters are furnished with biblical quotations underlining the importance of prophetic and priestly frank counsel, suitable for reuse in other letters. Moreover, they provide samples of classical rhetorical strategies of free speech, which are tailored

---

[87] Ambrose, *De obitu Theodosii* 34, ed. Faller, p. 388, lines 5, 6: 'Dilexi virum, qui magis arguentem quam adulantem probaret.'
[88] Ambrose, *De obitu Theodosii* 35, ed. Faller, p. 389, lines 10, 11.
[89] See the discussion on the composition and manuscript transmission of the letter collection above, pp. 87–99.

Part I

to Christian principles of pastoral admonition. And yet, Ambrose's letter collection was more than a compendium of suitable models. It was also a form of self-advertisement. Especially in the letters of Book Ten, he presents himself as a man who continued to speak out against injustice, regardless of attempts to silence him. Ambrose was successful in constructing an image of himself as a courageous truth-teller, and of Emperor Theodosius as an ideal Christian ruler who was willing to listen to the advice of a critic. In the eyes of his biographers and of later generations of bishops who aimed to follow his example, Ambrose stood out as a champion of free speech.[90] His self-presentation may also have influenced modern perceptions of his position at Theodosius' court. In his letters to Theodosius, and particularly in the Thessalonica letter, Ambrose claims that he was an outsider, someone whose prophetic voice of warning was not heard and who was excluded from deliberations that took place in the palace. Modern scholars take Ambrose's word for it that he was a *persona non grata* at Theodosius' court.[91] Moreover, it is held that his efforts to be included in the emperor's consistory suffered a major setback after his unwarranted intervention in the Callinicium affair.[92] Although this may have been the case, it is also possible that Ambrose deliberately styled himself as an outsider because it was a speaker-position that worked well in a speech or letter of frank criticism. As we have seen in previous chapters, many parrhesiasts from the past were, or were purported to be, marginal figures: philosophers, hermits, wandering holy men, who spoke with a voice of authority from the fringes of society. A truth-teller such as Ambrose, who, as bishop of Milan, could lay a claim to institutionalised authority, posed as an outsider to play the game of *parrhesia* according to its cultural rules. This does not necessarily mean that Ambrose was not welcome at Theodosius' court in reality, or that the emperor considered him a meddler in his affairs. It was part of the rhetorical performance of free speech to represent the relationship between a superior and his critic in this way. Just as criticism was supposed to be offered in private, but was rarely private in reality, the outsider–parrhesiast was rarely an outsider.

---

[90] See chapter 8.
[91] Kolb, 'Der Bussakt von Mailand', p. 49, McLynn, *Ambrose of Milan*, p. 318.
[92] Zelzer, *Epistolarum liber decimus, Prolegomena*, p. xiii; Klein, 'Kaiserbriefe', p. 352, n. 38; Liebeschuetz, *Ambrose of Milan: Political Letters and Speeches*, p. 18; McLynn, *Ambrose of Milan*, p. 318.

5

THE SILENT ASCETIC

> Freedom of speech and freedom of silence are equal.
> Pacatus Drepanius

As has been seen in the previous chapters, Christians assimilated the classical tradition of free speech and turned it into a Christian practice. Church historians and hagiographers glorified the words and deeds of martyrs and holy men and praised their *parrhesia*, while bishops recognised the significance of free speech as a means of connecting to the traditions and values of Greco-Roman society. Bishops found their authority increased if their confrontations (real or staged) with Roman emperors were acknowledged as acts of *parrhesia*. Their political criticism was couched within a framework of biblical references and Christian metaphors, but the rhetoric they employed and the parrhesiastic traditions they drew upon were pre-Christian, and familiar to the audience they aimed to persuade. Bishops such as Hilary of Poitiers and Ambrose of Milan made use of *parrhesia*'s symbolic capital to legitimise their criticism of imperial policy. By claiming the right of free speech, they spoke out for what they considered to be the right political course of a Christian empire.

Not all Christians, however, held free speech in high esteem. Some church leaders warned against its possibly disturbing effect on Christian communities. Michel Foucault points to what he called the 'développement d'un pôle anti-parrèsiastique' in Christian texts of the fifth and sixth centuries, and ascribes what he sees as a growing negative evaluation of free speech to a process of institutionalisation of the church. Over the course of the fifth century AD, Foucault argues, the rapidly expanding church required new structures of authority, in which obedience was valued over frankness.[1] When the public figure of the martyr disappeared, Foucault maintains, ascetics rose in prominence, who

---

[1] Foucault, *Le courage de la verité*, pp. 305–6.

Part I

regarded (free) speech as a disruptive force that scattered the concentration of a mind set on meditation and silent contemplation of things divine.[2] Foucault's suggestion that *parrhesia* was increasingly evaluated in a pejorative way is persuasive at first sight. A significant number of ascetic texts from the fifth and sixth centuries do indeed warn against the dangers of *parrhesia* in no uncertain terms. It needs to be investigated, however, whether the objections and reservations that we encounter in this period are part of a trend towards a negative interpretation of *parrhesia* overall, and if so, whether that trend can be related to the rise of asceticism and to the 'institutionalisation' of the church, as Foucault suggests. In the previous chapters, I showed how the words and deeds of martyrs and holy men were interpreted as *parrhesia*, while bishops followed in the footsteps of the free-spoken philosophers. In this chapter, I shall explore the other end of the spectrum of the Christian reception of classical free speech, and investigate the doubts and reservations that were expressed in some Christian communities, especially in ascetic milieus from the fifth to the seventh centuries.

THE COUNSELLOR WHO RAN OFF TO THE DESERT

After the persecution of Christians had ended, a new class of witnesses of the Christian faith emerged. Monks who fled into the desert, first to escape persecution and later to flee society and its temptations in order to dedicate their lives to solitude and contemplation, came to be regarded as the new heroes of the Christian faith. Anecdotes about their lives and wise sayings were gathered in collections and were popular reading in late Antiquity and the early Middle Ages, as well as in later periods. Among the themes addressed in these collections was the importance of silence. For authors who recorded the trial and death of Christian martyrs, *parrhesia* had been a vital instrument to state a Christian identity, to proclaim Christ's truth, and to measure the authority of Christ against the authority of secular judges and magistrates. In the descriptions of the lives of the desert fathers, by contrast, free speech is rarely mentioned.

According to the authors who recorded the lives and saying of the desert fathers, the heroes of the desert were not as highly educated as the Christian apologists and many of the protagonists of the early martyr acts had been. Fathers of the desert such as Anthony (d. 356 AD) and Pachomius (d. 347 AD) were depicted as simple men, who spoke in

---

[2] For a full account I refer to Foucault's lecture of March 28 1984, published in *Le courage de la verité* pp. 297–328 and to Árpád Szakolczai's discussion of Foucault's views on the negative reception of *parrhesia* in relation to the rise of monasticism, in *Genesis of Modernity*, p. 239.

The Silent Ascetic

a clear and accessible manner, if they spoke at all. It was held that speech only distracted the monk from contemplation, which was best practised in silence. In the *Verba seniorum*, a sixth-century Latin translation of a Greek collection of anecdotes and sayings of the desert fathers, ascribed to Pope Pelagius I (d. 561), we find the following anecdote about one of the desert fathers, Abba Arsenius of Scetis. When Arsenius was still living at the palace, he asked God how he could be saved. He heard a voice saying: 'Flee from men and you will be saved.' After he had withdrawn to the desert to live a solitary life, he heard the same voice again: 'Flee, say nothing, be at peace. For these are the roots of sinlessness.'[3] The assumption underlying this anecdote is that speech and the company of men can easily lead to sin and disturb one's inner tranquillity. The fact that these words are spoken to a former courtier, who, according to tradition, had been a counsellor of Emperor Theodosius and tutor to the imperial sons, gives the story an interesting edge.[4] These details were probably added so that readers would marvel at the conversion of a highly educated counsellor, who was used to moving in the corridors of power, from the hustle and bustle of the palace to a life of silence and seclusion.[5] Many of the narratives contained in the fifth- and sixth-century Greek and Latin collections of sayings mention Arsenius' almost complete withdrawal from human company and his gift for silence, which puzzled the people who met him.[6] Admirers came to visit the silent saint in the desert, only to find that, indeed, he did not want to see them, and did not want to speak to them.

MONKS SHOULD NOT SPEAK FREELY

Reservations about the usefulness or desirability of frank speech are expressed in both Latin and Greek ascetic literature. Outspokenness, frankness, courage and boldness were considered vital for preaching and spreading the word of Christ in a world that was hostile to Christianity, or

---

[3] Pelagius, *Verba seniorum* 2, 3, ed. *PL* 73, col. 858: 'Abbas Arsenius, cum adhuc esset in palatio, oravit ad Dominum, dicens: Domine, dirige me ad salutem. Et venit ei vox, dicens: Arseni, fuge homines, et salvaberis. Idem ipse discedens ad monachilem vitam, rursum oravit, eumdem sermonem dicens. Audivit vocem dicentem sibi: Arseni, fuge, tace, quiesce: haec enim sunt radices non peccandi.' Cf. *Apophthegmata patrum*, *PG* 65, cols. 71–440, at col. 88. The story is also recorded in Ps-Rufinus' *Verba seniorum* 190, ed. *PL* 73, col. 801.

[4] The oldest source to record that interpretation in writing dates to the ninth century, but according to Dmitry Afinogenov the tradition was much older. Afinogenov, 'To the origins of the legend about St Arsenius'.

[5] On Arsenius' education, his knowledge of Latin and Greek and the splendid garments he wore in the palace, see *Apophthegmata patrum* 4 and 6.

[6] *Apophthegmata patrum* 13, 26, 37, *PG*, col. 88; Ps-Rufinus' *Vitae Patrum* and Paschasius of Dumium's *Questions and Answers of the Desert Fathers*.

Part I

to combat heterodox views in the ensuing age of fierce theological controversies, but were not regarded as particularly beneficial to a quiet, ascetic life. Such reservations applied to the anchorites of the desert as well as to those who chose to live within the confines of a monastery. In monastic communities, silence took precedence over speech. Three of the most important monastic virtues, next to chastity and poverty, were humility, silence and obedience to the authority of the abbot. These virtues were held to be incompatible with the audacity and frankness of *parrhesia* or *fiducia*. Among monks, frank speech and bold conduct were considered to be disruptive to a well-organised communal life.

In ascetic texts, a pejorative meaning of *parrhesia* (or *fiducia* in Latin translations and adaptations) took precedence over other, more positive connotations of free speech. Speaking without considering whether one's words or actions might be inappropriate or offensive could harm the balance and peace of the monastic community. In fact, speech as such was held to be a destabilising force, ready to throw monastic order and quiet into confusion. It is telling that in the *Rule of Benedict* (c. 530 AD) frankness (in words or in action) is denoted by the word *praesumptio,* that is, stubbornness or arrogance.[7] A monk should conquer this bad habit and free himself of the urge to speak his mind. As the sixth chapter of the *Rule of Benedict* has it, permission to talk (*licentia loquendi*) should rarely be granted to perfect disciples, for silence is the best remedy against sins of the tongue.[8] However, the *Rule of Benedict* did not propagate silence as a goal in itself, but as a means to a higher end. In silence and obedience, the monk practised the humility of the Lord and learned how to discipline his thoughts and words. The *Rule of Benedict* grants permission to speak on certain occasions, provided that one does not engage in rude and frivolous conversations, but speaks moderately.[9] Neither should the monk use his permission to speak to defend himself. Following the example of Jesus, who was silent during his trial, the monk should hold his tongue rather than speak up for himself.[10]

The moment a monk entered the monastery, he abandoned his right to speak. Just like the slave, the foreigner and the exile, who had had no right of speech in Greco-Roman law, so the monk left his licence to speak at the monastery's threshold. He subordinated his will to the will of the abbot. From now on, he was permitted to speak only at certain times and places. Speech, and free speech in particular, could easily lead to impure

---

[7] Steidle, '*Parrhesia-praesumptio*'. [8] *Regula Benedicti* 6, ed. Holzherr, pp. 86, 87. [9] Ibid.
[10] Holzherr, *The Rule of Benedict*, p. 87, with reference to Matt. 26:63.

The Silent Ascetic

words and improper behaviour. It was a sign of stubbornness (*contumacia*), bad manners and lack of self-control.[11]

One of the most strongly worded warnings against *parrhesia* among monks is attributed to the desert father Abba Agathon. The author/compiler of the *Apophthegmata patrum* records the story of a brother who came to Agathon's cell to ask him how he should live with the brothers. Abba Agathon advised him always to think and behave as the stranger he was on the first day he joined the community, and never have too much familiarity (*parrhesia*) with his brothers. He compared *parrhesia* with a strong burning wind, that sends everything flying and destroys the fruit of the trees. Abba Macarius, who was present at this conversation, asked if familiarity (*parrhesia*) was really as bad as all that. Abba Agathon replied: 'No passion is worse than *parrhesia*, because it is the mother of all the passions.'[12]

Abba Agathon, or the author who recorded this story, thus compares the habitus of the solitary monk to that of a stranger. As in the *Rule of Benedict,* speaking (freely) is a privilege that a brother should be willing to give up the moment he joins the community. In Pelagius' sixth-century Latin translation of the *Apophthegmata patrum*, Agathon's *parrhesia* is translated as *fiducia*.[13] Recent translators of the *Apophthegmata patrum* have struggled to render the pejorative sense of Agathon's *parrhesia* into modern English, for the word takes different shades of meaning as Agathon's argument proceeds. Benedicta Ward alternates between 'familiarity', 'speaking too freely' and 'an uncontrolled tongue', while John Wortley chooses to translate all four occurrences of *parrhesia* in this passage as 'familiar talking'.[14] But Abba Agathon's *parrhesia* does not only pertain to speaking, but also to behaviour associated with people who are at ease with each other. While such familiarity was acceptable and essential for other social groups, it was not considered beneficial to the solitary life of the anchorite monks. Although ascetic literature often uses the language of the family household to describe the relationship of the solitary monks to each other (father, brothers), it was held that too much intimacy and openness should be avoided. Familiarity in speech and behaviour gave rise to feelings that stood in the way of one's dedication to a life of contemplation.

In spite of the undeniably pejorative meaning of *parrhesia* in the story about Abba Agathon, the author or compiler of the *Apophthegmata patrum* acknowledges that *parrhesia* (in the sense of familiarity) existed between

---

[11] Steidle, '*Parrhesia-praesumptio*'.
[12] *Apophthegmata patrum*, ed. *PG* 65, col. 109, trans. Ward, *The Sayings of the Desert Fathers*, p. 20.
[13] Pelagius, *Verba seniorum*, *PL* 73, col. 913.
[14] Ward, *The Sayings of the Desert Fathers*, p 20; Wortley, *The Book of the Elders*, p. 20.

brothers with a special spiritual bond. In another anecdote, recorded in the same collection, Abba Isaac is said to have enjoyed *parrhesia* with Abba Poemen. Isaac was at liberty to ask Poemen critical questions about his behaviour, which Abba Poemen did not take amiss. Here, *parrhesia* is not used in a negative sense, but taken as the mark of their special spiritual friendship. We find such positive descriptions of *parrhesia* in earlier lives of desert fathers as well, but not frequently. In Athanasius' *Life of Anthony* (c. 360), for example, the verb *parrhesiazesthai* is used once to indicate that Anthony spoke bold words of help to the brothers when he shared a meal with them, and once when Anthony prophesies that the orthodox faith will soon speak boldly everywhere with all freedom.[15] Although positive interpretations of *parrhesia* among monks do occur in ascetic literature, they are presented as the exceptions that confirm the rule. The close spiritual bond between Abba Poemen and Abba Isaac, who enjoyed *parrhesia* with each other, was thus a remarkable exception in a community of solitary strangers.

The notion that *parrhesia* was the mother of all passions was taken up by several other authors of ascetic literature. Antiochus the Monk (fl. early seventh century), of the monastery of St Saba near Jerusalem, author of a collection of moral sayings, devotes one chapter to *parrhesia*.[16] He builds on the idea that *parrhesia* opens the door to other passions, but he connects it with new metaphors and images. Like Agathon, Antiochus interprets *parrhesia* as too much intimacy between monks, as audacious speech and pride, but also as an inappropriate familiarity towards things divine. There are, according to Antiochus, certain boundaries that should be respected with regard to the holy. He draws on the biblical story of Uzzah (2 Samuel 6:6), who touched the ark of the covenant and died on the spot. Although Uzzah, says Antiochus, had gripped the ark with the best of intentions when the oxen carrying the ark stumbled, he had crossed a line. Uzzah acted with *parrhesia* towards a sacred object, when he should have maintained a respectful distance.

Some decades before Antiochus the Monk collected his sayings, Abba Dorotheus of Gaza (505–65 AD) also described *parrhesia* as the mother of all passions. His *Directions on the Spiritual Life* makes explicit what was already suggested in the *Apophthegmata patrum* by Abba Agathon, namely that *parrhesia* in the pejorative sense of 'too much familiarity' not only applies to speech, but refers to an overall free mode of behaviour. In Abba Dorotheus' view, such familiar behaviour is not conducive to a life of devotion to God:

---

[15] Athanasius, *Vita Antonii* 45, 4, and 82, 12, *PG* 26, pp. 909 and 960.
[16] Antiochus the Monk, *Peri parrhesias*, *PG* 89, pp. 1476–7.

The Silent Ascetic

Parrhesia may have many forms. *Parrhesia* is shown by word, gesture, or look. It may lead a man to chatter, to worldly talk, to doing something ridiculous, provoking others to unseemly mirth.[17] It is *parrhesia*, too, if a man touches another without need, points at someone who is laughing, pushes him, snatches something out of his hands, shamelessly stares at him; all this is the work of *parrhesia*, all this comes of having no fear of God in the soul and so little by little a man becomes utterly careless. [...] Hence nothing is more harmful than *parrhesia*; it is the mother of all passions, since it banishes reverence, drives the fear of God away from the soul, and gives birth to carelessness.[18]

The behaviour that resulted from *parrhesia* was, in Dorotheus' view, unfitting for a monk. If a monk spoke or acted with *parrhesia*, it was as an indication he had no fear of God or respect for his brother. Although Dorotheus is outspoken about the dangers of *parrhesia*, we should bear in mind that his warnings were aimed at those who were dedicated to a life of contemplation, not at all Christians. This is often the case with ascetic literature that warns against the harmful effects of *parrhesia*, or against the dangers of speech as such: it is directed at a specific audience of (prospective) ascetics and does not offer general directions on how all Christians should live and behave. Abba Dorotheus' cautions against *parrhesia*, moreover, pertained to a particular form of *parrhesia*, the type of free speech and bold conduct that sprang from lack of self-control. Self-control was the all-important factor that determined whether one should speak out or keep silent. For both activities, speech and silence, self-control was of vital importance: one needed to be in control of one's tongue to be able to remain silent *and* to speak moderately.

PARRHESIA BEFORE GOD

In contrast to Abba Dorotheus, Isaac of Nineveh (fl. c. 650) proposes a rather positive conception of *parrhesia* in his *Mystical Treatises*, written, like Dorotheus' *Directions on the Spiritual Life,* for those who were dedicated to a life of contemplation. Isaac does not address the issue of familiarity between monks; his reflections on *parrhesia* pertain to the intimate relationship between man and God. In Isaac's view, the measure of frankness a monk may adopt when speaking to God in prayer depends on the purity of his conscience. One has to search one's own heart, for, as Isaac writes: 'If our heart does not despise us, then we are frank with God. Frankness has its origin in firm behaviour and an

---

[17] Compare *Regula Benedicti* 6.
[18] Dorotheus of Gaza, *Directions on the Spiritual Life* 4, 53, trans. Kadloubovsky, Palmer, p. 160.

Part I

unstained mind.'[19] The link between *parrhesia* and a clear conscience, first addressed by Philo of Alexandria and later elaborated by Origen, became a frequent theme in ascetic literature.[20] Just like the martyr, the ascetic monk was believed to enjoy privileged *parrhesia* before God on account of his suffering. But, whereas the martyr had suffered torture and martyrdom by the hands of others, the ascetic suffered self-enflicted deprivations. Through suffering and ascetic practices, the monk could hope to regain the *parrhesia* that Adam had enjoyed in paradise, but lost after the Fall. Baptism was an essential first step on the path of recovery. At the moment of baptism, God adopted man and gave him the gift of *parrhesia*. Because of sin, however, the baptised lost that precious gift little by little, just as Adam had lost his *parrhesia* when he was expelled from paradise. Through ascetic practices of mortification and self-control, by curbing the tongue and remaining silent, the ascetic strove to diminish sin and thus gradually restore his *parrhesia* before God.[21]

Isaac and other ascetic authors developed and framed their ideas on *parrhesia* before God in analogy with the model of the family.[22] A monk could speak freely to God just as a son could speak to his father.[23] Familiarity was central to the positive interpretation of monastic *parrhesia* as frankness towards God, just as it was central to its negative construction, familiarity between monks. Another model for imagining freedom of speech before God was the court of the ruler. Just as a courtier who enjoyed privileged access to a ruler can speak his mind to the sovereign, according to Isaac, so a monk who spends much time with God in contemplation can address the heavenly ruler frankly. In the *Mystical Treatises*, Isaac elaborates on this analogy. When speaking of the difference between those who are in the active service of God and those God chooses to 'minister before himself', Isaac writes:

We do not only see, in the affairs of earthly kings, that those who are constantly with the king and participate in his secrets are more glorious and elevated in their ranks than those who accomplish their outward affairs with love, but also in divine affairs it is easy to see what freedom of speech those possess who, in intercourse with him, possess the mysteries of prayer at all times.[24]

---

[19] Isaac of Nineveh, *Mystical Treatises* 38, trans. Wensinck, p. 194. For all instances of *parrhesia* and its cognates in the Greek translation of Isaac's Syriac text, see Pirard, Kindt, *Concordance*, p. 2567–8.
[20] Bartelink, *Quelques observations sur* παρρησία, pp. 14–26.   [21] Ibid., pp. 12–14.
[22] Ibid., pp. 14, 23.   [23] Isaac of Nineveh, *Mystical Treatises* 4, trans. Wensinck, p. 38.
[24] Ibid. 19, trans. Wensinck, pp. 102, 103.

The Silent Ascetic

In Isaac's view, ascetics had a clear advantage over other ministers of the supreme Ruler when it came to freedom of speech and the possibility of participating in his secrets. The comparison with earthly rulers and their courts, however, held only up to a point. The ascetic's spiritual *parrhesia* before God had nothing to do with criticising God or offering Him unasked advice, as those truth-tellers did who spoke and acted with *parrhesia* before secular power. And yet, to question God's decisions was not as unthinkable as might appear at first sight. We find critical *parrhesia* towards God in the Book of Job, where Job takes God to account for his ordeals, and for allowing the devil to heap them upon him in order to test his loyalty.[25] This biblical notion of criticising God, however, is not taken up by Isaac, nor by other ascetic authors. For Isaac, tribulations and temptations are nothing to complain about; overcoming them only helps the ascetic to achieve the desired goal: getting nearer to God and having freedom of speech in prayer.[26]

SAINT BABYLAS CONFRONTS AN EMPEROR

Ascetic advisory literature discusses *parrhesia* as familiarity before God or, negatively, *parrhesia* as familiarity between monks, but rarely raises the issue of critical *parrhesia* to secular power. It would appear that ascetic authors such as Isaac, Antiochus, Dorotheus and the anonymous authors/compilers of the various collections of *Sayings of the Desert Fathers* did not envisage a duty or obligation for monks to leave their solitude to speak truth to secular authorities, or at least they do not explicitly address such an obligation. We do find this social expectation, however, in other sources of the period. As we have seen, the church histories of Socrates, Sozomen and Theodoret feature truth-telling ascetics who, in imitation of the solitary philosophers of old, ventured to the court to give the emperor a piece of their mind.

To understand the interconnection between ascetic virtues and political free speech, we need to turn back to the period when bishops, guided by ascetic ideals, reflected on the necessity to speak the truth to those power, as discussed in chapter 3. John Chrysostom (d. 407), bishop of Constantinople, who wrote much about *parrhesia*, wrote a panegyric on Saint Babylas around 380.[27] Babylas, the ascetic bishop of Antioch (d. c. 250), was considered a martyr because he died in prison under obscure circumstances.[28] John's *Discourse on Babylas* shows how the values

---

[25] Job 22:21–6.   [26] Isaac of Nineveh, *Mystical Treatises* 46, trans. Wensinck, p. 224.
[27] John Chrysostom, *De sancto Babyla*, ed. Schatkin.
[28] Schatkin, *Jean Chrysostome, Discours sur Babylas*, pp. 16–17.

Part I

connected to martyrdom, now enriched with ascetic virtues, continued to inform the discourse of free speech long after the days of persecution. In his panegyric, John recounts how Babylas once refused an unnamed emperor permission to enter the church, demanding that he first do penance for committing murder. Later adaptations of John Chrysostom's story of Babylas have it that this emperor was Philip the Arab (r. 244–249), but John does not mention his name, in accordance with the conventions of the panegyric genre.[29] In Eusebius' *Ecclesiastical History*, we find a similar story about an emperor who was not permitted to enter the church. Eusebius gives the name of the emperor, Philip, but not the name of the bishop who sent him away to do penance.[30] Perhaps Eusebius records the same story that John Chrysostom had recounted, but it is also possible that several similar stories circulated about bold bishops denying emperors access to their church, such as the story of Ambrose confronting Emperor Theodosius in the porch of the church of Milan.

John emphasises the idea that Saint Babylas showed great self-restraint when he confronted the ruler with his sins. Unlike the Cynic philosopher Diogenes, John argues, who was rude to Alexander the Great, Babylas was a well-mannered truth-teller.[31] While Greek philosophers, according to John, were ruled by irrational passions and employed more liberty than was necessary or less than was required, Babylas' *parrhesia* was well measured, because it was governed by moderation and discretion.[32] As John has it, the holy man never acted on impulse, but carefully analysed each situation first. Like a skilled surgeon, he took care not to jeopardise the health of his patient by a too radical cutting, but 'adapted the operation to the sickness and thus effected the best cure'.[33] 'If I may say something paradoxical,' John writes, 'I admire the blessed one not so much because he confronted the sovereign's fury, as because he recognized the limit to which he should go, and did not exceed this limit in deed or in word.'[34] What exactly Babylas said to the emperor, John cannot and will not say. He invites his audience to imagine the scene. He encourages them to picture the spearmen, the military men, the

---

[29] According to the seventh-century *Chronicon pascale*, the emperor was Philip the Arab; according to the *Acta S. Babylae* it was Numerian, while others say it was Decius. See Schatkin, Introduction to *Jean Chrysostome, Discours sur Babylas*, pp. 52–9.
[30] Eusebius, *Historia ecclesiastica* VI, 34.
[31] Against Diogenes (again without mentioning his name), John Chrysostom, *De sancto Babyla* 45–9, ed. Schatkin, pp. 148–55.
[32] John Chrysostom, *De sancto Babyla* 37, ed. Schatkin, pp. 136–9.
[33] Ibid. 37, ed. Schatkin, pp. 138, 139, trans. Harkins, Schatkin, *Saint John Chrysostom, Apologist*, p. 96.
[34] Ibid. 38, ed. Schatkin, pp. 138, 139, trans. Harkins, Schatkin, *Saint John Chrysostom, Apologist*, p. 96.

governors, the men of the palace and the rest of the retinue, the king resplendent in their midst, and then to picture the holy man approaching, wearing a simple garment, pushing aside the guards and laying his right hand on the emperor's breast. What Babylas then said to the emperor, John does not venture to put into words. *Parrhesia*, he says, is something that one should experience, not reproduce in writing. 'For such *parrhesia* cannot be grasped by language or sight, only by experience and practice.'[35] Those who have reached the same degree of liberty as the holy man, he continues, can fully comprehend this.[36] Thus, John underlines the importance of the outer performance as well as the inner practice of *parrhesia*.

John's *Discourse on Babylas* is interesting for two reasons. First, it demonstrates that although ascetic advisory literature itself does not show any explicit appreciation of bold *parrhesia* before rulers, we do find it in texts *about* ascetics, in which they are presented as heirs of the martyrs and the apostles. To John's mind, monks were the inheritors of their *parrhesia*: when necessary, they left the solitude of their cells on the mountain tops to intercede with authorities on behalf of the suppressed.[37] Although John's panegyric on Babylas dates to the late fourth century, it is relevant to the period under scrutiny here, as his story began to circulate widely from the fifth century onwards in many different versions and languages (Syriac, Latin, Greek, Armenian, Georgian) and was adapted and extended to reflect the interests of later generations.[38] The story about the ascetic saint–bishop who sent a ruler away from the church to do penance, and rebuked him firmly but respectfully, apparently appealed to readers precisely during the centuries when, as Foucault maintains, free speech gave way to silence and obedience.

Second, John's story about Babylas and the unnamed ruler, including its later adaptations, exemplifies how ascetic ideals did not replace, but rather reframed the traditional discourse of *parrhesia*. Ascetic virtues of self-renunciation and self-control were taken to transform and improve the practice of *parrhesia*. We encounter this type of reframing mainly in the writings of ecclesiastical authors who had strong sympathies for the ascetic life but were no solitary monks themselves. Bishops such as John

---

[35] Ibid. 33, ed. Schatkin, pp. 132–3; trans. Harkins, Schatkin, *Saint John Chrysostom, Apologist*, p. 94.
[36] Ibid.
[37] Harkins, Schatkin, *Saint John Chrysostom, Apologist*, p. 94, n. 66, with reference to John Chrysostom, *Homily on the Statues* 17, 7. On monks as the inheritors of the martyrs' *parrhesia* see also Bartelink *Quelques observations sur* παρρησία, p. 28.
[38] Schatkin, Introduction to *Jean Chrysostome, Discours sur Babylas* III, pp. 49–60, listing several versions and adaptations from the early fifth to the eleventh century. See also (not in Schatkin's list): Aldhelm of Malmesbury (639–709), *Carmen de virginitate*, with an extensive section on Babylas reprimanding the emperor and turning him away.

Part I

Chrysostom, Gregory Nazianzen, Basil of Caesarea and Gregory the Great brought the ascetic values of silence, self-control and moderate speech to bear on classical ideals of free speech. In the remainder of this chapter, we shall see how they went about adjusting the free speech tradition to meet their ascetic ideals as well as their pastoral responsibilities. It is in their texts that we find another interpretation, or rather application, of *parrhesia*: namely, to admonish one's flock with frankness.

PASTORAL FRANKNESS

When Bishop Gregory Nazianzen resigned from his episcopal office and turned to a life of contemplation, he wrote a poem in praise of silence. Looking back on his life in office, in which speech had played such a prominent role, Gregory lauds the beneficial effects of silence. Periods of withdrawal into silence, he writes, had taught him as a bishop to guard his tongue and speak with moderation.[39] Earlier, in an oration on the duties of the priesthood, Gregory had argued that self-control was a necessity for every priest and bishop with pastoral obligations. A priest should keep his anger in check if he wants his admonitions to be effective and sincere. The mouth that speaks the words of God has to be pure. In Gregory's orations, the ascetic values of silence, self-control and contemplation feed back into ideals of speaking well. By withdrawing into silence, according to Gregory, one takes care of one's own soul, re-emerging prepared to take care of the soul of others. Gregory's oration on the duties of the priesthood (also known as the *Apologetica*) was translated into Latin by Rufinus of Aquileia (d. 410) and was used by Gregory the Great (d. 604) in his *Pastoral Rule*, which was the most frequently used handbook on pastoral care throughout the Middle Ages. Especially the second and fourth books of the *Pastoral Rule*, with their emphasis on self-control and self-reflection, owed much to Gregory Nazianzen's *Apologetica*. Thus, Gregory Nazianzen's ideas on the relative merits of silence and speaking, and on the importance of self-knowledge in finding the right balance between the two poles, found their way into the Latin Middle Ages.

Late antique ascetic literature tends to emphasise the beneficial effects of silence versus the dangerous power of the tongue. As Conrad Leyser has argued, the ascetic technologies that had been developed in the fourth century to control the body came to be deployed against speech.[40] Speaking was dangerous, especially for the speaker himself. And yet,

---

[39] Gregory Nazianzen, *On Silence,* lines 123–151, trans. White, pp. 175–7.
[40] Leyser, 'Let me speak, let me speak', p. 176.

The Silent Ascetic

monastic communities could not do entirely without speech. According to Basil of Caesarea, silence is appropriate for certain persons and on certain occasions, but rightly measured speech is to be valued above everything. For Basil, mutual correction is an important aspect of monastic life. Monks should help improve each other, and they can do so only by speaking out, not by remaining silent.[41] Likewise, Gregory the Great in his *Pastoral Rule* warns against the dangers of overzealous silence. To his mind, people who remain silent when others are clearly in need of admonition 'withdraw so to speak medicine from visible wounds and become authors of death'.[42] The medical metaphor that Gregory employs was used by Epicurean philosophers to describe the health-bringing effect of frank speech. The moral philosophers compared frank speech (*parrhesia*) to a surgeon's knife that cut away the sick parts in order to ensure that the body of the community remained healthy and vital.[43] According to Gregory, immoderate silence is not only harmful for community life, but can also damage one's own soul.[44] Passions should be governed, he argues, not suppressed by silence. If passions do not find an outlet, they will continue to boil inside and poison the inner person.[45] 'Ideally', Gregory writes, 'the tongue should be discreetly curbed, not completely closed. For it is written: "The wise hold their tongue until the proper time [Wisd. 20:7]".'[46]

Gregory holds that moderate speech is to be preferred over silence. It should, however, be kept in mind that he expresses these views in a text that was not written for monks. Although Gregory's *Pastoral Rule* was widely read in monasteries, it was primarily intended for priests and bishops, or rather, for spiritual leaders (*rectores*). Its purpose was to advise the clergy on how to provide pastoral care and admonish lay people. As spiritual leaders, priests and bishops should correct, steer and admonish their flock. The *rectores*, in their turn, needed to be corrected themselves. A *rector* was not above sin, and he had to accept being corrected if his admonitions were too harsh.[47] Gregory did not consider it below the dignity of a spiritual director to let himself be corrected. Did the Apostle Peter not accept the censure of the Apostle Paul? Even when censure

---

[41] See the *Rule of Basil of Caesarea (Asketikon)* 47 and 208, trans. Frank, pp. 307, 308.
[42] Gregory the Great, *Regula pastoralis* III, 14: '... quasi conspectis vulneribus usum medicaminis subtrahunt, et eo mortis auctores fiunt'; ed. Judic, vol. 2, p. 344. Trans. Demacopoulos, p. 122.
[43] Malherbe, 'Medical imagery', pp. 19–31, especially pp. 24–6.
[44] Gregory the Great, *Regula pastoralis* III, 14, ed. Judic, vol. 2, p. 344.
[45] Ibid.; compare Gregory Nazianzen, *On Silence*, pp. 140–5.
[46] Gregory the Great, *Regula pastoralis* III, 14: 'Lingua itaque discrete frenanda est, non insolubiliter obliganda. Scriptum namque est: Sapiens tacebit usque ad tempus', ed. Judic, vol. 2, p. 344. Trans. Demacopoulos, p. 123.
[47] Gregory the Great, *Regula pastoralis* II, 8.

comes from a subordinate, Gregory says, a *rector* should be willing to accept criticism, for it will teach him humility. In this respect, a leader should follow the example of King David, who humbly accepted rebuke. He should not love himself more than he loves truth. Lay people were allowed to admonish and correct their pastors, to temper the harshness of their rule, provided that their admonitions stayed within certain bounds. Otherwise, their freedom of speech (*libertas*), when granted too liberally, could easily develop into arrogance, which is an argument familiar from the treatises of ascetic leaders such as Dorotheus of Gaza.[48]

EZEKIEL'S WATCHMAN

Gregory the Great considered it the duty of every spiritual leader to be a 'watchman of the house of Israel' (Ezek. 3:17). He drew upon this biblical metaphor to maintain that it was a *rector*'s duty to warn the people entrusted to his care against the dangers of sin. He ascribed the role of the Old Testament prophet, and in particular that of the prophet Ezekiel, to every Christian *rector*, and especially to the bishop. Gregory's invocation of the watchman image from the Book of Ezekiel functions as a 'mission statement' to encourage bishops to continue speaking, admonishing and preaching. We find this notion of an episcopal duty to admonish and reprove already in the *Apostolic Constitutions,* a Greek text written in Syria in the third century AD. This pseudo-epigraph, allegedly written by the twelve apostles at the time of the Council of Jerusalem, offers instructions to bishops to 'reprove and admonish with *parrhesia*' with reference to Ezekiel's watchman.[49] The expression *noutheteite meta parrhesias* (admonish with *parrhesia*) or *elegxein meta parrhesias* (to reprove with *parrhesia*) does not occur either in the Old or in the New Testament, but was projected upon it later in Christian literature.[50] The fourth-century Latin version of the originally Greek text of the *Apostolic Constitutions,* known as the *Didascalia,* translated the prophetic and apostolic duty to 'admonish and reprove with *parrhesia*' as 'monete et corripite palam'.[51] The *Constitutions*

---

[48] Gregory the Great, *Regula pastoralis* II, 8.
[49] *Constitutiones apostolicae* 2, 6, 12, ed. Funk, p. 40: 'noutheteite kai elegxete meta parrhesias', followed by an extensive quotation from the Book of Ezekiel.
[50] Bartelink, *Quelques observations sur* παρρησία, p. 38. We do find *elegxe, elegxein* ('reprove') in 1 Tim. 5:20, 2 Tim. 4:2, Tit. 2:13, Tit. 2:15, discussing the responsibilities of those who lead the communities of Christians, but without the addition *meta parrhesias*. *Noutheteite* ('admonish') occurs in 1 Thess. 5:14, 2 Thess. 3:15, Rom. 15:14, Acts 20:31, 1 Cor. 4:14, Col. 1:28, Col. 3:16, but again without the addition *meta parrhesias; Constitutiones apostolicae* 2, 6, 12, ed. Funk, p. 40.
[51] *Didascalia* 2, 6, 16, ed. Funk, p. 42. On other occasions *meta parrhesias* is translated as *cum fiducia, Didascalia/Constitutiones* 2, 8, 4 (Greek text, ed. Funk, p. 45, Latin text, ed. Funk p. 44).

The Silent Ascetic

emphasise the responsibility of bishops to admonish, and, if need be, to firmly reprimand those who give offence by their behaviour, stray from correct doctrine or touch the freedom of the church.[52] The theme was taken up by fifth- and sixth-century authors, who consistently refer to Ezekiel's wachman to corroborate this widening of the field of *parrhesia* to include pastoral frankness. The watchman should not only speak boldly to those of higher authority, which was the traditional direction of *parrhesia,* but also preach with *parrhesia* to those entrusted to his care.

While Gregory the Great propagated the bishop's duty to speak out, he did not fail to acknowledge the hazards involved in being a watchman. A watchman was not at liberty to remain silent, but by calling out to save others he put the salvation of his own soul at risk. The act of speaking was, after all, not without danger. If a preacher was not careful, pride in his preaching could get the better of him, or idle words might enter his sermon, polluting his mouth and making it an unfit vessel to proclaim the word of God.[53] To diminish the risk of pollution, Gregory recommends that bishops strive towards a language that is pure and moderate. Following Gregory Nazianzen, Gregory believed a pastor could learn to control his tongue and master his pride in quiet periods of self-examination in which he returned to himself.[54]

In fifth- and sixth-century ascetic literature, monastic ideals of complete silence coexisted with an ideology of pure and moderate speech.[55] As we have seen in the discussion of the martyr acts of the third and early fourth centuries in chapter 1, plain and pure speech that was devoid of rhetorical intricacies became the new rhetorical ideal. Augustine (d. 430 AD) promotes this type of speech in the fourth book of his *On Christian Doctrine*, while Cassian (d. 435 AD) does the same in his *Conferences,* Caesarius of Arles (d. 542 AD) in his sermons and the North African grammarian Pomerius (fl. fifth century AD) in his treatise *On the Contemplative Life*.[56] Augustine, Caesarius and Pomerius invoke the image of the watchman of the house of Israel (Ezek. 3:17–19) in their promulgation of this new rhetorical ideal.[57] The *speculator* of Ezekiel was identified with the *episcopus* who had a responsibility for his flock on

---

[52] See the second book of the *Constitutiones apostolicae* and *Didascalia*, dedicated to the duties and responsibilities of bishops, ed. Funk, pp. 30–191, especially pp. 38–42.
[53] See Gregory's lament in *Homilies on Ezekiel* I, 11, 5–6 and Conrad Leyser's discussion of this passage in 'Let me speak, let me speak'.
[54] Gregory the Great, *Regula pastoralis* IV, ed. Judic, vol. 2, pp. 532–40.
[55] Leyser, *Authority and Asceticism*, especially pp. 59–61 (Cassian), pp. 95–100 (Caesarius of Arles), pp. 168, 189 (Gregory), pp. 68–9 (Pomerius). See also Diem, Müller, '*Vita, regula, sermo*' on the *Regula magistri* and the *Regula Benedicti*.
[56] Augustine, *De doctrina Christiana* 27, 29, 38; Leyser, *Authority and Asceticism*, pp. 54–5.
[57] Caesarius of Arles, *Sermo* 1, 11; see further references in Leyser, *Authority and Asceticism*, pp. 28, 29.

the Day of Judgement. This identification was not far-fetched, seeing that the Greek word *episkopos* literally means 'watchman' or 'overseer'.[58] The watchman passage from the Book of Ezekiel became a key text in the rhetoric of admonition and political criticism, as we have seen in the chapters on Hilary of Poitiers and Ambrose of Milan. The passage was often used in combination with Paul's command to Timothy ('reprove, entreat, rebuke', 2 Tim. 4:2), with Psalm 118:46 ('I spoke of thy testimonies before kings, and I was not ashamed'), or with a passage from the Book of Isaiah ('Lift up your voice as a trumpet', Isa. 58,:1).[59] Bishops, who appropriated the role the Old Testament prophet–watchman to themselves, were to speak plainly and openly when they raised their voice to warn others away from the dangers of sins. It was their prophetic calling to uncover sins that were hidden for others and to admonish people in a language that was clear to understand for all: a language that was, moreover, so sincere and pure that it did not corrupt the speakers themselves with false rhetoric.

This rhetorical ideal of pure and plain speech was related to an ascetic technique of self-examination by which the bishop–watchman constantly investigated his ethical position as a speaker, in relation to God and to his audience, and the quality of his speech.[60] This rhetorical ideal of plain speech was not novel. It had been part of the tradition of *parrhesia* at least from the days of Socrates. Fifth- and sixth-century ascetic authors cultivated a connection between pure speech and self-knowledge that was reminiscent of the close link between *logos*, truth and *bios* that was inherent in the Socratic practice of truth-telling.[61] In contrast to Socrates' technologies of the self, the kind of soul-searching that Gregory propagated was couched in terms of ascetic contemplation.[62] A pastor who contemplated God's love and wisdom and explored the depths of his own soul on a regular basis guarded the purity of his language and the sincerity of his intentions. 'From speaking in the public forum, we must return to the court-room of the heart', Gregory writes.[63] This was the best protection against the sins of pride and ambition that, as it was seen at the time, went hand in hand with rhetorical prowess. By a constant process of critical self-examination, a bishop could continue

---

[58] Mohrmann, 'Episkopos-Speculator'.
[59] I thank Courtney Booker for his suggestion to look at this specific cluster of biblical texts.
[60] See for example Gregory the Great, *Homilies on Ezekiel* I, 11, 5–6, discussed in Leyser, 'Let me speak, let me speak'.
[61] On Socratic *parrhesia* and the interconnection between *logos*, truth and *bios* see Foucault, *Fearless Speech*, pp. 91–107.
[62] Leyser, *Authority and Asceticism*, pp. 160–87 and 'Let me speak, let me speak'.
[63] Gregory the Great, *Moralia* 35, 20.49, quoted after Markus, *Gregory the Great*, p. 24. Cf. *Regula pastoralis* 1, 9.

to fulfil his prophetic duty to speak out against sin, while at the same time protecting himself against the allurements of rhetoric and the danger of condemning himself out of his own mouth.

Authors such as Basil of Caesarea, Gregory Nazianzen and Gregory the Great, who were familiar with both the contemplative and the active life, with the merits of silence as well as with the virtues of speech, pointed to the advantages of both. Although they longed for a silent life of contemplation, they acknowledged that without speech the Church would get nowhere. Preaching, instructing, admonishing and correcting were important activities for maintaining and expanding the Church of Christ. Without preaching one could not spread the word of Christ; without mutual exhortation there would be no spiritual growth. While some ascetic authors considered frank speech disruptive to the smooth working of monastic community life, it was still highly appreciated as a means of moral and spiritual improvement within the community of Christ at large, and a vital instrument in preventing rulers from taking the wrong decisions and steering their policy in the right direction.

CONCLUSION

As mentioned at the beginning of this chapter, Michel Foucault associates the doubts and misgivings about free speech that we find in late antique Christian texts with the rise of monasticism and the Christian need for new structures of authority.[64] He points out that, when the days of persecution were over and the public figure of the martyr disappeared, the increasing prominence of ascetic ideals gave reservations against free speech a foothold in the Christian world. Speaking frankly clashed with ascetic self-control and with obedience to authorities. When the Christian Church went into a phase of institutionalisation, Foucault argues, and asceticism 'took over' the Christian ideals, the classical tradition of free speech came under attack. Foucault thus couches the change in the Christian's evaluation of *parrhesia* in terms of Weber's process of 'routinisation', or *Veralltäglichung*.[65]

As has become clear in this chapter, significant shifts took place in the Christian reception of *parrhesia* after the fourth century. With the progressive Christianisation of the Roman Empire, the status of *parrhesia* in society became more problematic than it had been in the age of the apostles and martyrs. However, the reservations against frank speech that we encounter in sources of the fifth and sixth centuries cannot be ascribed solely to the emergence of ascetic trends in Christianity. Christian ascetics

[64] Foucault, *Le courage de la verité*, pp. 305–6.   [65] Szakolczai, *Genesis of Modernity*, p. 239.

were not the first to express doubts about the benefits of speaking freely. Some Roman historians, such as Tacitus, had already questioned the merits of frank speech for the Roman state, and early Christian martyr acts show martyrs, whom Foucault considers charismatic parrhesiasts par excellence, seeking a new balance between free speech, respect for authorities and reticence. The process of re-evaluating the importance of frankness in relation to other values, such as obedience and moderation, was not set in motion by the arrival of monks and hermits. It was a process that had started long before.

Another objection to Foucault's thesis is that the tradition of free speech never lost its importance for Christian society in the first place. In late antique and early medieval Christian society, criticism was held in high regard in politics, in friendship and in spiritual relationships. The extent to which it was appreciated (or not) depended on the person who used it and the situation in which it was employed. This was nothing new either, as the normative rules for proper use of free speech set down in rhetorical treatises, which were discussed in the introduction, demonstrate. Rhetoricians reminded speakers to heed the person, time, circumstances and occasion before speaking out. The art of frank criticism was itself not beyond criticism. It was considered an unwholesome activity when it was seen to put the tranquillity of the soul at risk or felt to undermine the stability of the order of Christian society. And yet, when it was performed according to the appropriate rhetorical and behavioral rules – for example, within a specific social setting in which priests admonished their flock, bishops spoke the truth to emperors and the members of monastic communities exhorted each other – frank criticism was still highly valued.

EPILOGUE PART I

The first part of this book has focussed on the complex process of adaptation and reinterpretation of the classical tradition of free speech between the third and seventh century AD. As I hope to have demonstrated, Christian interpretations of *parrhesia* were diverse, and not all of these interpretations were exclusively spiritual. In Christian conceptualisation(s), *parrhesia* kept many of the moral and political aspects that had been part of its pre-Christian tradition. In analogy with Roman citizens drawing their licence to speak from their free status within the Roman Empire, Christians laid a claim to freedom of speech because they regarded themselves as free citizens in the kingdom of Christ. Christians conceived of their *parrhesia* as a tool to spread the gospel, to state their Christian identity, to combat heresy or to imagine the relationship between man and God. Although these fields of application can indeed be regarded as religious domains, we should not ignore the inherently political dimensions of Christian *parrhesia*. The free speech of the martyr narratives, of Hilary's invective, of John Chrysostom's speeches and Ambrose's letters was as much political as it was religious. When, over the course of the fourth century, the heavenly kingdom of Christ, from which Christians drew their citizen's privilege to speak freely, was seen to acquire an earthly counterpart in a Christian empire, *parrhesia* became a prominently political instrument once more.

Not all Christian authors who drew on the classical tradition of free speech felt the need to adapt it to Christian standards. Whether they chose to reframe *parrhesia* in a prominently Christian way or used it in a more traditional form depended on their outlook, and on the audience they aimed to persuade. Some Christian truth-tellers distinguished their free speech emphatically from Greco-Roman pagan *parrhesia*, while others did not. It would appear that in the period when Christianity was not yet an accepted religion, Christians were keen to demonstrate that their free speech was part of a classical tradition they shared with other Roman

Part I

citizens, while they later felt the need for differentiation, when traditional Roman religion and Greco-Roman culture were seen as rivals to Christianity. But this is no clear-cut explanatory model, given that different Christian interpretations of *parrhesia* existed side by side. Cases in point are the story of Ambrose and Theodosius and the nearly identical story of Babylas and the unnamed ruler, discussed in chapters 4 and 5. The stories started to circulate around the same time, that is, in the fifth century, and both feature a bishop who speaks boldly to a ruler and denies him access to the church. And yet, although the narrative patterns of the two accounts are very similar, the framing is different. While Ambrose presents his free speech towards Theodosius as traditional *libertas dicendi*, the right of a Roman citizen freely to address a Roman Emperor, John Chrysostom places his story about Babylas in an ascetic context, and distinguishes his protagonist's free speech from the *parrhesia* of Greek philosophers. Babylas' *parrhesia*, John emphasises, was a manifestation of apostolic boldness. John's evaluation of the free speech and behaviour of Babylas, bishop and martyr, is reminiscent of Hilary of Poitiers's *libertas apostolicae* a few decades earlier, rather than of his contemporary Ambrose, who drew on Roman tradition to frame his own freedom of speech. Different constructions and representations were feasible within the field of Christian free speech, and were connected to different types of truth-tellers. The philosopher, the prophet, the apostle, the martyr, the holy man and the ascetic bishop all provided role models for the performance of free speech. The transformation of the classical tradition of free speech thus did not develop in a linear manner from a political to a fully spiritual interpretation, from the model of the philosopher to the exemplar of the bishop, but formed different clusters of ideas and models that existed side by side, strengthening each other's symbolic capital.

Before closing the first part of this book, a few words are needed to elucidate the different structure and methodology of the second part. Up to now, Greek as well as Latin texts have been discussed. Greek texts throughout the period under investigation used the term *parrhesia* to denote the theory and practice of free speech in a variety of ways. New interpretations of *parrhesia* were grafted onto older ones and acquired aspects of the term's history. Isaac of Nineveh's mystical treatises, for example, established a specific ascetic interpretation of *parrhesia* – namely, an intimate relation between man and God – but Isaac's reconfiguration incorporated previous configurations of *parrhesia*, such as the boldness and confidence of martyrs, the intimacy between family members and the courtier's privileged access to the ruler. Sometimes the old meanings travelled along with the metaphors that were used to explain the new interpretation (or new application) to an audience not yet familiar with it.

Epilogue

Over the course of time, *parrhesia* accumulated ever more layers, while older and recycled meanings gave it coherence, strength and appeal.

The second part of this book is dedicated to the reception and further transformation of the tradition of free speech in the early Middle Ages. We leave the late antique Mediterranean, a period and area in which Greek and Latin cultures were entwined, to turn to medieval western Europe, where the two cultures grew apart. Latin was the dominant language of the intellectuals of the early medieval west who engaged with the free speech tradition. Knowledge of the Greek language and familiarity with Greek culture dwindled in this period, although it never entirely disappeared. The different circumstances and conditions of the region and period under investigation in the second part of this book thus call for a different method of investigation. Although close attention will continue to be paid to the words used to describe the phenomenon of free speech, the main focus of the second part lies on narrative patterns of representation, and on the reception of the late antique stories that have been introduced in the first part. Tracing the cultural memory of late antique truth-tellers, such as the memory of Bishop Ambrose confronting Emperor Theodosius, or of Hilary inveighing against Emperor Constantius II, offers a lens through which to study processes of adoption and adaptation, of continuities, discontinuities and further transformations of the classical tradition of free speech in the medieval Latin West.

PART II

6

THE FRANK HOLY MAN

'You are defeated and bound, because you are the son of the devil and an enemy of righteousness', Bishop Nicetius of Trier (d. 561) said to the Byzantine emperor Justinian (r. 527–65).[1] Around the mid-sixth century (the precise date is unknown), Nicetius wrote Justinian a letter in which he called the emperor to repentance. The bishop wanted to have the emperor know that 'all of Italy, the whole of Africa as well as Spain and Gaul curse your name as they weep about your damnation'.[2] The occasion that drove Nicetius to write his strongly worded letter was an edict Justinian had issued in 544, which sparked a dispute commonly known as the Three Chapters Controversy, named after three theological writings that were condemned by Justinian's edict.[3] The condemnation led to a wave of protests in the Latin West.[4] Nicetius accused Justinian of being a supporter of the heretics Nestorius and Eutyches, and called, or rather commanded, the emperor to recant: 'If you will not retract what you have taught and proclaim openly, "I have erred, I have erred, I have sinned; anathema upon Nestorius and Eutyches", you have surrendered yourself to eternal suffering along with them.'[5]

It is not known whether Justinian ever read Nicetius' letter. If he did, John Moorhead maintains, 'it is hard to imagine the emperor losing any sleep over this letter from a backwoods bishop outside the empire'.[6] Trier, once the capital of the emperor Magnus Maximus and seat of the

---

[1] Nicetius of Trier, *Epistola ad Iustinianum imperatorem*, ed. Gundlach, p.119, line 24: 'Victus es et vinctus, sed inde, unde filius diabuli et inimicus iustitiae.'
[2] Ibid, line 25: 'Nam notum tibi sit, quod tota Italia, integra Africa, Hispania vel Gallia coniuncta nomen tuum cum deperditione tua plorant, anathematizant.'
[3] On the Three Chapters Controversy, see Chazelle, Cubitt (eds.), *The Crisis of the Oikoumene*.
[4] Moorhead, *Justinian*, pp. 138–40.
[5] Nicetius, *Epistola*, ed. Gundlach, p. 119: 'Et si non, quae docuisti, distruxeris et publica voce clamaveris: Erravi, erravi, peccavi; anathema Nestorii, anathema Euticis! cum ipsis te ad supplicia sempiterna tradidisti.'
[6] Moorhead, *Justinian*, p. 40.

Part II

Gallic prefecture, was now a prominent city in the Merovingian kingdom of Austrasia. Nicetius' letter is commonly regarded as rude, tactless and too direct: an attestation to declining standards of decorum in this region of the former Roman Empire. Nicetius certainly does not mince his words as he upbraids the emperor for what he considers a serious theological mistake, and does not hesitate to use epithets of abuse.[7] Even in the more friendly parts of the letter, his tone is patronising rather than respectful.[8] The unsophisticated style of Nicetius' letter to Justinian is taken as evidence of the rapidly deteriorating culture of Gaul after the closure of the public schools.[9] In the estimation of Hans Pohlsander, Nicetius' letter is 'undiplomatic, ill-informed and intemperate'.[10] A similar judgement led Nancy Gauthier to conclude that, with Nicetius, 'we have arrived in the middle ages'.[11]

Yet if we look past (modern) stylistic judgements, and pay attention to the content of Nicetius' letter, it should be noted that the bishop of Trier was not exaggerating when he wrote that his objections against Justinian's edict were widely shared in Italy, Spain, Gaul and Africa. We have evidence of protests from other areas, among which is a pamphlet from the hand of Facundus, bishop of Hermiane in North Africa (fl. mid-sixth century).[12] In this pamphlet, Facundus encourages his fellow bishops to speak out against the emperor, calling upon the example of Bishop Ambrose as a model of Christian *libertas*. 'I am of the opinion', Facundus states firmly, 'that if God would raise another Ambrose in our days, we would soon have another Theodosius too'.[13] Facundus' pamphlet is replete with the familiar rhetoric and exemplary models of free speech. In Nicetius' letter, by contrast, we do not encounter any terms or expressions from the classical vocabulary of free speech, although this particular vocabulary was still in use among Gallo-Roman bishops one generation earlier.[14] Nonetheless, although Nicetius' admonitory letter is devoid of the traditional terms and models, it cannot be taken as evidence that the rhetoric of free speech disappeared in the course of the sixth century in the regions under Frankish rule. In the seventh century,

---

[7] See the terms of abuse in the quotation in note 1.
[8] For example, Nicetius, *Epistola,* ed. Gundlach, p. 119, line 2: 'dulcis et dulcis noster Iustiniane'.
[9] Pohlsander, 'A call to repentance', p. 463.   [10] Ibid., p. 470.
[11] Gauthier, *L'évangélisation des Pays de la Moselle,* p. 177: 'nous sommes déjà ici au Moyen-Age'.
[12] Facundus, *Pro defensione trium capitulorum ad Iustinianum*. On Facundus and the Three Chapters Controversy, see Modéran, 'L'Afrique reconquise et les Trois Chapitres'.
[13] Facundus, *Pro defensione* XII, 5, 10, ed. Clément, Vander Plaetse, p. 396, lines 74, 75: 'Unde credendum est quia si nunc Deus aliquem Ambrosium suscitaret, etiam Theodosius non deesset.' See also ibid. XII, 3, 21, p. 386, lines 184, 185: *libertas christiana*.
[14] Expressions such as *libertas eloquii* and *libera lingua loqui* occur for example in the letters and poems of Avitus of Vienne (d. 518) and Magnus Felix Ennodius of Arles (d. 521).

The Frank Holy Man

Nicetius' letter to Justinian was incorporated into a collection of letters, known as the *Epistolae Austrasiacae,* which provided models for correspondence. The collection contains a few epistolary examples of how to offer advice and criticism to high-placed persons.[15] Apparently, Nicetius' contemporaries did not share the judgement of modern scholars that the letter was tactless and too direct. They must have considered it an example worthy of imitation to have included it in this collection of model letters.

In this chapter, I shall discuss the lives and letters of saints and bishops who were considered truth-tellers by their contemporaries. I have selected letters and saints' lives that were written in Francia between c. 550 and c. 750. In addition, I have included two hagiographic texts from Italy and Visigothic Spain, to compare the developments that we see in Merovingian Francia with other kingdoms and regions of the former Western Roman Empire. In the selected sources, we encounter Gallo-Roman, Frankish, Visigothic, Anglo-Saxon and Irish holy men who ventured to criticise those in power. Although the rhetoric of these truth-tellers does not conform to classical standards, at least not according to the norms of modern literary critique, their frank speech and behaviour, as I hope to demonstrate, was very much related to the late antique tradition of free speech.

THE SUFFERINGS OF LEUDEGAR

In Merovingian hagiography, we encounter different types of truth-telling holy men: wandering monks (*peregrini*) who left the enclosure of the monastery to devote themselves to spreading the word of Christ and building new communities, or hermits who offered words of comfort, advice and criticism from their places of solitude. Gregory of Tours (d. 594), the most prolific producer of hagiography of this period, tells us that his friend, the recluse Leobard of Marmoutier (d. c. 583), 'had solicitude for the people, reproof for kings and assiduous prayer for all God-fearing clerics'.[16] The truth-tellers of Merovingian hagiography were not always solitary figures, but could also be, and in fact frequently were, bishops who were actively engaged in high politics and took part in the councils of kings. According to hagiographic tradition, they were often exiled, tortured and killed for expressing a contrary opinion or reprimanding a king. Narrative conventions aside, exile and murder were

---

[15] The *Epistolae Austrasiacae* will be discussed further on in this chapter. See the literature cited below.
[16] Gregory of Tours, *Life of Leobard, Vita patrum* 20, 3, ed. Krusch, pp. 292, 293: 'eratque ei sollicitudo pro populis, inquesitio pro regibus, oratio assidua pro omnibus ecclesiasticis Deum timentibus'; trans. James, p. 128.

Part II

a very real part of the career expectations of a Merovingian bishop, as Paul Fouracre has pointed out. Fouracre identifies eighteen bishops who were murdered in Francia between 580 and 754, often as a result of their opposition to a ruler.[17] The seventh century saw a veritable surge in martyrdom narratives, with the execution of bishops Desiderius of Vienne (d. 611), Aunemund of Lyon (d. c. 660), Sigobrand of Paris (d. c. 665), Leudegar of Autun (d. c. 676) and Praejectus of Clermont (d. 676).[18] Not every murdered bishop received his own *vita* or *passio*, but many did. The *passio* devoted to Saint Leudegar, bishop of Autun, merits a closer look, for it reveals a blend of high politics, local interests and ideals of martyrdom that is characteristic of the hagiography of the period.

The *Passio of Leudegar* was written in the early 680s, shortly after the death of the protagonist.[19] According to the author of the *passio*, Bishop Leudegar rebuked King Childeric II for changing the customs of the kingdom and for marrying his first cousin. The text does not specify what 'customs' Leudegar defended, but the author emphasises the fact that the saint was very much opposed to Childeric's decision, especially since the king, so it is said, had previously ordered these customs to be conserved.[20] Leudegar warned Childeric that, unless he made amends, divine vengeance would soon be upon him. Initially, the author says, Childeric was prepared to 'listen freely' to what Leudegar had to say.[21] His hangers-on, however, were none too pleased with Leudegar's influence on the king, and persuaded Childeric to bring the holy man to death. From then on, according to the author, Childeric began to look for an opportunity to kill Leudegar. The author blames the king's change of heart on the envy of the magnates at his court, who were worried about losing their comfortable position if the king continued to pay heed to the criticism and advice of the saint.[22]

Leudegar had encountered opposition and setbacks before, according to the author of his *passio*, but this was the turning point in the narrative that set off the tragic events of his suffering and martyrdom. Leudegar was banned from the court, sent to the monastery of Luxeuil, tortured and blinded. Later on in the narrative, his tongue and lips are cut to stop him from speaking the truth. Yet Leudegar somehow retained his capacity to

---

[17] Fouracre, 'Why were so many bishops killed?', pp. 13 and 17.
[18] Fouracre, 'The origins', p. 156, 'Why were so many bishops killed?'; see also Fouracre, 'Merovingian history'.
[19] Fouracre, Gerberding, *Late Merovingian France*, p. 195.
[20] *Passio Leudegarii* 8, ed. Krusch, p. 290, lines 10–14.
[21] Ibid., ed. Krusch, p. 290, lines 15, 16: 'Et quidem primitus libenter coeperat auscultari'. On listening freely as the counterpart of speaking freely, see also the *Martyrium Polycarpi*, discussed in chapter 1 pp. 21, 22.
[22] *Passio Leudegarii* 8, ed. Krusch, p. 290, line 15–p. 291, line 5.

The Frank Holy Man

speak in spite of this mutilation, which demonstrated that his power of speaking came directly from God and could not be stopped by human intervention or physical impediment. Later, his tongue and lips miraculously grew back again, but this miracle did not mark the end of his sufferings. Leudegar was condemned to further exile, endured more physical abuse and, finally, was murdered. The narrative moment the author chooses as a catalyst to Leudegar's tribulations makes it clear that, in his view, the holy man paid the price for his outspokenness to King Childeric. Leudegar's suffering is presented as the unavoidable fate of the truth-teller, who fell victim to the envy of courtiers and the fickleness of a king, and died as a martyr for the truth.

The narrative plot of the *Passio of Leudegar* and other seventh-century *passiones* of bishops is very similar to that of the late antique narratives that have been discussed in previous chapters.[23] And yet, the *Passio of Leudegar* does not present us with the timeless portrait of a holy man who could have lived in any age, but offers a glimpse of the rough and tumble of high politics and local strife, of religious ideals combined with pragmatic actions. 'The integrity of a priest does not fear the threats of a king', the author of the *passio* assures his readers.[24] The strong emphasis on integrity amidst political turbulence was probably a response to contemporary criticism of the participation of bishops in politics, and an attempt to justify their political engagement.[25] Stories such as the *Passio of Leudegar* demonstrate that the rectitude of these holy bishops, themselves members of the political elite, was not compromised by their involvement in the affairs of the palace.

In Merovingian hagiography, just as in late antique hagiography, the ideal of frank criticism as a corrective to power is firmly attached to ideals of martyrdom. But the hagiographers portray their protagonists and their heroic deeds also with an eye to the pragmatic needs of contemporary society. The new martyr for the truth no longer needed to be radically separated from the world. Naturally, he was expected to think little of material gain, honour and worldly pleasures, in keeping with the traditional expectations inherited from late Antiquity. But if he happens to be a bishop, authors stress, he should not shy away from the

---

[23] For a parallel (and competing) account, see the *Passio Praejecti*, discussed in Fouracre, Gerberding, *Late Merovingian France*, esp. pp. 203, 288, 289.

[24] *Passio Leudegarii* 8, ed. Krusch, p. 290, line 10: 'sacerdotalis integritas minas regis nescit metuere'. The same proverb, in slightly different wording, occurs in the *Passio Praejecti* 24, ed. Krusch, *MGH SRM* 5, p. 239, line 21. The origin of the proverb has not been identified.

[25] Here I build on the argument of Paul Fouracre, 'The origins', p. 155; see also Kreiner, *The Social Life of Hagiography*.

responsibilities that come with his position in society. We find a similar appreciation of the duties of a leader, and a sympathetic understanding for the predicaments of holy men in politics, in the *Dialogues* of Sulpicius Severus, dedicated to the memory of Saint Martin of Tours (d. 397).

SAINT MARTIN'S PREDICAMENT

The narratives about the life and deeds of Saint Martin, known as 'the apostle of Gaul', provided an important model for Merovingian hagiography.[26] Sulpicius Severus (d. 425), the author of the *Dialogues* on Saint Martin, was born in Aquitaine and was a contemporary of his protagonist Martin. Inspired by Martin's lifestyle, he established an ascetic household on his estate Primulacium in Southern Aquitaine. In an earlier hagiographic text dedicated to Martin, the *Life of Martin,* Severus describes a scene in which the saint attended a banquet in the palace of Emperor Maximus at Trier and passed a cup of wine not to the emperor, as he was supposed to do, but to a priest. It is probably the best-known episode from the *Life of Martin,* showing him as an independent man of God, who was impervious to the machinations of power and had a blatant disregard for social conventions and court protocol. In the *Dialogues,* however, Sulpicius Severus presents a different side of the holy man. Here, Martin is not blissfully ignorant of the demands and expectations of his environment, but is confronted with the need to balance the interests of different parties.

The *Dialogues* relate a conversation between the author, Sulpicius Severus, his friend Postumianus, and Gallus, a disciple and confidant of Martin. Their conversation takes place on Severus' estate, Primulacium. On the second day of the conversation, Gallus shares his memories of his teacher Martin with his interlocutors. He recounts how one day, when Martin visited Emperor Valentinian I (r. 364–75), the emperor kept the doors of the palace closed, because he did not want to be bothered by Martin's petitions. A miracle blew the doors off their hinges and the throne of the emperor caught fire, which forced the unwilling Valentinian to jump up and greet the holy man.[27] After the shock, Gallus says, the emperor treated Martin with respect and granted every request he put before him. Yet Gallus also remembers another, less successful visit that Martin paid to the imperial palace in Trier: an

---

[26] Vielberg, *Der Mönchsbischof;* Stancliffe, *St. Martin and his Hagiographer.*
[27] Sulpicius Severus, *Dialogues,* II, 5, 5, ed. Fontaine, Dupré, p. 241.

The Frank Holy Man

event, Gallus hastens to add, that Martin himself always concealed.[28] Emperor Maximus (r. 383–8), Gallus begins his story, was led astray by the advice of some bishops. They had persuaded him to give his protection to Bishop Ithacius of Ossanuba, the main instigator of the execution of Priscillian, bishop of Avila (d. 385). Martin was one of the bishops who protested against the execution.[29] While the supporters of Bishop Ithacius were still assembled at the palace in Trier, Gallus says, Martin was on his way to the palace with several petitions to present to the emperor. The bishops were alarmed when they heard of Martin's coming, because they feared that his visit spelled trouble, and they plotted to prevent Martin from entering the palace. Their scheme, however, failed, and Martin managed to get access to the emperor. He pleaded with the emperor not to continue persecuting heretics in Spain.[30] The emperor did not immediately respond, says Gallus, but kept Martin waiting for two days. In the meantime, Martin went to the chapel to pray, alone, and abstained from having communion with Ithacius and his supporters, which they interpreted as a condemnation of their political advice and actions. The bishops, fearing that others would soon follow Martin's example, threw themselves weeping at the emperor's feet. They begged Maximus not to grant any of Martin's requests until he had agreed to have communion with them first.[31] The emperor did as he was asked, called Martin to him, and presented him with arguments as to why he should make his peace with Bishop Ithacius and his supporters. Martin was not impressed, Gallus says, and refused to comply with the emperor's urgent request. The emperor became inflamed with anger and stormed out of the room.[32]

Normally such a dramatic scene would present the climax of the narrative. But the story that Severus here presents to his audience does not follow the conventional pattern of the 'a holy man goes to the palace' narrative, in which the holy man speaks his mind to the ruler, remains unperturbed by either promises or threats, and leaves again, unshaken. Earlier visits by Martin to the palace that Severus recounts do indeed follow that traditional pattern. This time, however, negotiations go less smoothly. Shortly after his meeting with Emperor Maximus, Gallus says, Martin heard that the emperor had already appointed executioners for the people in Spain on whose behalf he had pleaded. He rushed to the palace and pledged that, if the people were spared, he would be prepared to have

---

[28] Ibid. III, 11, 1, ed. Fontaine, Dupré, p. 328.
[29] On Martin's involvement in the Priscillianist affair, see Burrus, *The Making of a Heretic*; Stancliffe, *St. Martin and His Biographer*; Chadwick, *Priscillian of Avila*.
[30] Sulpicius Severus, *Dialogues*, III, 11, 9, ed. Fontaine, Dupré, p. 334.
[31] Ibid. III, 12, 1–2, ed. Fontaine, Dupré, p. 336.
[32] Ibid. III, 12, 4, ed. Fontaine, Dupré, p. 338.

Part II

communion with Ithacius and his supporters. Now that Martin had agreed to the emperor's condition, Maximus was willing to grant all his requests. The next day, Martin took part in the communion. From that time onwards, Gallus says, Martin avoided getting mixed up with the party of Ithacius, but he was never the same man thereafter. Whenever he cured one of the possessed, recovery was slower than before and with less grace than usual. He lived for another sixteen years after this event, 'but never again did he attend a synod and he kept far from all assemblies of bishops'.[33]

Sulpicius Severus wrote his *Dialogues* in response to growing criticism of Martin and the ascetic lifestyle he had promoted in Gaul.[34] In the *Dialogues*, he draws a portrait of Saint Martin as a man of flesh and blood. Being a bishop, Martin carried responsibility for people entrusted to his care, which meant that he had to be willing to negotiate and compromise. Sticking to the part of the unbending holy man, Severus seems to argue, was not in the interest of his clients. In this account of Martin's confrontation with emperor Maximus, Severus does not offer his protagonist the escape route of a miracle to get out of this deadlock and walk away with his integrity intact, as he had done on previous occasions. This time, no throne miraculously catches fire. In Severus' narrative, the concession Martin is willing to make saves people's lives, but harms his good reputation (*fama*), his inner tranquillity and the efficacy of his healing powers. Severus does not explicitly condone or justify Martin's decision, but expresses a sympathetic understanding for the predicament of his protagonist and, by extension, perhaps also of other bishops who, like Martin, got their hands dirty when dealing with the unsavoury reality of politics.[35]

It is this pragmatic outlook, balanced against undiminished high religious ideals, that we also find in later hagiography in Merovingian Francia. Without suggesting that this outlook is unique and directly inspired by Sulpicius Severus' *Dialogues*, it should be noted that Severus' texts on Martin had a significant influence on Merovingian hagiography. The image of Martin of Tours, created by Sulpicius Severus, provided the main model of sanctity for hagiographers of this period and region.[36] Severus' *Life of Martin* was, however, much more popular than his *Dialogues*; it circulated widely shortly after it was written. In the fifth century, Paulinus of Perigueux wrote a metrical adaptation of

---

[33] Ibid. III, 13, 6, ed. Fontaine, Dupré, p. 342: 'nullam synodum adiit, ab omnibus episcoporum conventibus se removit.'
[34] Fontaine, Dupré, *Dialogues*, pp. 66, 67.
[35] See especially Sulpicius Severus, *Dialogues* III, 13, 4, ed. Fontaine, Dupré, p. 342.
[36] Fontaine, 'Hagiographie et politique', p. 113; see also Vielberg, *Der Mönchsbischof*.

Sulpicius' *Life of Martin,* and so did Venantius Fortunatus in the sixth century. The *Dialogues* fared less well. It was put on Pseudo-Gelasius' list of 'books not to be received by the church' (c. sixth century).[37] Gregory of Tours, however, a great admirer of Martin and promotor of his cult, did know the *Dialogues* and referred to the sensitive episode I have just discussed in his *Histories,* as we shall see in the next chapter.

HILARY AND NICETIUS: MARTYRS WHO LIVED

Earlier in this chapter, I pointed out that Merovingian hagiographers continued to connect the social value of frank criticism to ideals of martyrdom and self-sacrifice. Late antique martyrdom accounts provided hagiographers with a cultural model for opposition that brought out sharply the desired qualities of integrity and truthfulness in the highly competitive climate of Merovingian courts.[38] The narrative patterns and literary tropes of martyr acts offered a frame for recounting the life and glorious deeds of their protagonists, especially if they were bishops who were killed in the line of duty. Some hagiographers, however, were confronted with the problem that the subject they portrayed as a valiant champion of truth had died of natural causes. They needed to reconfigure the ideal of dying as a martyr for the truth to match the reality of the life of their protagonists.[39] Evidently, this had already been an issue for hagiographers writing in the post-persecution age, but in the Merovingian period it became an issue again, when so many, but not all, bishops suffered a violent death.[40]

The poet Venantius Fortunatus (d. 610) wrote a *Life* of Hilary of Poitiers, the teacher of Martin of Tours, around 566. Fortunatus was born in Italy, and moved to the Merovingian court in Metz to offer his services as a court poet. Fortunatus, who would later become bishop of Poitiers, had a penchant for the tropes of martyrdom. He cast the lives and deeds of his protagonists in terms of a militant martyr's life by preference, as becomes clear in his metrical version of Severus' *Life of Martin.*[41] In his *Life of Hilary,* Fortunatus recounts how Hilary 'threw himself undaunted

---

[37] (Ps-)Gelasius, *De libris recipiendis et non recipiendis,* ed. Dobschütz, p. 12: 'Opuscula Postumiani et Galli apocrypha'.
[38] I have borrowed the expression 'cultural model for opposition' from Philippe Buc, *Dangers of Ritual,* p. 152.
[39] On the reconfiguration of the ideals of martyrdom, see Stancliffe, 'Red, white and blue martyrdom'. For the earlier post-persecution period, see Markus, *End of Ancient Christianity,* pp. 85–94; Lössl, 'An early Christian identity crisis.'
[40] Fouracre, 'Why were so many bishops killed?'; see also the literature cited in the previous note.
[41] Roberts, 'The last epic of Antiquity', pp. 270, 271.

amidst the swords of the heretics' and 'approached the tribunal of the empire without fear of torture'.[42] In Fortunatus' opinion, Hilary surely would have gained the martyrdom he desired had times been different.[43] But God could not allow Hilary to be killed, he postulates, because he still had an important task to fulfil in Gaul. When heresy had brought the whole world into disorder, Fortunatus says, Hilary convened several synods in Gaul and brought people back to the way of truth.[44] The bishop could not have done that had he been killed or forced to remain in exile, though that would have brought more personal glory to him. What is better, Fortunatus asked rhetorically: to gain martyrdom and eternal life for oneself, or to live longer so that others may not perish?[45]

Fortunatus solved the tension between Hilary's courageous life and his quiet death and made him a different type of martyr for the truth, in accordance with the scenario sketched by Hilary himself. In fact, the similarities between Fortunatus' presentation of Hilary and Hilary's self-presentation in his invective *Against Constantius*, discussed in chapter 2, suggest that Fortunatus was familiar with this invective.[46] Hilary received the desired *palma martyrii*, Fortunatus argues, because he was willing to save the souls of others who were in danger of succumbing to heresy, rather than prematurely taking the glory of martyrdom for himself.[47] Dying as a martyr was heroic, certainly, but a Christian society also needed a few brave men who, although ready to die for the truth, stayed alive so that they could continue fighting to preserve the orthodoxy of the Christian faith, combat injustice and uphold the law and morals of the church.

Another bishop whose desire for martyrdom was thwarted was the aforementioned Bishop Nicetius of Trier (d. c. 566). Nicetius is credited with reprimanding the Merovingian king Theuderic for his sins on several occasions, taking a stand against King Theudebert in church, excommunicating King Chlothar more than once for his wrongful deeds and proclaiming imminent death to anyone who did not obey the commands of God.[48] According to his biographer Gregory of Tours (d. 594), who recorded Nicetius' deeds in his *Life of the Fathers*, some

---

[42] Venantius Fortunatus, *Vita Sancti Hilarii* 5 (14), ed. Krusch, p. 2, lines 37, 38: 'inter haereticos gladios se ingerebat intrepidus'.
[43] Ibid. 8 (30), ed. Krusch, p. 4, lines 26–8. [44] Ibid. 8 (31), ed. Krusch, p. 4, line 28–30.
[45] Ibid. 8 (3), ed. Krusch, p. 4, line 30–p. 5, line 1: 'Quid autem sibi interest, vel pro aeterna vita factum fuisse martyrem; vel amplius vixisse, ne reliqui perirent?'.
[46] Compare for example Venantius Fortunatus, *Vita Sancti Hilarii*, ch. 8 to Hilary, *In Constantium*, ch. 4.
[47] Venantius Fortunatus, *Vita Sancti Hilarii* 8 (32), ed. Krusch, p. 5, lines 1, 2.
[48] Gregory of Tours, *Vita patrum* 17, 1, ed. Krusch, p. 278, lines 24, 25; Ibid. 17, 2, ed. Krusch, p. 279, lines 17–23; Ibid. 17, 2, ed. Krusch, p. 280, lines 8, 9; Ibid. 17, 2, ed. Krusch, p.279, lines 14, 15.

people whose wicked deeds he had exposed hated him enough to kill him. Gregory says he heard that Nicetius' wish to die for justice was so deeply felt that he tried to give fate a hand and presented himself voluntarily to his persecutors, offering his neck to their raised swords.[49] Nonetheless, the martyrdom Nicetius desired was never granted to him, for God, says Gregory, did not allow that he be killed. On one occasion he was exiled, when he excommunicated King Chlothar once too often, but he was able to return the next day, because the king had died during the night.[50]

When Nicetius was still abbot, Gregory tells us, he became acquainted with King Theuderic I (r. 511–33/4). Theuderic respected and honoured the abbot because, in Gregory's words, he had often 'revealed to him his sins and by reprimanding his faults offered him a chance of improvement'.[51] The king was so taken with Nicetius' forthrightness that he offered him the bishopric of Trier. Nicetius accepted the offer, but made it clear from the start that he had no intention of becoming a puppet of King Theuderic's rule, and would not hesitate to oppose him if he did not agree with the king's decisions.[52] If we are to believe Gregory, King Theuderic appreciated Nicetius' critical, independent attitude and chose him precisely because of this quality.[53]

Gregory credits Nicetius with a special talent for detecting hidden vices and virtues that were not clear for everyone to see. The holy men whose lives Gregory narrates in his *Life of the Fathers* are often able to discern what is concealed to others.[54] Nicetius sees and knows things that others cannot, because God reveals them to him.[55] Another character trait that Gregory ascribes to Nicetius is immunity to the machinations of power. Nicetius is impervious to threats of violence and to the deception of flattery,[56] so nothing can stop him from rebuking kings or refusing commands that he thinks are unjust. In Gregory's words, Nicetius 'never honoured the person in power, but feared God alone, in his heart and in his deeds'.[57] Gregory ascribes this independent quality also

---

[49] Ibid. 17, 2, ed. Krusch, p. 280, lines 5–7.   [50] Ibid. 17, 3, ed. Krusch, p. 280, lines 17–22.
[51] Ibid. 17, 1, ed. Krusch, p. 278, lines 24, 25: 'saepius vitia eius nudaret, ac crimina castigatus emendatior redderetur'. Trans. James, p. 106.
[52] Ibid. 17, 1, ed. Krusch, p. 279, lines 4–6
[53] Ibid. 17, 1, ed. Krusch, p. 278, lines 24–27 ('ob hanc gratiam').
[54] Uhalde, 'Proof and reproof', p. 3.
[55] Gregory of Tours, *Vita patrum* 17, 4, ed. Krusch, p. 282, lines 5, 6.
[56] Ibid. 17, 3, ed. Krusch, p. 280, line 25: 'nec minitantem timuit, nec a blandiente dilusus est.' The same quality of integrity is ascribed to Bishop Leudegar of Autun; see *Passio Leudegarii* 8, ed. Krusch, *MGH SRM* 5, p. 290, line 10 (see the quotation in note 24) and ibid. 4, ed. Krusch, p. 287, lines 3–5; *Passio Praejecti* 24, ed. Krusch, *MGH SRM* 5, p. 239, line 21.
[57] Gregory of Tours, *Vita patrum* 17, 1, ed. Krusch, p. 279, lines 8, 9: 'Non enim honorabat personam potentis, sed Deum tantum et in corde et in operibus metuebat.'

Part II

to Bishop Quintianus of Rodez (d. 525), when he says in his *Life of Quintianus*: 'He never feared the person of the powerful man, but he always had in everything a holy liberty (*libertas*).'[58] Here, *libertas* does not refer to free speech, at least not directly, but to an inner disposition that makes it possible to speak truth to power. It is this independence of mind that, in Gregory's narratives, enables a holy man to detect hidden virtues and vices in others. We have encountered a similar claim in Themistius' oration to Emperor Constantius II.[59] Moral authority, a pure heart, a free mind and the ability to discern true from false formed the preconditions for telling the truth.

At the beginning of the *Life of Nicetius*, Gregory has Nicetius, then still abbot, deliver a speech to his monastic community in which he stresses the importance of speaking aright. Nicetius admonishes the monks to avoid jokes and idle words and open their mouths only to praise God. Just as the monks present their bodies entirely pure to God, he says, so their mouths should be pure too.[60] In Gregory's account of Nicetius' life, following this opening chapter, his speaking voice is prominently present. But it is not the temperate voice of the former abbot that we hear throughout the rest of the narrative, but the thundering voice of the prophet. No sooner has Nicetius been made bishop than he threatens sinners with excommunication, reprimands the powerful and reveals their secret sins 'in the voice of a public crier' (*voce praeconia*).[61]

We have seen evidence of this strident voice, which Gregory ascribes to Nicetius, in the outspoken letter the bishop sent to Emperor Justinian, discussed at the beginning of this chapter. If one measures the Latinity and style of the letter against classical standards, or compares his rhetoric of free speech with learned precedents, Nicetius' letter may be found wanting. But we can also measure his letter against a different standard, namely that of the frank holy man in Merovingian hagiography. Nicetius speaks to Emperor Justinian as a prophet to a sinner, warning him of impending doom unless he repents. Thus, Nicetius conforms to the image of the holy man that we find in the hagiographical narratives of the time. In previous chapters, we often saw a discrepancy between narratives describing the brisk speech of a critic before a ruler and the effusive rhetoric of actual letters and speeches of criticism.[62] Such a discrepancy cannot be found between the letter of Nicetius and the

---

[58] Gregory of Tours, *Vita patrum* 4, 5, ed. Krusch, p. 227, lines 6, 7: 'nec metuit personam potentis, sed una eademque ei fuit in omnibus sancta libertas.'
[59] See chapter 3, p. 73. [60] Gregory of Tours, *Vita patrum* 17, 1, ed. Krusch, p. 279, lines 16–21.
[61] Ibid. 17, 1, ed. Krusch, p. 279, lines 3, 4; Ibid. 17, 2, ed. Krusch, p. 280, line 15.
[62] See for example the contrast between the polite rhetoric of Ambrose's letters to Theodosius and the description of his rebuke of the emperor in the ecclesiastical histories, discussed in chapter 4.

protagonist of Gregory's *Life of Nicetius*. In his admonitory letter to Justinian, Nicetius speaks to the emperor with the bellowing voice of the prophet, just as Gregory says he did and just as other frank holy men are reported to have done before him.

FRANK HOLY WOMEN

Merovingian hagiography also features a few truth-telling holy women. This is quite remarkable, seeing that women are hardly ever acknowledged as truth-tellers in classical and medieval narratives. Although some of the prerequisites for free speech, such as sincerity, constancy, lack of ambition and imperviousness to wealth and power are also ascribed to (holy) women, other virtues and character traits that were traditionally associated with free speech, such as independence and disregard of authority, were not considered desirable attitudes for women. When, from late Antiquity onwards, free speech became progressively entwined with the priestly office, and especially with the office of bishop, women were automatically excluded, since they had no access to the priesthood. The stock text on frank speech from the Book of Ezekiel, in which God commands the prophet to be a watchman of the house of Israel and warn people against sin, was not applied to holy women. There was no concept of the 'watchwoman'. And yet, female martyrs had been credited with *parrhesia* and *libertas* in early martyrdom accounts, as we have seen in chapter 1. They were reported to have resisted fearlessly secular authority when their faith and integrity as Christians was under threat.

We see a similar frank attitude ascribed to holy women in Merovingian hagiography. The female protagonists, often queens and aristocratic women, display attitudes that were considered appropriate for women (obedience to their husbands and to priests, modesty, reticence), but their social role was very similar to that of holy men. Just like their male colleagues, female saints were expected to bring the suffering and complaints of their 'clients' to the attention of authorities. They interceded on behalf of prisoners, they were able to discern what was hidden to others, they worked miracles that testified to their privileged access to God and they spoke out in defence of truth to those very same authorities to whom they owed obedience and deference.[63] It was generally acknowledged that obedience to God's will superseded obedience to earthly authorities. This rule of exception, which applied to both men and women, creates some leeway for frank speech in the narrative

---

[63] See for example the *Life of Radegund* II, 2, the *Life of Eustadolia* 6, the *Life of Rusticula* 5, 10 and 15, the *Life of Balthild* 4, trans. McNamara et al., *Sainted Women*, pp. 87, 109, 125, 128, 130, 270.

representations of the lives of holy women, even if speaking frankly to authorities was not in accord with the norms of proper female behaviour.

Merovingian female saints' lives were modelled after the same examples as the male saints' lives, namely martyrdom narratives and the lives of late antique holy men, in particular the *Life of Martin*. In the sixth-century *Life* of the holy virgin Genovefa of Paris (d. c. 520), the author, who may have been a monk or cleric from the *schola* of Tours,[64] explicitly compares the virtues and deeds of Genovefa to those of Martin of Tours.[65] Like Martin, Genovefa cures the sick, drives out demons, frees prisoners, represents the interests of the poor and the oppressed, and comes to the rescue when her city is under siege. According to the author, King Childeric held the holy virgin of Paris in high esteem, although sometimes he wished to avoid her meddling in his affairs.[66] One day, when she went out of the city, the author recounts, Childeric ordered the gates closed so that Genovefa could not rescue the captives he meant to execute. When Genovefa was informed of the king's intentions, she immediately set off to save the lives of the captives. The people were amazed, the author explains, when they saw the city gate opening by itself when Genovefa 'touched it without a key'.[67] She gained the king's presence and persuaded him not to behead his captives.

The story bears a remarkable similarity to the story that Sulpicius Severus recounts about Saint Martin visiting the palace of Valentinian. There, the doors miraculously blow open; here, they open by themselves by the mere touch of the virgin. The message of the story is that one cannot stop a saint on a mission. No doors or locks are solid enough to keep holy men, or women, from bringing petitions on behalf of those in need of their intercession to the attention of the ruler and speaking their mind in his presence.

MASONA OF MÉRIDA

Let us now turn to Visigothic Spain to see how the person and the performance of a frank holy man is portrayed in other Latin regions of the former Roman Empire.

The *Lives of the Holy Fathers of Mérida* narrates the lives of the bishops of Mérida in the second half of the sixth and first half of the seventh century. The text is taken to have been written in the seventh century and is commonly attributed to Paul the Deacon of Mérida, an author

---

[64] McNamara et al., *Sainted Women*, p. 28, n. 1.
[65] *Vita Genovefae* 14, ed. Krusch, p. 220, lines 15–21.   [66] Ibid. 26, ed. Krusch, p. 226, lines 6, 7.
[67] Ibid. 26, ed. Krusch, p. 226, lines 11–12: 'se porta civitatis inter manus eius sine clave reseravit'.

The Frank Holy Man

otherwise unknown. In the *Lives of the Holy Fathers of Mérida,* special attention is paid to the life of Bishop Masona (d. c. 606), who held the bishopric of Mérida from about 570 until his death. In his *Life of Masona,* Paul looks back to a period when the Visigothic kingdom was ruled by an Arian king, and the city of Mérida had an Arian as well as a Catholic bishop. Bishop Masona is reported to have supported Arianism before he converted to Catholicism. Paul describes Masona as a man of steadfast character 'who rebuked the Arian king [Leovigild] as was his duty and repudiated his heresy'. He tells us that King Leovigild (r. 568–86) called for a debate between Masona and his rival Sunna, bishop of the Arian community of Mérida. At stake was the church of Saint Eulalia, which both parties coveted for their own. Paul recounts how Masona won the debate thanks to his superior eloquence and debating skills, and thus won the church of Eulalia for the Catholic party.[68] But Sunna was a poor loser, says Paul, and started scheming against the man of God, whispering accusations in the ears of the Arian king.[69] Leovigild removed Masona from his see and had him brought before him. Paul's description of their confrontation reads like a scene from a martyr's acts, with a tyrant interrogating a martyr and putting him under pressure to renounce his faith:

When he [Masona] arrived at Toledo and stood in the presence of the fierce tyrant, the king reviling him with many insults and assailing him with many threats sought with all the power of his depraved will to draw him to the Arian heresy. Although the man of God willingly bore all the abuse that was heaped upon him and calmly put up with everything he gently but without hesitation answered what the rabid dog barked at him and, disregarding personal insults but pained at the outrage to the Catholic faith, resisted the tyrant bravely.[70]

Like a true martyr for the (Catholic) faith, the steadfast bishop cannot be persuaded to abandon his position. While the king is raging, he remains cool and undisturbed. Masona's equanimity is reminiscent of the composure of the polite martyrs of the early martyr acts discussed in chapter 1. Masona does not lose control over his emotions but replies 'gently but without hesitation' to the king's threats, which maddens Leovigild even

---

[68] Paul the Deacon of Mérida, *De vita patrum Emeritensium* 11, *PL* 80, cols. 141B–143C. I thank Stuart Airlie for the reference to this debate.
[69] Ibid. 12, *PL* 80, col. 144A.
[70] Ibid. 12, *PL* 80, col. 144C: 'Cumque pervenisset ad civitatem Toletanam, et atrocissimi tyranni conspectibus astitisset, plurimis eum rex lacessens conviciis, multisque terroribus pulsans, ad haeresim Arianam omni adnixu pravae intentionis pertrahere cupiebat: sed cum vir Dei omnes sibi illatas contumelias libenter toleraret, coepit tamen adversus ea, quae rabidus canis oblatrabat, cum omni mansuetudine incunctanter respondere, et omissis propriis contumeliis, pro injuriis catholicae fidei condolens, ipsi tyranno audaciter resistere.' Trans. Garvin, *Medieval Iberia,* p. 9.

further.[71] Enraged by Masona's imperturbability (*constantia*) the king eventually dismisses him from his presence and put him away in a monastery.[72] After Masona had been in exile for three years, Paul tells us, the holy virgin Eulalia appeared to Leovigild in a dream. Paul presents Eulalia in a militant manner, much as Prudentius had in his *Crowns of Martyrdom,* as we have seen in chapter 1. There, Eulalia appeared as a formidable martyr, who stood no nonsense from a tyrant and spit in the eyes of her interrogator. In Paul's narrative, Eulalia is no meek lady either. She physically assaults the king and demands that Masona be reinstated in Mérida. Leovigild, who fears further beatings from the saint, releases Masona from exile.

Paul's *Lives of the Fathers of Mérida* is in many respects very similar to Gregory's *Lives of the Fathers* and other Merovingian saint's lives and martyrdom accounts. The narrative patterns of the two series of biographies are close to those of late antique martyr acts. Perhaps in the case of Paul's *Lives* the tropes of martyrdom stand out even more prominently, given that he describes the lives of Catholic bishops under Arian rule. Although Arianism was certainly an issue for Gregory of Tours, generally speaking the frank bishops and holy men of Merovingian hagiography dealt with kings who were perhaps sinful and unjust, but were still Catholics, from King Clovis onwards.[73] Because of this different religious situation, not so much of the authors, but of the local truth-tellers whose lives they narrated, the problems that provoke their protagonists into action and that provide the topics of their truth-telling differ. Paul's Bishop Masona holds his own against the Arian king, but we do not hear him upbraid the king in order to improve his behaviour or change the course of his politics, as Leudegar and Nicetius are reported to have done. Paul's holy men are more concerned with heresy and orthodoxy than with moral improvement or with political policy in a wider sense. That said, the similarities between Paul's *Lives* and Merovingian hagiographies exceed the differences, which is hardly surprising seeing that the authors borrowed from the same late antique sources and shared the same cultural heritage. When it comes to local power structures and competition for resources, as Paul Fouracre observes, 'Visigothic Mérida is very much like Merovingian Poitiers'.[74]

---

[71] Less polite is Masona in ibid. 12, *PL* 80, col. 146B, where he mocks King Leovigild.
[72] Ibid. 12, *PL* 80, col. 144D and col. 145C.
[73] For Gregory's issues with what he perceived as the Arian threat, see Goetz, 'La compétition entre catholiques et ariens'.
[74] Fouracre, 'Why were so many bishops killed?', p. 29.

The Frank Holy Man

Let us now return to Francia for another example of cultural entanglement across different kingdoms and areas of the former Roman Empire, and turn to Saint Columban, an Irish *peregrinus* in Merovingian Francia, whose life and deeds were narrated by an author operating in the Lombard kingdom.

AN IMPUDENT BABBLER

Between 639 and 643, Jonas of the monastery of Bobbio in the Lombard Kingdom wrote a biography of the Irish *peregrinus* Columban (d. 615). As one of his influences, Jonas mentions Venantius Fortunatus' *Life of Hilary*, in which Hilary of Poitiers is portrayed as a champion of truth and tireless defender of orthodoxy against the Arians.[75] Columban was born in Meath, a kingdom in Ireland. When he reached the age of forty, his abbot gave him permission to travel to the Continent. When the reputation of the holy man reached the ears of the Merovingian king Sigebert (r. 561–75), Jonas recounts, the king invited Columban to his court to see for himself what kind of man he was. The king was much impressed by Columban's learning and held him in high honour, as did the rest of his court.[76] When the day came that Columban wished to leave the palace again, the king begged him to remain in the kingdom of Austrasia. Although the king respected the holy man's need to withdraw into solitude, he asked him not to wander too far away. He would not like to see the prosperous influence of Columban's counsel, prayers and mere presence go to one of the neighbouring kingdoms, so he pleaded with the holy man to stay, at least within the borders of the kingdom.[77]

Columban complied with the king's wish and settled with his disciples near an abandoned Roman fortress at Annegray in the Vosges, a place which Jonas claims to be a great wilderness. From this allegedly lonely spot, Columban continued to advise and admonish Sigebert's successor Theuderic. Theuderic thought himself fortunate to have Columban in his kingdom and regularly came to visit the holy man in his hermitage to ask for his prayers.[78] Columban, however, gave him more than the prayers and spiritual counsel Theuderic asked for: he rebuked the king sternly for sharing his bed with concubines instead of with a lawful wife. King Theuderic promised to mend his ways, but

---

[75] Kreiner, *The Social Life of Hagiography*, p. 99.
[76] Jonas of Bobbio, *Vita Columbani* 6, ed. Krusch, p. 162, l. 16–p. 163, line 1.
[77] Ibid. 6, ed. Krusch, p. 163, lines 1–15.   [78] Ibid. 18, ed. Krusch, p. 186, lines 9–12.

Part II

when Brunhild, the dowager queen, who was according to Jonas a second Jezebel, incited her grandson against the man of God, it came to a conflict between the king and the holy man.[79] When Columban refused to give in to threats and intimidations, he was taken prisoner and sent to Besançon.

In his *Life of Columban,* Jonas creates an image of Columban as an outspoken and morally upright man of God, who is not easily intimidated by kings or queens. In a liturgical poem which he attached to his *Life of Columban,* Jonas describes Columban as a 'philosopher among nobles and prophet among kings'.[80] Jonas places his description of Columban explicitly in the tradition of biographies of holy men, such as Athanasius' *Life of Anthony,* in the Latin translation of Evagrius, and Sulpicius Severus' *Life of Martin*.[81] As Albrecht Diem has noted, 'Columban the *peregrinus* is described as an outsider who refuses to become part of any social structure.'[82] The historical Columban was at least as frank as Jonas makes him out to be, as would appear from the letters that have survived from his hand.[83] Although no letters are extant in which Columban reprimands a king, there are several directed at bishops and popes. In these letters, Columban adopts the stance of the outspoken outsider. He presents himself as a stranger who had come from the other end of the world, and spoke his mind in the way he had been wont to do back in his own country.[84]

In a letter to Pope Boniface IV (608–15) Columban admonishes the pope, urging him to end the schism that separated Lombard Italy from communion with Rome. The aforementioned edict of Emperor Justinian, against which Nicetius protested and which had sparked the Three Chapters Controversy, resulted in a schism that divided East and West and also led to opposition from the churches of Northern Italy against Rome. The Lombard king Agilulf (r. 590–616), an adherent of 'Arianism', appears to have been concerned about the disruptive effects that the schism had on the churches under Lombard rule.[85] He asked Columban, who had recently arrived in Italy, to write to Pope Boniface

---

[79] Ibid. 19, ed. Krusch, pp. 187–93. This episode is discussed in Diem, 'Monks, kings and the transformation of sanctity', pp. 531–5; O'Hara, *The Legacy of Columbanus,* pp. 50–4; Heydemann, 'Zur Gestaltung der Rolle Brunhildes', pp. 79–80; Nelson, 'Queens as Jezebels', pp. 28–30.

[80] Wood, 'The *Vita Columbani*', p. 71; see Jonas of Bobbio, *Versus in eius festivitate,* ed. Krusch, p. 224, line 11: 'Te sofum proceres, te vatem dixere reges.'

[81] Diem, 'Monks, kings and the transformation of sanctity', p. 524.   [82] Ibid., p. 524.

[83] On Columban's frankness, see Mary Garrison's forthcoming study on 'Insular parrhesiasts'.

[84] Columban, *Ep.* 5, 11, ed. Walker, p. 48, lines 10, 11: 'et libertas paternae consuetudinis, ut ita dicam, me audere ex parte facit'.

[85] In particular, the churches of Aquileia and Milan. On the 'Aquileian schism', see Sotinel, 'The Three Chapters and the transformations of Italy' and Pohl, 'Heresy'. On Columban's involvement, see Gray, Herren, 'Columbanus and the Three Chapters controversy.'

and ask him to mediate in the conflict. In his letter to the pope, Columban states quite frankly that it is high time that the pope deals with the problem. Conflicts such as these are detrimental to the unity of the Church, Columban argues, and keep Arians such as King Agilulf from embracing the Catholic faith.[86] Columban shows he is aware of the incongruity of the fact that he, a foreign monk, is telling the pope what to do, and begins his letter by introducing himself in a self-deprecating manner: 'Who would listen to a bald man? Who would not say at once: who is this impudent babbler that dares to write such things without being asked?'.[87] After this self-consciously ironic opening, he silences his imaginary critic before he can even open his mouth to ask why this exile, this *peregrinus*, should venture to address the pope on such a delicate matter.[88] Columban's response to that critic, in whose mouth he puts objections that he imagines the pope and the audience of the letter will have to his frankness, is that one should not pay attention to the lowly status of the speaker, or to the impudence of his speech, but only to the worthiness of the topic. 'There is no impudence', Columban argues, 'where there is a need to edify the Church.'[89] He appeals to Boniface to do everything in his power to reunite the Church and resolve the division caused by the papacy's condemnation of the Three Chapters.[90] He asks the pope to believe him when he says it was not vainglory or impudence that inspired him to write, but sadness and sorrow.[91] He assures him that he is his friend and disciple, and for this reason he would not speak as a stranger (*non alienus loquar*) but speak out freely (*libere eloquar*) as a friend.[92] Although Columban presents himself as an outsider in the salutation of the letter, introducing himself to Pope Boniface as a foreigner writing to a native (*peregrinus indigenae*), he here reverses his position and assures the pope that the person who addresses him this frankly is not an *alienus* (an outsider, a stranger to the family) but a friend and close follower. Speaking freely as a friend is contrasted to speaking as a stranger; a friend could say things a stranger could not. At the same time, it was his outsider position that enabled Columban to address

---

[86] Columban, *Ep.* 5, 8, ed. Walker, p. 44, lines 25–8.
[87] Columban, *Ep.* 5, 2, ed. Walker, p. 36, lines 22, 23: 'Quis poterit glabrum audire? Quis non statim dicat: quis est iste garrulus praesumptuosus, qui non rogatus talia scribere audet?'.
[88] On Columban's self-designation as *peregrinus*, see Johnston, 'Exiles from the edge?'.
[89] Columban, *Ep.* 5, 2, ed. Walker, p. 36, lines 26, 27: 'non esse praesumptionem ubi constat esse necessitatem ad ecclesiae aedificationem'.
[90] Ibid. *Ep.* 5, 12, 13, ed. Walker, pp. 49–50; O' Hara, *Jonas of Bobbio and the Legacy of Columbanus*, p. 56.
[91] Columban, *Ep.* 5, 1 and 16, ed. Walker, pp. 35 and 54.
[92] Ibid. *Ep.* 5, 3, ed. Walker, p. 38, lines 11, 12: 'Ego enim ut amicus, ut discipulus, ut pedisequus vester, non ut alienus loquar; ideo libere eloquar.'

the pope on this controversial topic.[93] Being a pilgrim and an Irishman, he had no part in the religious struggle that divided the churches of Italy, which made him a suitable broker to mediate in the conflict.

Before the conflict can be solved, however, some issues have to be brought out in the open. As the pope's friend and supporter, Columban feels it is his duty to inform Boniface of the rumours that are circulating about him. People are calling him a schismatic and a supporter of heretics behind his back. Naturally, says Columban, when he heard these accusations soon after he had arrived in Italy, he defended the pope against these critics who reviled him.[94] Although he does not personally believe these accusations to be true, he advises the pope to convene a council and silence these critical voices once and for all. Rumours and suspicions, he says, tarnish the pope's authority and the doctrinal orthodoxy of the papal see.

Throughout the letter, Columban continues appealing to the pope to acknowledge the awkward position that he, Columban, has found himself in. He was but a blunt Irish pilgrim, a bald babbler, an inhabitant of the world's end, and yet he was the one who took up the courage to speak out to him. Where others have remained silent, or slandered him in private, he berates the pope openly.[95] He asks Boniface to trust his good intentions; if his words have come across as thoughtless or excessive, he should not set it down to arrogance but to the tactlessness (*indiscretio*) of a stranger.

Walker, the editor of Columban's letters, suspects that it was the Irish saint's outspokenness that often landed him in quarrels and conflicts. He attributes Columban's frankness to the 'tenacious independence' of his mind.[96] Columban himself put the audacity of his speech down to the customs of his country. In the same letter to Pope Boniface, he writes: 'The freedom of my country's customs (*libertas paternae consuetudinis*), to put it so, is partly the cause of my audacity.'[97] This could be read as a mild denigration of his Irish *libertas*, if it were not followed by this proud statement: 'For amongst us it is not a person's standing but his reasonable judgment that counts.'[98] Columban implies that in his home country there is no strict hierarchy that determines who is allowed to speak to

---

[93] Compare 'non ut alienus loquar' (ibid. 3) to 'noli despicere consiliolum alienigenae' (ibid. 4). Columban is a foreigner (*alienigena*) but not a stranger (*alienus*).

[94] Ibid. Ep. 5, 3, ed. Walker, p. 38, lines 31–6.

[95] Ibid. Ep. 5, 14, ed. Walker, p. 52, line 31: 'peregrinum Scotum hebetem'; Ep. 5, 1, ed. Walker, p. 36, line 23: 'garrulus praesumptuosus'; Ep. 5, 8, ed. Walker, p. 44, line 16: 'Ego enim de extremo mundo veniens'.

[96] Walker, *Sancti Columbani opera*, p. xxi.

[97] Columban, Ep. 5, 11, ed. Walker, p. 48, lines 10, 11: 'libertas paternae consuetudinis, ut ita dicam, me audere ex parte facit'.

[98] Ep. 5, 11, ed. Walker, p. 48, lines 11, 12: 'Non enim apud nos persona, sed ratio valet.'

whom on the basis of status (*persona*), as is the case on the Continent, but rather on the basis of sound judgement (*ratio*). Mary Garrison has suggested that Columban's *libertas* may well testify to an insular learned tradition which kept classical–biblical rhetorical knowledge alive that was lost elsewhere.[99] Columban's letters, but also the letters of Boniface and Alcuin, she argues, reveal a classical vocabulary of free speech that had virtually disappeared from contemporary Continental letters.[100] One could, however, also relate the frank tone that stands out in the letters of Columban, Boniface and other insular *peregrini* to their status as outsiders, rather than to any indigenous tradition of frank speech. Kings and popes were perhaps more inclined to accept a breach in decorum from a foreigner than from someone of their own circle who could be expected to know how to behave and how to strike the right tone. As Paul Fouracre observes, unlike Merovingian bishops who clashed with rulers, foreigners who ran afoul of those in power were never killed, probably because they were not considered a political threat.[101] Following this line of reasoning, a foreigner such as Columban could get away with more frankness than a local truth-teller who was part of the network of high or local politics, and therefore a possible rival or contender for positions of power.

Nonetheless, when comparing Columban's letter to Pope Boniface with Bishop Nicetius' letter to Emperor Justinian, or to any of the other letters written in Francia in this period, one cannot fail to notice that the Frankish letters do not contain any terms or phrases from the classical lexicon of free speech, whereas Columban's letters do. A similar contrast can be observed between Columban's own letters and Jonas' description of Columban's frankness in his *Life of Columban*. Words and expressions that Columban uses to refer to his freedom of speech (*libertas, libere eloqui*) in his letters do not occur in Jonas' *Life of Columban*, although Jonas gives ample room to his saint's verbal clashes with Merovingian kings.

Columban's letters were, however, not all about frankness. In reading the letter he wrote to Pope Boniface, or the letter he wrote to Pope Gregory the Great, it becomes clear that Columban combined frank speech with deference, erudition, rhetorical refinement, flattery and, last but not least, self-directed irony. In the salutation of his letter to Pope Boniface he introduces himself with many different denigrating self-descriptions. He is a peasant (*agrestis*), a prattler (*micrologus*), a poor creature (*pauperculus*), a rare bird (*rara avis*). When he finally reveals his name at the end of the salutation, he does so in yet another act of self-

---

[99] Garrison, 'The Insular parrhesiasts: Alcuin, Boniface, Columbanus – Free speakers abroad', paper delivered at the International Medieval Congress, Leeds, 15 July 2009; Garrison, 'An aspect of Alcuin', p. 150.
[100] Ibid.   [101] Fouracre, 'Why were so many bishops killed?', p. 29.

Part II

mockery: 'the Pigeon dares to write to Pope Boniface.'[102] Pigeon (*palumbus*) is a pun on his name Columbanus, 'dove', and carried as a second meaning 'the one who is easily fooled'. The effect of such little self-directed ironic jokes in a letter of criticism should not be underestimated. By presenting himself as an 'impudent babbler', or a 'blunt Irishman', while profusely apologising for his impudence, he takes the sting out of his frankness. As John Martyn has suggested, the 'Irishman's erudite and very rhetorical letter would have tickled the Pope's fancy rather than offend him'. Columban's simultaneously self-styled and real position as a foreigner and outsider served him in his role as critic and as an intermediary for others. Being a *peregrinus* without ties, possessions or a home, he was free to go where he pleased, to say what he pleased and to rebuke whom he pleased. The only punishment rulers or bishops could impose on him was exile and exclusion, but being a pilgrim he was in a perpetual state of exile anyway.

LETTER TO A QUEEN

The hagiographical texts that have been discussed so far in this chapter testify to a continued appreciation of late antique ideals on frank speech as a corrective to politics. Merovingian biographies display narrative tropes that are familiar from late antique hagiography, especially with regard to the character and performance of the truth-telling holy man, which suggests that these tropes continued to embody ideas and social values that were relevant to a contemporary audience. Letters written by Merovingian bishops can be seen to reflect norms and values that were propagated in late antique and contemporary biographies of frank holy men speaking truth to power. Bishop Remigius of Rheims, for example, in a letter to King Clovis, persuades the king to get rid of flatterers and surround himself with sound advisers: a topical piece of advice that we find in biographies of frank holy men and in ceremonial speeches to emperors.[103] There were other long-standing conventions that guided the rhetoric of the authors of these letters. Merovingian bishops were expected to act as spokesmen for their cities and report rumours to the ruler, just as their late antique episcopal predecessors had done, who, in turn, had inherited this responsibility from the pagan philosophers.[104] It was the bishops' duty to represent the interests of the poor and the oppressed, ask for the release of prisoners and speak for those who had

---

[102] Columban, *Ep.* 5, 1, ed. Walker, p. 36, lines 20, 21: 'Scribere audet Bonifatio Patri Palumbus'.
[103] Remigius of Rheims, *Epistola ad Chlodoveum regem*, ed. Gundlach, *MGH ep.* 3, III, 2, p. 113.
[104] Brown, 'Gregory of Tours: Introduction', pp. 24–7.

no voice in political councils and decisions. The fact that bishops were expected to report rumours to a ruler offered letter-writers the rhetorical possibility of presenting criticism in the guise of rumour reports ('I am not saying this, of course, but I heard people say that ... '). We have just seen an example of this type of indirect criticism by means of a rumour report in the letter of Columban to Pope Boniface, which shows that it was not only bishops who employed this rhetorical device.

Around 575, Bishop Germanus of Paris (d. 576) wrote a letter to Queen Brunhild, in which he makes clever use of this strategy to distance himself from the unpleasant message he had to deliver. He implores the queen to persuade her husband, King Sigebert I of Austrasia, to put a stop to the violence that has been ravaging the Austrasian kingdom during the fraternal war between Sigebert and his brother Guntram, king of Burgundy. Rumour had it that Brunhild was the instigator of this violence and had pitted Sigebert against his brother.[105] Germanus greets the queen respectfully, addressing her as 'daughter of the church'. Immediately after the respectful opening, Germanus comes straight to the point: he wishes to make a suggestion. He wastes no time with further pleasantries to warm up his addressee before broaching the topic. Although the statement of purpose is rather abrupt, suggesting the author is about to speak frankly without beating about the bush, the language in which Germanus phrases his purpose is ornate and deferential: 'Since love (*caritas*) rejoices in truth and sustains all things and never transgresses, therefore with a troubled heart (*contribulato corde*) but with deepest love from the spirit (*ex intima animi dilectione*) we dare to make a suggestion.'[106] Germanus justifies his daring initiative to offer a suggestion, to the queen of all people, with a reference to the two traditionally acceptable emotional motives for speaking frankly: sorrow and love. He combines them with a third emotional motive that prompts him to speak the truth: Christian *caritas*, which, he says, quoting from Paul's letter to the Corinthians, 'rejoices in truth and endures all things and never transgresses'.[107]

Germanus, however, offers more than a suggestion. He confronts Brunhild with the rumoured allegation that she has instigated her husband, Sigebert, to wage war against his brother. The region and the people, Germanus would have Brunhild know, are now on the verge

---

[105] Germanus of Paris, *Epistola ad Brunhildam reginam*, ed. Gundlach, *MGH, Epp.* 3, III, 9, p. 122.
[106] Ibid., ed. Gundlach, p. 122: 'Quia "caritas congaudet veritati et omnia sustinet et numquam excedit" [1 Cor. 13:6–8], propterea et contribulato corde, sed ex intima animi dilectione audemus suggerere.'
[107] The Vulgate has 'caritas numquam excidit' ('love never dies'), but Germanus probably knew a version of the Vetus Latina which had 'excedit' ('love never transgresses').

Part II

of destruction as a result of this fraternal war. It is a serious charge to put before a queen to suggest that she is responsible for this, so Germanus goes about it carefully. He assures Brunhild of his spiritual love for her and his concern for her well-being, and emphasises that he is not accusing her of anything; he is only reporting what people are saying about her, so as to give her a fair warning.[108]

Germanus refrains from naming the persons responsible for spreading these rumours, as if to protect his sources.[109] He distances himself from the content ('we do not say this because we believe it') and assures Brunhild that he takes no pleasure in bringing this allegation to her attention.[110] However, he cannot be reticent, seeing that Brunhild's prosperity and reputation are in danger. He advises her to take the biblical queen Esther as an example, who pleaded with her husband, King Ahasuerus, to spare her people.[111] Brunhild, says Germanus, should likewise persuade her husband Sigebert to stop the violence and protect the inhabitants of the ravaged regions of the Austrasian kingdom. He draws an implicit comparison between Esther's outsider status as a Jewish queen at a Persian court and Brunhild's position as a queen of Visigothic descent at a Frankish court. Germanus reminds Brunhild of the warm welcome she received when she first arrived in Francia to marry Sigebert. The people of Austrasia, Germanus says, rejoiced when they received her, to which he adds bleakly: 'for it seemed to see salvation, not destruction through you'.[112] With this emotional appeal to Brunhild's honour and sense of gratitude, Germanus persuades the queen to represent the interests of the people of this region, who once put their hope in her. He encourages her to speak to Sigebert on their behalf, mitigate his rage, and prove the rumours wrong.[113] If not, Germanus adds prophetically, Brunhild and her children will derive no triumph from the destruction of the kingdom.[114] Germanus emphasises again that he does not enjoy saying this, but he has to speak out 'since it is ordered to priests: "Like a trumpet raise your voice and declare their works to my people"'.[115]

By writing this letter, Germanus did indeed show that he did not hesitate to raise his voice and confront Brunhild with rumours about the wrongs she had allegedly committed, and yet he does not call her to repentance. Such a call would have been rather difficult to make, seeing

---

[108] Germanus, *Ep.*, ed. Gundlach, p. 122, line 35–p. 123, line 3.   [109] Ibid. p. 123, line 8.
[110] Ibid. p. 123, lines 10–12: 'Non propterea haec dicimus, quasi a nobis credatur.'
[111] Ibid., p. 124, line 15.
[112] Ibid., p. 123, line 27: 'ut per vos salutem, non interitum percipere videatur'.
[113] Ibid., p. 123, lines 27, 28.   [114] Ibid., p. 123, lines 25, 26.
[115] Ibid., p. 124, lines 2–4: 'Sed quia sacerdotibus praeceptum est: "Ut tuba exalta vocem tuam et adnuntia populo meo opera eorum [Isa. 58:1]".'

The Frank Holy Man

that he did not write as a critic but as a rumour reporter. Germanus does not adopt the persona of the truth-telling holy man, but that of a diligent bishop, who is doing his duty in bringing rumours of discontent among the people entrusted to his care to the attention of the court. He concludes his letter by commending the bearer of the letter, a man by the name of Gundulf, to the queen and he presses her to listen to the words that he has sent orally through him.[116]

The duty to report rumours, which Germanus uses as a shield of protection, was more than a rhetorical device to veil criticism and create a safe distance from the unpleasant message. As Peter Brown points out, it was a long-established practice, connected to the late antique institution of the *audientia episcopalis,* to bring rumours to the attention of a ruler or magistrate. As the fourth chapter of first book of the *Codex Iustinianus* of 529 has it, in a section dedicated to the jurisdiction exercised by bishops, bishops should intercede with magistrates or with the emperor on behalf of others. 'If a bishop fails to do so', the Code of Justinian warns, 'he incurs both God's and the emperor's anger, because by remaining silent in a servile manner he is not worthy of the free speech (*libera lingua, parrhesia*) that is fitting for a bishop.'[117]

Germanus' letter to Brunhild reveals a rhetoric that is reminiscent of late antique letters and speeches of admonition, such as the appeal to sorrow and love as prime motives for speaking frankly that we find recommended in the rhetorical treatise *Ad Herennium*. It is, however, not likely (although not impossible) that Germanus was familiar with the precepts of rhetorical treatises, for he had not received a traditional rhetorical education. Germanus was born in Autun at a time when the public schools of rhetoric had already disappeared from Gaul.[118] He went to a local school at Avallon and received further education under the guidance of his cousin, a priest. But the fact that Germanus was not trained in rhetoric, at least not in the same way as his earlier Gallo-Roman contemporaries or late antique Mediterranean colleagues had been, does not mean that he did not know how to write a letter of criticism and advice, with all the proper rhetorical trimmings, as is evident from his letter to Brunhild.

Germanus may have learned the rhetoric of frankness via a different route. For the art of how to speak frankly was not necessarily learned by

---

[116] Ibid., p. 124, lines 22–5.
[117] *Codex Iustinianus* I, 4 (*De episcopalis audientia*), 26, 5, Latin version: 'quod si religiosissimus episcopus praetermittit, dominum deum infensum habebit et imperatoriam indignationem expectet quod servilem in modum et indignum libera lingua [the Greek version of the *Codex Iustinianus* has *parrhesia* here], qualis sacerdotem decet, tacuerit.'
[118] Riché, *Education and Culture*, pp. 177–291.

reading theoretical treatises or by practising declamation in schools; it could also be mastered through imitation. In the words of Mary Garrison: 'Just as early medieval people of the era before the *ars dictaminis* learned to write letters by copying models rather than using a dictaminal manual, so, too, would the practice of *parrhesia* have been understood and acquired more by model than by precept.'[119] Although the term *parrhesia* probably meant little or nothing to Germanus, he did know how to speak frankly to a ruler in a manner that was both clear and safe, and he may well have learned this particular rhetorical practice from imitating models. As Ian Wood suggests, fifth- and sixth-century letter collections such as those of bishops Avitus of Vienne, Ennodius of Arles, Ruricius of Limoges and Sidonius Apollinarus of Clermont may have functioned as handbooks of style.[120] The letter collections, which also contained poems, secular speeches and sermons, were probably put together to provide models for correspondence, poetry, administration and perhaps also for the composition of public speeches.[121] These letter collections, assembled between the fifth and seventh century, met a need for written models for letters and speeches and provided an alternative form of rhetorical education after the Roman schools of rhetoric disappeared.[122]

Germanus' letter to Brunhild was incorporated into a seventh-century letter collection, known as the *Epistolae Austrasiacae*. Besides Germanus' letter to Brunhild, the collection of Austrasian letters also contains several other letters of Merovingian bishops to kings and queens to offer them criticism or advice, such as a letter of Bishop Remigius to King Clovis, of Bishop Aurelian to King Theudebert and of Bishop Nicetius to Princess Chlodosinda. It also includes Nicetius' letter to Emperor Justinian, with which I started this chapter. It is possible that these letters were included to provide epistolary models of frank criticism that fitted the circumstances of Post-Roman Gaul.

CONCLUSION

The holy men and women of the Merovingian period, who corrected their kings and other superiors bravely and frankly, acted as intermediaries for the poor and oppressed or spoke out in defence of truth, are presented in accounts of their lives in roughly the same manner as their late antique counterparts. As has been pointed out on several occasions in this chapter,

---

[119] Garrison, 'An aspect of Alcuin', p. 149, with reference to Lanham, 'Freshman composition'; Garrison, 'Letters to a king'.
[120] Wood, 'Letters and letter-collections' pp. 41, 42. See also, on the *Epistolae Austrasiacae*, Garrison, 'Letters to a king' and Hen, 'The uses of the Bible'.
[121] Wood, 'Letters and letter-collections', p. 42.   [122] Ibid., p. 42.

The Frank Holy Man

the narrative patterns of Merovingian saints' lives closely resemble those of late antique narratives. Martyr acts, the lives of the desert fathers, church histories and other narratives about free-spoken heroes of the Christian past offered Merovingian hagiographers a route to become acquainted with the rhetoric of free speech. These texts imparted ideas and ideals of free speech to the audience that read them or heard them being read. They transmitted legitimacy as well as codes of conduct to those who wished to be known as truth-tellers, or to the authors recording their deeds. By rendering directly or indirectly the words that the bishop or holy man had addressed to the ruler, hagiographers transmitted notions of acceptable modes of delivering criticism. Rhetorical knowledge and ideals of free speech thus travelled via routes other than rhetorical tracts and school education alone. When, in the fifth century, the public schools of rhetoric closed and the availability of a rhetorical education could no longer be taken for granted in every major city of the early medieval West, ideas on how one should, or could, speak frankly to superiors were passed on through stories about free-speaking bishops, holy men and martyrs, and through model letters.

Merovingian frank holy men were thus represented in much the same way as their late antique predecessors. The language, however, in which the speech of Merovingian saints is described is different. Regardless of how frankly these holy men and women spoke to kings or other authorities, no mention is made of *libertas dicendi, libere loqui, licentia, oratio libera* or any other term or expression by which frank speech was usually denoted in late antique literature. Nor does one come across any of these terms in letters of admonition or exhortation that bishops and other authors in the Merovingian period wrote to kings and queens to correct and encourage them. Columban's letter to Pope Boniface, in which he refers to a tradition of free speech (*libertas*) in his country to justify the frank tone of his letter, is a remarkable exception.[123]

In Merovingian saints' lives and letters the traditional vocabulary of free speech does not occur. We do find the term *constantia* or the adverb *constanter* as a stock attribute of a saint who is impervious to threats and promises, but it is rarely used in connection with frank speech. Traditional terms for free speech do not occur in the *Life of Martin* either, the main model of Merovingian hagiography, even though that text was written in the fifth century by an author steeped in classical learning. Although Sulpicius Severus' *Life of Martin* is in all other respects very much part of the late antique tradition of representing truth-telling holy

---

[123] Another exceptional case is that of the writings of Pope Gregory the Great (d. 604), who was born and educated in Rome. See for example *MGH, epistolae, Gregorii papae registrum* I, 24, p. 31.

men, specific terms to denote free speech are lacking. But the absence of words in a certain language does not imply that the concepts to which these words refer are absent as well.[124] A semantic field is not identical to a conceptual field. People can talk about, think about and discuss concepts, even without using exactly corresponding words for them. As the linguist David Crystal puts it: 'The fact that [a certain language] has no word for an object, does not mean it cannot talk about that object; it cannot use the same mechanical means to do so, but it can utilise alternative forms in its own structure for the same end.'[125] Therefore, if the authors of Merovingian saints' lives and letters do not employ particular words to denote the concept of free speech it does not automatically imply that the authors and their audiences did not think about or discuss free speech. Or, to put it plainly: the fact that people did not say it, does not mean they did not do it.

In Merovingian saints' lives, in letters to kings and emperors, and, as we shall see in the next chapter, in historiography, critics speak and behave in ways that closely resemble classical and late antique free speech, but they describe and discuss these actions using different words. Straightforward criticism is contrasted to flattery and insincerity, or to figured or indirect speech. The positive paradigmatic references of frankness are still constancy, steadfastness, equanimity and confidence, while the negative paradigmatic references are arrogance, impudence and presumption. I should like to suggest that this stable structure of representation of free speech provided a lasting framework for people in Merovingian Gaul and other areas of the former Roman Empire to think about, discuss and use free speech, after the traditional words for 'free speech' went out of use.

---

[124] It is a misconception to think that the unit of translation-equivalence is the word. Concepts can be translated to another language, without the word that denoted the concept being translated by another single word. Thiselton, *Thiselton on Hermeneutics*, p. 205, referring to David Crystal, 'Language, linguistics and religion'.

[125] Crystal, 'Language, linguistics and religion', p. 144, quoted in Thiselton, *Thiselton on Hermeneutics*, p. 205.

7

GREGORY OF TOURS

In 580, Bishop Gregory of Tours (d. 594) was charged with treason and summoned to appear before a council.[1] The former count of Tours, Leudast, had informed King Chilperic (r. 561–84) that Gregory was plotting against the king and planned to hand the city of Tours over to his nephew Childebert II. According to Leudast, Gregory had also been spreading malicious slander about Queen Fredegund, alleging that she had had an affair with Bishop Bertram of Poitiers. This accusation put Gregory in a tight spot. Although it was a bishop's duty to report rumours to the court, spreading slander was quite a different matter.[2] In the competitive climate of Merovingian courts, gossip and defamation were factors of considerable political significance. Rumours informed political strategies and could be used as weapons against one's adversaries.[3] King Chilperic, who considered a slur on his wife to be a direct insult to himself, did not take the accusations lightly. He convened a council of all the bishops of his kingdom in his villa at Berny-Rivière to investigate the matter, and summoned Gregory to defend himself. Meanwhile, Count Leudast, who apparently had an axe to grind with his former bishop Gregory, rounded up witnesses from among Gregory's own clergy to testify against him. At the trial, Gregory denied all charges of treason and slander. He declared that he had never said anything of the sort, he would not listen to such talk and the idea had never even crossed his mind. In the meantime, an uproar arose among the people assembled outside the villa. They demanded to know why the king had proceeded with this case and why these attacks were being made on the priest of the Lord. They were of the opinion that it was not right to accept the

---

[1] On Gregory's trial, see Wood, *Gregory of Tours*, pp. 48–50; Halsall, 'Nero and Herod?', Heinzelmann, *Gregory of Tours: History and Society*, pp. 47, 48. This paragraph follows Gregory's description of the events in Gregory, *Liber historiarum* V, 49, ed. Krusch, Levison, pp. 258–61.
[2] On the bishop's duty to report rumour, see chapter 6 pp. 154–157.
[3] Dolan, "You would do better to keep your mouth shut."

Part II

evidence of inferiors against a bishop, and that the king ought to accept Gregory's statement of innocence. The king decided to listen to the people and offered Gregory the opportunity to clear himself by a sworn statement and offer Mass at three different altars. Thus, the trial had a positive outcome for the bishop, who was cleared of all suspicion, and for the king, who had shown himself to be a just ruler. According to Gregory, all those who had gathered at the villa admired the king's discretion and patience.[4]

Among the guests at the villa was the poet Venantius Fortunatus, who delivered a panegyric to Chilperic and the assembled clergy in defence of his patron Gregory.[5] He lauded the queen's virtues, praised the king's piety and godly rule, and strongly advised him to let bygones be bygones.[6] Fortunatus' panegyric thus countered the tainted honour of the king and queen, and replaced it with the image of a virtuous and successful royal couple. By presenting Chilperic with the ideal of magnanimous kingly behaviour, Fortunatus offered him an opportunity to distance himself from the charges against Gregory without loss of face.[7]

Gregory recounts the story of his trial at Berny-Rivière in one of the many autobiographical episodes that are woven into the narrative of his *Histories*.[8] His *Histories* present a history of the church from Creation to the present day, with a strong focus on recent events in the Merovingian kingdoms and in his own diocese, Tours.[9] In the first book of the *Histories*, he treats the period from Adam and Eve until the death of Saint Martin, after which he moves on to Frankish history, and then to contemporary history. Gregory describes direct confrontations between bishops and kings, between political opponents and between bishops amongst themselves. Regularly Gregory was personally involved in the confrontations he describes, especially from book five onwards. At the

---

[4] Gregory, *Liber historiarum* V, 49, ed. Krusch, Levison, p. 261, lines 5–6: 'Mirati sunt omnes regis vel prudentiam vel patientiam simul.'
[5] Venantius Fortunatus, *Carmen* 9, 1. On Gregory's relationship to Fortunatus as friend and patron, see Roberts, 'Venantius Fortunatus and Gregory of Tours'.
[6] George, 'Venantius Fortunatus: Panegyric in Merovingian Gaul', p. 241.
[7] Ibid., p. 240. For a different interpretation, see Roberts, 'Venantius Fortunatus and Gregory of Tours', pp. 45–46, who suggests that the panegyric was delivered at the end of the proceedings, to celebrate the restoration of order. Gregory does not mention the panegyric, offered in his defence, in his *Histories*.
[8] See note 1. On the function of autobiographical elements in Gregory's historiographical narrative, see Heinzelmann, *Gregory of Tours: History and Society*, pp. 36–88.
[9] On the *Histories*, see Goffart, *Narrators of Barbarian History*; Mitchell, Wood, *The World of Gregory of Tours*; Wood, 'Secret histories'; Wood, *Gregory of Tours*; Heinzelmann, *Gregory of Tours: History and Society*; De Nie, *Views from a Many-Windowed Tower;* Breukelaar, *Historiography and Episcopal Authority*; Van Dam, *Saints and Miracles*; Reydellet, *La royauté*; Buc, *Dangers of Ritual*, pp. 88–122; Murray, 'The composition', and now Reimitz, *History, Frankish Identity,* especially pp. 27–43.

Gregory of Tours

end of the last book, Gregory entrusts his *Histories* to the care of the bishops who were to succeed him in Tours. He calls on them to see to it that the books are copied faithfully, just as he has written them, without omitting, rewriting, selecting or abridging anything.[10] But the intended audience of his *Histories* was probably much wider than the future bishops of Tours. The political criticism expressed throughout the work suggests that Gregory also wrote his chapters with an eye to the successors of the kings he had dealt with in the course of his episcopal career. In his *Life of the Fathers*, discussed in the previous chapter, Gregory had put bishops and holy men in the spotlight who were not afraid to reprimand a king. In the *Histories* he pictures himself as such a brave bishop, whose courage towards rulers is in no way inferior to the fearlessness of the saints and bishops whose lives he had recorded.

All case studies in this book focus on letters of one particular author who criticised a person in power. This chapter is the exception, in that it treats not letters but a historiographical narrative, Gregory's *Histories*, to see how the author presents himself as a truth-telling actor in the historical events he describes. It examines the models that may have inspired Gregory to present himself as a fearless defender of truth, and analyses the ways in which he embeds criticism in the autobiographical parts of his narrative. Two well-known episodes that Gregory describes in his *Histories* in which he confronts a Merovingian king will be studied in more detail; one concerns a clash with Chilperic I (d. 584), king of Neustria, and the other a brush with Guntram (d. 592), king of Burgundy. A question that will be addressed towards the end of this chapter is that of how Gregory's professed ideal of telling the truth frankly relates to the reports of rumours and gossip in his *Histories*.

A PLAIN SPEAKER

Gregory of Tours was born in 539 in Clermont in the Auvergne, as Georgius Florentius. He was born into an influential senatorial Gallo-Roman family that had held the see of Tours for generations. Gregory was entrusted to the household of his uncle, the bishop of Clermont, where he received his education. In his writings, Gregory complains about his lack of education and rhetorical training, which he blames on a general decline of the study of the liberal arts in Gaul.[11] In the preface to

---

[10] Gregory, *Liber historiarum* X, 31, ed. Krusch, Levison, p. 536, lines 2–15.
[11] Gregory, *Liber historiarum*, preface, ed. Krusch, Levison, p. 1, lines 1, 2, but see also ibid. X, 31, ed. Krusch, Levison, p. 536, lines 8–14.

his *Histories,* he apologises for his unpolished style, but also highlights the advantages of his colloquial speech. 'A few people understand a philosophising rhetorician', he writes, 'but many can follow a plain speaker.'[12] The 'rustic' character of Gregory's Latin should, however, not be exaggerated. Although his writings have long been regarded as symptomatic of the deteriorating quality of education in Gaul, today scholars are re-evaluating Gregory's idiosyncratic style, his creative agency and the episodic quality of his *Histories.*[13] In the opinion of Neil Wright, Gregory may not have been well-versed in classical literature and his grasp of grammar may have been shaky, but his prose was carefully structured and he made effective use of rhetorical figures.[14]

In 573, Gregory was ordained bishop of Tours, during the reign of King Sigebert of Austrasia (r. 561–75). Being a descendant of prominent Gallo-Roman senatorial families, Gregory was a valuable ally to the Merovingian kings, who in turn supported his episcopacy in Tours.[15] Helmut Reimitz describes Gregory as a 'cultural broker', who mediated between the people of Tours, his *civitas,* and the representatives of the Merovingian *regnum.*[16] He was on intimate terms with four Merovingian kings, although his relations with them were not always friendly. He often found himself at odds with them, especially with King Chilperic, who ruled Tours from 575. Next to the *Histories* and the *Life of the Fathers,* discussed above, Gregory wrote the *Miracles of Saint Martin,* the *Book of Martyrs* and the *Book of Confessors,* in which he collected the life stories and miracles of the saints and martyrs of his day. Gregory was very interested in holy men, confessors and martyrs, and in the ways in which these saints continued the history of salvation. He was especially devoted to Saint Martin, the patron saint of his church and the city of Tours, and actively promoted his cult. In his *Histories* he intersperses his narration of the main political events of his day with stories about martyrs, saints and holy bishops, and records their deeds in the service of the Church. The literary models he drew on for this type of history writing were Eusebius' *Ecclesiastical History* (in Rufinus' Latin translation), the chronicle of Eusebius-Jerome and Orosius' *Histories against the Pagans.* In the first chapter of the *Histories,* Gregory indicates that he places his own work in the tradition of these

---

[12] Ibid., preface, ed. Krusch, Levison p. 1, line 14: 'Philosophantem rhetorem intellegunt pauci, loquentem rusticum multi.'
[13] For an overview of recent, more appreciative views on the composition of Gregory's *Histories,* see Murray, 'The composition', especially pp. 71–3, and for the current re-evaluation of his Latinity and style of writing, see Hen, *Roman Barbarians,* pp. 6–10.
[14] Wright, 'Columbanus's epistulae', p. 38. On Gregory's style of writing, see also Beumann, 'Sermo rusticus'.
[15] Reimitz, *History, Frankish Identity,* p. 32. [16] Ibid., p. 29.

ecclesiastical authors.[17] Yet, as Walter Goffart and Marc Reydellet have observed, the later books of Gregory's *Histories* that focus on contemporary events resemble classical Roman histories such as those of Tacitus and Ammianus rather than Eusebius' school of Christian historiography.[18]

In the *Histories* as well in the *Life of the Fathers*, Gregory includes stories about holy men who spoke frankly to their rulers. In his *Life of Nicetius*, as we have seen in the previous chapter, he recounts how Bishop Nicetius of Trier did not shrink from excommunicating King Chlothar for his unjust deeds.[19] Gregory's stories are highly illustrative of ideas that were prevalent in sixth-century Gaul on the importance of frank speech and political criticism. Particularly telling in this respect is Gregory's account of the trial of Praetextatus, bishop of Rouen, who was accused (in Gregory's eyes, falsely) of having committed an act of treason against King Chilperic.[20] The main protagonist in this story is, however, not Bishop Praetextatus, but Gregory himself. Gregory recounts how he stood up against the king and told him frankly that he would not remain silent when an innocent man and fellow bishop was sent into exile. Before he squared up to Chilperic, however, Gregory confronted his fellow bishops, who had gathered for a council in Paris to decide upon Praetextatus' fate.

THE TRIAL OF PRAETEXTATUS

Bishop Praetextatus of Rouen (d. 586) was accused of handing out bribes to induce people to murder King Chilperic. Rumour had it that he planned to hand over the kingdom to Merovech, Chilperic's son. When the accusation came to Chilperic's attention, he ordered Praetextatus to be removed from his see, until his case was heard by a council of bishops. Praetextatus was already in Chilperic's black books, for the bishop had recently married Merovech to his aunt, Brunhild, much to the annoyance of his father Chilperic. In 577, bishops convened in the church of St Peter in Paris to investigate the matter. At the first day of the trial, Gregory tells us, after King Chilperic had interrogated Bishop Praetextatus in the presence of the bishops and had returned to his lodgings, all the bishops sat together in the *secretarium* of the church to

---

[17] Goffart, *Narrators of Barbarian History*, p. 157; Gregory, *Liber historiarum* I, 1, ed. Krusch, Levison, p. 3, lines 16, 17.
[18] Reydellet, *La royauté*, p. 434; Goffart, *Narrators of Barbarian History*, p. 118.
[19] Gregory, *Vita patrum* 17, 3, ed. Krusch, p. 280, lines 17–22.
[20] On the trial of Praetextatus, see Buc, *Dangers of Ritual*, pp. 100–6; Wood, 'Secret histories', pp. 268–9, Reimitz, *History, Frankish Identity*, pp. 39–43.

discuss the matter amongst themselves. Then Archdeacon Aetius of Paris entered the consistory and addressed the bishops. He urged them to raise their voices and speak out in defence of their brother. If they failed to do so, Aetius said, they were not worthy to be called priests of God.[21] According to Gregory, no bishop dared to reply, because they feared the fury of Queen Fredegund, whom they suspected of being the instigator of the malicious rumours against Praetextatus and the origin of the charges against him.[22] They remained seated with 'their finger pressed to their lips', the common sign for silence and a physical expression of their obstinate refusal to speak out.[23] Since none of the bishops responded to Aetius' challenge, Gregory joined in and reminded the bishops of their duty to give the king good advice:

'I beg you, most holy priests of the Lord, pay attention to my words, and especially you who seem to be in the king's confidence. Give him holy and priestly advice, so he will not burst out in fury at God's servant and be destroyed by his anger and lose his kingdom and fame.' When I said this all remained silent. As they sat there tight-lipped, I added: 'Be mindful, my lord bishops, of the word of the prophet when he says: "If the watchman sees the iniquity of a man and does not announce it, he shall be guilty for a lost soul." Therefore do not be silent but speak out and place the king's sins before his eyes, lest some disaster should occur and you should be responsible for his soul.'[24]

Gregory calls the bishops to account for neglecting their priestly task as royal anger-managers. They should prevent the king from 'bursting out in fury at God's servant'. Their task, as presented by Gregory, is a familiar one: just like the philosophers of old, bishops should help the king control his anger. By giving him 'holy and priestly advice', they were to soothe the king's anger and keep him from committing a serious offence against one of God's ministers. As Gregory reminds the bishops, the consequences of royal sin could be disastrous. If Chilperic were to commit this atrocious act, he might lose his kingdom and his fame, and 'be destroyed by his anger' (*pereat ab ira eius*). Quoting a key passage from the stock repertoire of biblical injunctions that were used to argue for

---

[21] Gregory, *Liber historiarum* V, 18, ed. Krusch, Levison, p. 217, lines 16–20.
[22] Ibid. V, 18, p. 217, lines 21–2.
[23] For the common sign of silence, see Dutton, *Charlemagne's Mustache*, p. 130.
[24] Gregory, *Liber historiarum* V, 18, ed. Krusch Levison, p. 218: '"Adtenti estote, quaeso, sermonibus meis, o sanctissimi sacerdotes Dei, et praesertim vos, qui familiariores esse rege vidimini; adhibite ei consilium sanctum atque sacerdotalem, ne exardiscens in ministrum Dei pereat ab ira eius et regnum perdat et gloriam." Haec me dicente, silebant omnes. Illis vero silentibus, adieci: "Memento, domini mi sacerdotes, verbi prophetici, quo ait: 'Si viderit speculatur iniquitatem hominis et non dixerit, reus erit animae pereuntes [Ezek. 3:17–19; 33:6].' Ergo nolite silere, sed praedicate et ponite ante oculos regis peccata eius, ne forte ei aliquid mali contingat et vos rei sitis pro anima eius."'

frank speech, Gregory recalls that bishops are the watchmen, the *speculatores*, who should warn people against sinning.[25] Although this passage from the Book of Ezekiel refers to the responsibility of 'the watchman' for all souls, not just for the souls of kings, the passage was often quoted specifically in reference to a bishop's responsibilities towards his ruler.[26] If bishops witness injustice and say nothing, Gregory argues, they will be responsible for a lost soul: in this case, the soul of King Chilperic.

Gregory recounts that he concluded his speech by reminding the bishops of the unfortunate fate of King Chlodomer, who murdered Sigismund and his wife and sons against the advice of Abbot Avitus of Micy, and was killed when he marched into Burgundy with his army. He then continues with another cautionary tale of what can happen to a ruler who does not listen to sound advice and acts unjustly towards a servant of God:

What of the emperor Maximus? He forced the blessed Martin to hold communion with a bishop who had committed murder. Martin consented to this impious ruler, for he hoped that he might more easily free those who had been condemned to death. Maximus, pursued by the judgment of the eternal king, was pushed from his *regnum* and condemned to a most cruel death.[27]

Gregory paraphrases this story about Saint Martin and Maximus, discussed in the previous chapter, which Sulpicius Severus had recorded in his *Dialogues*, a work with which Gregory was well acquainted.[28] Just like Emperor Maximus, who was led astray by the false advice of flattering bishops, King Chilperic was now about to commit a crime against a servant of God, while his bishops did nothing to hold him back. Helmut Reimitz interprets Gregory's comparison between the Praetextatus case and the Saint Martin story as part of a strategy to make himself and Chilperic part of the same history as Saint Martin and Maximus, and promote a radical Christian vision of the world.[29] Meinolf Vielberg suggests that Gregory chose this particular story to

---

[25] The reference is to Ezek. 3:17–19 or to Ezek. 33:6. The two passages in Ezekiel are rather similar in wording.

[26] See for example Facundus of Hermiane, *Pro defensione* XII, 5, 5; Ambrose, *Ep. extra collectionem* 1a, 2 or *Ep.* 74, 2; Columban *Ep.* 5, 5; Boniface, *Ep.* 78. For late antique references to Ezek. 3:17–19 in the context of a discussion of the bishop's duty to speak out, see chapter 5, pp. 122–124.

[27] Gregory, *Liber historiarum* V, 18, ed. Krusch, Levison, p. 218: 'Quid Maximus imperator? Cum beatum Martinum compulisset communicare cuidam homicide episcopo, et ille, quo facilius addictus morte liberaret, regi impio consensisset, prosequente regis aeterni iudicio, ab imperio depulsus Maximus morte pessima condemnatus est.'

[28] Gregory, *Liber historiarum* X, 31, ed. Krusch, Levison, p. 527: 'De cuius vita tres a Severo Sulpicio libros conscriptos legimus.' This is a reference not to Sulpicius Severus' *Life of Martin*, as it is sometimes interpreted to be, but to the three books of his *Dialogues* about Martin.

[29] Reimitz, *History, Frankish Identity*, p. 43.

Part II

cast himself in the role of Saint Martin, who fiercely resisted the condemnation and execution of Bishop Priscillian against a majority of bishops at great personal risk, much as Gregory was now defending Praetextatus.[30] The analogy between the two cases is indeed striking, but if it had been Gregory's intention to compare himself to Martin, he should perhaps have quoted another passage from the *Dialogues* or from Sulpicius Severus' *Chronicle,* where the author actually discusses Martin's intervention on behalf of Priscillian. For, in the passage from the *Dialogues* that Gregory paraphrases here, Martin does not forcefully resist the emperor and his sycophant bishops, but does the exact opposite and gives in to the ruler's wishes. In Gregory's words, Martin 'consented to an impious ruler' and agreed to do what he knew was wrong, that is, to hold communion with a murderous bishop, in the hope of gaining pardon for the lives of others. Perhaps Gregory chose this particular contentious episode in the life of Martin to underline the importance of accepting a compromise and giving in to a ruler's demands to obtain a greater good, but I do not think so. It is more likely that the moral of the story that he wished to underline concerned Emperor Maximus, who was struck by God's vengeance for the way he treated Martin, just as King Chilperic was about to treat Praetextatus unfairly. Whatever the reason that Gregory picked this particular story, it did not have the desired effect on the assembled bishops. According to Gregory, no one answered. Instead they sat there, 'stunned and petrified'.[31]

CRITICISM GOES BOTH WAYS

When Gregory had finished his speech, two of the bishops immediately rushed off to the king to report what Gregory had said. Thus, they brought into the open what the bishops had discussed among themselves in the church's *secretarium*. Gregory calls them *adulatores,* flatterers. The bishops maintained that no one was more hostile to the king than Gregory. Thereupon, King Chilperic sent one of his courtiers to summon Gregory to appear before him. When Gregory arrived, Chilperic called him to account for his alleged attempt to incite the other bishops against him. He asked Gregory why he was behaving unjustly towards him. Gregory answered:

'O king, if any of us [bishops] should want to overstep the path of justice, it is for you chastise him. But if it is you who should transgress, who will censure you?

---

[30] Vielberg, *Der Mönchsbischof*, pp. 127, 128.
[31] Gregory, *Liber historiarum* V, 18, ed. Krusch, Levison, p. 218: 'sed erant omnes intenti stupentes'.

Gregory of Tours

For we can speak to you, and if you wish to do so, you listen. But if you refuse to listen, who condemns you, except he who has proclaimed he is justice?'[32]

Gregory's phrase 'loquimur enim tibi', 'we can speak to you' is an allusion to Psalm 118:46: 'et loquebar in testimoniis tuis in conspectu regum et non confundebatur', 'I spoke of thy testimonies before kings: and I was not ashamed', another biblical text from the standard repertoire of frank speech and admonition.[33] Psalm 118:46 was traditionally associated with martyrs, who freely and openly testified to their faith in Christ before their interrogators.[34] Perhaps because of this association with the courage and free speech of martyrs, late antique and early medieval authors came to think of this particular psalm verse as referring to priests and bishops who spoke freely before kings.[35]

In his reply to Chilperic, Gregory indicates that he considers criticism to be a reciprocal undertaking between a king and his bishops.[36] Just as the king chastises (*corrigere*) bishops if they have committed an injustice, so the bishops should censure (*corripere*) their king if he has acted unjustly. Against the king's accusation that he, Gregory, has put the bishops up against their legitimate ruler, Gregory counters that he has merely done his duty as a bishop to monitor the dispensing of justice in the kingdom. Gregory's answer did not placate the enraged king. Far from it: their altercation turned into an most unpleasant argument, with Chilperic threatening to unmask Gregory before the inhabitants of Tours as an unfair man, at whose hands not even a king could find justice, while Gregory in turn threatened Chilperic with the judgement of God if he did not heed the law and the canons.[37] This was not the first, nor the last time that Gregory and Chilperic locked horns.[38] Gregory's unbending attitude, his refusal to be intimidated by the king's anger or persuaded by

---

[32] Ibid., p. 219: 'Si quis de nobis, o rex, iustitiae tramitem transcendere voluerit, a te corrigi potest; si vero tu excesseris, quis te corripiet? Loquimur enim tibi, sed si volueris, audis; si autem nolueris, quis te condemnavit, nisi is qui se pronuntiavit esse iustitiam?'.

[33] See chapter 5, p. 124.

[34] See Augustine, *Enarrationes in psalmos, In psalmum* 118, *sermo* 14 and Hilary of Poitiers, *Commentary on Psalm 118*, 6, 10, here associated with saints, discussed in chapter 2.

[35] See for a later example the ninth-century *Third Life of Saint Liudger* (after 864), where this psalm verse is applied to *sacerdotes* and the adverb *libere* has been added to the Psalm's verb *loqui*: 'Sacerdotes libere de testimoniis Dei in conspectu regum loquantur'. Altfrid, *Vita Liudgeri tertia*, II, 42, ed. Diekamp, p. 111.

[36] On mutual correction of bishops and rulers, see De Jong, *The Penitential State*, especially pp. 112–47; De Jong, 'Transformations of penance', pp. 211–15; De Jong, '*Admonitio* and criticism of the ruler', especially pp. 319, 322–7.

[37] Gregory, *Liber historiarum* V, 18, ed. Krusch, Levison, pp. 219, 220.

[38] Heinzelmann, *Gregory of Tours: History and Society*, pp. 140–4 lists their confrontations in his summary of the structure of book five.

flattery or bribes, exasperated King Chilperic and fuelled his anger, at least according to Gregory's representation of events.

In spite of Gregory's efforts on his behalf, the trial did not end well for Bishop Praetextatus. Some of Chilperic's sycophants tricked Praetextatus into making a false confession and admitting that he indeed was an evil murderer who had planned to kill the king and place his son on the throne.[39] King Chilperic demanded that Praetextatus should have his tunic torn, that Psalm 108(109) with its maledictions against Judas Iscariot should be recited over his head, that he should be excommunicated and that his verdict should be recorded in writing. Gregory protested that this procedure was not according to the canons, but to no avail. Praetextatus was thrown into prison and later sent into exile.[40] A few years later he was murdered in his own church. According to Gregory, it was Queen Fredegund who sent the assassins.[41]

Not long after the trial of Praetextatus, another event provoked a heated discussion between Gregory and Chilperic.[42] King Chilperic had issued a decree on the Trinity, which stated that no distinction should be made between persons in the Holy Trinity. From now on, Chilperic declared, people should refer to the Trinity simply as God. Chilperic had the decree read out to Gregory and ordered him to accept his pronouncement as an article of his own faith. Gregory refused and tried to persuade Chilperic to abandon what he considered to be an ill-founded belief, for the apostles and the church fathers had taught differently. According to Gregory, Chilperic was annoyed by his refusal to accept his decree and replied in a huff that he would put the matter to men who were wiser than Gregory. To this, Gregory replied: 'Anyone who is prepared to accept your proposals will not be a wise man but a fool.'[43] The king gnashed his teeth, and turned to Salvius, the bishop of Albi, to propound his views to him instead. Salvius, however, rejected the king's proposals even more vehemently than Gregory had done. According to Gregory, he would have torn the decree into shreds, had he been able to reach the sheet of parchment on which it was written.[44] Thus, King Chilperic was forced to change his mind. According to Guy Halsall, this altercation took place at the villa Berniers-Vizelle, during the days of Gregory's trial.[45] The

---

[39] Gregory, *Liber historiarum* V, 18, ed. Krusch, Levison, p. 222.   [40] Ibid., p. 223.
[41] Gregory, *Liber historiarum* VIII, 31 and 41, ed. Krusch, Levison, p. 223.
[42] Ibid. V, 44, ed. Krusch and Levison, pp. 252–4.
[43] Ibid., p. 253: 'numquam erit sapiens, sed stultus, qui haec quae proponis sequi voluerit'.
[44] Ibid. pp. 253, 254: 'Quod ille audiens, ita respuit, ut, si cartam, in qua haec scripta tenebantur potuisset attingere, in frustra discerperit.'
[45] Halsall, 'Nero and Herod?', p. 341.

relevance of this date and location, which puts their relationship in a different light, will be discussed below.

GOOD RULERS, BAD RULERS

After Chilperic was murdered in 584, his half-brother Guntram, king of Burgundy, ruled Tours. Once Chilperic was dead, Gregory wrote a damning obituary in which he calls Chilperic the 'Herod and Nero of our time'. This has been interpreted as a sign that Gregory could finally express his true feelings, now that Chilperic was dead and could no longer threaten his position.[46] Scholars have come up with several plausible theories to explain the sudden change of sentiment. Martin Heinzelmann postulates a break between what he calls a 'Chilperic cycle' and a 'Guntram cycle'. He proposes that books four and five of the *Histories*, in which Gregory describes events under Chilperic's rule, were written while the king was still alive, whereas books six to nine were written after Chilperic's death, when 'good king Guntram' ruled Tours and Gregory could at last speak his mind. However attractive this and other theories about the composition of the *Histories* are, it should be noted that we do not know when exactly Gregory completed or revised the different books of his *Histories*, nor do we know with any certainty who the intended (or feared) recipients of his books were.[47] It is no longer accepted without question that Gregory wrote as a diarist, describing events as they unfolded, under the watchful eyes of whoever ruled at the time.[48] His working methods are still under debate. This uncertainty should be kept in mind in the discussion of the various interpretations of Gregory's apparent change of heart below.

Guy Halsall offers a different explanation of what happened at the turn of book five to six. Rather than postulating that Gregory could finally speak his mind now that Chilperic was dead, he argues that Gregory wrote his scathing obituary of Chilperic to ingratiate himself with the new ruler, not to express his true, long-oppressed opinion of the dead king. Guntram had just invaded Tours, so it was in Gregory's interest to remain on his good side. This argument, however, makes sense only if we assume that Guntram was the intended recipient of book six, or at least that he could have read or heard the obituary. Halsall maintains that Gregory could in fact speak more freely during Chilperic's reign than under Guntram's rule. Even when he stood trial on an accusation of

---

[46] See for example Wood, 'Secret histories', p. 259.
[47] Although Gregory indicates that he finished book 6 in 580, it is not clear how much he revised afterwards and which parts of book 6 reflect opinions he held in 580.
[48] Murray, 'The composition', pp. 71–5.

slander, the account of which forms the dramatic closure of book five, Gregory was never in any real danger, at least not from King Chilperic. He had more to fear from Count Leudast and his own clergy. If Gregory's altercation with Chilperic on the Trinity did indeed take place in the villa at Berniers-Vizelle during the very days of the trial, as Halsall surmises, then Gregory was apparently sufficiently sure of his standing with Chilperic to engage in a heated discussion with the king and oppose his decree. Chilperic, who could have used this opportunity to get rid of Gregory, just as he got rid of Praetextatus, was not quick to believe the accusations made against Gregory, and acquitted him. In Gregory's narrative, the uproar of people gathered outside forces the king's hand, turning the people, not the king, into his benefactors. Yet Gregory does praise Chilperic for his 'discretion and forbearance'.[49] Thus he acknowledges that the king could have acted differently, had he wanted Gregory out of the way. Instead Chilperic restrained his anger over the insult to his honour and listened to advice.

On the whole, Gregory's portrait of Chilperic is rather balanced. He criticises the king's faults, but also praises his good deeds. Martin Heinzelmann describes Gregory's self-presentation in the chapters that describe Chilperic's rule as that of an Old Testament prophet before an ungodly king, a stance that Sulpicius Severus had popularised with his stories about Saint Martin before the Roman emperors Valentinian and Maximus.[50] I agree with Heinzelmann that Gregory styled himself as an Old Testament prophet, but not necessarily before an unjust king. Just like Emperor Maximus in the narrative of Sulpicius Severus, Chilperic could be a good ruler, or a bad ruler, depending on the counsel he received from his bishops. This rule of thumb equally applied to King Guntram, who received his own share of criticism from Gregory's pen.[51] The frank and honest counsel of bishops was what made, or unmade, a good king. It is true that Chilperic was the king with whom Gregory most often and most vehemently disagreed, but the point is that he *could* disagree with him. As he tells Chilperic at Praetextatus' trial: 'You are the king and we can say what we think to you.'[52] If we are to believe Gregory's version of events, he could even call Chilperic a fool to his face if the orthodoxy of the Christian faith was at stake. He may not have had that same understanding with King Guntram. As Guy

---

[49] See the quotation in note 1.
[50] Heinzelmann, *Gregory of Tours: History and Society,* pp. 41, 42.
[51] Passages in which Gregory criticises Guntram are listed in Wood, 'Secret histories' and Halsall, 'Herod and Nero'.
[52] Gregory, *Histories* V, 18, ed. Krusch, Levison, p. 219: 'Loquimur enim tibi, sed si volueris, audis.'

Gregory of Tours

Halsall notes, Gregory has Count Guntram Boso say to King Guntram: 'You are the king, and therefore we *cannot* speak our mind to you.'[53] It is the exact opposite of what Gregory had told King Chilperic. It makes one wonder which ruler allowed Gregory more freedom to speak: 'good king Guntram' or Chilperic, the 'Herod or Nero of our time'. As always with Gregory, things were never black and white, and his opinion of rulers changed as events developed.

For whom did Gregory write these stories about his dealings with kings? As already mentioned in the introduction to this chapter, Gregory identifies the readers, or rather the custodians, of his work in the epilogue of his *Histories* as 'the bishops of the Lord who will govern the church of Tours after my unworthy self.'[54] And yet, his intended audience was probably wider than the circle of his direct successors. Perhaps he even kept the possibility open that members of the Merovingian family, either the present rulers or their successors, would read his *Histories,* and draw some lessons from his portraits of rulers. Although it is hard to imagine that the fifth book of Gregory's *Histories,* which contains some unfavourable descriptions of Chilperic, was intended for the king's eyes, Gregory had to reckon with the possibility that it could come to his attention.[55] But perhaps any king who heard or read Gregory's account of his confrontations with Chilperic was meant to realise that an unbending, morally upright and 'I give it to you straight' bishop like Gregory was a pain to have around, but indispensable if one wanted honest advice and criticism.

RUMOUR AND SECRETS

In spite of his frequent praise of frank speech and straightforward counsel, Gregory was a master of indirection. In an article with the intriguing title 'The Secret Histories of Gregory of Tours', Ian Wood shows that Gregory rarely expresses his criticism of contemporary politics directly. More often, he vents his opinions by reporting the speeches of others, recounting dreams and visions, juxtaposing events or reporting rumours.[56] Although at his trial Gregory firmly denied the accusation that he had spread slander about Queen Fredegund, his *Histories* are full of

---

[53] Ibid. VII, 14, ed. Krusch, Levison, p. 335: 'Cui ille: "Tu", inquid, "dominus et rex regali in solio resedis et nullus tibi ad ea quae loqueris ausus est respondere".' Halsall, 'Herod and Nero', p. 347.
[54] Not only of his *Histories,* but of all his writings. Gregory, *Histories* X, 31, ed. Krusch, Levison, p. 536: "Omnes sacerdotes Domini, qui post me humilem ecclesiam Turonicam sunt recturi."
[55] Wood, 'Secret histories', p. 257.
[56] For Gregory's strategies of indirect criticism, see Wood, 'Secret histories', especially pp. 266 and 270.

Part II

gossip and rumour. He has no qualms about revealing the rumour that Fredegund was unfaithful to her husband, tortured the suspected killers of her son, and was a multiple murderer. This observation leads Wood to conclude that 'although Gregory takes a stand for honesty and frankness at the trial of Praetextatus, it can scarcely be said that his *Histories* uphold that ideal.'[57] As mentioned above, Gregory could not write everything he wanted and had to be careful about what he revealed, to protect his own position. And yet, when reading his *Histories,* one cannot escape the impression that there was much he could reveal with impunity and that he frequently disclosed secrets and sensitive information. Gregory put into writing what he heard others talk about and he divulged information that could make and break reputations. It would appear that he had few reservations about bringing into the open what others, notably the rulers he criticises, would have preferred to stay hidden.

In the letters and narratives that have been discussed in this book so far, rumours and secrets are a regular topic of discussion. Letter-writers refer to their duty to bring rumours to the attention of the ruler, while hagiographers emphasise the gift of holy men for detecting inner secrets and hidden vices. By appealing to the necessity of discussing openly what others kept silent or gossiped about, critics highlighted the virtue of frank speech against the dark background of rumours and secret accusations.[58] Gregory also explicitly juxtaposes open speech and secret accusations, when he quotes Guntram Boso as saying: 'If there is anyone of my status who accuses me of the crime in secret (*occulte*), let him speak openly (*palam*) now.'[59] Occasionally, in letters of admonition and narratives about truth-tellers, a tension is brought into play between the public and the private sphere, to emphasise the sincerity of the critic. Ambrose, in his letter to Theodosius on the Thessalonica incident, creates an atmosphere of confidentiality, when he tells the emperor that he has written him a private letter with his own hand, because he did not want to berate him in public.[60] The fact that this privacy was relative, since letters were read out loud, is conveniently overlooked in order not to break the illusion of intimacy. Sulpicius Severus, in his *Dialogues* on Saint Martin, evokes a similar atmosphere of confidentiality when he has his interlocutor Gallus reveal a story that Martin himself always kept

---

[57] Ibid., p. 269.
[58] Examples are the speech of Themistius before Emperor Constantius II (chapter 2), Hilary of Poitiers' invective against the same emperor (chapter 3) and Columban's letter to Pope Boniface (chapter 6).
[59] Gregory, *Liber historiarum* VII, 14, ed. Krusch, Levison, p. 336: 'At si aliquis est similis mihi, qui hoc crimen inpingit occulte, veniat nunc palam et loquatur.'
[60] See the discussion in chapter 4, pp. 96, 97.

174

hidden.[61] By framing this story in the setting of an intimate conversation between three friends at a private location, his own estate Primulacium, Sulpicius Severus creates the illusion that there are no readers and no audience listening in.[62] The three interlocutors of the *Dialogues* discuss a delicate matter that could harm Saint Martin's *fama,* as if it will not move beyond the sphere of private conversation. The information they share as Martin's confidants is meant to acquire extra value by being presented as confidential. Thus, the *Dialogues* offer a prime example of what is called the secrecy paradox: Saint Martin's secrets are discreetly and privately discussed, in a literary work that is meant for publication.

Gregory creates no such illusion of privacy and confidentiality in his *Histories.* As a historiographer of contemporary events, it was his business to provide information and report news. The fact that news of recent events often came from hearsay automatically brought him into the realm of rumour and talk. In the words of Ian Wood, 'Gregory seems to be little more than a recorder of rumours and assertions which were politically motivated.'[63] Although Wood makes this observation with regard to one particular episode in the *Histories*, and not as a general characterisation of Gregory as a historian, Gregory can be seen to make use of the full potential of rumour and gossip as political manipulative devices.[64] He employs the narrative strategy of reporting rumours to express his criticism indirectly and deflect any responsibility for content to unnamed sources (*ut aiunt, ut fertur*). Another strategy he turns to in order to express criticism safely is to report dreams and visions. As a reporter he cannot be held to account for the content of a dream or vision, except perhaps for its interpretation. In book seven of the *Histories,* Gregory recounts such a dream that conveyed criticism of a ruler, but instead of deflecting responsibility, Gregory gives himself the lead role in this dream, as we shall see below.

ANOTHER AMBROSE?

In a confrontation with King Guntram, Bishop Gregory shows once more that he had the courage to resist a ruler who was about to commit an act which he, Gregory, the Lord's bishop, could not condone.[65] This time, however, his heroic act of resistance takes place in a dream. Gregory

---

[61] Discussed in chapter 6, pp. 138–139.
[62] Apart from a few members of his ascetic household, who came to listen to their conversation on the second day.
[63] Wood, 'Secret histories', p. 276, in a discussion of Gregory's references to the murder of Sigebert.
[64] See the note above and Dolan, 'You would do better to keep your mouth shut.'
[65] Heinzelmann, *Gregory of Tours: History and Society,* p. 43.

Part II

interprets his dream as a vision, perhaps foretelling a future event, and decides to relate the dream to Eberulf, the former chamberlain of Chilperic, who had sought sanctuary in the church of Saint Martin to escape the revenge of King Guntram.[66] Guntram believed Eberulf had murdered his half-brother Chilperic. This is how Gregory recounts his dream:

> I imagined myself in this consecrated church, as if celebrating the solemn rite of Mass. When the altar, with the holy offerings upon it, was already covered with a silken cloth, I suddenly noticed King Guntram walking in, who shouted with a loud voice: 'Drag out this enemy of my family! Remove this murderer from God's sacred altar!' When I heard him, I turned to you [Eberulf] and said: 'Hold tight, unfortunate man, to the altar cloth which covers the holy offerings, so you will not be cast out from here.' You seized it, but with a feeble hand, instead of grasping it manfully. I spread my own hands wide and pressed my chest against that of the king, saying: 'Do not drag this man out of the sacred church, on peril of your life, lest the saintly bishop [Martin] slay you with his miraculous power! Do not destroy yourself with your own weapon, for if you do you will lose not only your present life but also eternal life!'[67]

Gregory continued 'manfully to resist the king' (*rege viriliter resisterem*) until he woke from his dream in fear and in trembling.[68] According to Philippe Buc, Gregory adopts Ambrose's persona in this vision, when he boldly refuses to hand over a fugitive who has sought refuge in his church.[69] It is indeed tempting to see parallels between the story of Ambrose, who stood firmly in front of his church blocking the emperor's way, and Gregory's representation of himself stopping King Guntram in his tracks, when this king comes barging into the church of St Martin. Gregory portrays his own act of defiance as a powerful, physical confrontation: he spreads his hands wide and presses his chest against that of the king, using his own body as a shield between the king and the fugitive,

---

[66] This episode is discussed in Meens, 'The sanctity of the Basilica of St. Martin'.

[67] Gregory, *Liber historiarum* VII, 22, ed. Krusch, Levison, p. 342: 'Putabam me quasi in hac basilica sacrosancta missarum solemnia caelebrare. Cumque iam altarium cum oblationibus palleo syrico coopertum essit, subito ingredientem Gunthchramnum regem conspicio, qui voce magna clamabat: "Extrahite inimicum generationis nostrae, evellite homicidam a sacro Dei altario". At ego, cum haec audirem, ad te conversus dixi: "Adpraehende palleum altaris, infelix, quo sacra munera conteguntur, ne hinc abiciaris." Cumque adpraehenderis, laxa eum manu et non viriliter detenebas. Ego vero, expansis manibus, contra pectus regis meum pectus aptabam, dicens: "Noli eiecere hunc hominem de basilica sancta, ne vitae periculum patiaris, ne te sanctus antestis sua virtute confodeat. Noli te proprio iaculo interemere, quia, hoc si feceris praesentem vitam aeternamque carebis".'

[68] Ibid., p. 342 : 'Dum hunc tu tepide reteneris et ego rege viriliter resisterem, evigilavi pavore conterritus, ignarus quid somnium indecaret.' See also Peter Brown's interpretation of this scene in 'Gregory of Tours: Introduction', p. 15.

[69] Buc, *Dangers of Ritual*, p. 114.

in a way not unlike that in which Rubens (1599–1641) would later depict Ambrose with a forbidding, outstretched arm touching Theodosius' chest, as he stops the emperor from entering his church. Perhaps this famous painting has influenced the interpretation of modern scholars, who are quick to see similarities between stories featuring Merovingian bishops who stand up to their rulers and Ambrose's courageous attitude towards Theodosius, as if Frankish authors deliberately copied the scene. Hans Pohlsander, for example, makes this comparison when discussing Gregory's description of Bishop Nicetius' conflict with King Clothar I: 'The whole matter recalls Ambrose of Milan confronting Theodosius.'[70] Jacques Fontaine suggests a link between Sulpicius Severus' representation of the confrontation between Saint Martin and Emperor Maximus and the story of how Ambrose induced Emperor Theodosius to do penance,[71] while Philippe Buc maintains that the 'Ambrosian tradition was alive and well in Gregory's writings.'[72]

Although this 'Ambrosian tradition' is indeed prominently present in Carolingian literature, as we shall see in the next chapter, there is little evidence that Merovingian truth-tellers, or the authors who recorded their acts, consciously modelled their behaviour after that of Ambrose, in spite of some remarkable similarities. Gregory recounts in his *Lives of the Fathers* how Bishop Nicetius refused to proceed with the celebration of Mass until King Theudebert had done his bidding. This story, perhaps even more than Gregory's dream, is reminiscent of Paulinus' description of Ambrose's clash with Theodosius after the Callinicium incident. In his *Life of Ambrose*, Paulinus recounts how Ambrose, when Theodosius visited his church, stopped in the middle of the celebration of Mass and only agreed to proceed after Theodosius had given him his solemn word that he would do as the bishop asked.[73] The parallels between the two stories are so striking that it is difficult to see how Gregory could *not* have been inspired by Ambrose's example. And yet there are no indications, either in the *Histories* or in Gregory's other writings, that Gregory was familiar with Paulinus' *Life of Ambrose*. In fact, Gregory does not once mention Ambrose in his *Histories*, not even in his section on the reign of Theodosius.

It is not impossible that the story of Ambrose denying communion to Theodosius was at the back of Gregory's mind. Stories travel via many routes and not only via texts. Nevertheless, there is no evidence to conclude that Gregory deliberately tried to imitate Ambrose. Although

---

[70] Pohlsander, 'A call to repentance', p. 459.   [71] Fontaine, 'Hagiographie et politique', p. 119.
[72] Buc, *Dangers of Ritual*, p. 114.
[73] Paulinus, *Vita Ambrosii* 23. The details of this particular story have been discussed in chapter 4.

Part II

it is clear that Gregory in his description of his confrontation with King Guntram adopts the persona of a courageous bishop who was not afraid to oppose a ruler, that bishop was not necessarily Ambrose. What Philippe Buc refers to as the 'Ambrosian tradition' was a much more widespread tradition of bishops and holy men who claimed the right of free speech and independent behaviour towards a ruler. For the sixth-century North-African bishop Facundus of Hermiane, the story of Ambrose rebuking Theodosius was *the* example of episcopal free speech and courageous behaviour.[74] His Gallo-Roman contemporary Gregory, however, may well have taken inspiration from other examples, such as Nicetius of Trier or Hilary of Poitiers, the teacher of his patron saint Martin of Tours.[75] Like the Merovingian letter-writers discussed in the previous chapter, Gregory seems to have had a preference for truth-tellers close to home, related to his own history and area, to serve as models of frank speech and courage.

CONCLUSION

Merovingian narratives about bishops, holy men and their confrontations with kings and prelates, which have been discussed in this chapter and the preceding one, reveal certain similarities with late antique narratives. Gregory reminds us of Ambrose, Nicetius bears a resemblance to Martin and, as Albrecht Diem has pointed out, Columban is much like Nicetius.[76] The question is how we should interpret these similarities. In my opinion, the parallels that we can detect between late antique and early medieval stories point to the continuation of a *tradition* of bishops and clerics behaving boldly towards rulers, which was itself a continuation of the tradition of the pagan philosopher–truth-teller. Apart from living on via stories and rhetorical theory, it persisted as a set of norms and expectations on which a Merovingian truth-teller could model his behaviour. Gregory probably realised that, if he described his act of resistance to King Guntram in the manner he did, his audience would admire him for it. His readers would not think him insubordinate, arrogant or presumptuous for not letting Guntram pass. On the contrary, they would consider him a brave bishop who defended God's justice and was not afraid of incurring the king's wrath. This was an image Gregory wanted to transmit. It is difficult to tell if he grafted his self-presentation onto a particular model, on an Old

---

[74] See chapter 6, p. 134.
[75] Gregory devotes one chapter to Hilary in his *Glory of the Confessors*, and two chapters in the *Histories* (I, 38 and 39), of which the second is based on Fortunatus' *Life of Hilary*. Apart from these chapters, nine references to Hilary and his church at Poitiers can be found in Gregory's *Histories*.
[76] Diem, 'Monks, kings and the transformation of sanctity', pp. 538–40.

Testament prophet, on Martin of Tours, Hilary of Poitiers, Nicetius of Trier or a combination of these types and persons. Neither is it possible to determine if the speech and demeanour he ascribes to himself in the autobiographical passages of the *Histories* are related to a specific rhetorical performance of free speech; Gregory knew that this image 'worked' and would trigger the response he was after. His readers will have recognised the significance of a bishop's bold and independent behaviour in the service of truth and justice. Gregory uses the symbolic potential of that image, and gives it a self-consciously ironic twist: his manly act of resistance to King Guntram is after all but a dream, and a dream from which he woke in fear and trembling.

8

THE WISE ADVISER

In the earlier chapters, we have encountered various types of truth-tellers who embodied the ideal of free speech and frank criticism in different periods and cultural settings: the steadfast martyr, the independent philosopher, the frank holy man and, an increasingly prominent figure, the Old Testament prophet. In the late eighth century, a new model or persona entered the stage: the wise adviser, who was closely connected to the ruler and used his privileged position to proffer disinterested, honest advice. Some traits of the persona of the wise adviser were already present in earlier ages: the philosopher Themistius fulfilled the role of counsellor in the service of several Roman emperors, while Bishop Ambrose cast himself as Theodosius' close adviser, who unabashedly told the emperor the truth. We have encountered the persona of the trusted adviser also in the writings of Isaac of Nineveh, who modelled his ascetic ideal of privileged free speech towards God on the image of the courtier who enjoyed closeness to the ruler and participated in his secrets. However, the credibility of advisers who claimed to speak frankly to rulers beneath or via the advice they offered was subject to continuous discussion and adjustment, as we have seen in the case of Themistius. There was a widely held assumption that court advisers, afraid of losing their position and status, told rulers exactly what they wanted to hear. Merovingian saints' lives abound with flattering, untrustworthy advisers, who serve as a foil to highlight the frankness and honesty of the outsider critic. Counsellors, who guarded their reputation as truth-tellers, needed to prove time and again that their advice was sincere, straightforward and not motivated by self-interest. Over the course of the eighth, and particularly during the ninth century, however, the adviser who spoke frankly from a privileged position of trust became a highly valued figure, both in political discourse and in hagiographic narratives.

In this chapter I shall explore how the rise of the persona of the wise adviser, who spoke up for justice and orthodoxy and who used his familiarity with the ruler to mediate on behalf of others, was connected to the reform movement that took off in the mid-eighth century. The Carolingian programme of renewal, which aimed to improve church discipline, education and justice, went hand in hand with a reinvigorated interest in classical and patristic learning. This cultural revival, generally known as the 'Carolingian Renaissance', led to an increased appreciation of ancient texts and traditions that, as we shall see in this chapter, shaped the representation of frank speech and provided the resources needed to construct the persona of the wise adviser.

Traditionally, historians have paid a lot of attention to the role of bishops in the Carolingian reform movement. It was the bishops who took up the reform agenda, formulated at general councils and assemblies, to discuss in their own diocesan synods how to implement and fine-tune the reform ideals.[1] A vital duty of bishops, as the reform statutes kept reiterating, was to admonish and correct the flock entrusted to their care and report rumours of abuse and injustice to the court. Bishops had performed this task since late Antiquity, and continued to do so under Merovingian rule.[2] The reformers put these traditional episcopal duties on the agenda with new vigour. As a result, bishops became more confident of their role as admonishers and as protectors of justice.[3] And yet, not all those who were involved in the early stages of the reform movement and who shaped the reform agenda that formulated the principle duties of bishops were bishops themselves.[4] Abbots, too, played a prominent and essential role in government as advisers to the king,[5] and so did poets and scholars who gathered at the Carolingian court and offered their counsel and words of warning in advisory literature and letters of admonition.[6]

This chapter looks into the profile of the court adviser in the age of ecclesiastical reform and cultural renewal between c. 790 and c. 840. Who were these counsellors who advocated and embodied frank speech and straightforward advice as agents of social and political change? What were the qualities and credentials that qualified them as competent advisers? And to what extent were advisers at liberty to express their admonitions, criticism and advice openly and directly? To answer these questions, I shall investigate the advice literature of the late eighth and the first half of the ninth century: that is, hortatory letters and mirrors for princes, written in response to, or as part of, attempts to create a well-organised, orthodox and just Christian society by educating its rulers.

---

[1] Davis, *Charlemagne's Practice of Empire*, p. 243.   [2] See chapters 6 and 7.
[3] Patzold, 'Redéfinir l'office épiscopal'; *Episcopus*.
[4] Nelson, 'The *libera vox* of Theodulf', p. 297.   [5] McKitterick, *Charlemagne*, especially p. 298.
[6] See especially Garrison, 'An aspect of Alcuin'.

Part II

INSULAR ADVISERS

To understand the advice literature that was produced in the heyday of Carolingian ecclesiastical reform and cultural renewal, we should start with the letters of admonition that were written in the early days of reform. As Giles Brown and Rosamond McKitterick have emphasised, the Carolingian reform movement did not start from scratch, but was preceded by earlier Merovingian, Visigothic and Northumbrian reforms, and by the initiatives of insular missionaries such as Willibord and Boniface.[7] It was the Anglo-Saxon bishop Boniface who received instructions from the Carolingian mayor Carloman I in the early 740s to convene a general council with the goal to 'emend and correct ecclesiastical discipline'.[8] Around 745, Boniface called another council, this time of Anglo-Saxon bishops on the Continent, to discuss ecclesiastical affairs in their homeland. On the agenda were 'evil rumours' that had come to their attention regarding the immoral behaviour of King Aethelbald of Mercia (d. 757), who was reported to have committed acts of fornication with nuns and consecrated virgins. In the aftermath of the council, Boniface wrote a letter of admonition to King Aethelbald. In this letter, written with the consent and approval of his fellow bishops, Boniface informs the king that it is rumoured that he has engaged in illicit sexual relations, stolen church property, annulled privileges, and treated monks and bishops with violence.[9] God forbid that this should be true, Boniface says, but if it is, he strongly advises the king to mend his ways: 'We beseech and appeal to your clemency, beloved son [...] that if it is true that you live in this guilt, you may correct your life by repentance and amend it by purification.'[10]

Boniface's letter to Aethelbald is often invoked as an example of fierce and outspoken criticism. And yet, if we subject the letter to closer scrutiny, Boniface calls the king to repentance in a rather indirect manner. His letter contains no open censure. Boniface dresses his objections against Aethelbald's immoral conduct as if in response to having heard a rumour, and adopts the tone of a well-meaning, pastoral adviser and supplicant, who offers his admonitions out of pure love for the king and sincere concern for his well-being. Boniface emphatically presents his

---

[7] Brown, 'The Carolingian Renaissance'; McKitterick, *The Frankish Church*.
[8] Brown, 'The Carolingian Renaissance', p. 11, with reference to Boniface, *Ep.* 50.
[9] Boniface, *Ep.* 73, ed. Rau, pp. 212–27. On the council, see Boniface's letter to Archbishop Ecberth of York, *Ep.* 75 (746/7), ed. Rau, pp. 230–3.
[10] Boniface, *Ep.* 73, ed. Rau, p. 218: 'Propterea obsecramus et contestamur, fili carissime [...] ut, si hoc verum sit, quod in isto scelere versaris, et vitam tuam penitendo corrigas et purificando emendes [...].'

The Wise Adviser

missive not as a piece of criticism, but as a 'letter of admonition or supplication'.[11] He adopts the role of adviser, not that of outspoken critic.

Boniface was careful not only in how he phrased his disapproval of Aethelbald's conduct, but also in the manner in which he brought his admonition to the king's attention. First, he sought the approval of his fellow-bishops on the Continent, Wera, Burchard, Werberht, Abel, Willibald, Hwita and Liafwin, and asked them to support and co-author the letter.[12] Then, he asked the archbishop of York, Ecberth, to correct the letter, which was a way of soliciting his support and commitment.[13] Finally, he approached the priest Herefrid, who apparently had a good standing at Aethelbald's court, to bring the letter to the king's attention and explain its content to him.[14] Boniface persuaded the priest to act as his messenger by appealing to his reputation as a truth-telling man of God. He had heard people say that Herefrid feared no man, and that the king from time to time listened to his admonitions.[15] By addressing Herefrid as a truth-teller, he expressed the expectation that the priest would behave as one. Boniface impressed upon Herefrid the importance of understanding one thing above all: 'Let it be known to your love that we have addressed these words of admonition to the king solely out of pure and loving friendship.'[16] The priest was to transmit their good intentions and love for the king to Aethelbald himself, as he stood in the king's presence and translated and explained the content of the admonitory letter to him.

Boniface's letter is of much interest, not only because its rhetoric is very similar to that of later letters of admonition, but also because it was written by an Anglo-Saxon missionary on the Continent, who signalled and addressed problems from which he was, at least geographically, far removed. It is a noteworthy feature of the hortatory letters that have been preserved from the early days of the reform of the Frankish church, that many of them were written not by Frankish but by insular authors, who were in a sense outsiders, and distanced from the issues that they confronted in their letters of admonition.[17]

Some twenty years after Boniface wrote his letter to King Aethelbald, another insular cleric on the Continent, Cathwulf, wrote an admonitory letter to a king. The otherwise unknown cleric directed his advice at

---

[11] Boniface, *Ep.* 75 (746/7), ed. Rau, p. 230: 'admonitoriam vel praecatoriam epistolam'.
[12] See Rau, *Briefe des Bonifatius*, p. 213 on the identity of the co-authors of the letter.
[13] Boniface, *Ep.* 75 (746/7), ed. Rau, pp. 230–2.
[14] Boniface, *Ep.* 73 (746/7), ed. Rau, pp. 228–30.   [15] Ibid., p. 228, lines 16–18.
[16] Ibid., p. 228, lines 18–20: 'Et notum sit caritati tuae, quia haec verba admonitionis nostrae ad illum regem propter nihil aliud direximus nisi propter puram caritatis amicitiam [. . .].'
[17] See Mary Garrison's forthcoming study on insular parrhesiasts.

Charlemagne, who was at the time a young Frankish king.[18] The letter, which can be dated to around 775, is commonly regarded as a mirror for a prince, a genre that already existed in Antiquity but gained in popularity in the Carolingian period. Cathwulf presents Charlemagne with a series of traditional exhortations, such as we have already encountered in Remigius' letter to Clovis, asking the king to protect the interests of the church, dispense justice, look after widows and orphans, and take counsel from wise advisers. And yet, beneath Cathwulf's traditional advice and conventional praise, one can detect a note of criticism. As Joanna Story has observed, Cathwulf's seemingly casual remark that queens deserve respect can be read as a barbed comment on Charlemagne's marital record.[19]

Cathwulf presents Charlemagne with a blueprint for the construction of a just kingdom, which he borrowed from the *Proverbia Graecorum*, a collection of wise sayings which, despite its name, was not of Greek but probably of Irish origin.[20] According to Cathwulf, ideal Christian kingship rests on eight pillars: truth, patience, largesse, persuasiveness, punishment for evildoers, praise for the innocent, mild taxation and fair administration of justice. If Charlemagne takes care of these eight columns of just rule, Cathwulf assures him, his reign will be prosperous. If not, calamities await his family and his entire realm, as the examples of Ahab, Achaz and other Old Testament kings have shown, as well as, more recently, those of Count Waifarus of Aquitaine and the Lombard king Desiderius and his son.[21] With the latter example, Cathwulf has selected an up-to-date political event to illustrate his point, since Charlemagne had just the previous year conquered Desiderius' realm. He encourages the king to draw a lesson from this example: namely, always to appreciate good counsel and hold council with those who fear God.[22] The Old Testament king Ahab, whom Cathwulf lists among his detterent examples, famously ignored the warnings of the prophet Elijah and other prophets and died ignominiously in battle. Cathwulf concludes his letter with a promise: Charlemagne will reign with good fortune and bliss, now and in eternity, if he will only heed Cathwulf's *consilium* and follow his instructions.

One of the pillars of just rule that Cathwulf describes to Charlemagne as a guarantee for a prosperous reign is eloquence. Two decades later, yet another insular adviser, the Northumbrian deacon Alcuin of York

---

[18] Cathwulf, *Letter to Charlemagne*, ed. Dümmler, pp. 501–4. See Garrison, 'Letters to a king'; Story, 'Cathwulf, kingship'.
[19] Story, 'Cathwulf, kingship', p. 7 [20] Ibid., p. 9.
[21] Cathwulf, *Letter to Charlemagne*, ed. Dümmler, p. 503, line 44–p. 504, line 2.
[22] Cathwulf, *Letter to Charlemagne*, ed. Dümmler, p. 504, lines 3–5.

(d. 804), also stressed the importance of eloquence and good counsel for fortunate and effective rule, in his dialogue *On Rhetoric and Virtues,* an advice manual intended, again, for King Charlemagne. In the 780s, Alcuin joined a group of scholars at the court, at the king's invitation, and became one of Charlemagne's chief advisers.

ADVICE MANUALS

Alcuin's *On Rhetoric and Virtues,* written in the mid-790s, is a fusion of a mirror for a prince and a rhetorical treatise. It takes the shape of a dialogue between Charlemagne, the eager student, and Alcuin, his teacher. In Alcuin's fictional setting, the king expresses his wish to be instructed in the art of rhetoric, because of its importance for the government of the kingdom and the palace. 'As you very well know,' Alcuin has Charlemagne say at the opening of the dialogue, 'we are constantly going round such questions because of the duties of the kingdom and the cares of the palace, and it seems silly not to know the rules of this art when we need to employ it every day.'[23] To comply with Charlemagne's wish to acquire more knowledge of the art of rhetoric, Alcuin explains the three branches of rhetoric: demonstrative, judicial and deliberative speech.[24] In his discussion of deliberative rhetoric, that is, the art of persuasion and dissuasion, he emphasises the importance of listening to (the right kind of) counsel.[25]

As we have seen, Cathwulf's exhortatory letter-cum-mirror was written in response to a recent political event: Charlemagne's annexation of Lombard Italy. Such a direct link between Alcuin's *On Rhetoric and Virtues* and contemporary politics is not easily discernable, unless we read the treatise against the background of Alcuin's letters of admonition, written in the same period. In the mid-790s, Alcuin wrote several letters of admonition in which he questions, ever so politely, Charlemagne's harsh treatment of the Saxons and the policy of forced conversion in the Christianisation of Saxony.[26] The letter (*Ep.* 110), which he addressed to Charlemagne in person, reads, in the words of Ian Wood, as

---

[23] Alcuin, *Disputatio de rhetorica et de virtutibus* 1, ed. Halm, p. 525: [Karlus] 'Sed ut optime nosti propter occupationes regni et curas palatii in huiscemodi questionibus assidue nos versari solere, et ridiculum videtur eius artis nescisse praecepta, cuius cotidie occupatione involvi necesse est.'

[24] On the sources of Alcuin's *Dialogue on Rhetoric and Virtues* see Kempshall, 'The virtues of rhetoric', especially pp. 24–5.

[25] Alcuin, *Disputatio de rhetorica et de virtutibus* 5, ed. Halm, p. 527. On the connection between Alcuin's rhetorical treatise and deliberative rhetoric, see Ramsey, 'A reevaluation of Alcuin's *Disputatio de rhetorica et de virtutibus* as consular persuasion'.

[26] Alcuin, *Epp.* 107 (796, to Bishop Arn of Salzburg), 110 (796, to Charlemagne) and 111 (796, to Meginfred), ed. Dümmler, pp. 153–4, 157–62.

Part II

a 'remarkably public statement' that was probably intended for the ears of the entire court.[27] People should receive proper cathechetical instruction, Alcuin maintains. They should be persuaded of the truth of the gospel, not forced into accepting Christianity. However, Alcuin presents his arguments not as open or confrontational criticism, but in the form of embedded questions and pastoral admonitions.[28]

Alcuin's letters of admonition reached the Carolingian court in 796.[29] Around the same time, perhaps even in exactly the same year, he published his *On Rhetoric and Virtues*, in which he presents eloquence and persuasion as powerful political tools.[30] Viewed against the background of Alcuin's letters of admonition, the dialogue *On Rhetoric and Virtues* can be read as a plea to the king to choose the way of persuasion instead of force, and perhaps as indirect criticism of Charlemagne's missionary policy of forced conversion. Whether Charlemagne changed his policy towards the Saxons in response to Alcuin's admonitions is difficult to tell, but it is striking that the second Saxon capitulary of 797 is much milder than the first.[31]

The late eighth and early ninth century saw a rise in the production of treatises, letters and poems in which kings, emperors and counts received instructions and moral guidelines on how to become wise, effective and eloquent governors.[32] Well-known examples are Theodulf of Orleans's *Exhortation to Judges* (c. 798), Smaragdus of Saint-Mihiel's *Royal Way* (between 811 and 814), Jonas of Orleans's *On the Instruction of the Laity* (818–28) and the same author's *Instruction for a King* (after 829). Hans Hubert Anton subsumes these texts under the umbrella term 'mirrors for princes', with the caveat that the technical term *speculum regum* or *speculum principum* is attested only from the twelfth century onwards.[33] As for the precursors of this genre of advisory literature that boomed in the Carolingian period, Anton points to the hortatory letters from the late antique and Merovingian period, some of which have been discussed in the previous chapters, and to seventh-century texts such as the Irish *On the Twelve Abuses of the World*, ascribed to Cyprian, and Isidore of Seville's

---

[27] Wood, *The Missionary Life*, p. 86.
[28] Alcuin, *Letter to Charlemagne, Ep.* 110 (796), ed. Dümmler, p. 158: 'His ita consideratis [...] si melius sit'; 'Illud quoque maxima considerandum est diligentia'. On Alcuin's pastoral style of admonition, see Garrison, 'An aspect of Alcuin'.
[29] Flierman, 'Religious Saxons', p. 177.
[30] Alcuin's *On Rhetoric and Virtues* is usually dated between 795 and 797; see Rädler-Bohn, 'Redating Alcuin's *De dialectica*', pp. 78, 79.
[31] Wood, *The Missionary Life*, p. 86.
[32] Anton, *Fürstenspiegel und Herrscherethos; Fürstenspiegel des frühen und hohen Mittelalters*; Stone, 'Kings are different'. On the Irish mirror tradition, see Meens, 'Politics, mirrors of princes and the Bible'.
[33] Anton, *Fürstenspiegel des frühen und hohen Mittelalters*, p. 5.

Etymologies, which contain discussions of the good king and just government.[34] In these texts, we find the notion that a ruler should above all be able to rule and correct himself, before correcting others.[35] This notion of rulership and (self-)correction is a recurrent theme in Carolingian mirrors for princes and letters of admonition. And yet, the ideas and ideals that informed the paraenetic genre go back much further than the seventh century. Ultimately, they sprang from the Greek ideal of *paideia* and from the belief that culture and learning could have a beneficial influence on the state by educating its rulers.[36]

Mirrors for princes present guidelines for a (young) ruler on how to become a good king. They usually include lists of virtues to cherish and vices to avoid. Mirrors and hortatory letters were, by virtue of their genre, no vehicles for direct criticism, but, as we have seen, criticism could hide beneath advice, just as it could be seen lurking under praise. Above all, mirrors prepared a ruler to *accept* advice and criticism. Often, the mirror's advice is of a very general nature. In discussions of the type of advisers and counsellors a ruler should choose, the king is usually advised to avoid flatterers and rely on wise, experienced and reliable counsellors. We rarely find explicit instructions for advisers on how to offer counsel to a ruler. Sometimes one encounters practical advice such as 'make sure your speeches are not too long', or 'never give counsel when you are angry or in a hurry',[37] but apart from such general profundities, advice to the advice-givers is not a topic treated in mirrors for princes.

COURT COUNSELLORS

We get a clearer picture of the profile of the adviser from a tract that is technically speaking not a mirror, but which shares some traits with that genre. The tract is called *De ordine palatii,* or *On the Organisation of the Palace.*[38] It describes the foundations of kingship, the workings of the palace, the social organisation of the court and the proceedings of assemblies. A treatise was originally written under this title by Adalhard of Corbie (d. 826), a cousin of Charlemagne and one of his principal counsellors. He may have written the text in 781 for Pippin of Italy, or

---

[34] Anton, *Fürstenspiegel des frühen und hohen Mittelalters,* pp. 10, 12.
[35] Ps-Cyprian, *De XII abusivis* ch. 9, ed. Hellmann, p. 54, lines 4–9; Isidore, *Etymologiae* IX, iii, 4–6. See also Isidore, *Sententiae* III, c. 48, 7.
[36] Jaeger, *Paideia: The Ideals of Greek Culture,* vol. 3, p. 85.
[37] Sedulius Scotus, *De rectoribus christianis* 6, ed. Hellmann, p. 40; cf. Heiric of Auxerre, *Collectanea,* ed. Quadri, p. 135: 'Duo maxime contraria esse consilio: festinationem et iram.'
[38] *De ordine palatii,* ed. Gross, Schieffer.

Part II

later, between 810 and 814, for Pippin's son Bernard.³⁹ The version that has come down to us, however, is a revision by Hincmar of Rheims (d. 882), dedicated to King Carloman (r. 882–4). Hincmar made a few alterations, and added three chapters and a preface, but it is generally accepted that the core of the treatise is Adalhard's tract.⁴⁰

The sixth chapter of the treatise discusses the organisation of assemblies (*placita*) that were convoked at the court to discuss and settle issues pertaining to order and justice in the entire realm. The author distinguishes between two kinds of assemblies: a general assembly, at which all the great men of the realm came together, ecclesiastical as well as lay magnates, and a restricted meeting, to which only the senior and foremost advisers were invited. This group of special advisers also consisted of laymen and clerics. During the restricted gatherings, the emperor asked the counsel of the *seniores* and his trusted advisers, the *consiliarii*, on issues that called for careful deliberation and confidentiality. Sometimes a restricted meeting involved an even smaller group of advisers, when the urgency of the matter did not allow for enough time to convene all the emperor's advisers. If a case needed immediate attention, courtiers (*palatini*) were called in for counsel, for they were present in the palace at all times and were the emperor's intimates.⁴¹ According to the author, these *palatini* are well equipped to give advice because of 'their constant familiarity with the decision-making process in public and household affairs'⁴² and because they are used to discussing matters through exhortation (*allocutio*), refutation (*responsio*) and deliberation (*consultatio*).⁴³

Advisers (*consiliarii*) are selected, the author says, on the basis of specific character traits: they are men who put the interest of the emperor and the realm before anything else, before friends or enemies, before relatives or bearers of gifts: in fact, before everything but eternal life.⁴⁴ They do not flatter or stir up discussion. They do not argue like sophists, nor do they think cunningly or according to the wisdom of the world, which is inimical to God.⁴⁵ Perhaps most importantly, they know how to keep a secret.⁴⁶ The author's ideal *consiliarius* sounds much like the ideal court

---

[39] McKitterick, *Charlemagne*, p. 152; Nelson, 'Aachen as a place of power', p. 10.
[40] Nelson, 'Aachen as a place of power', pp. 10, 11. For a more cautious judgement, see McKitterick, *Charlemagne*, pp. 144–8.
[41] *De ordine palatii* 6, 542–52, ed. Gross, Schieffer, p. 88.
[42] Ibid., 546, 547, ed. Gross, Schieffer, p. 88.   [43] Ibid., 548, ed. Gross, Schieffer, p. 88.
[44] Ibid., 510, 511, ed. Gross, Schieffer, p. 86. On the representation of the ideal adviser in *De ordine palatii*, see Althoff, *Kontrolle der Macht*, pp. 57–67.
[45] *De ordine palatii* 6, 512–14, ed. Gross, Schieffer, p. 86: 'non blandientes, non exasperantes, non sophistice vel versute aut secundum sapientiam solummodo huius saeculi, quae inimica est Deo sapientes.'
[46] Ibid., 519–24, ed. Gross, Schieffer, p. 86.

The Wise Adviser

philosopher of Antiquity: he was trustworthy, could not be bribed with gifts and was impervious to manipulation. These qualities enabled him to give disinterested, honest advice. The only aspect that is absent from this otherwise traditional list of adviser's virtues is frank speech. One could argue that frank speech follows automatically from the absence of flattery, sophism and cunning thought, but it should be noted that frankness is not mentioned here explicitly as a virtue in itself. What a Carolingian *consiliarius* does have, however, is *familiaritas*: a term that regularly crops up in this treatise, either to refer to the unreserved relationship of the adviser to the ruler, or to the confidential and open way in which matters between the advisers are discussed.[47]

Counselling the ruler was an honorary task that could last a lifetime. According to the authors of the lives of two famous counsellors, Alcuin of York (d. 804), the author of *On Rhetoric and Virtues,* discussed above, and Benedict of Aniane (d. 821), both men expressed the wish to withdraw into solitude after years of service at the court, but their emperors were not prepared to let them go. The *Life of Alcuin,* written in Ferrières not long after Alcuin's death, tells us that Alcuin expressed the wish to enter the monastery of Fulda as a monk, but Charlemagne made him abbot of the monastery of St Martin at Tours instead, where he could come to visit him and hear his counsel.[48] During one of Charlemagne's visits with his sons in Tours, Alcuin prophesied, according to the author of the *Life,* that Louis would be the next emperor.[49] Ardo's *Life of Benedict* (c. 822/3) contains a topical scene in which Benedict tempers the anger of the emperor and the jealousy of the courtiers.[50] The author describes how Louis had the monastery of Inda, later known as Kornelimünster, built near the palace of Aachen, so that he could keep his adviser close. According to the *Life of Benedict,* Benedict visited the palace frequently, after he had withdrawn to Inda, to counsel the emperor and intercede on behalf of others.[51] These two Carolingian lives show that the old ideals of the independent truth-teller who could not be 'captured' in an institutional setting were still present. Yet, at the same time, their position was becoming more institutionalised and their regular presence at the court needed less justification than before. The *Lives* of Alcuin and Benedict and the treatise *De ordine palatii* indicate that the notion had taken hold that a man of God could accept the position of counsellor and live at court for a longer period of time, without compromising his integrity.

[47] *De ordine palatii* 7, 596, 597, ed. Gross, Schieffer, p. 92, see also 6, 519, p. 86 and 6, 547, p. 88.
[48] *Vita Alcuini* (c. 820–30) 11, and see 9 and 15.   [49] *Vita Alcuini* 15.
[50] Ardo, *Vita Benedicti* 29.
[51] Ardo, *Vita Benedicti* 35. See also Ermoldus Nigellus on Benedict of Aniane in *Carmen in honorem Ludovici* (before 830).

Part II

ADMONITION AND REFORM

The Carolingian period saw a rise in the production of mirrors for princes and other types of advisory literature. As mentioned in the introduction to this chapter, there is a strong link between the Carolingian programme of ecclesiastical and educational renewal and this flourishing of advisory literature. Mirrors for princes express concerns that coincide with the topics of many of the major reform councils of the ninth century, such as the outlines of episcopal admonition and the responsibilities of bishops in reforming society.[52] From late Antiquity onwards, pastoral admonition had been a widely acknowledged duty of priests and bishops. Equally long-standing was the notion that rulers should admonish and reprove their subjects. Ferrandus of Carthage (d. 545/4) wrote in his mirror for secular governors that a wise leader should imitate the good deeds of Samuel, and 'acquire the outspoken boldness of truthful and honest freedom of speech, so that he is worthy to speak with a frank countenance to those who are subservient to him'.[53] During the reform councils of the late eighth and early ninth century, the duty to admonish and reprove was articulated anew, both for bishops and rulers. Bishops were expected to admonish their rulers frankly, just as rulers corrected their subjects.[54] As we have seen in the previous chapter, Gregory of Tours gave expression to this ideal of mutual admonition when he told King Chilperic that it was up to him to chastise bishops if they veered from the path of justice, and suggested that the king, in turn, should listen freely to the censure of his bishops.[55] This old ideal, laid down in conciliar acts as a fundamental episcopal task, became part of the Carolingian programme of reform. Charlemagne's promulgation of the *Admonitio generalis* (789), formulated with the assistance of a select number of bishops and with his counsellors (*consiliarii nostri*), among whom were Alcuin and Theodulf, gave the impetus to a range of further statutes and capitularies.[56] At regional reform councils, the basic outline of Charlemagne's programme was discussed and further elaborated. The duty to admonish and correct was connected to the task of bishops to protect the poor and the oppressed.[57] Bishops should act as watchmen or overseers over their flock, and bring

---

[52] According to Anton, *Fürstenspiegel des frühen und hohen Mittelalters*, p. 6, the following councils gave rise to the production of specific mirrors: Paris 829, Yütz 844 and Quierzy 858.

[53] Ferrandus of Carthage, *Ep.* 7, ed. *PL* 67, col. 934 C: 'comparet sibi liberam fiduciam verecundae et honestae libertatis, ut ingenua fronte dicere valeat subjectis sibi'.

[54] De Jong, *The Penitential State*, especially chapter 3, pp. 112–47; Althoff, *Kontrolle der Macht*, pp. 39–56.

[55] Gregory, *Liber historiarum* V, 18, ed. Krusch, Levison, p. 219, lines 9–11; see the discussion in chapter 7.

[56] Nelson, 'Charlemagne and the bishops', p. 345.   [57] Ibid., p. 349.

The Wise Adviser

any injustices they witnessed in their diocese to the ruler's attention. Again, this was an old ideal, but it was articulated anew in episcopal statutes from the late eighth century onwards. The treatise *De ordine palatii* also gives rather precise instructions on the best moment to bring rumours and reports of injustice before the ruler in a discreet manner.[58] At the Council of Reisbach in 798, convoked by Bishop Arn of Salzburg to discuss the essentials of Charlemagne's reform,[59] the contribution of bishops to the creation of a just and most Christian society was phrased in terms of 'audacious resistance'.[60] Bishops were called to speak out against injustice and admonish corrupt judges without fear. If these corrupt officials failed to listen, the bishop was to turn to the king himself.[61] The acts of the reform council of Arles of 813 phrased this episcopal duty in similar wording:

> When (bishops) see judges and powerful men behaving as oppressors of the poor, they must first refute them with priestly admonition, and then, if those men look down on being corrected, their insolence should be brought to the ears of the king, so that those whom episcopal admonition cannot bend to justice, royal power shall restrain from wickedness.[62]

Much weight was put on the reforming effect of episcopal admonition to guarantee justice for the poor and the powerless, backed up by the promise (or threat) of royal intervention in the event that offenders failed to listen to the bishop's admonitions. If persuasive means failed, royal coercion could bring oppressors back to the path of justice. Such checks on abuse of power as were envisaged in episcopal statutes and capitularies could only work, as the acts of the Council of Reisbach pointed out, if bishops were willing to speak out against local powers and royal officials without fear of repercussion.[63] Naturally, the first condition was that bishops not be engaged in corruption and scandal themselves and that it should be possible to trust them to speak as disinterested ambassadors of the oppressed.[64]

---

[58] *De ordine palatii* 7, 619–621, ed. Gross, Schieffer, p. 94.
[59] Davis, *Charlemagne's Practice of Empire*, p. 243.
[60] Council of Reisbach (*Concilium Rispacense*), 798, ch. 9, ed. Werminghoff, *MGH Conc.*, p. 200: 'ut facientibus mala cum summa audacia resistere'.
[61] Council of Reisbach, 798, ch. 9, ed. Werminghoff, *MGH Conc.*, p. 200.
[62] Council of Arles (*Concilium Arelatense*), 813, ch. 17, ed. Werminghoff, *MGH Conc.*, p. 252: 'dum conspiciunt iudices ac potentes pauperum obpressores existere, prius eos sacerdotali ammonitione redarguant et, si contempserint emendari, eorum insolentia regis auribus intimetur, ut quos sacerdotalis ammonitio non flectit ad iusticiam regalis potestas ab inprobitate coerceat.' I owe the reference and the translation to Jinty Nelson, who discussed the councils of 813 in a paper she gave in Utrecht in 2012. On the reform councils of 813, see also Kramer, 'Order in the church'.
[63] Council of Reisbach, 798, ch. 9, ed. Werminghoff, p. 200.
[64] See the capitularies of 811, discussed in Nelson, 'Charlemagne and the bishops', p. 348.

Part II

Carolingian mirrors for princes can be seen to reflect ideals that were discussed at length during reform synods, concerning just government and the importance of episcopal admonition. Some mirrors even began their lives as parts of episcopal statutes.[65] As always, it is difficult to tell what was ideology and what was political reality. The fact that long-standing social expectations regarding proper episcopal conduct and the reforming power of admonition and correction were laid down in statutes and capitularies, and were endorsed by a reform programme initiated from the palace, does not mean that they became part of 'law' as we understand it today, let alone of daily reality. And yet, the Carolingian programme of educational and ecclesiastical reform, even though it may not have achieved its high ambitions, was a serious attempt to implement these high-sounding moral ideals, to enforce them at a local level, and to change society. The same argument applies to mirrors and other paraenetic literature for rulers that highlights the importance of frank speech and honest counsel in a Christian empire. Mirrors reflect ideals, not necessarily political realities. That said, it is nonetheless clear that *admonitio* was a highly valued form of advice and criticism from Charlemagne's reign onwards. Ideals informed political reality; there was no point in stressing the values of correction and admonition in advice literature for rulers if these rulers did not share these values, at least in theory.

A NEW VOCABULARY

Admonitio became something of a buzzword in the late eighth and early ninth century. Bishops, but also court scholars such as Alcuin and Einhard, offered *admonitio* to rulers according to accepted codes of delivery that were rooted, or believed to be rooted, in the Old Testament world.[66] Although one can also detect the influence of classical rhetoric in their letters of admonition, authors rarely invoke a Cicero or Hermogenes as the model they wish to emulate. Rather, they strive to imitate the language of the Old Testament prophets, who had fearlessly reprimanded their kings. A prime example of such a fearless prophet was the prophet Elijah, who warned King Ahab of impending doom, the example that Cathwulf uses in his hortatory letter to Charlemagne to underline the importance of listening to one's counsellors.

---

[65] Anton, *Fürstenspiegel des frühen und hohen Mittelalters*, pp. 6 and 12.
[66] De Jong, *The Penitential State*, pp. 112–47. On the continued importance of *admonitio* and clerical counsel in the epistolary culture of the high Middle Ages, see Weiler, 'Clerical *admonitio*'.

The Wise Adviser

As pointed out in the previous chapter, the classical vocabulary of frank speech went out of use during the Merovingian period. We find references to *libertas (dicendi)* in the writings of Gallo-Roman authors until the early sixth century, in the letters of Pope Gregory the Great and in those of the Irish monk Columban, but not in Merovingian letters and hagiography. In the advisory literature of the late eighth and ninth century, however, we do occasionally encounter references to the classical and New Testament vocabulary of free speech. Mary Garrison has shown that Alcuin uses the word *fiducia* and its cognate *fiducialiter* in his letters of admonition to bishops and kings in a way that strongly suggests that his *fiducia* referred not only to trust and self-confidence, but also to courageous and frank speech.[67] Alcuin's student Candidus praises the *libera vox* of Theodulf of Orleans (d. 821) at the assembly of Rome in 800/1, when he urges Pope Leo, accused of perjury and adultery, to purge himself with an oath.[68] Radbert of Corbie (d. 865) employs the word *constantia* and its cognate *constanter* in reference to frank speech when describing the lives and deeds of his favourite abbots, Adalhard and Wala, about whom we shall hear more later in this chapter.[69]

Although the evidence should not be overstated, it is safe to say that some knowledge of the classical vocabulary of free speech was around. It re-entered the world of letters along with the revival of learning promoted by Charlemagne's reform programme. Rhetorical handbooks that discussed *parrhesia, licentia* or *oratio libera*, such as the *Rhetorica ad Herennium* and Quintilian's *Institutes of Oratory*, were not widely available and may only have been known to a handful of scholars.[70] By the ninth century, however, nearly every library in the Carolingian realm owned a copy of Isidore of Seville's *Etymologiae,* which contained a definition of *parrhesia* as 'speech full of freedom and boldness'.[71] But even though knowledge of these specific terms was available, at least to some scholars,

---

[67] Garrison, 'An aspect of Alcuin', pp. 149–51. Einhard employed *fiducia* in a similar sense, see below, p. 205.
[68] Nelson, 'The *libera vox* of Theodulf', p. 293.
[69] Radbert of Corbie, *Vita Adalhardi* 15, PL 120, col. 1516; *Epitaphium Arsenii* 2, 5, ed. Dümmler, p. 65.
[70] Excerpts from the *Rhetorica ad Herennium* and Quintilian's *Institutio oratoria* can be found in Sedulius' *Collectaneum*, ed. Simpson. Hadoard, the librarian of Corbie, listed the *Rhetorica ad Herennium* in an inventory of classical manuscripts drawn up in the second half of the ninth century. Lupus of Ferrières had access to a copy of Quintilian's *Institutio oratoria* (now Bern, Burgerbibliothek, Cod. 351 (s. IX$^{2/3}$), which, although incomplete, does contain the sections on *licentia* and *parrhesia* in books 3 and 9. I thank Evina Steinová who checked the Bern manuscript for me. On the medieval manuscripts of these rhetorical treatises, see Van Renswoude, *Licence to Speak*, pp. 364–8, Reynolds, *Texts and Transmission,* pp. 98–100, 332–4.
[71] Isidore of Seville, *Etymologiae* 2, *De rhetorica* 21: 'parrhesia est oratio libertatis et fiduciae plena'. See Reydellet, 'La diffusion des Origines d'Isidore de Séville'.

Part II

Carolingian authors preferred to use different words when discussing the social value and transformative power of frank speech.

Between the sixth and ninth century, a new vocabulary developed that was considered suitable for reprimanding a king and a society in need of reform. The central terms in the discourse of advice and criticism, as Mayke de Jong has shown, were *admonitio*, *correctio* and *increpatio*, the last two of which derived from Scripture, notably from the books of the Old Testament.[72] In place of the New Testament and patristic vocabulary of *fiducia* and *constantia*, the qualities par excellence of the apostles and martyrs, Carolingian authors use the language of the Old Testament, and prefer the words that had characterised the discourse of the prophets: *correctio* and *increpatio*. The word *admonitio*, with its Old Testament ring, was strictly speaking no biblical term.[73] *Admonitio* was instead part of the late antique discourse of frank speech, used in particular of friends advising and reprehending each other. The word frequently occurs in the writings of patristic authors, such as Tertullian, Cyprian, Lactantius, Ambrose and Augustine, and also in the works of Ambrosiaster, Marius Victorinus Firmicus Maternus and Gregory the Great. Gregory's *Pastoral Rule* had a major influence on the development of the discourse of admonition. It offers practical advice on how to admonish different groups and types of people, tailored to the interests of every type of governor who admonishes, encourages and preaches to those under his care.[74] From the sixth century onwards, the term *admonitio* moved from the field of encouragement and preaching into the field of warning and (moral) correction, until, in the ninth century, it could often be found in connection with criticism of rulers. By that time, the discourse of *admonitio*, now firmly associated with Old Testament prophets, had merged with late antique Christian ideals of frank speech. This particular blend of early medieval *admonitio* and late antique notions of frank speech can be gleaned from ninth-century adaptations of the late antique story of the confrontation between Bishop Ambrose and Emperor Theodosius, as will be shown below.

AMBROSE AND THEODOSIUS

References to Ambrose's courageous behaviour towards Theodosius in the Thessalonica incident had almost disappeared by the end of the sixth

---

[72] De Jong, *The Penitential State*, pp. 118–22. [73] Ibid., p. 118.
[74] On Gregory the Great's *Regula pastoralis*, see above, pp. 120–3 and Suchan, *Mahnen und Regieren*.

century. One of the sources of Epiphanius-Cassiodorus' *Tripartite History* which recorded that particular confrontation between the bishop and the emperor was banned by Pope Gregory the Great, in response to the Three Chapters edict of Emperor Justinian in 553. Gregory did not so much condemn the *Tripartite History* itself, but strongly advised against reading one of its main sources, Sozomen's *Ecclesiastical History*.[75] According to Walter Jacob, the pope's negative reading advice constrained the reception of the *Tripartite History*.[76] However, one may well wonder to what extent a papal ban in this period could stop a book from being read. It is, for example, well known that texts and authors that were put on the list of 'books not to be received' ascribed to Pope Gelasius were copied and read in spite of what was believed to be a genuine papal decree.[77] Although Jacob's explanation thus does not seem entirely plausible, it is true that there are hardly any references to the *Tripartite History* after the sixth century.[78] Over the course of the ninth century, however, the *Tripartite History* started to circulate again, and references to the confrontation between Ambrose and Theodosius abound in ninth-century advisory literature and in the acts of councils.[79] The notebook of Sedulius Scotus (fl. 840–60), a collection of excerpts from which he drew when composing his mirror for Charles the Bald, contains more than ninety excerpts from the *Tripartite History*, ranging from single lines to substantial paragraphs.[80]

Alongside the increased interest in the *Tripartite History*, manuscripts of Paulinus' *Life of Ambrose* started to proliferate in this period.[81] The story of how Ambrose rebuked Theodosius for the massacre of Thessalonica in particular resurfaced in mirrors for princes, letters of exhortation and other types of advice literature for rulers.[82] In these texts, Emperor

---

[75] Gregory the Great, *Ep.* 7, 31 (June 597).   [76] Jacob, *Die handschriftliche Überlieferung*, p. 3.
[77] Rose, *Ritual Memory*.
[78] Jacob, *Die handschriftliche Überlieferung*, p. 4; Laistner, 'The value and influence', but see Paulinus of Aquileia, *Ep.* 18b, ed. *MGH epistolae* 4, p. 526; *Collectio Flaviniacensis*, ed. *MGH formulae* 1, pp. 474–5.
[79] Council of Paris (*Concilium Parisiense*), 825, ed. Werminghoff, *MGH Conc.*, pp. 487, 503, 517, 538.
[80] Sedulius, *Collectaneum*, ed. Simpson.
[81] Michele Pellegrino's edition of Paulinus's *Vita Ambrosii* is based on forty-two manuscripts, twelve of which date to the ninth and tenth century. Pellegrino, *Paulino di Milano*, pp. 27–8.
[82] Jonas of Orléans, *De institutione laicali* (between 822 and 828) 2, 20, ed. *PL* 106, cols. 208–11; Hrabanus Maurus(?), *Epistola ad Humbertum episcopum*, ed. Dümmler, *MGH Epp.* III, p. 526; Freculf of Lisieux, *Historiae* (829) II, 4, 27, ed. Allen, pp. 659–60; Agobard of Lyon, Bernard of Vienne and Faof of Chalon-sur-Saône, *De Iudaicis superstitionibus et erroribus* (826/7) 2, ed. Van Acker, pp. 200–1; Astronomer, *Vita Hludowici imperatoris* (c. 840) 35, ed. Tremp, p. 406; Sedulius Scotus, *De rectoribus Christianis* (c. 843) 12, ed. Hellmann, pp. 54–6; Hincmar of Rheims, *De divortio Lotharii regis et Theutberga reginae* (c. 863), ed. Böringer, pp. 201–2, 253–6; Hincmar of Rheims, *Pro ecclesiae libertatum defensione* (c. 868), ed. *PL* 125, cols. 1056–7; Hincmar of Rheims, *De fide Carolo regi servanda* (875), ed. *PL* 125, cols. 961–3; Pope Stephen V, Letter to the Byzantine

Part II

Theodosius was held up to rulers as an example of a most Christian ruler, who was not too proud to do penance after a bishop had told him to do so. Sedulius Scotus, in his mirror for Charles the Bald, *On Christian Rulers* (after 843), expresses the opinion that in the Thessalonica case both Ambrose and Theodosius deserved admiration, Ambrose for his courage to speak out, Theodosius for his willingness to listen. Quoting verbatim from the *Tripartite History,* Sedulius writes: 'Hence both the bishop and the emperor, both of whose deeds were admirable, shone forth with excellent and manifold virtue, particularly in the boldness and fervent zeal of the former and the obedience and pure faith of the latter.'[83] Around 868, Archbishop Hincmar of Rheims wrote to the same emperor: 'Fortunate was that emperor to have in his days such a bishop [...] and fortunate was that bishop of God Ambrose to have such an emperor in his days.'[84]

This renewed interest in the story of the confrontation between Ambrose and Theodosius may have been related to an event that took place in the 820s and which made quite an impact on the public imagination. At the Assembly of Attigny in 822, Emperor Louis atoned for the wrongs he had done to members of his family, whom he had removed from the political scene when he succeeded to the throne of his father Charlemagne.[85] The sins he had committed against his relatives, so it was perceived, had called God's displeasure onto the Empire. It is possible that Louis wished to emulate the example of the penance of Emperor Theodosius: an idea that either he or his advisers may have taken from one of the late antique narratives that recounted the event. Emperor Theodosius had become the model Christian emperor who was presented to rulers for emulation, surpassing even Emperor Constantine.[86] The authors who refer to Theodosius' penance as a shining example of admirable imperial behaviour often choose the version in the *Tripartite History*, which gives much credit to Ambrose, rather than the version in Rufinus' *Ecclesiastical History*, in which Ambrose plays no role

---

emperor Basil I (c. 885), ed. Dümmler, *MGH Epp.* V, p. 374. For an overview and excerpts of all references to the story of Ambrose and Theodosius in ninth-century letters and narratives, see Van Renswoude, *Licence to Speak*, pp. 371–81.

[83] Sedulius Scotus, *De rectoribus Christianis* 12, ed. Hellmann, p. 56: 'Tali ergo tantaque et praesul et imperator virtute clarescebant, quorum opus valde fuit admirabile, illius fiducia, huius autem oboedientia, illius zeli fervor, huius fidei puritas.' Compare Epiphanius-Cassiodorus, *Historia ecclesiastica tripartita* 9, 30, ed. Jacob, Hanslik, p. 546, l. 145–7.

[84] Hincmar of Rheims, *Pro ecclesiae libertatum defensione* (868), ed. *PL* 125, cols. 1056–7: 'Felix ille imperator qui suo tempore talem habuit sacerdotem [...] Et felix sacerdos Dei Ambrosius, qui in tempore talis fuit imperatoris.'

[85] On the penance of Louis the Pious in 822 and again in 833, see De Jong, *The Penitential State* and Booker, *Past Convictions*, with references to older literature.

[86] On the rising popularity of Theodosius in the ninth century, eclipsing the fame of Constantine, see Anton, *Fürstenspiegel und Herrscherethos*, pp. 443–6.

whatsoever.[87] The *Tripartite History* highlights the crucial role of Bishop Ambrose's admonitions and offers the most elaborated version of the event, with much attention on Theodosius' catharsis through crisis, changing from an angry, vengeful emperor to a humble, pious ruler. According to the *Tripartite History*, Theodosius had discovered that there was a difference between an emperor and a bishop, and that Ambrose was a 'master of truth'.[88] For ninth-century authors, the story had an extra appeal: the *Tripartite History* makes much of the confrontation between the bishop and the emperor, elaborately describing the words, gestures and demeanour of Ambrose on this occasion, thus giving a clear idea of how one could, or perhaps even should, imagine a bishop's admonitions.

The renewed interest in the Ambrose–Theodosius affair was probably also related to changing ideas about the organisation of society. Ambrose's example became highly relevant to the Carolingian programme of reform. As the relationship between ecclesiastical and secular power changed and the responsibilities of bishops were redefined, Ambrose exemplified the kind of episcopal behaviour that the acts of the councils of Reisbach, Arles and many other reform councils promoted: namely, to protect orthodoxy and advocate justice. When Freculf of Lisieux recounts the Thessalonica incident in his *Histories* (829) for Louis's young son Charles, he explicitly states that Ambrose approached Theodosius because he had witnessed an injustice. It was an injustice the emperor had committed himself, but it was Ambrose who brought it to his attention, just as the episcopal statutes said a bishop should.[89] Hincmar, who makes a similar point about Ambrose's initiative in approaching Theodosius, adds a biblical quotation to elucidate Ambrose's motives: 'Blessed is the man who explains justice to the ear of one who listens.'[90] With this quotation, Hincmar stresses Theodosius' willingness to listen to Ambrose's admonitions, which was a quality he considers to be just as admirable as the courage to admonish. Ninth-century authors admired Ambrose's frank speech and bold behaviour, and often retold the story as recounted by the *Tripartite History*, with much emphasis on Ambrose's salutary admonitions. Each of the authors who turned to the account of Ambrose's confrontation with Emperor Theodosius in the *Tripartite History* used the story differently, adapting

---

[87] Rufinus, *Historia ecclesiastica* II, 18; see chapter 4, n. 12.
[88] Epiphanius-Cassiodorus, *Historia ecclesiastica tripartita* 9, 30, ed. Jacob, Hanslik, p. 546, lines 153–5: '"Vix", [Theodosius] inquit, "potui discere, quae differentia sit imperatoris et sacerdotis; vix enim veritatis inveni magistrum."'
[89] Freculf of Lisieux, *Historiae* (829) II, 4, 27, ed. Allen, *CCCM* 169A, pp. 659–60.
[90] Hincmar of Rheims, *Pro ecclesiae libertatum defensione*, addressed to Charles the Bald c. 868, ed. *PL* 125, col. 1057: 'Scriptum est enim: Beatus qui enarrat justitiam auri audienti [Eccles. 25:12].'

Part II

it to fit the moral lesson they wished to transmit. They omitted some scenes, rewrote others, paraphrased or summarised scenes in their own words, and reinterpreted the story to match the political–religious circumstances of their own time. The authors also paraphrased Ambrose's *fiducia* (the word that was used in the *Tripartite history* to translate Ambrose's *parrhesia*) with the words *increpatio*, *correctio* and *(ad)monitio*. These were the new words with which they framed and interpreted frank speech.[91]

FEARLESS DEFENDERS OF JUSTICE AND TRUTH

There may be an even more direct link between Emperor Louis's penance in 822 and the *Tripartite History*. This connection can perhaps be found in the person of Abbot Adalhard of Corbie (d. 826), the aforementioned (first) author of *De ordine palatii*, former adviser to Emperor Charlemagne, and one of the relatives who fell victim to Louis's political cleansing when he became emperor in 814.[92] Louis exiled Adalhard to the island of Noirmoutier (Hero), where he stayed between 814 and 821. While Adalhard was in exile, a copy of the *Tripartite History* was made for him, or so it would appear from an inscription in a ninth-century manuscript that used to belong to the monastery of Corbie and is now in St Petersburg. In the eleventh century, a colophon was added to this manuscript, saying that Abbot Adalhard commissioned this copy of the *Tripartite History* 'while he was living in exile' in Noirmoutier.[93] The *Tripartite History* would no doubt have been a comforting book to read in exile, given that it abounds with stories about courageous men of God, who were exiled for speaking the truth to a ruler, just as Adalhard was reported to have done. After his death, Adalhard was remembered in the monastery of Corbie as an *assertor veritatis*, advocate of truth, who was not afraid to rebuke the mighty and reveal their faults.[94] The expression *assertor veritatis* derives from the judicial vocabulary of the Roman courtroom, and was adopted by Christians to refer to those who fearlessly proclaimed the truth in the

---

[91] Jonas of Orléans, *De institutione laicali* (818–28) 2, 20, ed. *PL* 106, col. 211: 'beati Ambrosii memorabilis viri monitis, et increpationibus ... parverit'; Freculf of Lisieux, *Historiae* (829) II, 4, 27, ed. Allen, p. 659: 'multis increpans eum' and p. 660: 'a venerabili episcopo correptionibus'; Hincmar of Rheims, *Pro ecclesiae libertatum defensione* (c. 868), ed. *PL* 125, cols. 1056: 'corripuit eum'; Sedulius Scotus retains the word *fiducia* as he found it in his source: Sedulius Scotus, *Liber de rectoribus Christianis* (c. 869/70) 12, ed. Hellmann, p. 56: 'illius fiducia, huius autem oboedientia'.

[92] On Adalhard of Corbie, see Cabaniss, *Charlemagne's Cousins* and De Jong, *The Penitential State*, pp. 122–9.

[93] Jacob, *Die handschriftliche Überlieferung*, p. 11; Ganz, *Corbie in the Carolingian Renaissance*, p. 143: St Petersburg, National Library of Russia, F.v.I. no. 11, fol. a recto: 'hic codex hero insula scriptus fuit iubente sco patre Adalhardo dum exularet ibi'.

[94] Radbert of Corbie, *Vita Adalhardi* 38 and 51, *PL* 120, cols. 1529 and 1535.

The Wise Adviser

face of opposition.[95] According to Adalhard's biographer, Radbert of Corbie (d. 865), Adalhard bore the verdict of exile patiently, 'giving thanks that he had been found worthy to suffer hardship on account of truth'.[96]

In his *Life of Adalhard,* written shortly after Adalhard's death in 826, Radbert models the image of his former abbot after the desert father Anthony, described in Athanasius' *Life of Anthony*.[97] The monks of Corbie knew Adalhard as 'Antonius', a name given to him by Alcuin, who started a fashion of bynames in Carolingian literature.[98] In his letters, Alcuin addresses his friend and fellow counsellor Adalhard affectionately as 'Antonius', which suggests that Adalhard was seen to typologically represent the desert father Antonius not only within the confines of Corbie, but also among the members of Charlemagne's court.[99] Like Abbot Adalhard, Abba Antonius (d. 356) had been an adviser to an emperor and his sons, namely to Emperor Constantine and his sons Constantius and Constans.[100] Athanasius' *Life of Anthony* (c. 360), which circulated widely in the Latin West in the translation of Evagrius Ponticus, records the life and virtues of the desert father Anthony, who sought martyrdom during the persecution under Emperor Maximinus. According to Athanasius, Anthony ministered to the confessors in prison and 'approached the judge with great freedom of speech', yet a martyr's death was not granted to him.[101] Athanasius praises Anthony's ascetic lifestyle but also his glorious deeds as a counsellor and truth-teller.[102] Just like Adalhard, who combined the responsibilities of an abbot with the duties of a magnate and court counsellor, Anthony balanced a life of silence and contemplation with his duty to teach and admonish: a task

---

[95] See the introduction. Lactantius, *Divinae institutiones*, 5, 1, 22; Gregory the Great, *Moralia in Job* 23, 14; see also, but without the connotation of fearlessness or justice, Isidore, *Etymologiae* 10, 275–6: 'veridicus, quia verum dicit et veritatis adsertor est'. I thank Rutger Kramer for the reference to Isidore.

[96] Radbert of Corbie, *Vita Adalhardi* 36, *PL* 120, col. 1528: 'Agebat namque gratias quod dignus inventus fuerit pro veritate contumeliam pati.'

[97] Athanasius, *Vita Antonii* (c. 360), ed. *PG* 26, cols. 823–976, translated into Latin by Evagrius Ponticus shortly before 374, ed. *PL* 73, cols. 126–170.

[98] Ganz, 'The *Epitaphium Arsenii* and opposition to Louis the Pious', p. 541; Garrison, 'The social world of Alcuin'.

[99] See Alcuin's letters to Adalhard, *Ep.* 175, 176, 181, 220, 222, 237, ed. Dümmler. *MGH Epp.* II. The first letter in which Alcuin addresses Adalhard as Antonius (*Ep.* 175) dates to 799. On nicknames at Charlemagne's court, see Garrison, 'The social world of Alcuin'.

[100] *Vita Antonii*, Greek version, ch. 81, *PG*, col. 955; Latin version, ch. 50, *PL* 73, cols. 126–70, at col. 162.

[101] See previous note. On Anthony seeking martyrdom, see *Vita Antonii*, Latin version, ch. 23 ('magna cum libertate ingrediens at iudicem'), *PL* 73, col. 143.

[102] On Anthony coming down from the mountain and going into Alexandria to warn against heresy and publicly (*publico sermone*) condemn the Arians, see *Vita Antonii*, Latin version, ch. 41, *PL* 73, col. 157; on his discernment and 'how he was counsellor to all', ch. 55, *PL* 73, cols. 165–6.

Part II

God had assigned to him when his desire for martyrdom was thwarted. According to the *Life of Anthony*, not only Anthony's brothers in the desert, but also visitors from the city of Alexandria came to ask for his advice and admonitions. Being a solitary desert monk, Anthony was not always approachable for those who sought his advice, but once in a while he left his cell and came down from his mountain to join his brothers, or to enter the city to admonish, rebuke, prophesy and warn against heresy.[103] On these occasions, Athanasius tells us, Anthony spoke the truth boldly, with *parrhesia*.[104]

In Radbert's *Life of Adalhard,* Adalhard is presented as a defender of truth, just like Anthony, whose name he carried. Radbert recalls how Adalhard, when he was still a young man 'trained in all prudence of the world among young recruits of the palace', strongly objected against what he considered to be the unlawful marriage of his cousin Charlemagne.[105] In an act of protest, he left the palace to lead the life of a monk. Notwithstanding his withdrawal, he became one of Charlemagne's principal advisers. According to Radbert, Adalhard was 'fertile in skilled counsel' and a stout defender of justice.[106] He was a pleader (*causidicus*), who settled differences of opinion and ensured that everyone's rights were respected.[107] Radbert praises Adalhard's eloquence and his skills of persuasion and dissuasion, which were highly valued qualities in a counsellor.[108] In Radbert's view, a court could not operate without competent advisers, as became painfully clear when Louis succeeded his father. The way Radbert saw it, everything went south when the new emperor banned his father's counsellors and exiled Adalhard. Once Adalhard, the *assertor veritatis*, returned to the court and the emperor publicly atoned for his misdeeds, order was restored, at least for the time being.[109] Radbert gives much credit to Adalhard for ensuring that the penance was done willingly and with the right intention. Drawing on

---

[103] See the references in the previous note.
[104] *Vita Antonii*, Greek version, ch. 82, PG 26, col. 960: Anthony prophesied that after the downfall of the Arians, Christians would 'speak boldly in every place with all freedom'; cf. Latin version, ch. 51, PL 73, col. 162. On Anthony speaking with *parrhesia* to his brothers, see *Vita Antonii*, Greek version, ch. 45, PG 26, col. 909.
[105] Radbert, *Vita Adalhardi* 7, PL 120, col. 1511: 'inter palatii tirocinia omni mundi prudentia eruditus'. On Adalhard's protests against Charlemagne's illicit marriage (*illicito thoro*), see further on in the same chapter, PL 120, col. 1511.
[106] Radbert, *Vita Adalhardi* 61, PL 120, col. 1539: 'Patet quia fecundus inventus est eruditionis consilio'.
[107] Ibid. 13, PL 120, col. 1515; 16, col. 1517; 38, col. 1529 ('inter omnium querimoniarum iura causidicus irrogantium'); 52, col. 1535.
[108] Ibid. 63, PL 120, col. 1540.
[109] Ibid. 51, PL 120, col. 1535: 'Sed nisi reversus esset veritatis assertor, interea minime paruisset, quo lethargio spiritu premerentur.'

The Wise Adviser

the traditional metaphor of frank speech, Radbert says that Adalhard cured the 'blindness' of the emperor and his entourage, and took care 'that the wound was treated in persuasion by the healthful antidote of Christ'.[110]

Perhaps it was Adalhard who, inspired by his reading of the *Tripartite History* during his years in exile, persuaded the emperor to follow Theodosius' illustrious example. And yet, apart from Radbert's suggestions, there is no corroborating evidence that Adalhard orchestrated Louis's penance.[111] The eleventh-century inscription in the Corbie manuscript of the *Tripartite History* that connects the copy to Adalhard and his place of exile may have been a reflection of a later literary tradition, in which Louis's penance, the account of Theodosius' atonement, and the theme of suffering exile for speaking the truth had become inextricably linked.

Some ten years after composing the *Life of Adalhard* in honour of his beloved abbot, Radbert wrote another tribute, this time to Adalhard's brother and successor, Wala (d. 836). It is a funeral oration, shaped as a dialogue between grieving monks of Corbie. Radbert presents Wala as a truth-teller at the court, who spoke with *constantia*, just as the prophets, the apostles, the martyrs and his own brother Adalhard had done.[112] While Adalhard's monastic name was Antonius, Wala took his byname from another desert father: Arsenius. The title that Radbert gave his funeral oration was *Epitaph for Arsenius*. According to the *Lives of the Desert Fathers,* Arsenius had been a counsellor at the palace before he ran off to the desert. The *Lives* do not mention the name of the emperor whose palace Arsenius left, but a later tradition has it that Arsenius was counsellor to Theodosius and tutor to his sons.[113] Arsenius was remembered as a champion of eloquence and of silence; he knew when to speak out and when to remain silent, just like Wala and his biographer Radbert.[114]

According to Radbert, Wala not only bore the image of Arsenius, but also that of Jeremiah, the Old Testament prophet who frequently called the people of Israel and her kings to repentance, and who lived in exile for a large part of his life.[115] Jeremiah advised, admonished and corrected

---

[110] Ibid. 51, *PL* 120, col. 1535: 'Unde etiam matura senectus caecitatis eorum vulnus salubri Christi antidoto mederi persuadendo curabat.'
[111] See in particular two accounts written shortly after the event: Agobard, *De dispensatione* 3 (c. 823/4), ed. Van Acker, and Radbert of Corbie, *Vita Adalhardi* 51 (after 826).
[112] Radbert, *Epitaphium Arsenii* II, 5, *PL* 120, col. 1613.
[113] See Pseudo-Rufinus, *Verba seniorum* III, 37, *PL* 73, cols. 762–763A. For a discussion of the development of this tradition, see De Jong, *Epitaph for an Era*.
[114] On Arsenius' silence, see chapter 5.
[115] De Jong, 'Becoming Jeremiah'; 'Jeremiah, Job, Terence and Paschasius Radbertus'.

Part II

with a vengeance, and did not hesitate to turn to invective when he deemed it necessary.[116] But, as Radbert points out, the invectives of both Wala and Jeremiah sprang from love, not from hatred.[117] In his *Epitaph* for Wala, Radbert draws on the vocabulary of judicial rhetoric to present Wala as an undaunted truth-teller and pillar of justice.[118] Inspired by the example of the subject of his biography, Radbert says he himself can no longer remain silent; the 'laws of truth' (*iura veritatis*) compel him to speak openly.[119] In the words of Matthew Kempshall, 'the prophetic conjunction of truth with justice runs right through [Radbert's] characterization of both Adalhard and Wala as advocates of justice and truth.'[120]

Much attention has been given in this chapter to the reception of the *Tripartite History* and to the story of Ambrose's bold admonition of Theodosius. Radbert's *Epitaph for Arsenius*, however, highlights the diversity of late antique resources that biographers had at their disposal in portraying a truth-teller. Many of the characters that populate the *Epitaph* carry the names of late antique emperors, poets and saints, such as Honorius, Gratian, Justina, Naso, Phasur, Antonius, Arsenius and Justinian. As Mayke de Jong has observed, these names cloak but simultaneously reveal the identity and moral status of the characters of Radbert's *Epitaph*, which breathes the world of late antique Christian and imperial history, as well as biblical history.[121] Scholars have pointed to the 'Ambrosian typology' of the characters in Radbert's dialogue, or referred to its literary setting as 'Ambrose's world'.[122] This characterisation is well-chosen, but we should bear in mind that the world of Radbert's *Epitaph* was also wider and more elusive than the world of Ambrose or the court of Theodosius. Ambrose, for one, does not figure as a character in Radbert's *Epitaph* and neither does Theodosius; their names are conspicuously absent.[123] Among Radbert's sources were Sulpicius Severus' *Dialogues* on Saint Martin and the *Lives of the Desert Fathers*,

---

[116] Radbert, *Epitaphium Arsenii* II, 11, ed. Dümmler, pp. 19, 20 and 24, discussed in Kempshall, *Rhetoric and the Writing of History*, p. 205 and in De Jong, *Epitaph for an Era*.
[117] Radbert, *Epitaphium Arsenii* II, 11, ed. Dümmler, p. 24, line 9,10.
[118] See the analysis of Kempshall, *Rhetoric and the Writing of History*, pp. 202–8.
[119] Ibid., p. 203. Compare Radbert, *Vita Adalhardi* 4, ed. PL 120, col. 1510.
[120] Kempshall, *Rhetoric and the Writing of History*, p. 205.
[121] On the function of aliases in Radbert's *Epitaphium Arsenii*, revealing the moral status of the characters, see De Jong, 'Becoming Jeremiah', pp. 186, 187; see also Garrison, 'The social world of Alcuin'.
[122] Booker, *Past Convictions*, p. 46; De Jong, 'Paschasius Radbertus and Pseudo-Isidore', p. 171; De Jong, 'Becoming Jeremiah', p. 186; De Jong, 'The resources of the past', pp. 131–51, Ganz, 'The *Epitaphium Arsenii* and opposition to Louis the Pious', p. 541.
[123] Radbert does mention Ambrose as a patristic author, but not as a historical figure or character in his dialogue. On the absence of the names of Ambrose and Theodosius, see De Jong, 'The resources of the past', pp. 140, 141, where she argues that both the assigning and the withholding of names created a *typus*.

featuring saints and abbots who performed the role of truth-tellers and counsellors just as confidently as bishops did. The biographies of desert fathers Anthony and Arsenius and the Old Testament books of the prophets supplied Radbert with *personae* or types for his free-speaking abbots, which he may have considered more appropriate than the example of Bishop Ambrose, promoted by the *Tripartite History*. There was more than one model or cultural resource from which to choose when drawing the portrait of a courageous truth-teller.

CONCLUSION

In the late eighth and ninth century, criticism of the ruler was tolerated, as long as it was expressed according to accepted modes of delivery.[124] Mirrors for princes encouraged rulers to accept criticism, and to be open to the contrary opinions of their advisers. This is not to say that all critics spoke 'freely' to their rulers. Critics had a variety of literary genres, rhetorical models and modes of delivery at their disposal to bring their warnings, advice or dissent to a ruler's attention. These modes were often indirect or circumspect. Very popular at the time, for example, was visionary literature, in which political criticism was expressed in the form of supernatural moral warnings.[125] Many of the authors of paraenetic literature and letters of admonition that we have encountered in this chapter expressed their criticism in a less than open and direct manner. Boniface dressed his rebuke of King Aethelbald in the guise of a rumour report, Cathwulf hid his critique underneath praise and traditional counsel, while Alcuin chose the role of pastoral adviser to influence policy in a most gentle yet persistent manner.

Carolingian authors probably did not value frank criticism higher than authors in the Merovingian period did, but there are some differences. For one thing, the position of the person who delivered criticism at the court had changed. Sixth- and seventh-century saints' lives feature wandering missionary monks, such as Columban, holy women such as Genovefa, or saintly bishops such as Leodegar, who offer advice and criticism to the ruler, but who are no regular presence at the court.[126] They came and they went, either voluntarily or by force, at least according to the authors who recorded their lives. Their criticism was the criticism of the charismatic outsider. Ninth-century narratives feature critics who are part of the 'establishment'; they take part in assemblies,

---

[124] De Jong, *The Penitential State*.
[125] On vision literature, see Dutton, *The Politics of Dreaming* and Keskiaho, *Dreams and Visions*.
[126] See chapter 6.

Part II

councils and restricted meetings and are the emperor's right-hand men. In Carolingian advice literature and letters of admonition, a different type of critic emerges, the wise adviser, who did not replace the charismatic outsider of late antique and Merovingian literature, but was another *persona* in the repertoire of truth-tellers. The position was open to anyone who could be trusted to offer disinterested, honest advice, had an expert knowledge of politics and the will of God, and was skilled in rhetoric.[127]

This period saw no new rhetorical treatises or theoretical reflections that prescribed modes of acceptable criticism, but there were models to imitate. The story of Ambrose rebuking Theodosius was such a model, for truth-telling bishops, for counsellors, and for those who harboured the ambition to be both. Ninth-century adaptations and interpretations fine-tuned the narrative model of the *Tripartite History* to fit the cultural needs of the time. The differences we can observe between Merovingian and Carolingian literature reflect more than just a change in literary taste; they also show that social roles had shifted, resulting in new settings, new interpretations and new performances of frank speech.

Admonitio became a highly important notion in the ninth-century discourse of frankness. The rhetoric of free speech, with its roots in Greco-Roman philosophy, was increasingly determined by the code model of the Old Testament prophet. The court of Theodosius is regularly invoked in advice literature as the ideal court, where critics and advisers spoke freely to rulers. That model court, however, was not historically specific. What scholars have called 'the world of Ambrose' was a cultural hybrid world, populated with fearless bishops, wise counsellors and outspoken prophets. For biographers constructing a portrait of a truth-teller, this cluster of ideas, values and role models offered a wealth of possibilities from which to choose. Authors of letters of admonition and mirrors for princes drew from the same pool of cultural resources, and mixed the language of the Old Testament prophet with a rhetoric of frankness that they ascribed to late antique bishops, but not exclusively to bishops. Desert fathers such as Anthony and Arsenius equally served as models of frank speech and bold behaviour, especially for those who had chosen the monastic life, but were also called upon to fulfil social and political duties, such as the abbots Adalhard and Wala.

In Carolingian literature of advice and criticism, the outsider position remained a popular stance. As Mary Garrison has pointed out with regard to Alcuin, and Jinty Nelson with regard to the poet Theodulf (before he became bishop), these authors took advantage of their lowly rank in the

---

[127] On the Christian ideal of public service, see Noble, 'Secular sanctity'. Laymen, especially the nobility, were expected to share in the burdens of the citizenship of the City of God on earth.

The Wise Adviser

clerical hierarchy to vent their opinions.[128] They offered advice and criticism from an unthreatening position below or outside the top regions where political power was wielded. Declarations of love for the ruler and concern for his well-being further softened the impact of criticism and removed any suspicion of presumption on the part of the speaker. As the court scholar and lay abbot Einhard assures Emperor Louis's son Lothar in a letter of admonition: 'God knows I love you, and this is why I admonish you this boldly. Do not consider the worthlessness of the person who admonishes, but the wholesomeness of the advice.'[129] The fact that such protestations of modesty were a literary topos should not lead us to dismiss it out of hand. The literary stance of the critic who professed that his status was far below that of the person he admonished was highly effective. Archbishop Agobard of Lyon (d. 840) was such an admoniser who presented himself as an outsider–critic, even though he occupied a higher rank in the ecclesiastical hierarchy than an Alcuin, Einhard or the poet Theodulf. His outsider status was of a different kind, as we shall see in the next chapter.

---

[128] Garrison, 'Les correspondants d'Alcuin'; Nelson, 'The *libera vox* of Theodulf'.
[129] Einhard, *Ep.* 11, ed. Dümmler, *MGH Epp.* III, p. 115: 'Amo vos, Deus scit, et ideo tam fiducialiter ammoneo; nec vos vilitatem personae ammonentis, sed salubritatem consilii considerare debetis.' Einhard's letter of admonition to Lothar dates to 829/30.

9

AGOBARD OF LYON

In the early years of the seventeenth century, the humanist Jean Papire Masson (d. 1611) visited a bookshop in Lyon.[1] When he entered the shop, he was just in time to stop a bookbinder from cutting up an old codex. As Masson later reported, the bookbinder had already taken up a knife to begin his destructive work.[2] Masson recognised the value of the codex and procured it. He found that it contained hitherto unknown writings of Agobard, archbishop of Lyon from 816 to 840. Masson recounts the story of his discovery in a prefatory letter to the church of Lyon, added to his edition of the manuscript in 1605.[3] The codex, written partly in a ninth-century, partly in a tenth-century hand (Paris, BnF, lat. 2853, ff. 1–212 s. IX, ff. 213–30 s. X, provenance Lyon), contained letters, theological treatises and polemical pamphlets of the archbishop, spanning his entire episcopal career. Among them were letters addressed to Emperor Louis the Pious (814–40), that were previously unknown. Some texts from Agobard's hand, dealing mainly with liturgy and church discipline, had been transmitted in other manuscripts.[4] The newly-discovered writings were of a different nature: they were of a political and, as it was perceived at the time, a highly contentious nature. These new finds revealed that Agobard, who was venerated as a saint in Lyon, had played a leading part in the deposition of Emperor Louis in 833 in Soissons. The fact that he had been involved in the revolt against Louis was already known from contemporary sources, but the extent of his

---

[1] This chapter owes much to the work of Mayke de Jong, Courtney Booker and Stuart Airlie, and to the conversations I have had with them.

[2] Masson, Prefatory letter to the church of Lyon, ed. *PL* 104, col. 18B. Masson's discovery and the debate that followed his edition of the manuscript are discussed by Boshof, *Erzbishof Agobard von Lyon*, pp. 1–6 and Booker, *Past Convictions*, pp. 98–100, 103.

[3] Masson, *Sancti Agobardi episcopi Ecclesiae Lugdunensis opera: quae octigentos annos in tenebris delituerant* [...] (Paris, 1605). Masson's edition, including the prefatory letter, is reprinted in *PL* 104.

[4] For the manuscripts, see Van Acker, *Agobardi Lugdunensis Opera omnia*, pp. xlviii–lv.

206

involvement came to light after Masson's discovery of the codex of Agobard's letters.[5]

This chapter studies a selection of letters from the extensive collection of Agobard's writings that were discovered by Masson. The selected letters represent different phases in Agobard's career. I shall explore the ways in which this 'insolent offender of the imperial majesty', as he would come to be viewed later, adopted different voices of admonition and speaker positions to advise and criticise his emperor.

Agobard's political career knew an unfortunate start. He was dismissed from court at the assembly of Attigny in 822, after having delivered what appears to have been an inappropriate speech. He managed to find his way back onto the political stage around 829. For a brief period of time he found himself in the centre of political action, when he sided with Lothar, Emperor Louis's eldest son, in the rebellion against his father in 833. In less than a year, Emperor Louis was back on the throne and Agobard was exiled. In this chapter, I shall focus mainly on Agobard's letters of admonition dating from before the rebellion, addressed to the emperor and his courtiers in the years during which he was shunned by the court. I shall address the question of whether Agobard was really an outsider, or merely styled himself as such in his letters to get his message across more effectively. A second question is the one that has informed every chapter of this book: that of the extent to which these letters can be situated in the framework of the rhetorical tradition of *parrhesia* or *libertas dicendi*. At the end of this chapter I shall turn to the polemical pamphlets that Agobard produced in 833, the year when he changed his position from self-appointed adviser, eager to get the emperor's attention, to one of the chief rebels in the revolt. To understand the range of his performances as adviser, critic, outcast and exile we first need to take a closer look at the details and circumstances of his career, and consider his relationship with the emperor and his court.

YOUR LOWLY SERVANT

When Agobard was elected archbishop of Lyon in 814, he was a relative newcomer in court circles. As successor to the highly respected Leidrad of Lyon (d. 816) he had big shoes to fill. Leidrad had been a *missus* and adviser of Charlemagne and had restored and reformed the Church of Lyon with the emperor's support and patronage.[6] Agobard may have taken the intimate relationship between Leidrad and Charlemagne as

---
[5] Booker, *Past Convictions*, p. 99.
[6] On Leidrad's reforms in Lyon, see Rubellin, *Église et société chrétienne*, pp. 148–9.

a model of the kind of bond he hoped to establish with the new emperor.[7] Agobard, however, had not been Emperor Louis's choice. It was Leidrad who had chosen him as his successor in the year that Louis ascended his father's throne. For some years, Agobard had been Leidrad's *coepiscopus* or *chorepiscopus*,[8] and although there is some discussion about what precisely that function entailed, it qualified Agobard to become the next archbishop of Lyon, at least in Leidrad's eyes. Louis eventually approved Agobard's election, but only after two years. Between 814 and 816, Agobard's position was uncertain: he was acting archbishop of Lyon, but his position was not formally confirmed. After the emperor and a council of bishops had approved his election, possibly at the Council of Aachen in 816, Agobard made every effort to curry the emperor's favour and establish his place in a network of bishops by sending them his writings as gifts.[9] Some of his texts were written upon request, but the greater part of his letter-treatises were composed and dispatched on his own initiative, to solidify bonds with his fellow bishops and with the emperor.

Agobard's early letters cover topics which he knew would interest those bishops with whom he wished to align himself, and which might attract the benevolent attention of the emperor. These topics range from the correct organisation and administration of the *ecclesia* to the fight against heresies and superstitions. In 818 or 819, he sent the emperor a treatise on the dangers of Adoptionism, a Hispanic Christology which had been condemned by Alcuin and others as heresy at the end of the eighth century. In this treatise, called *Against the Teachings of Felix*, Agobard deals with the ideas of Felix, bishop of Urgel (d. 818), who had recently died in Lyon in exile. Felix's teachings had been refuted by Alcuin during a public disputation at the court in Aachen in 799.[10] Felix was put into the custody of Leidrad, and when Agobard succeeded Leidrad, he 'inherited' Felix. It is somewhat curious that Agobard decided to combat Felix's heretical views this late in the day, when the man was already dead. He may have been worried that Felix still had supporters in Lyon, and that his ideas continued to pose a threat to orthodoxy. Agobard says he had found a document written by Felix that indicated that Felix had maintained his Adoptionist views after he had formally denounced them in Aachen.[11] Since Felix enjoyed some freedom of movement in Lyon, it is not unthinkable that he had been able to spread his teachings.

---

[7] Langenwalter, *Agobard of Lyon*, p. 57.   [8] Boshof, *Erzbishof Agobard von Lyon*, pp. 33, 34.
[9] Langenwalter, *Agobard of Lyon*, pp. 57–9.
[10] Van Renswoude, 'The art of disputation', pp. 38–40.
[11] Agobard, *Adversum dogma Felicis* 1, 1–13, ed. Van Acker, p. 74 and Boshof, *Erzbishof Agobard von Lyon*, p. 60.

As the annotations of a tenth-century reader show, jotted down in the margins of the manuscript of Agobard's *Against the Teachings of Felix*, interest in this particular heresy and its refutation was long-lived.[12] And yet, concern about the spread of Felix's teaching need not have been the main reason why Agobard sent the text to Louis. Doubtless he wanted to establish his authority, display his theological abilities and demonstrate to the emperor in what ways his writing skills, sharp wit and concern for the Church could be of use.

In the dedicatory letter attached to this treatise, Agobard offers his text to Louis for correction and asks him to approve or disapprove his work.[13] He had made a similar request in his treatise *Against the Law of Gundobad* (written c. 818/19), in which he asks the emperor to correct him if he has said something unsuitable.[14] Such requests for correction were an approved and tested means of confirming hierarchy and seeking the favour of a patron or solidifying the relationship between correspondents.[15] As Gertrud Simon has argued, in her study of medieval dedicatory letters, the several replies to dedicatory letters requesting corrections and literary judgement that have been preserved confirm the genuine communicative function of such letters.[16] Moreover, revised versions of texts have survived in which the suggestions and corrections of a patron–proofreader have been incorporated.[17] Archbishop Hincmar, for example, proofread a draft of the theological report of Ratramnus of Corbie, and indicated with signs in the margin where he thought the text should be revised.[18] Submitting a text for approval and correction was therefore no mere rhetorical nicety, but part of an actual editorial practice.

The main aim of Agobard's letter-preface to Louis, however, was to seek the emperor's approval and favour. Letters, especially letters of petition, confirmed hierarchy and reflected the kind of relationship desired by the author of the letter.[19] Letters thus also had a performative function, establishing, or at least trying to establish, the relationship they proclaimed.[20] Asking for correction was furthermore an effective

---

[12] Paris, BnF, lat. 2853, ff. 4r–v, 8v, 10r, 11v.
[13] Agobard, *Adversum dogma Felicis*, preface, ed. Van Acker, p. 73, lines 13–17.
[14] Agobard, *Adversus legem Gundobadi* 5, ed. Van Acker, p. 21, line 23–p. 22, line 7.
[15] Simon, 'Untersuchungen zur Topik der Widmungsbriefe', pp. 112–36, especially pp. 125–9; Steckel, 'Between censorship and patronage'; Janson, *Latin Prose Prefaces*, pp. 106–16, especially p. 109.
[16] Simon, 'Untersuchungen zur Topik der Widmungsbriefe', p. 133.
[17] See for example Bishop Echberth's revision of Boniface's letter of admonition to King Aethelbald, discussed in Rau, *Briefe des Bonifatius*, p. 212, n. 10; p. 226, n. 23.
[18] Hincmar, *Epistola ad Odonem Bellovacensem* (868), ed. Lambot, p. 270.
[19] Poster, 'A conversation halved', p. 26.   [20] Ibid., 27.

Part II

rhetorical means of mitigating any possible offence the letter might cause the addressee. This literary strategy was known as *praecedens correctio*.[21] By saying something along the lines of 'if I speak inappropriately, do tell me', the speaker/writer could take the edge off his criticism or advice if he feared the message would not go down well with the addressee.[22] Used in combination with a humility formula such as 'pardon my presumption', which one often finds in epistolary salutations, a letter invoked the physical setting and ritual of a formal petition to a superior.[23] The author of the letter offered a gift, a text, and if it was received well, he could expect a favour in return: namely, to be listened to.[24]

Agobard's early letters and treatises, written between 817 and 822, are remarkably diplomatic. There is an air of subservience to his early letters that we do not find in the more confident letters of admonition written after his fall from grace in 822, or in the polemical pamphlets that he wrote in 833. In the letters that can be dated to the early phase of Agobard's episcopal career, when he still hoped to curry Louis's favour, he refers to himself as Louis's lowly servant, who is unworthy to talk about worthy topics and too insignificant to speak about great things.[25] He voices strong opinions about justice and orthodoxy, but takes care not to offend Louis, apologising in advance for any offence his advice and admonitions might cause. In the light of Agobard's reputation as a fierce and outspoken critic of Louis, it is interesting to see that his early communications do not reveal any inclination towards frank criticism. Agobard presented himself to Louis in writing as someone who was capable of pointing out injustice, who was eager to defend orthodoxy, and dedicated to admonition and correction, which were all qualities that were expected of a bishop, as we have seen in the previous chapter. He wanted to be known, moreover, as an admonisher who was open to be corrected himself, if his opinions did not meet with the emperor's approval.

The letters that Agobard sent to Louis in the early years of his episcopacy suggest that he envisaged a role for himself as Louis's adviser on matters concerning orthodoxy, justice and the right organisation of the church. He may even have met with some initial success in establishing such a position for himself. In 821, after the death of Louis's chief adviser

---

[21] On *correctio* as a rhetorical figure and its relation to free speech (*licentia/parrhesia*), see Lausberg, *Handbook of Literary Rhetoric,* par. 786, 4 and Lanham, *Handlist of Rhetorical Terms,* p. 110.
[22] Aquila Romanus (fl. third century AD), *De figuris* 1: 'prodiortosis. praecedens correctio'.
[23] Lanham, *'Salutatio' Formulas,* pp. 63–6.
[24] On admonition perceived as a precious gift, see M. Garrison, 'An aspect of Alcuin'.
[25] Agobard, *Adversum dogma Felicis,* ed. Van Acker, p. 73, lines 4, 5; *Adversus legem Gundobadi* 5, ed. Van Acker, p. 21, lines 23–5.

Agobard of Lyon

Benedict of Aniane, Agobard was entrusted with the supervision of the election of a new abbot in the royal monastery of Aniane, together with Bishop Nibridius of Narbonne. It was Agobard who informed Louis that the election of the new abbot of Aniane had taken place in good order, and he may have done so personally at the assembly of Diedenhofen in 821.[26] The events in Attigny taught Agobard, however, that he could not simply take over Leidrad's privileged position at the court.

A FAILED SPEECH

In 822, Agobard attended a general assembly in Attigny.[27] This was the occasion on which Emperor Louis performed public penance to atone for sins committed against his family, as discussed in the previous chapter. Louis's confession and subsequent penance were not the only issues on the agenda; other topics that were discussed at Attigny were schooling, preaching, simony and the pervasive problem of negligence of duties.[28] It was at this meeting that Agobard delivered his first public speech. He had also been present at the assembly of Aachen in 817, shortly after he officially acceded to the see of Lyon in 816, but there is no record that on that occasion he spoke publicly. Perhaps it was his ambition to be acknowledged as a reformer and a valuable adviser to the emperor that led him to address the gathering on a contentious issue, namely, the inalienability of church property. This was not the safest topic to tackle in a maiden speech. Agobard's speech did not go down well, as the events that shortly followed showed.

A year or so after assembly, Agobard described his failed speech in a letter to an unnamed friend, a bishop from Provence or Septimania, the region Agobard originally came from.[29] Agobard provides his friend with a rather elaborate account of the assembly, with much attention to the manner in which people spoke. He recounts to his friend how Emperor Louis first conducted an enquiry into the affairs of the realm.[30] When Louis finished his address to the assembly, some of the leading men got up to speak. Among them was the 'venerable old man Adalhard', who had just returned from exile.[31] Adalhard delivered a speech in which he stated

---

[26] Boshof, *Erzbischof Agobard von Lyon*, p. 82.
[27] The events of Attigny and Agobard's role at this assembly are discussed by Airlie, 'I, Agobard' and De Jong, *The Penitential State*, especially pp. 142–7.
[28] See the capitulary of the assembly of Attigny, *Concilium Attiniacense 822*, MGH Conc. 2,2, ed. Werminghoff, pp. 471–2.
[29] Agobard, *De dispensatione ecclesiasticarum rerum*, dated to 823 or 824. On the identity of the addressee of Agobard's treatise on church property, see Boshof, *Erzbischof Agobard von Lyon*, pp. 83–5.
[30] Agobard, *De dispensatione* 2, ed. Van Acker, pp. 121, 122.   [31] See chapter 8.

Part II

that he had never seen such glorious progress of the public cause since the days of King Pippin.[32] He admonished all who were present to stand together and support the emperor, and invited the participants of the assembly to come up with suggestions for further improvement. If anyone had anything to say, said Adalhard, then he should 'proclaim [this] audaciously' (*confidenter edicite*), without a doubt in his mind that the lord emperor would give satisfaction.[33]

Then Agobard got up to speak, for indeed he had a few suggestions in response to Adalhard's call. By the time he delivered his speech, the emperor had already withdrawn from the general meeting.[34] In his speech, Agobard argued for a different policy regarding church property, and warned of the moral danger of handing out to laymen what belonged to the Church. At first, Agobard writes to his friend, he had the impression that his speech went down well, and that two of the leading men who were close to the emperor, the abbots Adalhard and Helisachar, agreed with him. Agobard hoped that they would pass on to the emperor what he had said, but, as he writes to his friend, he was not sure whether they had actually done that.[35] But he soon found out that his speech had not made a favourable impression, for he was neither allowed to repeat his points in the presence of the emperor, nor invited to attend subsequent assemblies.

Agobard's letter to his unnamed friend is the only account we have of the speech he delivered at the assembly of Atttigny. Therefore, if we want to establish what exactly went wrong, and why his speech was so inappropriate, we have to take Agobard's own report as a starting point. In the letter to his friend, Agobard includes the full speech, suggesting that these were the very words he spoke. The letter is an epistolary preface to a treatise *On the Right Administration of Church Property,* which he wrote at his friend's request in 823 or 824. His friend had heard from reliable sources in Septimania and Provence that Agobard's public performance at the assembly of Attigny had caused quite a stir. Rumour had it that Agobard had instigated an 'unheard-of contention and discord' (*inauditam contentionem et discordiam*) when defending the integrity of church property. His friend warned Agobard that people were not talking favourably about him.[36] Agobard replies that these rumours overstate his influence at court. His position or reputation, he says, is not such that he could cause such discord. He is but an inexperienced and timid person, he writes,

---

[32] Agobard, *De dispensatione* 3, ed. Van Acker, p. 122, lines 1–5.
[33] Ibid. 3, ed. Van Acker, p. 122, lines 7–12.
[34] This can be concluded from Agobard, *De dispensatione* 4, ed. Van Acker, p. 123, lines 54, 55.
[35] Ibid. 4, ed. Van Acker, p. 123, lines 53–5.   [36] Ibid. 1, ed. Van Acker, p. 121, lines 1–7.

who hardly dares to open his mouth in the company of great and better men.[37]

Agobard presents himself here as an inexperienced speaker, and contrasts his own cautious way of speaking with the agreeable speech of the leading men who had spoken before him.[38] 'When our leading men had spoken these and similar things in an agreeable fashion', Agobard writes, 'I, surely the most humble and lowest of them all, began to offer suggestions, in a certain cautious way, as one speaks to great men.'[39] Agobard characterises his mode of speaking with the adverb *pedetemptim* (cautiously, feeling one's way) to indicate the careful manner in which he had phrased his viewpoints. Yet the speech that followed, which Agobard reproduces in this letter in the direct mode, as if he is quoting himself word for word, comes across as a confident speech. He points out the dangers for the church if laymen continue to administer church goods for their own purposes. Back in the old days, according to Agobard, nobody dared to oppose the canons of the church concerning church property, because it was agreed that whoever did so, opposed God and the universal Church. Touch the canons, says Agobard, and you touch God himself.[40] If, however, the participants of the assembly were to collectively acknowledge and regret the current abuse of church goods, then perhaps God, in his mercy, would grant a pardon. Agobard closes his speech with a direct address to all who were present, calling upon them (strongly, in the imperative mode) to support the emperor and carry the responsibility for undoing the wrongs of the recent past together.[41] Although Agobard emphasises that the present deplorable situation is not Louis's personal fault, but should rather be blamed on his predecessors, he makes it perfectly clear that he consideres it the emperor's responsibility to do something about it. He implies that the emperor will be punished for transgressing the sacred canons if he does not act against the abuse of church property, and so will all the participants in the assembly, if they do not warn the emperor and convince him that he has to correct a wrong.

Agobard was dismissed from court and not invited to assemblies in the following years. No discussion on church property is mentioned in the acts of the Council of Attigny, nor in any other contemporary sources, which may be taken as an indication that Agobard's speech was formally ignored. If we are to believe Agobard's letter to his friend, however,

---

[37] Ibid. 1, ed. Van Acker, p. 121, lines 14–18.
[38] An observation made by Stuart Airlie in 'I, Agobard', p. 177.
[39] Agobard, *De dispensatione* 4, ed. Van Acker, p. 122, lines 1–3: 'Haec et his similia cum primores nostri iocundissime loquerentur, ego, ut scilicet humillimus omnium et extremus, coepi quodammodo pedetemptim, utpote magnis viris, ita suggerere.'
[40] Ibid. 4, ed. Van Acker, p. 123, lines 26–30. [41] Ibid. 4, ed. Van Acker, p. 123, lines 46–52.

people in Septiminia and Provence did talk about it, and not favourably. Egon Boshof attributes the failure of the speech to Agobard's unrealistic expectations.[42] Being a new actor on the political stage, he was not familiar enough with the diplomatic situation and the specific sensitivities of the lay magnates. He may have stepped on some people's toes without realising it.[43] Boshof judges Agobard to be an idealist, using canons and examples from the past that no longer matched the realities of his own time. Six years later, however, at the Assembly of Aachen in 829, Abbot Wala of Corbie delivered a speech on the same topic, the inalienability of church property, using similar arguments to Agobard's, and yet Wala's speech was well received.[44] Was this topic all of a sudden not contentious anymore?

Agobard's come-down at Attigny was probably above all a matter of bad timing. After all, this was the very assembly where Louis confessed his sins and asked for forgiveness for his involvement in the blinding of his nephew Bernard of Italy, for exiling his relatives, and for all the wrongs that either he or his father had committed in the past. The bishops followed his example, and confessed that they too had failed to live up to their task; they had been negligent in administering their duties.[45] Agobard, strangely enough, does not mention this part of the meeting in the letter to his friend, although the atonement of the emperor and the bishops must surely have made quite an impression on all who were present. Whatever the reason that Agobard passed over this aspect of the meeting in silence, it will have been obvious to all who were present at the time that the assembly was meant to create unity and solidarity. The speech that the emperor's kinsman Adalhard gave appropriately underlined the theme of solidarity. Then it was Agobard's turn, and instead of giving the kind of positive 'let's move on' speech that Adalhard had delivered, he pointed out, perhaps following Adalhard's call to speak out audaciously, what else was wrong in the empire.[46] Although some may have felt there was some truth in what Agobard said, this was not the occasion to utter it.[47] Next year, at the assembly of Compiègne, the issue of church property was discussed in the general assembly, but by that time Agobard was no longer invited to participate. For the time being, he was excluded from the decision-making process.

---

[42] Boshof, *Erzbishof Agobard von Lyon*, p. 87.   [43] Ibid., p. 89.
[44] It should, however, be noted that it was Wala's staunch supporter Radbert of Corbie who maintained that Wala's speech was well received. De Jong, *The Penitential State*, pp. 167, 168. On Wala's speech at the assembly of Aachen 828, see Boshof, *Erzbishof Agobard von Lyon*, pp. 88–9.
[45] The procedure of Louis's penance in Attigny is described in the *Royal Frankish Annals* and in the Astronomer's *Life of Louis;* see De Jong, *The Penitential State,* pp. 122, 123.
[46] Agobard, *De dispensatione* 3: 'confidenter edicite', ed. Van Acker, p. 122, lines 1–5.
[47] De Jong, *The Penitential State,* p. 143.

Agobard of Lyon

THE MUMBLING PROPHET

After his luckless performance at Attigny, Agobard sent several hortatory treatises and letters of admonition to the court. The first of these was a letter to Louis's three counsellors, Wala, Helisachar and Adalhard, in which he complains about the growing influence of the Jewish community in Lyon and at the court – another topic that was high on Agobard's agenda during the first years of his episcopacy.[48] He looks back on the conversation he had with these men on this topic after the general assembly was over, shortly before everyone returned home again:

Recently, when the time to leave the palace had already been granted to us, your sweetest kindness sat down and listened to me, mumbling rather than speaking against those who support the complaints of the Jews. And when these words had been heard by you and when what had been said by both sides had been modified, you got up, and I did so after you. You entered into the presence of the ruler, I stood behind the door. After a while you signalled that I could enter, but I heard nothing, except for the permission to leave. What you said about the aforementioned matter to the most clement prince, how he reacted, and what he replied, I have not heard. Afterwards I did not go to you, lamed by embarrassing shame and fatigued by the trouble that by all means assailed me, not because of the difficulty of the matter but because of lack of nobility of mind. I therefore went away troubled, I began my journey uncertain, I arrived home confused, and I settled back down afflicted. I would describe the causes of this affliction, but I fear to belabour your kindness. Nevertheless, the bearer of this letter can tell you all about it, if your patience allows.[49]

Before Agobard was granted an audience with the emperor, he had to present his problem before the courtiers Wala, Adalhard and Helisachar. Their discussion appears to have been the kind of preparatory discussion described in the treatise *De ordine palatii,* to establish beforehand if a topic was worthy to bring 'to the ruler's tender ears'.[50] Agobard describes how

---

[48] This topic has been discussed in detail elsewhere; see Pezé, 'Amalaire et la communauté Juive de Lyon' and the literature cited there.

[49] Agobard, *De baptismo*, ed. Van Acker, p. 115, lines 3–19: 'Nuper cum a palatio tempus redeundi nobis iam fuisset indultum, suavissima dilectio vestra sedit et audivit me, musitantem potius quam loquentem contra eos, qui quaerelas Iudaeorum astruebant. Cumque audita fuissent a vobis et modificata quae dicebantur altrinsecus, surrexistis; et ego post vos. Vos ingressi estis in conspectu principis, ego steti ante ostium; post paululum fecistis ut ingrederer, sed nihil audivi, nisi absolutionem discedendi. Quid tamen vos dixeritis clementissimo principi prefata de causa, qualiterque acceperit, quidve responderit, non audivi. Ad vos postea non accessi, praepediente pudore ignavo, et molestia fatigante me, quae mihi utique accessit non tam ex involutione rerum, quam ex ignobilitate mentis. Quamobrem recessi turbatus, arripui iter incertus, perveni domum confusus, resedi afflictus. Causas vero huius afflictionis scriberem, sed timeo mansuetudini vestrae laborem ingerere. Portitor tamen harum litterarum potest vobis edicere, si patitur longanimitas vestra.' The translation is based on De Jong, *The Penitential State*, pp. 142, 143.

[50] *De ordine palatii* 5, 425, 426, ed. Gross, Schieffer, pp. 78, 79.

Part II

the three courtiers sat down with him to listen to his complaint. After they had heard what he had to say, they began 'to moderate what we had said to each other'.[51] This is an interesting choice of words. The verb *modificare* means 'set limits' or 'keep within bounds', which suggests that Wala, Adalhard and Helisachar tempered Agobard's viewpoints. Then the three courtiers rose and went inside to talk to the emperor, while Agobard waited outside the door. After waiting for some time, while Wala, Helisachar and Adalhard put in a good word for him (or so he hoped) with the emperor to arrange an audience, he was allowed to enter, but heard nothing but 'a permission to leave'.

In his letter to Louis's counsellors, Agobard describes the humiliation he felt when he was dismissed in this brusque manner. He quietly left the palace without seeking out the three men to ask them how their conversation with the emperor went and what the emperor had answered. The self-critical tone of the letter is striking, especially in those passages where Agobard describes his own mode of speaking. He says he did not speak clearly when he talked to Wala, Adalhard and Helisachar, but 'mumbled rather than speaking out'. The verb *mussitare,* which is used here, refers to a mode of speaking somewhere between silence and speech. Agobard may have spoken in a low tone out of fear that his words were overheard. It is, however, more likely that he is deliberately presenting himself in his letter to these high-ranking courtiers, and via them to a wider audience, as a mumbler who did not speak confidently. By referring to his own mode of speaking as *mussitare*, Agobard deprecates himself before his audience. He stresses his loss of honour when he confesses to feelings of humiliation and shame when he was not granted a hearing. Why did he choose to do that? He could have ignored his dismissal and never brought it up again, but for some reason Agobard wished to make his shame publicly known.

Stuart Airlie proposes that Agobard's frankness about his embarrassing shame may have been 'designed to sting his readers into forming an emotional community with him'.[52] Indeed, it may well have been Agobard's intention to get the sympathy of his audience, but there is also another explanation as to why he stresses the humiliation of his dismissal: namely, to deliberately cast himself in the role of the dejected prophet. Agobard's 'mumbling' voice is reminiscent of the stuttering voice of the prophet Jeremiah, who could speak clearly and unhampered only if God spoke through him. Old Testament prophets were often depicted as notoriously bad speakers. Moses, for example, had a stammer.

---

[51] Agobard, *De baptismo*, ed. Van Acker, p. 115, line 6: 'modificata quae dicebantur altrinsecus'.
[52] Airlie, 'I, Agobard', p. 177.

When God sent him to see the Pharaoh, Moses brought his eloquent brother Aaron along to speak for him. The first words the prophet Jeremiah spoke to God are not even proper words but stuttering sounds: 'A ... a ... a, my Lord God, I'm too young and I do not know how to speak.'[53] This is not exactly the type of confident speech of which a Greek or Roman orator would have been proud.

The rhetorical ideals expressed in the Old Testament, and to a certain extent also in the New Testament, were markedly different from Greco-Roman rhetorical ideals. Eloquence was appreciated in both cultures, but while Greco-Roman rhetoricians cultivated talent through an intense training programme, the Old Testament rhetorical ideal rested on divine inspiration. The prophet did not need to excel in rhetoric; he was chosen to be a (passive) conduit for the voice of God. His way of speaking was presented as unaccomplished, unless he was inspired by God's spirit. Thus it was stressed that true eloquence came directly from God, not from the prophet himself.[54] Seen from this perspective, naturally accomplished speakers or trained orators were suspect. It was believed they would be easily tempted to trust in their own persuasive capacities and cease to acknowledge their dependence on God. In his treatise *On Rhetoric and Virtues,* Alcuin highlights this difference between Christian and classical ideals of eloquence by juxtaposing the straightforward speech of the Apostle Paul with the learned speech of the trained orator Tertullus.[55] It is remarkable that Alcuin draws this contrast in a treatise that presents and promotes knowledge of classical rhetoric. As George Kennedy has pointed out, Christians used rhetoric to denounce rhetoric.[56] This is an important observation that should warn us against taking loud protests against rhetoric too literally, but we should not dismiss them as meaningless either. It was a recurrent motif for Christian speakers and authors to emphasise that they had no natural talent for speaking and were not properly educated in the art of rhetoric. This was no hollow humility topos, but a coded and formalised expression of commonly shared values. After such a statement of incompetence, the audience knew that whatever sensible words came out of the mouth (or pen) of the speaker must derive directly from God.

---

[53] Jer. 1:6: 'et dixi a a a Domine Deus ecce ego puer sum, nescio loqui'. Jonas of Bobbio took this very quotation from Jeremiah and drew on the example of Moses' speech impediment, to call attention to the fact that the prophets chosen by God to be a vehicle of his message were no naturally gifted speakers, *Vita Columbani,* ed. Krusch, p. 246: 'Hieremias etenim Domini electione praemissus, se dignum denegat, dicens: A, a, a, domine Deus, ecce ego puer sum, nescio loqui; Moyses electus a Domini se tardum linguae testator [Exod. 4:10].'

[54] Kennedy, *Classical Rhetoric,* p. 139, and see the quotation in the previous note.

[55] Alcuin, *De rhetorica et de virtutibus* 5, ed. Halm, p. 527. [56] Kennedy, *Classical Rhetoric,* p. 196.

Part II

Agobard reflects on this biblical notion of prophetic speech resulting from divine inspiration in a letter–treatise addressed to his friend Bernard, bishop of Vienne. He attributes divinely inspired speech to priests in particular, citing a verse from the Book of Ezekiel, where God tells the prophet: 'I will make your tongue cling to the roof of your mouth so that you shall be speechless and unable to rebuke them, for they are a rebellious house.'[57] This verse is followed by the words (not quoted by Agobard, but perhaps filled in from memory by his readers): 'but when I have something to say to you, I will give you back the power of speech'.[58] To underline the God-given nature of prophetic speech, Agobard brings up the example of the high priest Caiaphas, who prophesied that Jesus would die for the people so that a whole nation need not be destroyed. Caiaphas, says Agobard, 'did not say this on his own' (*hoc autem a semetipso non dixit*), but being a high priest, he could not but prophesise the truth.[59] Priests spoke the word of God, whether they wanted to or not, and they could only speak when God loosened their tongue.

I suggest that Agobard adopted this model of prophetic speech to characterise his own speaking. In his letters, he downgrades his eloquence, and stresses that he is, like many Old Testament prophets, no naturally accomplished speaker, but a mumbler. During his public speech at the assembly of Attigny, he could not speak as confidently and agreeably as the *seniores,* or so he says in his letter to his friend. When, at last, he had a chance to talk to the three great men of the palace, he claims he did not speak up, but muttered. Perhaps Agobard really was not a gifted public speaker, but he must have had a reason to stress it so often. In the letters of admonition he sent to the court after 822, which were less subdued than his earlier letters, Agobard held on to the stance of the unwilling speaker who would rather have remained silent, but had to speak out.[60] He was compelled to break the silence, not because he was an eloquent speaker or a gifted writer, but because, like a true prophet, his concern for the well-being of God's people forced him to speak. Like the prophets Elijah and Jeremiah, he became an outcast (or so he claimed) when he ventured to speak the truth in the palace.[61]

---

[57] Agobard, *De privilegio et iure sacerdotii* 4 (between 817 and 822), ed. Van Acker, p. 55, lines 3–5: 'Linguam tuam adherescere faciam palato tuo, et eris mutus, nec quasi vir obiurgans: quia domus exasperans est [Ezek. 3:26].'
[58] Ezek. 3:27: 'cum autem locutus fuero tibi aperiam os tuum'.
[59] Agobard, *De privilegio et iure sacerdotii* 4, ed. Van Acker, p. 55, line 6: Cf. John 11:51.
[60] Agobard, *De baptismo*, ed. Van Acker, p. 117, lines 75–85; *De insolentia Iudaeorum*, ed. Van Acker, p. 191, lines 21–4; *De Iudaicis superstitionibus* 1, ed. Van Acker, p. 199, lines 15–24.
[61] 3 Kgs 18, 19:1–3 and 21:17–27. Agobard refers to this last passage in his *Liber apologeticus* II, 5, ed. Van Acker, p. 318, lines 3–7.

Agobard of Lyon

Agobard's letter to Louis's trusted advisers of 823, written after the failure in Attigny, marked a transition to a new role, namely that of the dejected and isolated prophet. He was no longer invited to court assemblies to discuss politics with his social peers face to face. He used this unfortunate circumstance to present himself as an outcast who offered advice and criticism through letters. In the years between 822 and 829, the year of his return to the political stage, he besieged the palace with letters of admonition. He wrote to the emperor's counsellors, to the high-ranking courtier Count Matfrid of Orléans and to the emperor himself, bombarding them with requests, unasked-for advice, implicit criticisms and admonitions. The first letter in this series of communications to the palace, addressed to Wala, Adalhard and Helisachar, discussed above, stands out as the letter of an outsider who speaks to a group of insiders. A question that needs to be asked is, did Agobard really consider himself an outsider? Did he look at himself as someone who did not fit in, and who could not speak as well as the great men of the palace could? Perhaps, but it is more probable that the role of dejected prophet suited him well. Agobard's self-presentation as a poor speaker and cast-out prophet whose message was not well received may have been a deliberate self-stylisation to mark this transition from public speaker to a voice crying in the wilderness. We should keep in mind, however, that this was not just a literary role. For a certain period of time, Agobard's situation actually was precarious. After his dismissal from court he did not attend further assemblies for some years. And yet, we should also not overstate the extent to which Agobard was shunned by the court. Between 823 and 826, he wrote a treatise at the request of Archbishop Ebo of Rheims, Louis's foster-brother, which indicates that Agobard cannot have been completely isolated from court circles.[62] But, as long as the outcast position more or less accorded with his actual circumstances, he styled himself as a dejected prophet.

RUMOURS AND LIES

After Attigny, Agobard flooded the palace with letters of admonition. In these letters, he implores, urges, advises and admonishes the emperor and his courtiers to remain committed to the lofty ideal of a unified empire. Agobard has the reputation of being one of Louis's most vociferous critics.[63] Indeed, in each letter Agobard sent to Louis, he emphasises the

---
[62] Agobard, *De spe et timore ad Ebbonem*, ed. Van Acker, pp. 429–54. This point is made by Langenwalter, *Agobard of Lyon*, p. 72.
[63] Boshof, *Erzbishof Agobard von Lyon*, pp. 132, 133; Airlie, 'I, Agobard', p. 175; Booker, *Past Convictions*, p. 99, with reference to older literature.

risk he is taking by giving his opinion on highly contentious topics.[64] But when push comes to shove, he minimises that risk with the help of a wide range of rhetorical safety measures. Agobard advised, interfered and criticised, but he did not speak openly, at least not in the letters he wrote to the court before 829. The people who get the full blast in his letters are always the others, not his correspondents. These others – for example, the Jews at the court, the flatterers at the palace or Louis's delegates – serve as contrast points in his rhetoric. Before 829, or in fact before 833, he does not directly or openly express his criticism of the emperor, or, for that matter, of his other addressees. Instead, he persuades them to change their behaviour or course of action through the instrument of rumour reports. In previous chapters, we have seen other authors, such as Columban, Germanus of Paris and Boniface, who used the same, well-worn rhetorical device and strategically employed rumour as a political instrument.[65] Agobard plays on his addressees' sense of honour and confronts them with whispers that could smear their reputation unless they do something about it. Around 828, for example, he informed Count Matfrid, a prominent member of the court, of a malevolent rumour that circulated about him. According to Agobard, many people believed he was a wall (*murus*) between the emperor and themselves, and that kept the emperor from correcting injustices.[66] By reporting this rumour, he in fact accuses Matfrid, albeit indirectly, of receiving bribes and leaving the emperor in the dark about corruption of justice, without uttering a single word of criticism himself. Instead, he pictures an ideal portrait of Matfrid as the kind of man who would never do such a thing, thus persuading the count to conform to the ideal image of him that he, the author of the letter, has created. 'O most outstanding of men', Agobard writes to Matfrid, just after he has informed him of what people are supposedly saying behind his back, 'strive instead to be a wall for the increase of happiness, a wall which defeats the harmful and protects the innocent'.[67] Agobard puts pressure on Matfrid to use his familiarity with the emperor to do good, and never use this privileged position for his personal advantage, without stating directly that he thinks this is exactly what Matfrid has been doing.[68]

In his letter to Emperor Louis *On the Insolence of the Jews* (c. 827), Agobard employs a similar strategy when he confronts the emperor with rumours

---

[64] See the references in note 60 and Agobard, *De iniusticiis*, ed. Van Acker, p. 226, line 49.
[65] See chapters 6 and 8.
[66] Agobard, *De iniusticiis ad Matfredum*, ed. Van Acker p. 226, lines 49–51. The letter was written in 827 or 828.
[67] Agobard, *De iniusticiis ad Matfredum,* ed. Van Acker, p. 226, lines 51–4: 'Quin potius, praestantissimae virorum, date operam, ut sitis murus in augmento felicitatum, qui noxios expugnet, innocentes tueatur, Deo congruat, ab inimico discrepet, supernam remunerationem accumulet.'
[68] Ibid., ed. Van Acker, p. 227, lines 67–70.

which he claims the Jews have spread in Lyon.[69] The Jews, he says, pretended that they had received clothes from Louis's female relatives and other high-born ladies of the palace.[70] They claimed, moreover, that they 'entered and left the emperor's sight with honour', which was more than Agobard can say for himself.[71] Undoubtedly, he implies, a most Christian emperor such as Louis would never condone such favouritism of non-Christians. The emperor probably did not know, or he would have put a stop to it. Agobard does not raise accusations; he only asks questions.[72] In his letters to the court, Agobard uses *mala fama* to construct a negative counter-image of the ruler and the palace.[73] He creates a distorting mirror based on rumours which he has heard, and which he puts into sharp contrast with the ideal ruler image that he holds up to the emperor, and to others to whom he writes about the emperor.[74] As Louis would not fail to see, these rumours were blemishes that did not fit the picture of an ideal Christian ruler and, moreover, tainted the image of the palace.[75]

Whenever Agobard confronts his addressees with a rumour, he hastens to add that, of course, he does not believe a word of it. He is just the messenger. It is evident that the rumours Agobard reports represent his own criticism, or at least concur with his own suspicions, notwithstanding his assurances to the contrary ('you should know without a doubt that I am not lamenting my own complaints').[76] He distances himself from what other people are saying about the emperor or his courtiers ('they lie', 'they say', 'they boast'), putting his own criticisms and suspicions in the mouth of others. Meanwhile, he offers advice on how best to counter these false accusations.[77] Agobard wanted his readers to know that he personally had nothing to do with these stories, and that in fact it displeased him to hear them. As he wrote to Emperor Louis in 829, after he had heard that Louis's magnates were required to swear new oaths

---

[69] On Agobard's campaign against the Jews of Lyon and his references to Ambrose's criticism of Theodosius' decision to rebuild the Jewish synagogue in Callinicium, see Van Renswoude, *Licence to Speak*, pp. 317–22.
[70] Agobard, *De insolentia*, ed. Van Acker, p. 194, line 121–4.
[71] Ibid., ed. Van Acker, p. 194, lines 111–12: 'ingrediantur in conspectu vestro et egrediantur.'
[72] Airlie, 'I, Agobard', pp. 179, 180.
[73] On Agobard's manipulation of the image of the palace to his own rhetorical and political advantage, see Airlie, 'I, Agobard', pp. 181–3; De Jong, 'Bride shows revisited' and *The Penitential State*, pp. 195, 196; see furthermore on rumours, whispers and gossip: Dutton, *Charlemagne's Mustache*, ch. 5, 'Whispering secrets to a dark age', pp. 129–50; Booker, '*Iusta murmuratio*'.
[74] Agobard, *De cavenda convictu et societate Iudaica*, ed. Van Acker, p. 233, lines 78–82.
[75] For a similar strategy, see Agobard, *Cartula de poenitentia*, ed. Van Acker, p. 324, lines 36–8.
[76] Agobard, *De iniusticiis*, ed. Van Acker, p. 226, lines 56, 57: 'absque ulla dubitatione sciatis me non proprias querelas deplorare'.
[77] See for example ibid., ed. Van Acker, pp. 226, 227.

Part II

to revisions that had been made to previous arrangements concerning the division of imperial rule: 'It seems to me that I should not conceal from your Excellency the fact that there is now great grumbling among men because of these diverse and contradictory oaths, and not only grumbling but also sadness and slander against you.'[78] After diligently reporting what he has heard, Agobard usually switches to the language of prophetic admonition to warn his reader(s) of God's impending judgement. Rarely, however, does he employ the language of open confrontation. His own criticisms are safely cloaked in anonymous reports. Before 829, Agobard is certainly no 'free speaker', but a rumour reporter, which was a relatively safe position to take. He presented himself as a concerned bishop who brought rumours into the open to dispel lies and bring out the truth, and deflected possible suspicions about his motives by pointing, for example, to Louis's own delegates. They were the real gossip mongers, for they were whispering into people's ears, filling their minds with all the wrong ideas about the emperor.[79]

UNANSWERED LETTERS

It is not known if Louis ever received any of Agobard's letters of admonition. No written replies from Louis have been preserved, nor is there evidence of any form of indirect response. This lack of response, however, did not keep Agobard from writing more letters. Why did he continue to harass the palace with letters of admonition, if he did not get any direct results? Mayke de Jong has suggested that Agobard used his letters of admonition to regain the emperor's favour and write himself back into the court.[80] This seems to be a plausible explanation. Since *admonitio* was considered an appropriate means by which to improve government policy and enhance the general well-being of the *res publica*, Agobard's letters of admonition may have served to display his talents as an advice-giver and a trustworthy critic. The letters had the potential to become his ticket back to the palace, if the emperor and his counsellors would only recognise Agobard's value as an admonisher. But there is also another way to read Agobard's letters: namely, as means of gathering support around a commonly shared agenda. His letters and the dossiers he attached to them, containing patristic and canonical quotations that

---

[78] Agobard, *De divisione* 7, ed. Van Acker, p. 250, lines 2–5: 'videtur mihi non celandum excellentiae vestrae, quod multa murmuratio est nunc inter homines propter contraria et diversa iuramenta, et non sola murmuratio, sed et tristitia et detractio adversum vos.' On *murmuratio*, see Booker, '*Iusta murmuratio*'.
[79] Agobard, *De insolentia Iudaeorum*, ed. Van Acker, p. 192, lines 53–6.
[80] De Jong, *The Penitential State*, p. 143.

support his case, may have been intended as discussion texts for a wider group of like-minded readers. This is not to say that Agobard's letters were never meant to reach the emperor and his circle, but they were probably not written for their eyes only. The letters of admonition that Agobard wrote between 822 and 829, during the years when he was presumably shunned by the court and excluded from deliberations, may have been part of a campaign to generate attention for issues he wished to be placed on the court's agenda. The fact that there are no traces of any reception of Agobard's letters of admonition outside Lyon does not exclude the possibility that Agobard intended his letters to be read by a wider group of readers who shared, or who might come to share, his interests. Agobard's letters of admonition could have served both purposes: they were actual letters, sent to the emperor and his courtiers, as well as discussion texts that were meant to be discussed among a select group of people.

In 829, Lyon was chosen as the venue for a major reform council, over which Agobard presided. The confident mood of the letters dating to this period reflects the change in his position. He no longer writes from the perspective of the outsider, but spoke with the voice of a worried bishop, who, although perhaps still not one of the emperor's intimates, was certainly one of his faithful men.[81] His main concern was now the unity of imperial rule, which he regarded as a precondition for the unity of the church. At the assembly of Worms in August 829, Louis revised the succession arrangements made in Aachen in 817. Agobard disapproved of these new arrangements and feared they would dislodge the stability of the realm. His fears were not unfounded: in 830, a revolt broke out. Agobard, who, it seems, was not involved in this revolt but remained loyal to the emperor, wrote a letter of admonition to Louis in which he expressed his concerns and warned the emperor of the dangers he saw ahead.[82]

Agobard continued to write letters of admonition to the emperor until he decided to withdraw his support from Louis and turn to the camp of his son, Lothar. His letter to Louis *On the Division of Imperial Rule,* in which he begs the emperor not to turn back on his decision to have Lothar succeed him as sole emperor, probably dates to 829. Shortly before Easter 833, he wrote his final letter to Louis, *On the Privilege of the Apostolic See,* to persuade the emperor to accept the pope's proposal to mediate in the negotiations with his rebellious sons.[83] Around this time, Agobard

---

[81] Two letters that Agobard wrote to Louis have been preserved from this period: *De divisione imperii* (829), ed. Van Acker, pp. 247–50, and *De privilegio apostolicae sedis* (833), ed. Van Acker, pp. 303–6.
[82] Agobard, *De divisione imperii* (829), ed. Van Acker, pp. 247–50.
[83] Agobard, *De privilegio apostolicae sedis*, ed. Van Acker, pp. 303–6.

Part II

appears to have lost his faith in the emperor's commitment to the cause of the unity of imperial rule. His last two letters to Louis, written shortly before he withdrew his support, were still every bit as respectful as his earlier letters had been. After he took Lothar's side and became involved in the next rebellion against Louis, however, the tone of his writings changed dramatically. Just like Hilary of Poitiers, who turned to invective when his petitions and admonitions to Emperor Constantius did not meet with a response, Agobard switched from admonition to forceful rebuke when he abandoned Louis in 833.

PAMPHLET OF DEFENCE

On the eve of the battle on the Rotfeld, Emperor Louis was abandoned by his troops. It is believed that Agobard delivered a sermon on that very night in the camp of the imperial sons who had taken up arms against their father.[84] The sermon is transmitted as the first part of Agobard's pamphlet of defence, his *Liber apologeticus*. In the speech, which Agobard supposedly gave to the magnates in the camp of Louis's sons, he calls out in the bellowing voice of a prophet:

> Hear this all peoples! Let the earth and her fullness hear, from the rising of the sun to its setting, from the north and from the sea; let all men learn and reflect at the same time on the fact that the sons of the lord and emperor Louis have been and are justly outraged and that they properly mean and plan to cleanse their father's palace of its filthy crimes and wicked factions and to cleanse the kingdom of its most bitter and turbulent disturbances![85]

The speech that follows, in which Agobard defends the rebellion of Louis's sons against their father, is much more outspoken and critical than any of his previous writings had been. No longer does he apologise for being presumptuous, or too lowly in status to dare criticise anyone, let alone the emperor, as he did in his early letters of admonition. This time, he expresses his criticism of the emperor and the palace unreservedly, in a tone of voice that can only be described as acrimonious. The mood of Agobard's *Liber apologeticus* matches the tenor of other texts of admonition that were produced in the same period. As Mayke de Jong has observed, admonition went into overdrive in the turbulent years of the 830s, and

---

[84] Patzold, *Episcopus*, p. 204; Boshof, *Erzbishof Agobard von Lyon*, pp. 228, 229 and (tentatively) De Jong, *The Penitential State*, p. 95.
[85] Agobard, *Liber apologeticus* I, 1, ed. Van Acker, p. 309, lines 1–6: 'Audite haec omnes gentes, audiat terra et plenitudo eius a solis ortu et occasu, ab aquilone et mari, et sciant et recogitent pariter, domni et imperatoris Luduuici filios iuste fuisse et esse indignatos, et bene sentire et intendere ad expurgandum paternum palatium a sordibus facinorum et iniquis factionibus, et regnum ab amarissimis et tumultuosis inquietudinibus.'

turned into virulent accusation.[86] This development can be observed particularly well in Agobard's writings. Compared to the deferential and subdued character of his earlier admonitory letters to Louis, the political pamphlets he wrote in 833 preserve little of the respect in which he had previously held the emperor.[87] Now he turns from rumour to outright slander. The image of Louis that he projects in his *Liber apologeticus* is that of a feeble old man, who can no longer satisfy the sexual needs of his young wife Judith, who has turned to other men for pleasure.[88] In Agobard's opinion, the emperor is under the spell of the sycophants of the palace and the flattery of the adulterous empress, who have corrupted his mind with bad counsel. Agobard's image of the palace as an unclean place of corruption, flattery and lasciviousness reads as a parody of the well-ordered palace described in *De ordine palatii*.[89] Although Agobard considers the wanton empress to be the main culprit in the present crisis, the emperor is to be blamed for letting things get out of hand. It is his duty to run a tight ship. If he cannot be trusted to keep the palace in good order, how can he be expected to maintain order in the realm? Agobard cannot but conclude that the emperor's mind has become unstable. He has listened to the wrong advice when he should have listened to the counsel of his faithful men. To Agobard, the solution is clear: Louis has to do penance to amend the wrongs which he has either committed himself, or which have come about through his negligence.[90]

In the *Liber apologeticus*, Agobard's criticism is bold and direct, especially in comparison to his earlier subservient and evasive letters of admonition. Exceptions are the last two letters that Agobard sent to Louis shortly before his about-face in 833. In these letters, *On the Division of Imperial Rule* and *On the Privilege of the Apostolic See*, he had confronted the emperor openly with his criticism, while assuring him that his impudence sprang from love for the emperor and from a genuine concern about the salvation of his soul.[91] Seeing that his *Liber apologeticus* was even more outspoken, it would appear that Agobard's writings reveal

---

[86] De Jong, *The Penitential State*, pp. 142–7, 'From *admonitio* to *increpatio*', especially p. 142.
[87] That is, parts I and II of the *Liber apologeticus* and Agobard's attestation to Emperor Louis's penance in Compiègne, the *Cartula de poenitentia*. On Agobard's *Cartula*, see Boshof, *Erzbischof Agobard von Lyon*, pp. 247–51; Airlie, 'I, Agobard', pp. 182, 183; Booker, *Past Convictions*, pp. 155–7, 176 and De Jong, *The Penitential State*, pp. 234–41, with a translation of this document at pp. 277–9.
[88] On Agobard slandering Judith, see De Jong, 'Bride shows revisited', pp. 267–72.
[89] This point is made by Airlie, 'I, Agobard', p. 180, in reference to Agobard's picture of the palace in his letter to Matfrid, but it also holds true of the *Liber apologeticus*.
[90] Agobard, *Liber apologeticus* II, 7, ed. Van Acker, p. 319.
[91] Agobard, *De divisione* 2 and 6; *De privilegio* 2 and 7.

Part II

a progressive tendency towards frank speech. But is that really the case? This question can best be answered by looking at both the form and the audience of Agobard's *Liber apologeticus*.

Agobard's polemical pamphlet has been edited in two parts, under the title *Liber apologeticus* I and II. The title is reminiscent of Tertullian's *Apologeticum* or Gregory Nazianzen's *Apologetica,* and evokes a late antique world of free-speaking bishops.[92] The title attributed to Agobard's pamphlet is, however, a modern one. In the manuscript that was discovered by Masson, Paris, BnF, lat. 2853, the only surviving manuscript to contain Agobard's political pamphlet, the text does not carry a title. The manuscript is written in several ninth-century hands. Only the last part of the manuscript, where the pamphlet is located (ff. 297r–230r), is written in a tenth-century hand, which indicates that the text was added to the collection at a later stage. Moreover, it is not mentioned in the list of titles written in a ninth-century hand on the first folio of the codex.

The first part of the *Liber apologeticus* is written as a sermon, directed at all nations of the earth. The second part resumes the arguments of part one, to argue why the emperor's sons justly rose up against their father, and continues with a list of all aspects of the emperor's negligence. Here, Agobard casts himself in the role of the prophet Elijah, who rebuked King Ahab for his sins. According to this biblical story (3 Kgs 20–7), God averted the disaster he intended to bring on Ahab's house, after the king humbled himself before God. Agobard implores the bishops of Louis's realm to call their emperor to repentance, just as the prophet Elijah had done, to prevent the Empire from falling into ruin.[93] Here we seem to be back on the familiar terrain of frank speech, as developed by late antique truth-tellers and propagated by church histories and saints' lives: a discourse that invoked examples of Old Testament prophets who rebuked kings as models of authority to legitimise criticism of a contemporary ruler, compelling him to reflect on his own behaviour and atone for his sins. Agobard ends his list of the emperor's sins in the *Liber apologeticus* with a most familiar plea: 'For all these sins it is necessary that the once most religious emperor return to his heart and do penance, humbling himself beneath the powerful hand of God.'[94] The language

---

[92] Agobard owned a codex of Tertullian's writings: Codex Agobardinus, Paris, BnF, lat. 1622 (ninth century, Lyon), which does not, however, contain Tertullian's *Apologeticum*.

[93] Agobard, *Liber apologeticus* II, 6, 7, ed. Van Acker, pp. 318, 319; cf. Agobard, *Cartula de poenitentia*, ed. Van Acker, pp. 323, 324.

[94] Agobard, *Liber apologeticus* II, 7, ed. Van Acker, p. 319, lines 7–10: 'pro quibus omnibus peccatis necessarium est religiosissimo quondam imperatori, ut redeat ad cor suum, agatque penitentiam humiliatus sub potenti manu dei.' Cf. Agobard, *Cartula de poenitentia*, ed. Van Acker, pp. 323, 324, lines 25–8.

that Agobard employs in his pamphlet contains all the ingredients that would enable his readers to recognise it as frank speech, except for one thing: he does not deliver his bold message in the emperor's face. In his political pamphlet, Agobard never addresses the emperor directly. Louis is consistently referred to as 'he', not as 'you'. The *Liber apologeticus* is not addressed to the emperor; it is *about* the emperor and the empress, which means that the criticism expressed in it, no matter how severely it is phrased, is no form of direct, open criticism delivered fearlessly before a superior.

I suggested earlier that Agobard's letters of admonition to the emperor may have served as discussion texts for a 'peer group' connected to the court. The *Liber apologeticus* was probably written with a similar purpose in mind. It has even been suggested that the second part was meant to provide a dossier in preparation of the assembly of Compiègne, the meeting that was convened in 833 to decide on Louis's fate.[95] If that is indeed the case, their function and purpose could be compared to that of Hilary of Poitiers's invective against Constantius, Ambrose's letters to Theodosius, or the speeches of Synesius and Libanius. It has long been established that the speeches of these famous orators who spoke with *parrhesia* to the emperor were never actually delivered before the emperor.[96] Instead, they were intended to circulate in written form among a select group of people who were of a similar mind regarding certain aspects of the emperor's policy. The question presents itself: why was it necessary for a Libanius, a Synesius, a Hilary, an Ambrose or, for that matter, an Agobard, to adopt the voice of a free speaker in the first place, if their messages were not written for their emperors' attention? What was the point of presenting oneself as an outsider–critic who was prepared to suffer exclusion, exile or execution for the right to speak one's mind if there was no actual risk? Perhaps the answer is: because that was how it was done. It was part of an established tradition to present criticism while wearing the robe of a parrhesiast or, in Agobard's case, the cloak of a fearless prophet, whether this criticism actually reached the ears of the emperor or not.

CONCLUSION

A variety of voices can be heard in Agobard's writings. There is the voice of the excluded prophet, the eager admonisher, the rumour reporter and

---

[95] Boshof, *Erzbischof Agobard von Lyon*, pp. 228–53; De Jong, *The Penitential State*, p. 229; Airlie, 'I Agobard', p. 181.
[96] Cameron, Long, *Barbarians and Politics*, p. 133.

Part II

the dissident. These different shades of voice, which belong to different literary personae, come together in one voice that can be recognised in nearly all of his writings: namely, the voice of the concerned bishop, who wishes to warn, advise and entreat the emperor on matters concerning the Church.[97] In his later writings, Agobard continued to report rumours, although in a different manner than before. In his early letters of admonition, he had presented himself as the outsider who confronted the insiders at the palace with rumours that circulated 'out there'. As soon as he managed to find his way back into the corridors of power, his voice grew more confident. When he sided with Lothar against Louis in 833, Agobard turned from rumour to slander. In the *Liber apologeticus*, he employed *mala fama* as an instrument of persuasion to convince others that action was needed to cleanse the palace, and that the rebellion of Louis's sons was justified.

When Agobard chose to join the rebels, he became one of the leading figures in the group of bishops involved in the proceedings of Louis's deposition and public penance. Yet his success in re-establishing a prominent position for himself at the court was not (only) the sudden result of his involvement in the rebellion. It was the outcome of a gradual process: a comeback which he had carefully prepared by writing letters of admonition. Within a year, however, the tide had turned, and Louis was back on the throne. Agobard was one of the bishops who took the fall for the rebellion of 833, not so much in the eyes of contemporaries, who put all the blame on Ebo of Rheims, but rather in the eyes of seventeenth- and eighteenth-century historians.[98] To their mind, Agobard had taken a wrong turn in his career. From an admonisher of Louis, he had become his opponent; from an adviser, he had turned into a political dissident.

After Louis had regained power, Lothar was sent back to Italy and Agobard disappeared from the scene. Archbishop Ebo of Rheims was removed from his episcopal see and sent to Fulda. Agobard would probably have met a similar fate, but he did not appear at the synod to which he was summoned. He was condemned in his absence for his part in the revolt, but formally because he had thrice failed to show up at the council.[99] Agobard remained in exile for five years, at an unknown location, probably in a monastery in or near Lyon, from where he continued to offer correction and admonition to his clergy via letters.[100] He even wrote a letter to Emperor Louis. This letter from

---

[97] Cf. Airlie, 'I, Agobard', p. 179: 'he is consistent in his pose as a concerned bishop. This was his role.'
[98] Booker, *Past Convictions*, pp. 99–100.
[99] Astronomer, *Vita Hludowici imperatoris* 54 and 57, ed. Tremp, pp. 502 and 516.
[100] Boshof, *Erzbischof Agobard of Lyon*, p. 271.

exile, written around 837, was not a letter of admonition, but a petition. Agobard asked the emperor to intervene in a conflict between Amalarius of Metz, who acted as interim bishop of Lyon in Agobard's absence, and the clergy of Lyon. He wrote the letter, he said, as a pastor, out of care for the flock that had been entrusted to him. This letter has not been preserved, but is cited by Agobard's deacon Florus.[101] In fact, this was the one letter to which Emperor Louis did respond. He put the conflict on the agenda of the assembly of Quierzy in 838.

In 839, Agobard was recalled from exile.[102] He was reinstated as archbishop of Lyon, but did not enjoy the restoration to his office for long. The chronicle of Ado of Vienne records that Agobard died in Saintes when on campaign with the emperor.[103] Apparently, Louis regained sufficient trust in the bishop to take him along in his retinue, which indicates that he thought less harshly about Agobard's political intervention than later generations of historians would do. In the ninth century, apparently, there was more room for criticism and political opposition than historians in seventeenth- and eighteenth-century France could imagine.

Much of what we know about Agobard's life revolves around the theme of correction. When he started his literary career, he asked the emperor to correct his theological writings; then he put himself forward as the emperor's corrector, only to be corrected himself by the disgrace of exile, until he was restored to his former position as archbishop of Lyon and once again entered the service of the emperor. In the seventeenth century, Masson's edition of Agobard's complete oeuvre was put on the list of forbidden books by the Sacred Congregation of the Index. The clause that was added to the verdict of the censors seems strangely appropriate in the light of the main motive of Agobard's life: *donec corrigantur*, 'until corrected'.[104]

---

[101] Florus of Lyon, *De causa fidei* (= *Relatio Flori*) 81, ed. Zechiel-Eckes, p. 85, lines 73-5.
[102] Ado of Vienne, *Chronicon*, ed. Pertz, p. 231; Boshof, *Erzbishof Agobard von Lyon*, p. 305.
[103] Ado of Vienne, *Chronicon*, ed. Pertz, p. 231.
[104] *Index librorum prohibitorum* (Rome, 1664), p. 5: 'Agobardi episcopi Lugdunensis Opera impressa studio Papirii Massonii, donec corrigantur.' For the precise instructions for the correction of Masson's edition of Agobard's writings, see the Spanish Index of 1612, *Index librorum prohibitorum et expurgatorum* (Madrid, 1612), p. 639.

10

POPE GREGORY

In 833, on the eve of the battle against his sons, Emperor Louis was abandoned by his troops. The defection took place on a plain in Alsace called the Rotfeld, which soon after came to be known as *Campus Mendacii*, the 'Field of Lies', the place 'where fidelity died'.[1] Contemporary authors gave widely divergent versions and interpretations of the conflict. Some blamed the defection of Louis's faithful men on treachery, others saw it as a divine judgement, by which God punished Louis for neglecting to protect the unity of the Empire. Negotiations were complicated by the unexpected arrival of Pope Gregory IV (827–44), who had made the journey across the Alps to mediate in the conflict between the emperor and his sons.[2] Bishops who were loyal to the emperor suspected the pope's visit was part of a shrewd political move on the part of Louis's son Lothar and questioned the pope's neutrality in the matter. Agobard of Lyon, who was at that time still a supporter of the emperor, was one of the bishops who did welcome Gregory's arrival. He wrote a letter to Emperor Louis in which he begged him to listen to Gregory and trust his good intentions.[3] At long last, Louis agreed to meet Pope Gregory, but their talks were unsuccessful. The pope returned to Italy empty-handed, and Louis's supporters, including Agobard, went over to the camp of his sons. To some contemporary interpreters, the two events were related: if Louis had only been willing to listen to the pope, the desertion might not have happened. But because the emperor closed his ears to his critics and even refused to listen to the advice of the pope, his men abandoned him.[4]

---

[1] Thegan, *Gesta Hludowici imperatoris* 42, ed. Tremp, p. 228: 'nominatur Campus Mendacii, ubi plurimorum fidelitas extincta est'. On the events on the Field of Lies, see Scherer, *Der Pontifikat Gregors IV*, pp. 165–95; De Jong, *The Penitential State,* pp. 224–8; Booker, *Past Convictions,* pp. 15–67.
[2] De Jong, *The Penitential State*, p. 217.
[3] Agobard, *De privilegio apostolicae sedis,* ed. Van Acker, pp. 301–6, see previous chapter.
[4] Agobard, *Liber apologeticus* 8, ed. Van Acker, p. 320; Radbert of Corbie, *Epitaphium Arsenii* II, 18, ed. Dümmler, pp. 88, 89.

Pope Gregory

When Jean Papire Masson discovered the manuscript containing the collected works of Agobard in the early seventeenth century, a letter, purportedly written by Pope Gregory IV in 833, was found among Agobard's letters.[5] The authenticity of the letter has long been disputed, but it is now generally accepted that the letter is probably a Frankish forgery.[6] Some scholars have considered Agobard to be its author, given the fact that the only extant copy of the papal letter had survived among his letters.[7] Although this is no longer the current opinion, the identity of the person (or perhaps group of persons) who did write the letter has not yet been established. The possibility that the letter is genuine cannot be ruled out, but there is no evidence to argue for or against its authenticity. The text has been transmitted without an exordium or conclusion, and hardly any letters of Pope Gregory IV have survived with which to compare the vocabulary or style. The few letters that have been attributed to Gregory IV are nearly all forgeries.[8] Gregory's letter to Archbishop Otgar of Mainz is probably genuine, but the letter is too succinct to offer sufficient material for comparison.[9]

What speaks against the (sole) authorship of Gregory is that the arguments used in the papal letter show a deep familiarity with the details of the conflict and with a particular discourse that had been employed over the years in discussions on the right administration of the Empire. The pope, who was until then an outsider to the events, could not have possessed such an intimate acquaintance with Frankish affairs, nor could his secretaries.[10] One of the theories that has been developed in recent years is that someone provided the pope with the necessary information and arguments. It has been suggested that this person was Wala of Corbie.[11] His biographer Radbert recounts how Wala handed Pope Gregory a dossier on the Field of Lies to assure him that it was his papal duty and responsibility to interfere in the conflict

---

[5] On the discovery of the manuscript, see chapter 9 pp. 206–7.
[6] See for example Scherer, *Der Pontifikat Gregors IV*, p. 182. More cautious is De Jong, *The Penitential State*, pp. 220, 221. See Boshof, *Erzbishof Agobard von Lyon*, pp. 225–8 for an overview of the arguments.
[7] For a summary of the arguments that speak against Agobard's authorship, see Boshof, *Erzbishof Agobard von Lyon*, pp. 227–8, but see now Harder, *Pseudoisidor und das Papsttum*, p. 57, who reconsiders Agobard's authorship.
[8] On forged letters attributed to Gregory IV, see Scherer, *Das Pontifikat Gregors IV*, pp. 184–95, Jasper, Fuhrmann, *Papal Letters*, p. 171, Harder, *Pseudoisidor und das Papsttum*, p. 181, especially n. 3.
[9] *MGH epistolae* 5, 13.
[10] On Gregory's pontificate, see *Liber pontificalis*, ed. Duchesne II, p. 81; Scherer, *Der Pontifikat Gregors IV*.
[11] Knibbs, 'Pseudo-Isidore on the Field of Lies'.

Part II

and restore peace.[12] However, Radbert wrote his account two decades after the event, and it is difficult to ascertain how reliable his version of the events is, all the more so since details about the dossier are missing.

In this final chapter, I shall discuss both the content and the details of the transmission of this papal letter of 833, because the text is highly relevant to the reception of ancient ideas on free speech. In this letter to the bishops of Francia, the author draws upon the late antique tradition of *libertas* in an attempt to persuade the bishops to speak out to the emperor. To maintain the option that the letter might be authentic, I shall refer to the author of the letter as (ps-)Gregory.

TO THE BISHOPS OF FRANCIA

(Ps-)Gregory's letter to the bishops of Louis's realm was written in reply to a missive they had sent him when he had just arrived in Francia. Their letter is no longer extant, but we can reconstruct its content from (ps-)Gregory's reply, in which are quoted or paraphrased parts of the letter he received. It appears that some bishops who were loyal to the emperor had threatened to place him under a ban and separate their churches from communion with Rome, if he acted towards the emperor in any way without their consent. (Ps-)Gregory counters that the bishops should listen to him rather than obey the orders of the emperor, for, he says, papal authority takes precedence over imperial government.[13] To his mind, the attitude of the bishops shows lack of courage and instability of mind.[14] Were they perhaps afraid to take a stand against the emperor? Did they not dare to speak out? (Ps-) Gregory urges the bishops to take their duties as bishops seriously. It is their responsibility to warn Louis and speak the truth at all times, not only as bishops, but especially as faithful men of the emperor, who have sworn an oath of fidelity to him. 'You promised him that you would act faithfully toward him in all things', (ps-)Gregory writes. 'Yet now, despite seeing him act contrary to the faith and rushing headlong into ruin, you do not recall him as much as you could.'[15]

Fidelity, *fides,* was a recurring issue discussed during the political crisis of the 830s.[16] (Ps-)Gregory argues that bishops who speak frankly to an

---

[12] Radbert, *Epitaphium Arsenii* II, 16, ed. Dümmler, p. 84.
[13] (Ps-)Gregory IV, *Epistola ad episcopos regni Francorum*, ed. Dümmler, p. 228, lines 39–41.
[14] Ibid., ed. Dümmler, p. 229, lines 33–4.
[15] Ibid., ed. Dümmler, p. 230, lines 16–19: 'Vos tamen [...] promittentes ei erga illum omnia fideliter vos agere, et nunc videntes illum agere contra fidem, et praecipitari in perniciem, non revocatis eum quantum ex vobis est.'
[16] De Jong, *The Penitential State*, p. 223.

emperor to correct the course of politics are in no way unfaithful to him. On the contrary, it is a mark of fidelity if bishops speak their mind and steer the emperor back onto the path of righteousness. Agobard had adopted the same line of argument in his letter *On the Division of Imperial Rule,* as would the bishops who would draft the report of the penance of Emperor Louis in 833.[17] Certainly, (ps-)Gregory writes, there is a chance that those who speak out will have to suffer the consequences of defending the truth, but so did the apostles and martyrs before them. He draws on the example of the high priest Caiaphas to argue that if even this cruel man prophesied the truth, righteous priests of God should do so even more.[18] Being ministers of the church and faithful men of the emperor, the bishops are obliged to proclaim the truth and endure the outcome. For, as the examples of the apostles and martyrs have shown, (ps-)Gregory writes, 'that which is done through the will of God, often leads to oppression and persecution.'[19]

LIBERTAS VERBI

In his plea to the bishops to break their silence and speak out against the emperor, (ps-)Gregory uses the expression *libertas verbi.* He has taken the expression from oration 17 of Gregory Nazianzen (d. 390), and embeds the quotation in the following manner:[20]

Gregory Nazianzen did not fear to preach this in church before emperors. For he spoke to those emperors thus saying: 'Will you receive the frankness of the word (*libertas verbi*)? Will you accept willingly that the law of Christ puts you under our sacerdotal power and our tribunals? For he gave us power, gave us dominion, I might add, that is a good deal greater than yours. Or does it rather seem just to you, if the spirit yields to the flesh, if the things of heaven are surmounted by terrestrial things, if human things are put before divine things?' Therefore why did you [this is Pope Gregory speaking again], as priests of truth – that is, not ministers of the worship of human things but of divine things – not respond to the emperor, whose sacred command, you say, forestalled you, just as the same blessed Gregory [Nazianzen] exhorted the emperor in person, saying: 'I ask that you accept our candour (*libertas nostra*) patiently. I know that you are a sheep of

---

[17] Agobard, *De divisione imperii* 2, ed. Van Acker, p. 247. See also the *Relatio episcoporum* 4, MGH Capit. II, 196.
[18] (Ps-)Gregory IV, *Epistola ad episcopos regni Francorum,* ed. Dümmler, p. 230. Agobard had used that same argument in *De privilegio et iure sacerdotii* 4, ed. Van Acker, p. 55.
[19] (Ps-)Gregory IV, *Epistola ad episcopos regni Francorum,* ed. Dümmler, p. 230, lines 36–7: 'Illud namque quod per voluntatem Dei fit, plerumque causa est pressure et persecucionis.'
[20] I thank Courtney Booker for allowing me to use his translation of this letter, which can be consulted at www.history.ubc.ca/documents/faculty/booker.

Part II

my flock, one rendered to me by the supreme shepherd Christ, and consigned to me by the Holy Spirit'.[21]

The Greek word that Gregory Nazianzen had used in oration 17 to denote frank speech was *parrhesia*.[22] In the Latin translation that (ps-)Gregory quotes from, *parrhesia* is translated as *libertas verbi*.[23] Inspired by Gregory Nazianzen, (ps-)Gregory reminds the bishops of their duty to confront their ruler with the truth. It ias true, (ps-)Gregory admits, that he has come to reprimand Louis for the crimes he has committed against the unity of the Church and the realm, but only because the bishops have failed to do so. They have been too afraid or self-serving to censure their emperor. (Ps-)Gregory reprimands his addressees remarkably harshly. He calls the bishops 'deceivers of truth', and dismisses their arguments as 'presumptuous', 'exceedingly stupid', 'wearisome' and 'nauseating'.[24]

Gregory Nazianzen's oration 17 had been translated into Latin by Rufinus of Aquileia in 399 or 400, some fifteen years after the speech was delivered. Only a few copies of the Latin translation of this oration dating from before the tenth century have been transmitted. It is worthwhile to see which libraries owned a copy of this particular oration, for this may give us a clue to the identity of Pope Gregory's ghostwriter. Finding out who had access to this manuscript may reveal who the person or persons were who reintroduced *libertas* in the explicit sense of frank criticism into medieval political discourse.

MANUSCRIPTS

In the first half of the ninth century, only two libraries north of the Alps are known to have possessed a copy of the Latin translation of Gregory

---

[21] (Ps-)Gregory IV, *Epistola ad episcopos regni Francorum*, ed. Dümmler, p. 229, lines 1–11: 'Beatus Gregorius Nazianzenus non hoc timuit coram imperatoribus in ecclesia praedicare. Sic enim ipsis imperatoribus loquitur dicens: "Suscipitisne libertatem verbi, libenter accipitis, quod lex Christi sacerdoctali vos nostrae subicit potestati, atque istis tribunalibus subdit? Dedit enim et nobis potestatem, dedit principatum multo perfecciorem principatibus vestris. Aut numquid iustum vobis videtur, si cedat spiritus carni, si a terrenis coelestia superentur, si divinis praeferantur humana" Quare igitur vos, sicut veri sacerdotes, divini videlicet cultus minystri, non humani, non respondetis imperatori, cuius sacra vos dicitis iussione preventos, sicut isdem beatus Gregorius alloquitur imperatorem dicens: "Pacienter, quaeso, accipe libertatem nostram. Scio te ovem esse gregis mei a Christo mihi summo pastore annumeratam, et a sancto Spiritu consignatam."' Cf. Rufinus, *Ad cives Nazianzenos* (= Rufinus' fourth-century Latin translation of Gregory Nazianzen, *Oratio* 17), ed. Engelbrecht, Wrobel, pp. 201, 202 ; cf. Gregory Nazianzen, *Oratio* 17, 8, *PG* 35, col. 976.

[22] Gregory Nazianzen, *Oratio* 17, 8, ed. *PG* 35, col. 976.

[23] More on this Latin translation below.

[24] (Ps-)Gregory IV, *Epistola ad episcopos regni Francorum*, ed. Dümmler, p. 230: 'hortatu praesumptione', 'nimis stolide', 'haec verba vestra exaggerare laboriosum est, eo quod plena sint nausiae'.

Pope Gregory

Nazianzen's orations, namely, the library of the church of St Stephen in Lyon and the library of the monastery of Corbie. The origin of a third manuscript that contains oration 17, now kept in the Vatican Library (BAV, Reg. lat. 141), is unknown.[25] This manuscript, which dates to the early ninth century, will be discussed further below.

The Lyon manuscript of Gregory's orations (Lyon, Bibliothèque municipale 599) dates to the late eighth or early ninth century. The manuscript was annotated by Deacon Florus of Lyon (d. 860), who closely cooperated with Agobard. According to a scribal annotation on the first folio, Bishop Leidrad of Lyon, Agobard's predecessor, donated the manuscript to the church of St Stephen. The codex is incomplete; in its present state it contains four orations of Gregory Nazianzen in Rufinus' translation, but not oration 17, which is number 6 in Rufinus' series. The manuscript breaks off at the end of the fourth oration. In the ninth century, the codex probably still contained oration 17, since two related manuscripts of the tenth and eleventh centuries (Bamberg Staatsbibliothek, Patr. 64 and Patr. 78), contain eight of Gregory's orations in Rufinus' Latin translation, including oration 17. As the two manuscripts contain the same interpolations as the Lyon manuscript, they are believed to be either direct copies of Lyon, Bibliothèque municipale 599, or part of the same tradition. At the time the letter of (ps-)Gregory was written, the Lyon codex may still have been complete.

The Corbie manuscript (St Petersburg, National Library of Russia, Lat. Q. v 46) dates to the ninth century, and contains all orations of Gregory Nazianzen in Rufinus' translation.[26] The presence of this manuscript in the monastery of Corbie could suggest a link with the so-called Pseudo-Isidorean decretals, a collection of fictitious and genuine papal letters, interspersed with authentic conciliar records, that were designed to reinforce the spiritual authority of bishops and the pope vis-à-vis secular power.[27] A forged letter of Gregory IV to Bishop Aldrich of La Mans, also dated to 833, was inserted into the Pseudo-Isidorean collection of a group of later ninth- and tenth-century manuscript copies known as the

---

[25] Bischoff assumes the origin of the manuscript is 'Nordostfrankreich', possibly Saint-Denis (*Katalog der festländischen Handschriften*, p. 423). Wilmart does not mention a place of origin, but identifies the scribe as a 'Gallicus vir', a man from Gaul. He dates the manuscript to before the middle of the ninth century. Wilmart, *Codices reginenses*, p. 243. According to the catalogue of the Vatican Library, the origin is 'Francia'.

[26] See Ganz, *Corbie in the Carolingian Renaissance*, p. 141.

[27] Zechiel-Eckes, 'Ein Blick in Pseudo-Isidors Werkstatt'. A prior scholarly tradition holds that the compiler(s) should be sought in the circle of Ebo of Rheims; see Canning, *A History of Medieval Political Thought*, p. 51 and Jasper, Fuhrmann, *Papal Letters*, p. 171.

Part II

'c-group'.[28] Klaus Zechiel-Eckes argues that Radbert of Corbie may have been the mastermind behind the composition of the Pseudo-Isidorean collection.[29] Although some scholars doubt Zechiel-Eckes' conclusions, the monastic library of Corbie does appear to have been an important resource for the compilers of the pseudo-Isidorean collection.[30] Was the letter attributed to Pope Gregory IV perhaps part of this large-scale forgery project, either as a spin-off, or as a source of inspiration?

The manuscript evidence could point to the involvement of either Agobard of Lyon or Radbert of Corbie, or persons close to them, in the creation of the papal letter. Both Agobard and Radbert express political views in their own writings that concur with those that (ps-)Gregory puts forward in his letter. Each had been a witness to the events of 833 and had been present at the Field of Lies. They were both concerned with the unity of the Church and the realm, they blamed Louis for failing to maintain that unity, they were opposed to the new arrangements on the division of imperial rule, and they both took the spiritual authority of the pope very seriously. But, as Mayke de Jong has noted, Radbert's firm belief in papal authority that we find expressed in his *Epitaph for Arsenius* may well reflect a later development in his thought.[31] Neither Radbert nor Agobard, moreover, went so far as to state that the authority of the pope exceeded that of the emperor, as (ps-)Gregory does in his letter, using the quotation from Gregory Nazianzen's oration to back up his claim.[32]

However, there is something odd about this quotation. Gregory Nazianzen never delivered his speech 'before emperors', as (ps-)Gregory says he did.[33] Gregory Nazianzen gave his speech in 373 before the citizens of Nazianzus and its prefect, to soothe heated feelings after a conflict over taxes. In the second half of his oration, he addresses the prefect directly, reminding him and other prefects of their duty to govern the city wisely. Gregory Nazianzen claimed the right to speak with *parrhesia*, which, as we have seen, Rufinus renders as *libertas verbi* in his

---

[28] Jasper, Fuhrmann, *Papal Letters*, p. 171.
[29] Zechiel-Eckes, 'Ein Blick in Pseudo-Isidors Werkstatt', p. 60.
[30] See for example Knibbs, 'Pseudo-Isidore on the Field of Lies' and the literature cited there. More cautious is De Jong, 'Paschasius Radbertus and Pseudo-Isidore' and now also Knibbs, 'Ebo of Reims, Pseudo-Isidore'.
[31] De Jong, *The Penitential State*, pp. 219, 220.
[32] Clara Harder revives the possibility that Agobard was the author of Pope Gregory's letter after all, but also points out that Agobard never argued for the primacy of the papal see. Harder, *Pseudoisidor und das Papsttum*, p. 57 and p. 51.
[33] (Ps-)Gregory IV, *Epistola ad episcopos regni Francorum*, ed. Dümmler, p. 230, line 1: 'coram imperatoribus in ecclesia'.

Pope Gregory

Latin translation. The person Gregory Nazianzen addressed, however, was a prefect, not an emperor, and certainly no emperors (plural). And yet, (ps-) Gregory maintains in his letter that Gregory Nazianzen preached frankness of speech 'before emperors' and adds the detail 'in church' (*coram imperatoribus in ecclesia*). This is a detail that cannot be found in Gregory Nazianzen's oration, nor in Rufinus' Latin translation of that oration.

The heading of Gregory Nazianzen's oration in Greek manuscripts is *Logos pros tous politeuomenous Naziantou agoniontas kai ton archonta orgizomenon* ('Speech to the Terrified Citizens of Nazianzus and the Angry Prefect'). According to Johann Wrobel, editor of Rufinus' Latin translation of Gregory Nazianzen's orations, Rufinus decided to change the title because he assumed that his Latin readers would not find the problematic relation of the citizens of Nazianzus with their prefect relevant to their own situation. Rufinus therefore, according to Wrobel, gave his Latin translation of this oration the heading *De Hieremia dicta praesente imperatore apud quem et intercedit pro quodam periclitante* ('A Speech on Jeremiah Delivered in the Presence of the Emperor to Intercede With Him on Account of a Certain Danger'). The first part of the new heading is quite fitting, since Gregory Nazianzen takes a verse from the Book of Jeremiah (Jer. 4:19) as the point of departure for his speech. But why would Rufinus add 'in the Presence of the Emperor on Account of a Certain Danger' if he knew very well, since he had translated the speech, that no emperor is mentioned in the entire oration? Was it really Rufinus who came up with that title, as Wrobel surmises, or was it rather an early medieval scribe who copied Rufinus' translation?

There are further intriguing circumstances that add up to the mystery of the letter attributed to Pope Gregory IV. As mentioned earlier, the only surviving copy of the papal letter was found between the letters of Agobard of Lyon, placed in a dossier of texts that pertain to the revolt of 833 and the penance of Emperor Louis.[34] That dossier (Paris, BnF, lat. 2853, ff. 213–30) was, however, not part of the ninth-century collection, but was added to it in the tenth century.[35] Agobard's editor, Lieven van Acker, has suggested that it was copied from a dossier that may already have existed in Lyon in the mid-ninth century.[36] Building on this

---

[34] Van Acker, 'Introduction to Agobard', *Opera*, p. xxi. This dossier is located at the end of the manuscript of Agobard's letters and treatises, Paris, BnF lat. 2853, and consists of the following texts: *De divisione imperii* (f. 187r–190r), *De privilegio apostolicae sedis* (f. 190r–192v), Letter of Pope Gregory IV (f. 192v–197r), *Liber apologeticus* (f. 197r–206r), *Cartula de Hludovici poenitentia* (f. 206r–208v).

[35] Van Acker, *CCCM* 52, p. LI.

[36] See previous note. Michel Rubellin's 2016 edition of Agobard's *Oeuvres*, in *Sources Chrétiennes* 583, reproduces Van Acker's critical edition and offers no new information on MS Paris, BnF, lat. 2853.

hypothesis, Courtney Booker surmises that it is likely that Agobard had had a hand in assembling such a dossier and may have included a copy of the papal letter because it justified his own position in the conflict.[37] Whatever the reason for preserving the pope's letter amidst Agobard's letters, thematically and stylistically it was well placed in the dossier of polemical texts at the end of the collection. (Ps-)Gregory's letter was positioned between Agobard's letter to Louis *On the Privilege of the Apostolic See*, written to persuade the emperor to accept the pope's mediation in the conflict, and his *Liber apologeticus*, in which he defends the right of bishops to censure a ruler if that ruler strays from the path of salvation and endangers the unity of the Church. In his letter to Louis *On the Privilege of the Apostolic See*, Agobard includes fragments from papal letters and canonical texts which underline the pope's spiritual authority to strengthen his case.

A THIRD SUSPECT

Earlier, I mentioned a third ninth-century manuscript of Gregory Nazianzen's orations, in addition to the two manuscripts that were kept in Lyon and Corbie. This manuscript of uncertain origin, which dates to the beginning of the ninth century, is now kept in the Vatican (BAV, Reg. lat. 141).[38] The title that Gregory Nazianzen's oration 17 carries in this manuscript is identical to the one Wrobel identifies as Rufinus' title: *de hieremia dicta presente imperatore aput quem et intercedit pro quodam periclitante*.[39] The margins of Vatican, BAV, Reg. lat. 141 are filled with annotations in a hand that is contemporary to that of the main text.[40] According to André Wilmart, the hand of the annotator is in fact identical to that of the scribe.[41] This manuscript, and especially its annotations, can be linked to Deacon Florus of Lyon.

This brings us to the third candidate who may have been involved in the production of the papal letter: Florus of Lyon (d. 860), who not only assisted Agobard in his literary pursuits, but was also the author of several polemical treatises and invectives in his own name.[42] Moreover, he

---

[37] See the hypothesis of Booker, *Past Convictions*, p. 133.
[38] Wilmart, *Codices reginenses*, p. 243.   [39] Vatican, BAV Reg. lat. 141, f. 124.
[40] I thank Mariken Teeuwen for sharing her observations on the hand of the annotator with me when I consulted this manuscript in the Vatican Library in June 2017.
[41] Wilmart, *Codices reginenses*, p. 243.
[42] Zechiel-Eckes, *Florus von Lyon*, on Florus' polemical writings, and see pp. 13, 14 on his co-authorship with Agobard.

owned the manuscript of Agobard's letters (Paris, BnF, lat. 2853) to which the papal letter was added.[43] Florus composed a collection of quotations from twelve church fathers, in which we find several excerpts from Gregory Nazianzen's oration 17.[44] One of the excerpts Florus included was the *libertas verbi* quotation that we also find in (ps-) Gregory's letter.[45]

The content of the annotations in the margin of Vatican, BAV, Reg. lat. 141, as Paul-Irénée Fransen has observed, bears a close resemblance to the titles that Florus gave to the different sections taken from Gregory Nazianzen's orations in his *Collection of Sayings of Twelve Fathers*.[46] The hand of the annotator, however, is not that of Florus, but belongs to an unidentified 'man of Gaul' (*gallicus vir*) according to André Wilmart.[47] On folio 127v of Vatican, BAV, Reg. lat. 141, next to the *libertas verbi* paragraph of Gregory Nazianzen's oration 17, which reads in full: 'Will you receive the frankness of the word? Will you accept willingly that the law of Christ puts you under our sacerdotal power and our tribunals?', we find the following annotation: 'Let the rulers of the present age hear this' and 'Let the pastors of the church hear this'.[48] A little further on, the annotator has written: 'Listen to this, rulers, with a humble mind, and be careful'.[49] Who was this annotator, and how was he connected to Florus of Lyon? Did Florus perhaps read these annotations when he was compiling his *Collection of Sayings of Twelve Fathers*, and did the annotation next to the *libertas verbi* paragraph prompt an idea that he perhaps later elaborated when he wrote, or helped to write, the letter attributed to Pope Gregory IV?

It has not been established when exactly Florus composed his collection of excerpts from the Church fathers.[50] The collection has been transmitted in a tenth-century manuscript, together with some of Florus' invectives (Paris, BnF, lat. 13371). Besides excerpts taken from Gregory Nazianzen's orations, Florus' *Collection of Sayings of Twelve Fathers* also contains extensive paragraphs from Hilary of Poitiers's invective against emperor Constantius, discussed in chapter 2. Did Florus collect these excerpts to have ready ammunition at hand when he was writing his own invectives? The invective that we find in Paris, BnF, lat.

---

[43] Besson, introduction to Rubellin (ed.), *Agobard de Lyon: Oeuvres*, p. 72.
[44] Florus, *Collectio ex dictis XII patrum*, ed. Fransen et al., pp. 49–54 and pp. 76–7.
[45] Ibid., pp. 76–7.   [46] Fransen, 'Florilège pastoral', p. 88.
[47] Wilmart, *Codices reginenses*, p. 243.
[48] Vatican, BAV, Reg. lat. 141, f. 127v: 'Suscipitisne libertatem verbi, libenter accipitis, quod lex Christi sacerdotali vos nostrae subicit potestati, atque istis tribunalibus subdit?'. In the margin: 'audiant haec seculi principes' and 'audiant ecclesiae pastores'.
[49] Vatican, BAV, Reg. lat. 141, f. 128r: 'audite et humili animi principes et caute agite'.
[50] Fransen, 'Florilège pastoral' does not mention a possible date of composition.

Part II

1337¹ was oddly enough also attributed to a pope and did not carry Florus' name.[51]

AFTERMATH

The connection between these different texts, authors, manuscripts and circumstances calls for further investigation. A careful study of the manuscripts is needed to answer some of the questions that have been raised in this chapter. For the present, let it suffice to conclude that, in the first half of the ninth century, someone was familiar with the late antique vocabulary of free speech, as found in the Latin translation of the orations of Gregory Nazianzen. This person, who may have been Radbert of Corbie, Agobard of Lyon, Florus the Deacon, the anonymous annotator of Vatican, BAV Reg. lat. 141, or Pope Gregory IV after all, reintroduced the term *libertas* to refer to free speech into early medieval political discourse. Since only one copy of the letter attributed to Pope Gregory IV has survived, it is unlikely that the letter itself exerted much influence on later literature. Nonetheless, its author(s) may have played a role in transmitting Gregory Nazianzen's *libertas verbi* to later ages. From the eleventh century onwards, the very same passage that (ps-)Gregory had selected from Rufinus' translation of Gregory Nazianzen's oration – that is, the passage starting with 'will you accept frankness of speech?' (*suscipitisne libertatem verbi*) – was incorporated into canon law collections, such as Ivo of Chartres' *Collectio tripartita* and the *Decretum Gratiani*. Like (ps-)Gregory in his letter to the bishops of Francia, the composers of these canon law collections situated Gregory Nazianzen's claim to *libertas verbi* in the context of a speech delivered before emperors (plural), and used it to promote the dignity of the episcopal office and the supremacy of the papal seat.[52]

The reference to *libertas* in the classical sense of frank speech in the papal letter of 833 was no isolated instance in the ninth century. Some thirty years after (ps-)Gregory persuaded the bishops of Louis's realm to take a stand, Pope Nicholas I (d. 867) used the term *libertas* in a circular letter (865 AD) to the bishops and archbishops of the realm of King Lothar II (d. 869) in which he admonishes the bishops to speak out against the king's attempted divorce.[53] The pope tells the bishops to put away their slavish fear, assume the *libertas episcopalis* to which

---

[51] Van Renswoude, 'Crass insults'.
[52] Ivo of Chartres, *Collectio tripartita* A2 xiv 6; *Decretum* V; *Decretum Gratiani*, Distichon X, 6: William of Ockham, *Dialogus* 3, 2, 2.
[53] On the divorce case, see Heidecker, *The Divorce of Lothar II*; Stone, West, *The Divorce of King Lothar*.

they were called, and speak out against the king's attempts to divorce his wife.[54] He reminds the bishops of their duty as watchmen (*speculatores*) and pastors to implore, beseech, persuade, encourage, correct and rebuke any sinner committed to their pastoral care, including the ruler.[55] In his letter, Pope Nicholas draws upon the standard repertoire of the Christian discourse of admonition.[56] He quotes the watchman passage from the Book of Ezekiel (Ezek. 3:17–19), and the well-known passage from the Book of Isaiah, 'Shout out! Lift up your voices like a trumpet!' (Isa. 58:1), to persuade the bishops to break their silence.[57] Pope Nicholas connects these biblical quotations to the dignity of sacerdotal *libertas*, which no emperor could deny a bishop, just as Ambrose had argued in his letter to Theodosius on the Callinicium affair.

Around the same time, and in response to the same political issue – that is, the attempted divorce of King Lothar II – Archbishop Hincmar was drawing on the story of Ambrose and Theodosius to exemplify the responsibility of bishops to point out a ruler's sins. Hincmar had not only read the *Tripartite History*, he was also familiar with the letter that Ambrose wrote to Theodosius concerning the Callinicium incident (*Ep.* 74) and even with Ambrose's letter to Theodosius after the Thessalonica massacre (*Ep. extra collectionem* 11), previously unattested in the early Middle Ages.[58] Hincmar justifies his frankness to King Lothar with an appeal to Ambrose's free speech (*libertas*), quoting liberally from both of Ambrose's letters to Theodosius.[59] About twelve years later, in a circular letter to the bishops and nobles of the archdiocese of Rheims, he once more used the example of Ambrose and Theodosius to convince his episcopal colleagues that they had the moral obligation to speak freely. In this letter of 875, which was dedicated to the topic of *fides* to the king, titled 'Why We Must Remain Faithful to King Charles', Hincmar quotes from Ambrose's letter to Theodosius (*Ep.* 74), saying: 'As it is not the part of an emperor to deny freedom of speech, so it is not that of a priest to refrain from saying what he thinks', and 'In a priest nothing is so dangerous before God or so disgraceful among men as not to state freely what he

---

[54] Nicolas I, *Epistola* 35, ed. Perels, *MGH Epp.* IV, p. 306.   [55] See the previous note.
[56] On the biblical quotations that made up the standard repertoire of the Christian discourse of admonition, see chapter 5.
[57] Nicolas I, *Epistola* 35, ed. Perels, p. 306: 'Clama quasi tuba exaltate voces vestras (et annunciate illi scelera sua, quibus peccat et peccare fuit Israel).'
[58] On Hincmar's knowledge of the *Tripartite History*, see Böringer, *De divortio*, p. 202. For more information on the manuscript transmission of the 'Thessalonica letter', see chapter 4.
[59] Hincmar, *De divortio*, Responsio 6, 7, 11 and 12, ed. Böringer, pp. 201, 249, 253, 254, quoting from Ambrose *Ep. extra collectionem* 11 and *Ep.* 74.

Part II

thinks.'[60] Hincmar continues his appeal to the bishops of Rheims by encouraging them to discuss the virtues and vices of the king openly, saying (this time in his own words): 'Let us therefore speak freely, bishops of the Lord, about what can be called admirable in our king and what can be declared open to censure.'[61]

CONCLUSION

As we have seen in the previous chapters, the use of the term *libertas* to refer to frank speech disappeared in Merovingian and Carolingian letters. In 833, we first encounter *libertas* again in the explicit sense of frank criticism in a letter attributed to Pope Gregory IV. Although it is still unclear who the person or group of persons were who composed this letter, or whether its author was Pope Gregory IV after all, the author was apparently familiar with the classical vocabulary of free speech and reintroduced the term *libertas* into political discourse. Within the ninth-century movement to bolster spiritual authority, the old vocabulary of free speech found a new place. In (ps-)Gregory's letter, the call for *libertas verbi* went hand in hand with a reminder to the bishops of the spiritual dignity of their office. Although *libertas verbi* was a direct quotation from a late antique source, the context in which these words were placed was new. Frank speech was presented as a virtue and a duty that not only came with the eminence of the episcopal office but also with the moral responsibility of being one of the emperor's faithful men. The social importance of fidelity, which in the ninth century applied as much to bishops as to any other magnates in the emperor's realm, was a new ingredient in the already well-stocked package of ideals of frank speech. The letters of (ps-)Gregory IV, Nicholas I and Hincmar of Rheims show that the vocabulary of free speech, which had figured so prominently in the writings of Ambrose of Milan, Hilary of Poitiers and many others, made a comeback in early medieval political discourse. As I hope to have shown in this book, the notion of free speech and the ideals it embodied had never disappeared from early medieval thought and political action, but now it once more went by the name of *libertas*.

---

[60] 'Non est imperiale, libertatem dicendi negare, neque sacerdotale, quid sentias non dicere [...] Nihil etiam in sacerdote tam periculosum apud Deum, tam turpe apud homines, quam quod sentiat non libere pronuntiare.' Hincmar of Rheims, *De fide Carolo regi servanda* 1, ed. PL 125, col. 962, quoting from Ambrose, *Ep*. 74, 2, ed. Zelzer, p. 71. See also *De divortio*, Responsio 7, ed. Böringer, p. 253.

[61] Hincmar, *De fide Carolo regi servanda* 1, ed. PL 125, col. 963: 'Igitur dicamus libere, Domini sacerdotes, quae dicuntur notabilia et reprehensibilia de rege nostro.'

EPILOGUE PART II

On the north-east edge of Hyde Park in London, near Marble Arch and Oxford Street, is a designated site for public speeches and debates, known as Speaker's Corner. Since the Act of Parliament of 1872, anyone who enters the Speaker's Corner is allowed to speak freely on any topic he or she chooses, offence to the British royal family excepted. The institution of a free speech zone in a public place is not unique, since free speech zones can be found in many major cities across Europe and America. What is remarkable about Speaker's Corner is its location: it was established on a previous site of execution. London tourist guides inform visitors that the Speaker's Corner's tradition of free speech took its beginning from the Tyburn gallows, which were located on this very spot. Prisoners who were sent to the Tyburn gallows were allowed to speak freely before they were executed. According to tradition, they were given the opportunity to address the crowd on topics that were otherwise taboo.

Stories about fearless speech in the face of persecution or execution have appealed to the imagination of people over centuries. Narratives about heroic martyrs who were prepared to die for the right or duty to speak the truth were more than 'just' narratives; they transmitted expectations about how defenders of truth were supposed to behave. Such norms and ideals of truth-telling were long-lived. During the Counter-Reformation, ideals of martyrdom prevailed that were modelled on early Christian martyr narratives. One recognised true martyrs of the faith by their steadfastness in the face of torture and their willingness, or even desire, to die for the truth.[1] These qualities were often denoted with the same terms and interpretative categories that had been used in early Christian martyr acts. Fearlessly, with great self-control, and without ostentatious emotional display, a martyr proclaimed the truth to the

[1] Gregory, *Salvation at Stake*.

Part II

very end. These norms of behaviour, which go back to Antiquity, not only prevailed in the Middle Ages and the early modern period, but are still normative today. Twenty-first century self-confessed truth-tellers, such as WikiLeaks founder Julian Assange, whistle-blower Edward Snowden and members of the Russian activist group Pussy Riot, style themselves as martyrs of the free word, or are described as such by the media. They place themselves, perhaps without fully realising it, in a historical tradition of free speakers who were thwarted and persecuted by established authorities, and yet remained steadfast in the face of opposition and continued to speak freely regardless of the consequences.

In this book, I set out to investigate the cultural rules and rhetorical performances that shaped practices of delivering criticism in late Antiquity and the early Middle Ages. I explored the processes of transformation by which classical traditions of free speech, known as *parrhesia* in Greek and *libertas dicendi* or *licentia* in Latin, were transmitted to the Middle Ages. Over the course of ten chapters, we have seen how ancient ideals of free speech and rhetorical strategies for delivering criticism travelled from Greek to Latin culture, from oral to written rhetoric, from the speeches of court philosophers to the letters of Christian bishops, from the late antique language of asceticism to the early medieval discourse of admonition, from the *parrhesia* of the free citizen of Athens, to the *libertas* of the free citizen of the kingdom of Christ. Along the way, ideals and practices changed shape and acquired new layers of meaning. As a result, early medieval *libertas dicendi* was conceptualised and practised in a way that, in spite of continuities, differed from the cultural construction of *parrhesia* in ancient Greece.

Of all the cultural strands explored in this book, codes of expectation concerning martyrdom proved to be particularly time-resistant, as is apparent in the example of the Tyburn gallows and the free-speaking martyrs of the Counter-Reformation. Another expectation that outlived Antiquity was the idea that the practice of truth-telling is connected to an outsider status. Not all those who appointed themselves as truth-tellers, or were acknowledged as such by their contemporaries, were necessarily social outcasts. Yet the normative force of this particular expectation was so persistent that even those who occupied a position of authority tended to present themselves as outsiders to make their role of truth-teller more convincing, and their words more persuasive. Bishop Ambrose, for example, portrayed himself in his letters as a *persona non grata* at the court of Emperor Theodosius. He complained about being excluded from the deliberations that went on in the emperor's council and stressed his position outside the charmed circle of Theodosius' intimates and counsellors. The Irish monk Columban presented himself as an

Epilogue

impudent, babbling foreigner who was not acquainted with the mores of Frankish society. By pretending not to be familiar with the cultural rules that determined what could and could not be said in the presence of superior authority, Columban created a licence to speak freely. Bishop Agobard publicised his dismissal from the court, which enabled him to adopt the voice of the cast-out prophet, calling out from the wilderness. These strategies for adopting the perspective of the social outsider, exile or foreigner enabled the delivery of sharp criticism, for which the speaker could not be held fully accountable. It created room to discuss matters outside the regulated spaces and rules of debate. Interestingly, the exile and the foreigner were precisely the people who did not have the right to speak freely in Roman law. By deliberately adopting these unconventional positions, early medieval truth-tellers found a voice to express unwelcome opinions. As these late antique and early medieval examples show, the outsider status became part of the performance of free speech.

Until bishops entered the public domain of truth-telling around the fourth century AD, parrhesiasts had always been solitary and eccentric figures: wandering philosophers or slightly crazy wise men like the Cynic Diogenes in the barrel, who told Alexander the Great to step out of his light. These free-thinking and free-speaking philosophers were not tied down by social norms and conventions, nor were they susceptible to the workings of power or the attractions of worldly preferment. That, at least, was the prevailing image to which a philosopher–truth-teller was expected to conform. Although one can doubt whether this idealised image ever matched reality, the norms and ideals really existed, and they were more than a narrative construction, in that they informed social and political behaviour. When bishops of the early Church took over the role of truth-tellers, they strove to assimilate the prestige of the pagan court philosopher and the charisma of the holy man, both of whom (according to popular narratives) had spoken with *parrhesia* to the powerful. The social status of a bishop, however, his responsibilities for his community and his position of (institutionalised) authority, differed considerably from that of the philosopher–parrhesiast of old and the truth-telling, ascetic holy man. A bishop was not a solitary figure who lived on the fringes of society, no matter how one looked at it. Bishops needed a free-speaking model, a person who held a position of authority, who was part of Church hierarchy, but who possessed the independence of mind to stand up to a ruler, notwithstanding the social responsibilities that went with his position. Bishop Ambrose of Milan (338–97) was one of the bishops who provided that model for later generations of truth-tellers. The story of his confrontation with Emperor Theodosius in the porch of the church of Milan, as recounted by late antique church historians who portrayed Ambrose speaking and behaving as a parrhesiast, showed later generations how to combine the traditional role of truth-teller with pastoral responsibilities.

Late antique stories about truth-telling bishops such as Ambrose of Milan, Gregory Nazianzen, Hilary of Poitiers and Martin of Tours show how the social roles and cultural rules of ancient *parrhesia* were adapted to fit the needs and circumstances of a newly Christianised society. In late Antiquity, major cultural shifts took place in the discourse of free speech, which not only involved a process of adaptation of social roles, but also concerned a change of language. One of the main challenges in this period of transition from classical to Christian free speech, from solitary philosophers to community leaders such as bishops and abbots, was the need to develop a Christian language of free speech that left room for both frank criticism and pastoral care – a language, moreover, that retained the charisma of the truth-telling outsider. The new Christian discourse of free speech relied heavily on the *parrhesia* of the pagan court philosophers, but also assimilated the language and ideology of pure speech of Christian ascetics. However, a friction was perceived between the two types of discourse, one being a rhetorically constructed, the other an inspired language that was in essence anti-rhetorical. Pure speech, so it was believed from the latter perspective, could not be mastered by rhetorical training. The mouth of the speaker could only be purified by contemplation and a constant examination of one's inner man. The more untrained and uneducated a person was, the better he or she could function as a pure vessel to transmit God's message, unhampered by pride in rhetorical prowess. In chapter 5 I showed how this tension between the classical rhetoric of *parrhesia* and the ascetic ideology of pure speech was overcome, without ever being entirely solved. In the early Middle Ages, speakers and authors continued to struggle with the tension between rhetoric and pure speech, a tension that had been inherent in the history of *parrhesia* from the very beginning.

During the early Middle Ages, the process of transformation of the discourse(s) of free speech continued. Quotations from the biblical books of the prophets (in particular Ezekiel, Isaiah and Jeremiah) made up the stock repertoire of letters of admonition. The language of Old Testament prophecy, which evoked associations with exiled bishops and cast-out prophets, was integrated into what can be termed a priestly language of frank speech, which can already be detected in the letters of Ambrose and in late antique ascetic literature. The biblical image of the 'watchman of the house of Israel' from the Book of Ezekiel was key to late antique and early medieval understanding of the relevance of frank criticism for society. By drawing on the charisma and authority of the Old

Epilogue

Testament prophets, critics legitimised the use of frank speech and enhanced its persuasive force.

The processes of transformation described and analysed in this book evidently involved not only strands of continuity but also of discontinuity. The latter can be observed in particular in the development of the vocabulary of free speech and frank criticism. Perhaps under the influence of the 'prophetic trend', the vocabulary and semantic field of frank speech changed. In the sixth and seventh centuries, words and expressions that used to be part of the classical repertoire of free speech (*libertas, licentia, parrhesia*) went out of use, and the New Testament vocabulary of free speech (*fiducia, constantia*) occurred less frequently. These words and expressions were replaced with a vocabulary associated with the Old Testament prophets (*correctio, increpatio, admonitio*). This observation might have led to the conclusion that the classical language of free speech slowly disintegrated until the memory of its traditional vocabulary and rhetoric was completely dissolved by the time of the ninth century. But the discovery of the letter attributed to Pope Gregory IV among the letters of Agobard shows that this is not the case. In this letter, dated to 833, free speech is once again being discussed and propagated under the name *libertas*, and reintroduced into early medieval political discourse.

Licentia, the other term that was traditionally used in handbooks of rhetoric and in Roman literature to denote the rhetorical figure of free speech, took longer to re-emerge. We encounter it in medieval rhetorical treatises from the mid-twelfth century onwards: for example, in Geoffrey of Vinsauf's *Poetria nova*, where *licentia* was again listed among the figures of thought. Geoffrey connected the rhetoric of free speech once more to the virtues of honesty and justice, when he defined *licentia* as the rhetorical figure with which one 'honestly and rightfully' censures one's superiors and friends without giving offence.[2] The Greek term *parrhesia*, which was last discussed in the Latin West by Isidore of Seville in the early seventh century, did not reoccur in Latin texts until the early modern period. In the mid-sixteenth century it was taken up again in rhetorical textbooks, such as the *Epitome of Tropes and Figures of Speech* of Johannes Susenbrot, printed in 1546.[3]

As this study has shown, there was no straight line of continuity between classical and early medieval constructions of free speech. Some cultural strands, terms and performances seem to have lost their

---

[2] Geoffrey of Vinsauf, *Poetria nova* 4, 2, ed. Faral, v. 1239: 'Licentia: cum culpat honeste et licite dominos vel amicos, nemine verbis offenso.' For other occurrences of *licentia* in medieval rhetorical handbooks from the mid-twelfth century onwards, see the *Colores rhetorici seriatim*, John of Garland's *Parisiana poetria*, Guido Faba's *Summa dictaminis* and the anonymous *Tria sunt*.

[3] Johann Susenbrot, *Epitome troporum ac schematum* 2.2.2.

significance at certain points in time, while other strands, such as the codes of expectation connected to the social role of the truth-teller, remained remarkably stable. The vocabulary, ethics, rhetorical strategies, cultural rules and social roles of free speech continued to be adapted and transformed to accommodate new religious and political ideals. This rich and multi-layered process of transformation continued into the early modern period. Scholars who study free speech in the early modern period, however, still do not acknowledge the medieval developments that went before and informed early modern constructions of free speech.[4] The topic of free speech and rhetoric invites further investigation, especially into the period between (Ps-) Gregory's letter, which propagated frankness of speech (*libertas verbi*) before emperors, and Geoffrey of Vinsauf's description of the rhetorical figure of frank speech (*licentia*) in his *Poetria nova*.

I started this book with Herodian's story of the unfortunate philosopher who jumped on the stage to warn Emperor Commodus and was executed for his ill-timed *parrhesia*. I should like to end with an anecdote by Niccolò Machiavelli that represents the other end of the spectrum and offers a counter-example to Herodian's story. In the early sixteenth century, Niccolò Machiavelli, statesman and political philosopher, warned counsellors not to speak their mind too openly. In his *Discourses on Livy* (1519), in the chapter *On Giving Advice*, he points out the risks of advising a prince.[5] If the advice leads to disaster, Machiavelli says, the counsellor will be held accountable and suffer the consequences. In his view, it is best to give one's opinion not too frankly, but to leave the ruler under the impression that he thought of it himself. Such opportunistic advice can be seen as typical of Machiavelli's pragmatism. Yet he ends his chapter *On Giving Advice* with an anecdote that demonstrates the opposite of what he has just said. The anecdote concerns King Perseus of Macedonia, one of whose close advisers had withheld his advice and spoken out only when it was too late, when the damage was already done; the king became so enraged that he killed his adviser on the spot. 'Thus', Machiavelli concludes, 'was a man punished for keeping silent when he ought to have spoken, and for speaking when he ought to have been silent.'[6] Machiavelli tells this story to argue that counsellors who are too careful and do not express their opinion at all are of no use to the republic or to their ruler. This shows that in the sixteenth century the traditional

---

[4] See for example Colclough, *Freedom of Speech in Early Stuart England* and '*Parrhesia*'; Parkin-Speer, 'Freedom of speech'.
[5] Machiavelli, *Discorsi sopra la prima deca di Tito Livio* I, 7, 23.
[6] Ibid. III, 35, 5, trans. Walker, p. 599.

Epilogue

values of frank speech and honest advice were still held in high esteem, even by a pragmatist such as Machiavelli.

In Machiavelli's age, *parrhesia* was once again explicitly discussed in handbooks on rhetoric, and in the early seventeenth century, freedom of speech became a significant civic virtue. The rhetorical tradition of *parrhesia* contributed to the formation of the active subject, allowing people to take on public identities as citizens.[7] As I hope to have demonstrated in this book, early modern rhetoricians did not need to go all the way back to Antiquity to see what free speech was about. They could draw on a tradition that had never disappeared during the Middle Ages.

---

[7] Colclough, *Freedom of Speech in Early Stuart England*, p. 1.

BIBLIOGRAPHY

MANUSCRIPTS

Bern, Burgerbibliothek
Cod. 351

Bamberg, Staatsbibliothek
Msc. Patr. 7
Msc. Patr. 64 (earlier B IV 6)
Msc. Patr. 78 (earlier B IV 13)

Copenhagen, Kongelige Bibliotek
Ms. Fol. 22

Lyon, Bibliothèque municipale
Ms. 599 (earlier 515)

Milan, Biblioteca Ambrosiana
Ms. J. 71 sup.

Paris, Bibliothèque nationale de France
Ms. Lat. 1622
Ms. Lat. 2853
Ms. Lat. 13371

St Petersburg, National Library of Russia
Ms. Lat. Q. v 46 (earlier Corbie 112)
Ms. F. v. I. no. 11

Vatican, Biblioteca Apostolica Vaticana
Ms. Reg. lat. 141

PRIMARY SOURCES

Acta Alexandrinorum, ed. H. Musurillo, *Acts of the Pagan Martyrs*, Greek Texts and Commentaries, new edn (New York, 1979)
Acta Cypriani, ed. A. A. R. Bastiaensen, in *Atti e passioni*, pp. 206–31

Bibliography

Acta Marcelli, ed. and trans. H. Musurillo, *ACM*, pp. 250–9
Acta Phileae, ed. G. A. A. Kortekaas, in *Atti e passioni*, pp. 280–337
Ado of Vienne, *Chronicon sive Breviarium chronicorum de sex mundi aetatibus de Adamo usque ad anno 869*, ed. (partial) G. H. Pertz, *MGH SS* 2, pp. 315–23
Agobard, *Opera*, ed. L. Van Acker, *Agobardi Lugdunensis Opera Omnia*, CCCM 52 (Turnhout, 1981), ed. M. Rubellin, *Agobard de Lyon, Oeuvres: Tome 1*, SC 583 (Paris, 2016)
Alcuin, *Disputatio de rhetorica et de virtutibus sapientissimi regis Karli et Albini magistri*, ed. C. Halm, *RLM*, pp. 523–50, trans. W. S. Howell, *The Rhetoric of Alcuin and Charlemagne* (Princeton, 1941)
  Epistolae, ed. E. Dümmler, *MGH Epistolae* 4, *Epistolae Carolini aevi* (Berlin, 1895), pp. 1–493
Altfrid, *Vita Liudgeri tertia*, ed. W. Diekamp, *Die Vitae sancti Liugeri. Die Geschichtsquellen des Bisthums Münster* 4 (Münster, 1881), pp. 85-134
Ambrose, *Apologia David*, ed. and trans. P. Hadot, *Ambroise de Milan, Apologie de David*, SC 239 (Paris, 1977)
  De obitu Theodosii, ed. O. Faller, *Sancti Ambrosii opera* 7, CSEL 73 (Vienna, 1955), pp. 372–401
  De officiis, ed. M. Testard, CCSL 15 (Turnhout, 2000), trans. H. de Romestin, NPNF-2, 10 (Peabody, 1980)
  Epistularum liber decimus, ed. M. Zelzer, *Sancti Ambrosii opera* 10, *Epistulae et acta* 3, CSEL 82.3 (Vienna, 1982), trans. (partial) J. H. W. G. Liebeschuetz, *Ambrose of Milan: Political Letters and Speeches* (Liverpool, 2005)
Ammianus Marcellinus, *Res gestae*, ed. W. Seyfarth with L. Jacob-Karau and I. Ulmann, Bibliotheca scriptorium Graecorum et Romanorum Teubneriana, 3 vols, new edn (Leipzig, 1999), trans. J. C. Rolfe, LCL 300, 315, 331 (Cambridge, MA; London, 1935–40)
Antiochus the Monk, *Homilia XVI, De immodica et audaciore fiducia loquendi (Peri parrhesias)*, PG 89, pp. 1476–8
Apophthegmata patrum, alphabetical collection, ed. PG 65, cols. 71–440, trans. B. Ward, *The Sayings of the Desert Fathers: The Alphabetical Collection*, Cistercian Studies 59, new edn (London, 1983)
Apophthegmata patrum, systematic collection, ed. J.-C. Guy, *Les apophtegmes des Pères: collection systématique*, SC 387, 474, 498 (Paris, 1993–2005), trans. J. Wortley, *The Book of the Elders: Sayings of the Desert Fathers*, Cistercian Studies 240 (Collegeville, 2012)
Aquila Romanus, *De figuris sententiarum et elocutionis*, ed. C. Halm, *RLM*, pp. 22–37
Ardo, *Vita Benedicti abbatis Anianensis et Indensis*, ed. G. Waitz, *MGH SS* 15 (Hanover, 1887), pp. 200–20
Astronomer, *Vita Hludowici imperatoris*, ed. E. Tremp, *MGH SRG* 64 (Hanover, 1995), pp. 280–554
Athanasius, *Vita Antonii*, ed. PG 26, cols. 835–976
  Vita Antonii versio Evagrii, ed. and trans. G. J. M. Bartelink, *Athanase d'Alexandrie, Vie d' Antoine*, SC 400 (Paris, 1994)
Athenagoras, *Legatio pro Christianis*, ed. and trans. J. H. Crehan, *Athenagoras, Embassy for the Christians* (Westminster, 1956).

Bibliography

Augustine, *Enarrationes in psalmos*, ed. E. Dekker, J. Fraipont, 3 vols, *CCSL* 38, 39, 40 (Turnhout, 1956)
Basil of Caesarea, *Asketikon*, trans. K. S. Frank, *Basilius von Caesarea, Die Mönchsregeln* (St. Ottilien, 1981)
Benedictus, *Regula Benedicti*, ed. and trans. G. Holzherr, *The Rule of Benedict: A Guide to Christian Living* (Dublin, 1994)
Biblia sacra iuxta Vulgatam versionem, ed. R. Weber, 2 vols (Stuttgart, 1969)
Bonifatius, *Epistulae*, ed. R. Rau, *Briefe des Bonifatius, Willibalds Leben des Bonifatius*, Ausgewählte Quellen zur Deutschen Geschichte des Mittelalters 4b (Darmstadt, 2011)
Cathwulf, *Epistola ad Carolum*, ed. E. Dümmler, *MGH Epistolae* 4, *Epistolae Carolini aevi, Epistolae variorum* (Berlin, 1895), pp. 502–5
Codex Iustinianus, ed. P. Krueger, *Corpus iuris civilis* 2 (Berlin, 1954)
Columban, *Epistulae*, ed. and trans. G. S. M. Walker, *Sancti Columbani Opera*, 2 vols, Scriptores Latini Hiberniae 2, new edn (Dublin, 1970)
Constitutiones apostolicae, ed. F. X. Funk, *Didascalia et Constitutiones Apostolorum* (Tübingen, 1905)
(Ps-)Cyprianus, *De XII abusivis saeculi*, ed. S. Hellmann, Texte und Untersuchungen zur Geschichte der altchristliche Literatur 34 (Leipzig, 1909)
Demetrius, *Peri Hermeneias*, ed. and trans. W. Rhys Roberts, *Demetrius, On Style: The Greek text of Demetrius Edited after the Paris Manuscript* (Cambridge, 1902)
De ordine palatii, ed. T. Gross, R. Schieffer (eds.), *Hincmarus, De ordine palatii*, MGH Font. Iur. Germ., 3 (Hanover, 1980)
Dorotheus of Gaza, *Directions on the Spiritual Life*, ed. and trans. L. Regnault, J. de Préville, *Dorothée de Gaza, Oeuvres spirituelles*, SC 92 (Paris, 1963), trans. E. Kadloubovsky, G. E. H. Palmer, *Early Fathers from the Philokalia* (London, 1981)
Einhard, *Epistolae*, ed. K. Hampe, *MGH Epistolae* 5, *Epistolae Karolini aevi* (Berlin, 1899), pp. 105–49
Epiphanius- Cassiodorus, *Historia ecclesiastica tripartita*, ed. W. Jacob, R. Hanslik, *CSEL* 71 (Vienna, 1952)
Epistolae Austrasiacae, ed. W. Gundlach, *MGH epistolae* 3, *Epistolae Merovingici et Karolini aevi* III (Berlin, 1892), pp. 110–153
Ermoldus Nigellus, *Carmen in honorem Ludovici*, ed. E. Dümmler, *MGH Poetae Latini aevi Carolini* 2 (Berlin, 1881–4), pp. 1–93
Eunapius, *Historia* (fragments), ed. and trans. R. C. Blockley, *The Fragmentary Classicising Historians of the Later Roman Empire* 2, Classical and Medieval Texts, Papers and Monographs 10 (Liverpool, 1983)
  Vita philosophorum et sophistarum, ed. and trans. W. C. Wright, *Philostratus and Eunapius: The Lives of the Sophists*, LCL 134, new edn (Cambridge, MA; London, 1968), pp. 317–596
Eusebius, *Historia ecclesiastica*, ed. E. Schwartz, in E. Schwartz, T. Mommsen (eds.) *Eusebius Werke, Zweiter Band, Die Kirchengeschichte*, 2 vols, *GCS* (Leipzig, 1903 and 1908), trans. K. Lake, LCL 153, 265 (Cambridge, MA; London, 1957–9)
Facundus of Hermiane, *Pro defensione trium capitulorum ad Iustinianum*, ed. J-H. Clément, R. Vander Plaetse, *Facundi episcopi ecclesiae Hermianensis opera omnia*, *CCSL* 90a (Turnhout, 1974)

Bibliography

Florus of Lyon, *Collectio ex dictis XII patrum*, ed. I. Fransen, B. Coppieters 't Wallant, R. Demeulenaare, *CCCM* 193 (Turnhout, 2006)

De causa fidei (= *Relatio Flori*), ed. K. Zechiel-Eckes, *Florus Lugdunensis Opera polemica*, *CCCM* 260 (Turnhout, 2014), pp. 83–90

Freculf of Lisieux, *Historiae*, ed. M. I. Allen, *Frechulfi Lexoviensis episcopi opera omnia*, *CCCM* 169A (Turnhout, 2002)

(Ps-)Gelasius, *De libris recipiendis et non recipiendis*, ed. E. von Dobschütz, *Das Decretum Gelasianum de libris recipiendis et non recipiendis im Kritischen Text herausgegeben und untersucht*, Texte und Untersuchungen 38 (Leipzig, 1912)

Geoffrey of Vinsauf, *Poetria nova*, ed. E. Faral, *Les arts poétiques du XIIe et du XIIIe siècle: Recherches et documents sur la technique littéraire du Moyen Age*, new edn (Paris, 1971), pp. 194–262, trans. E. Gallo, *The Poetria Nova and its Sources in Early Rhetorical Doctrine* (The Hague; Paris, 1971)

Germanus of Paris, *Epistola ad Brunhildam reginam*, ed. W. Gundlach, *MGH Epistolae* 3, *Epistolae Merowingici et Karolini aevi* 3, *Epistolae Austrasiacae* 9, pp. 122–4

(Ps-)Gregory IV, *Epistola ad episcopos regni Francorum*, ed. E. Dümmler, *MGH Epistolae* 5, *Epistolae Karolini aevi*, *Agobardi Lugdunensis archiepiscopi epistolae* 17 (Berlin, 1899), pp. 228–32

Gregory the Great, *Epistolae*, ed. P. Ewald, L. M. Hartmann, *MGH epistolae*, *Gregorii papae registrum*, 2 vols (Berlin, 1899–1900)

Regula pastoralis, ed. and trans. B. Judic, *Grégoire le Grand, Règle pastorale*, 2 vols, *SC* 381, 382 (Paris, 1992), trans. G. E. Demacopoulos, *St. Gregory the Great, The Book of Pastoral Rule* (New York, 2007)

Gregory Nazianzen, *Oratio 17, Ad cives Nazianzenos*, ed. *PG* 35 (Paris, 1857), cols. 964–81

Ad cives Nazianzenos gravi timore perculsos et praefectum irascentem, Latin translation by Rufinus of Aquileia, ed. A. Engelbrecht, J. Wrobel, *Tyrannii Rufini Orationum Gregorii Nazianzeni novem interpretatio*, *CSEL* 46, new edn (Vienna; Leipzig, 1965)

Apologetica – Oratio II, ed. *PG* 35, cols. 407–514, trans. C. G. Brown *NPNF-2*, 7, new edn (Peabody, 1995)

Apologeticus, Latin translation by Rufinus of Aquileia, ed. A. Engelbrecht, *CSEL* 36 (Vienna; Leipzig, 1910)

De vita sua, ed. *PG* 37, cols. 1030–64, trans. C. White, *Gregory of Nazianzus, Autobiographical Poems*, Cambridge Medieval Classics (Cambridge, 1996), pp. 2–153

In silentium jejuniii, ed. *PG* 37, cols. 1307–22, trans. C. White, *Gregory of Nazianzus, Autobiographical Poems*, Cambridge Medieval Classics (Cambridge, 1996), pp. 165–82

Gregory of Tours, *Liber historiarum*, ed. B. Krusch, W. Levison, *MGH SRM* 1, 1, new edn (Hanover, 1992)

Vita Patrum, ed. B. Krusch, *MGH SRM* 1, 2, VII, new edn (Stuttgart, 1969), pp. 211–94, trans. E. James, *Gregory of Tours, Life of the Fathers*, new edn (Liverpool, 1991)

Heiric of Auxerre, *Collectanea*, ed. R. Quadri, *Spicilegium Friburgense* 2 (Freiburg, 1968)

Bibliography

Herodian of Antioch, *Historia Romana*, ed. and trans. C. R. Whittaker, *Herodian of Antioch, History of the Empire*, 2 vols, LCL 454, 455 (Cambridge, MA, 1969–70)

Hilary of Poitiers, *Liber II ad Constantium imperatorem*, ed. A. Feder, *S. Hilarii episcopi Pictaviensis opera, Pars quarta*, CSEL 65 (Vienna, 1916), pp. 197–205, trans. L. R. Wickham, *Hilary of Poitiers, Conflicts of Conscience and Law in the Fourth-Century Church*, Translated Texts for Historians 25 (Liverpool, 1979), pp. 104–9

Liber in Constantium imperatorem, ed. A. Rocher, *Hilaire de Poitiers, Contre Constance*, SC 334 (Paris, 1987), trans. R. Flower, *Imperial Invectives against Constantius II: Athanasius of Alexandria, Hilary of Poitiers and Lucifer of Cagliari*, Translated Texts for Historians 67 (Liverpool, 2016)

Preface to the Opus historicum, ed. P. Smulders, *Hilary of Poitiers' Preface to his Opus historicum: Translation and Commentary* (Leiden; New York; Cologne, 1995)

Tractatus super Psalmos, ed. and trans. J. Doignon, P. Descourtieux, *Commentaires sur les psaumes*, 2 vols, SC 515, 565 (Paris, 2008, 2014)

Tractatus super Psalmos in Psalmum CXVIII, ed. M. Milhau, *Commentaire sur le Psaume 118*, 2 vols, SC 344, 347 (Paris, 1988)

Himerius, *Orationes*, ed. R. J. Penella, *Man and the Word: The Orations of Himerius (c. 310–c. 390*, (Berkeley, 2007)

Hincmar of Rheims, *De divortio Lotharii regis et Theutberga reginae*, ed. L. Böringer, MGH Concilia 4, suppl. 1 (Hanover, 1992), trans. R. Stone and C. West, *The Divorce of King Lothar and Queen Theutberga: Hincmar of Rheims's De divortio*, Manchester Medieval Sources (Manchester, 2016)

Epistola ad Odonem Bellovacensem, ed. C. Lambot, 'L' homélie du Pseudo-Jerome sur l'Assomption et l'Évangelie de la Nativité de Marie d'apres une lettre inédite d'Hincmar', *Revue Bénédictine* 46 (1934), p. 270

De fide Carolo regi servanda, ed. PL 125, cols 961–84

Irenaeus of Lyon, *Adversus haereses*, ed. W. W. Harvey, *Sancti Irenaei episcopi Lugdunensis Libros quinque adversus haereses*, 2 vols (Cambridge, 1857)

Isaac of Nineveh, *Mystical Treatises*, ed. P. Bedjan, *Mar Isaacus Ninivita de perfectione religiosa* (Leipzig, 1909) pp. 582–639, trans. A. J. Wensinck, *Mystic Treatises by Isaac of Nineveh: Translated from Bedjan's Syriac Text*, Verhandelingen der koninklijke Akademie van Wetenschappen te Amsterdam, Afdeeling Letterkunde, n. s. 23, 1 (Amsterdam, 1923)

Isidore of Seville, *Etymologiae*, ed. W. M. Lindsay, *Isidori Hispalensis episcopi, Etymologiarum sive originum*, Scriptorum classicorum bibliotheca Oxoniensis, new edn (Oxford, 1957), trans. P. K. Marshall, *Isidore of Seville, Etymologies* 2 (Paris, 1983)

Jerome, *De viris illustribus*, ed. G. Herding, *Hieronymi de viris illustribus liber: Accedit Gennadii catalogus virorum illustrium*, Bibliotheca Scriptorum Graecorum et Romanorum (Leipzig, 1924)

John Chrysostom, *De incomprehensibilitate Dei*, ed. and trans. F. Cavallera and J. Danielou, *Sur l'incomprehensibilité de Dieu*, SC 28 (Paris, 1951). English trans. W. Harkins, *On the Incomprehensible Nature of God*, The Fathers of the Church 72 (Washington, DC, 1984)

De sancto Babyla, ed. M. Schatkin, *Jean Chrysostome, Discours sur Babylas*, SC 362 (Paris, 1990), trans. M. Schatkin and P. W. Harkins, *Saint John Chrysostom, Apologist*, The Fathers of the Church 73 (Washington, DC, 1985)

Bibliography

Jonas of Bobbio, *Versus in eius festivitate*, ed. B. Krusch, *MGH SRG in usum scholarum* 37 (Hanover, 1905), pp. 225–7

Vita Columbani, ed. B. Krusch, *MGH SRG in usum scholarum* 37 (Hanover, 1905), pp. 144–294

Jonas of Orléans, *De institutione laicali*, ed. *PL* 106, cols. 121–278

Iulius Rufinianus, *De figuris sententiarum et elocutionis*, ed. C. Halm, *RLM*, pp. 38–62

Julius Victor, *Ars rhetorica*, ed. C. Halm. *RLM*, pp. 371–448

Justin Martyr, *Apologia I, II*, ed. and trans. C. Munier, *Justin, Apologie pour les Chrétiens*, *SC* 507 (Paris, 2006). English trans. L. W. Barnard, *The First and Second Apologies*, Ancient Christian Writers: The Works of the Fathers in Translation 56 (New York; Mahwah, NJ, 1997)

Liber Pontificalis, ed. L. Duchesne (Paris, 1886)

Machiavelli, Niccolò, *Discorsi sopra la prima deca di Tito Livio*, trans. L. J. Walker, *The Discourses of Niccolò Machiavelli*, 2 vols (London; New York, 1950, repr. 1991)

Martyrium Apollonii, ed. and trans. H. Musurillo, *ACM*, pp. 90–105

Martyrium Dasii, ed. and trans. H. Musurillo, *ACM*, pp. 272–9

Martyrium Iustini et sociorum, ed. and trans. H. Musurillo, *ACM*, pp. 42–61

Martyrium Lugdunensium, ed. A. P. Orbán, *Atti e passioni*, pp. 58–95, trans. H. Musurillo, *ACM*, pp. 62–85

Martyrium Pionii, ed. A. Hilhorst, *Atti e passioni*, pp. 150–91, trans. H. Musurillo, *ACM*, pp. 136–67

Martyrium Polycarpi, ed. A. P. Orbán, *Atti e passioni*, pp. 7–31, trans. H. Musurillo, *ACM*, pp. 2–21

Menander Rhetor, *Treatises*, ed. and trans. D. A. Russell, N. G. Wilson, *Menander Rhetor*, (Oxford, 1981)

Nicetius of Trier, *Epistola ad Iustinianum imperatorem*, ed. W. Gundlach, *MGH epistolae* 3, *Epistolae Merowingici et Karolini aevi* 3, *Epistolae Austrasiacae* 7, pp. 118–19

Origen, *Contra Celsum*, ed. M. Borret, *Contre Celse*, 5 vols, *SC* 132, 136, 147, 150, 227 (Paris, 1967–76)

Paschasius of Dumium, *Interrogationes et responsiones Graecorum patrum*, ed. *PL* 73, cols. 1025–1062, trans. C. W. Barlow, *Iberian Fathers* I, The Fathers of the Church (Washington 1969), pp. 113–71

Paschasius Radbertus, see Radbert of Corbie

Passio Leudegarii episcopi et martyris Augustodunensis, ed. B. Krusch, *MGH SRM* 5, Hanover, 1910), pp. 282–322, trans. P. Fouracre, R. A. Gerberding, *Late Merovingian France: History and Hagiography 640–720* (Manchester, 1996), pp. 215–53

Passio Montani et Lucii, ed. and trans. H. Musurillo, *ACM*, pp. 213–39

Passio Praejecti Episcopi et Martyris Arverni, ed. B. Krusch, *MGH SRM* 5 (Hanover, 1910), pp. 223–248, trans. P. Fouracre, R. A. Gerberding, *Late Merovingian France: History and Hagiography 640–720* (Manchester, 1996), pp. 271–300

Passio Sanctarum Perpetuae et Felicitatis, ed. J. Amat, *Passion de Perpétue et de Félicité; suivi des Actes*, *SC* 417 (Paris, 1996)

Paul the Deacon of Mérida, *De vita patrum Emeritensium*, ed. *PL* 80, cols. 117–64, trans. A. T. Fear, *Lives of the Visigothic Fathers*, Translated Texts for Historians 26

Bibliography

(Liverpool, 1997), pp. 45–106; trans. J. N. Garvin, 'A Catholic bishop and an Arian king: Lives of the Holy Fathers of Merida', in O. R. Constable, D. Zurro (eds.), *Medieval Iberia: Readings from Christian, Muslim and Jewish Sources* (Philadelphia, 2012), pp. 5–12

Paulinus of Milan, *Vita Ambrosii*, ed. M. Pellegrino, *Paulino di Milano, Vita di S. Ambrogio: Introduzione, testo critico e note a cura di Michele Pellegrino*, Verba seniorum n. s. 1 (Rome, 1961); ed. and trans. M. Kaniecka, *Vita Sancti Ambrosii Mediolanensis Episcopi, A Paulinus Eius Notario* (Washington, DC, 1928)

Pelagius, *Verba seniorum*, ed. PL 73, cols. 855–1024, trans. B. Ward, *The Sayings of the Desert Fathers: The Alphabetical Collection*, Cistercian Studies 59, new edn (London, 1983)

Philostratus, *Vitae sophistarum*, ed. and trans. W. C. Wright, *Philostratus and Eunapius: The Lives of the Sophists*, LCL 134, new edn (Cambridge, MA; London, 1968), pp. 3–315

Plato, *Apologia Socratis*, ed. and trans. H. N. Fowler, LCL 36, new edn (Cambridge, MA; London, 1982), pp. 68–145, trans. G. M. A. Grube, *Five Dialogues* (Indianapolis, 2002), pp. 21–44

Plutarch, *Quomodo adulator ab amico internoscatur*, ed. and trans. F. C. Babitt, *Plutarch's Moralia*, LCL 197 (Cambridge, MA; London 1960)

Prudentius, *Peristephanon liber*, ed. and trans. H. J. Thomson, LCL 102, new edn (Cambridge, MA; London, 1961), pp. 98–345

Quintilian, *Institutio oratoria*, ed. and trans. D. A. Russell, 5 vols, LCL 124–127, 494, new edn (Cambridge, MA; London, 2001)

Radbert of Corbie (Paschasius Radbertus), *Epitaphium Arsenii*, ed. E. L. Dümmler, Abhandlungen der königlichen Akademie der Wissenschaften zu Berlin, Philosophische und historische Classen 2 (Berlin, 1900)

Vita Adalhardi, ed. PL 120, cols. 1507–56

Rhetorica ad Herennium, ed. and trans. H. Caplan, LCL 403, new edn (Cambridge, MA; London, 2004)

Rufinus, *Historia ecclesiastica*, ed. T. Mommsen, *Die lateinische Übersetzung des Rufinus*, in E. Schwartz, T. Mommsen (eds.), *Eusebius Werke, Zweiter Band, Die Kirchengeschichte*, 2 vols, GCS (Leipzig, 1903, 1908), trans. P. R. Amidon, *The Church History of Rufinus of Aquileia, Books 10 and 11* (New York; Oxford, 1997)

Ps-Rufinus, *Verba seniorum*, ed. PL 73, cols. 741–810

Rutilius Lupus, *De figuris sententiarum et elocutionis*, ed. C. Halm, RLM, pp. 3–21

Sedulius Scotus, *Collectaneum*, ed. D. Simpson, *Sedulii Scotti Collectaneum miscellaneum*, CCCM 67 (Turnhout, 1988)

De rectoribus Christianis, ed. S. Hellmann, Quellen und Untersuchungen zur lateinischen Philologie des Mittelalters 1 (Munich, 1906), trans. E. G. Doyle, *Sedulius Scottus, On Christian Rulers and The Poems*, Medieval and Renaissance Texts and Studies 17 (New York, 1983)

Socrates, *Historia ecclesiastica*, ed. PG 67, cols. 30–842, trans. A. C. Zenos, NPNF-2, 2, new edn (Peabody, 1995)

Sozomen, *Historia ecclesiastica*, ed. J. Bidez, G. Hansen, *Sozomenus, Kirchengeschichte*, GCS 50 (Berlin, 1960); ed. PG 67 (Paris, 1864), cols. 843–1724, trans. C. D. Hartranft, NPNF-2, 2, new edn (Peabody, 1995)

Bibliography

Suetonius, *De vita Caesarum*, ed. and trans. J. C. Rolfe, revised by K. R. Bradly, 2 vols, *LCL* 31, 38, new edn (Cambridge, MA, 1997)

Sulpicius Severus, *Dialogues*, ed. J. Fontaine, N. Dupré, *Gallus ou Dialogues sur les 'vertus' de Saint Martin*, SC 510 (Paris, 2006)

Vita Martini, ed. J. Fontaine, *Sulpice Sévère, Vie de Saint Martin*, 3 vols, SC 133–5 (Paris, 1967–9)

Synesius of Cyrene, *De regno*, ed. *PG* 66, cols. 1053–1108, trans. A. Fitzgerald, *The Essays and Hymns of Synesius of Cyrene* 1 (Oxford; London, 1930), pp. 108–210

Thegan, *Gesta Hludowici imperatoris*, ed. E. Tremp, *MGH SRG* 64 (Hanover, 1995), pp. 168–258

Themistius, *Orationes*, trans. P. Heather and D. Moncur, *Politics, Philosophy, and Empire in the Fourth Century: Select Orations of Themistius*, Translated Texts for Historians 36 (Liverpool, 2001)

Private Orations, ed. and trans. R. J. Penella, *The Private Orations of Themistius* (London, 2000)

Theodoret, *Historia ecclesiastica*, ed. L. Parmentier, G. C. Hansen, *CGS* n. s. 5 (Berlin, 1998), trans. P. Canivet, *SC* 501, 530 (Paris, 2006, 2009), trans. B. Jackson, *NPNF*-2, 3, new edn (Peabody, 1995)

Venantius Fortunatus, *Carmina*, ed. M. Reydellet, *Venance Fortunat: Poèmes*, 3 vols (Paris, 1994–2004)

Vita Sancti Hilarii, ed. B. Krusch. *MGH AA* 4, 2 (Berlin, 1885), pp. 1–11

Vetus Latina: die Reste der altlateinischen Bibel, ed. B. Fischer, J.-C. Haelewijck, P. Sabatier, H. J. Frede, R. Gryson (Freiburg, 1949)

Vita Alcuini, ed. W. Arndt, *MGH SS* 15 (Hanover, 1887), pp. 182–97

Vita Genovefae, ed. B. Krusch, *MGH SRM* 3, pp. 204–38, trans. J. A. McNamara, J. E. Halborg and E. G. Whatley, *Sainted Women of the Dark Ages* (Durham; London, 1992), pp. 17–37

Xenophon, *Apologia Socratis*, ed. and trans. O. J. Todd, *LCL* 168, new edn (Cambridge, MA; London, 2002), pp. 642–63

SECONDARY LITERATURE

Afinogenov, D., 'To the origins of the legend about St. Arsenius: The tutor of the emperors Arcadius and Honorius' (in Russian), *Vestnik drevnei istorii* (= *Journal of Ancient History*) 2004, 49–60

Ahl, F., 'The art of safe criticism', *American Journal of Philology* 105 (1984) 174–208

Airlie, S., 'I, Agobard, unworthy bishop', in R. Corradini, M. Gillis, R. McKitterick, I. van Renswoude (eds.), *Ego Trouble: Authors and Their Identities in the Early Middle Ages*, Forschungen zur Geschichte des Mittelalters 15 (Vienna, 2010), pp. 230–43

Althoff, G., *Kontrolle der Macht: Formen und Regeln politischer Beratung im Mittelalter* (Darmstadt, 2016)

Anton, H. H., *Fürstenspiegel des frühen und hohen Mittelalters* (= *Specula principum ineuntis et progredientis medii aevi*) (Darmstadt, 2006)

Fürstenspiegel und Herrscherethos in der Karolingerzeit, Bonner Historische Forschungen 32 (Bonn, 1968)

Bibliography

Auerbach, E., *Literary Language and Its Public in Late Latin Antiquity and in the Middle Ages*, new edn (Princeton, 1993)

Balot, R. K., 'Free speech, courage and democratic deliberation', in I. Sluiter and R. M. Rosen (eds.), *Free Speech in Classical Antiquity* (Leiden; Boston, 2004), pp. 232–59

Baltussen, H. and P. J. Davis, 'Parrhesia, free speech, and self-censorship' in H. Baltussen, P. J. Davis (eds.), *The Art of Veiled Speech: Self-Censorship from Aristophanes to Hobbes* (Philadelphia, 2015), pp. 1–17

Barnes, T. D., *Early Christian Hagiography and Roman History*, Tria Corda 5 (Tübingen, 2010)

  'Early Christian hagiography and the Roman historian', in P. Gemeinhardt and J. Leemans (eds.), *Christian Martyrdom in Late Antiquity (300–450 AD): History and Discourse, Tradition and Religious Identity*, Arbeiten zur Kirchengeschichte 116 (Berlin, 2012), pp. 15–33

  'Hilary of Poitiers on his exile', *Vigiliae Christianae* 46 (1992) 129–40

  'Himerius and the Fourth Century', *Classical Philology* 82:3 (1987), pp. 206–25.

Bartelink, G. J. M., *Quelques observations sur παρρησία dans la littérature paléo-chrétienne*, Graecitas et Latinitas Christianorum primaeva, Supplementa 3 (Nijmegen, 1979)

  'Die *Parrhesia* des Menschen for Gott bei Johannes Chrysostomus', *Vigiliae Christianae* 51 (1977) 261–72

Bastiaensen, T., Introduction to V.J.C. Hunink, E. Ketwich Verschuur, A. Akkermans, T. Bastiaensen (eds.), *Eeuwig geluk: De passie van de vroegchristelijke martelaressen Perpetua en Felicitas en drie preken van Augustinus* (Zoetermeer, 2004), pp. 9–23

Beard, M., 'The public voice of women', in M. Beard, *Women and Power* (London, 2017), pp. 1–46

Beckwith, C., *Hilary of Poitiers on the Trinity: From De Fide to De Trinitate* (Oxford, 2008)

Benz, E., 'Christus und Sokrates in der alte Kirche: Ein Beitrag zum altkirchlichen Verständnis des Märtyrers und des Martyriums', *Zeitschrift für die neutestamentliche Wissenschaft und die Kunde der älteren Kirche* 43:3–4 (1950, 1951) 195–224

Beumann, H., 'Gregor von Tours und der sermo rusticus', in H. Beumann, *Wissenschaft vom Mittelalter: Ausgewählte Aufsätze* (Cologne, 1972), pp. 41–70

Bischoff, B., *Katalog der festländischen Handschriften des neunten Jahrhunderts (mit Ausnahme der wisigotischen)*, 3 vols, Veröffentlichungen der Kommission für die Herausgabe der mittelalterlichen Bibliothekskataloge Deutschlands und der Schweiz (Wiesbaden, 1998–2014)

  Manuscripts and Libraries in the Age of Charlemagne, trans. from the German by M. Gorman, Cambridge Studies in Palaeography and Codicology 1 (Cambridge, 1995)

Bishop, E. F. F., 'The unreserved frankness of privilege', *The Bible Translator* 18 (1967) 175–8

Bohak, G., 'Acts of the Alexandrian martyrs', in R. J. Zwi Werblowsky, G. Wigoder (eds.), *The Oxford Dictionary of the Jewish Religion* (Oxford, 1997)

Bibliography

Booker, C. M., 'Iusta murmuratio: The sound of scandal in the early middle ages', *Revue Benedictine* 126:2 (2016), 236–70
  Past Convictions: The Penance of Louis the Pious and the Decline of the Carolingians (Philadelphia, 2009)
Borchart, C.F.A., *Hilary of Poitier's Role in the Arian Struggle*, Kerkhistorische Studiën 12 (The Hague, 1966)
Boshof, E., *Erzbishof Agobard von Lyon: Leben und Werk*, Kölner historische Abhandlungen 17 (Cologne, 1969)
Bourdieu, P., *Language and Symbolic Power*, ed. and introduced by J. Thomson, translated by G. Raymond and M. Adamson (Cambridge, 1991)
Bouwsma, W. J., 'Liberty in the Renaissance and Reformation', in R. W. Davis (ed.), *The Origins of Modern Freedom in the West* (Stanford, 1995), pp. 203–34
Bowersock, G. W., *Greek Sophists in the Roman Empire* (Oxford, 1969).
  Martyrdom and Rome. The Wiles lectures given at the Queen's University Belfast (Cambridge, 1995)
Boyarin, D., *Dying for God: Martyrdom and the Making of Christianity and Judaism* (Stanford, 1999)
Braund, S., 'Libertas or licentia? Freedom and criticism in Roman satire', in I. Sluiter and R. M. Rosen (eds.), *Free Speech in Classical Antiquity* (Leiden; Boston, 2004), pp. 409–28
Breukelaar, A., *Historiography and Episcopal Authority in Sixth-Century Gaul: The Histories of Gregory of Tours Interpreted in their Historical Context* (Amsterdam, 1991)
Brown, G., 'The Carolingian Renaissance', in R. McKitterick (ed.), *Carolingian Culture: Emulation and Innovation* (Cambridge, 1994), pp. 1–51
Brown, P., 'Gregory of Tours: Introduction', in K. Mitchell and I. Wood (eds.), *The World of Gregory of Tours*, Cultures, Beliefs and Traditions 8 (Leiden, 2002), pp. 1–28
  Power and Persuasion in Late Antiquity: Towards a Christian Empire. The Curti Lectures (Madison, 1992)
Brunner, K., *Oppositionelle Gruppen*, Veröffentlichungen des Instituts für Österreichische Geschichtsforschung 25 (Vienna,1979)
Buc, P., *The Dangers of Ritual: Between Early Medieval Texts and Social Scientific Theory* (Princeton Oxford, 2001)
Burns, P. C., *A Model for the Christian Life: Hilary of Poitiers' Commentary on the Psalms* (Washington, DC, 2012)
Burrus, V., *The Making of a Heretic: Gender, Authority, and the Priscillianist Controversy*, Transformations of the Classical Heritage 24 (Berkeley, 1995)
Cabaniss, A., *Charlemagne's Cousins: Contemporary Lives of Adalhard and Wala* (New York, 1967)
Cain, A., 'Vox Clamantis in deserto: Rhetoric, reproach, and the forging of ascetic authority in Jerome's letters from the Syrian desert', *Journal of Theological Studies*, n. s., 57:2 (2006), 500–25
Camargo, Martin, *Ars Dictaminis, Ars Dictandi*, Typologie des sources du Moyen Âge occidental 60 (Turnhout, 1991)
  'Latin composition textbooks', in V. Cox and J. O. Ward (eds.), *The Rhetoric of Cicero in Its Medieval and Early Renaissance Commentary Tradition*, Brill's

Bibliography

Companions to the Christian Tradition 2 (Leiden; Boston, 2006), pp. 267–88

Cameron, A., *Christianity and the Rhetoric of Empire: The Development of Christian Discourse,* Sather Classical Lectures 55 (Berkeley; Los Angeles; Oxford, 1991)

Cameron, A. and J. Long, *Barbarians and Politics and the Court of Arcadius* (Berkeley, 1993)

Campenhausen, H. von, *Die Idee des Martyriums in der alten Kirche,* new edn (Göttingen, 1964)

Canning, J., *A History of Medieval Political Thought 300–1450* (London; New York, 1996)

Carter, D., 'Citizen attribute, negative right: A conceptual difference between ancient and modern ideas of freedom of speech', I. Sluiter and R. M. Rosen (eds.), *Free Speech in Classical Antiquity* (Leiden; Boston, 2004), pp. 197–220

Chadwick, H., *Priscillian of Avila: The Occult and the Charismatic in the Early Church* (Oxford, 1976)

Chazelle, C. and C. Cubitt (eds.), *The Crisis of the Oikoumene: The Three Chapters and the Failed Quest for Unity in the Sixth-Century Mediterranean,* Studies in the early Middle Ages 14 (Turnhout, 2007)

Claassen, J.-M., *Displaced Persons: The Literature of Exile from Cicero to Boethius* (Madison, 1999)

Close, F., *Uniformiser la foi pour unifier l'Empire: La pensée politico-théologique de Charlemagne* (Brussels, 2011)

Colclough, D., *Freedom of Speech in Early Stuart England* (Cambridge, 2005)

'Parrhesia: The Rhetoric of Free Speech in Early Modern England', *Rhetorica* 17 (1999), 177–212

Constable, G., *Letters and Letter-Collections,* Typologie des sources du Moyen Âge occidental 17 (Turnhout, 1976)

Cooper, K., 'The martyr, the matrona and the bishop: The matron Lucina and the politics of martyr cult in fifth- and sixth-century Rome', *Early Medieval Europe* 8 (1999), 297–317

Copeland, R. (ed.), *Criticism and Dissent in the Middle Ages* (Cambridge, 1996)

Copeland, R. and I. Sluiter, *Medieval Grammar and Rhetoric: Language Arts and Literary Theory, AD 300–1475* (Oxford; New York, 2009)

Crook, J., *Consilium Principis: Imperial Councils and Counsellors from Augustus to Diocletian* (Cambridge, 1955)

Dam, R. van, *Saints and Their Miracles in Late Antique Gaul* (Princeton, 1993)

Dartmann, C., A. N. Pietsch and S. Steckel (eds.), *Ecclesia disputans: Die Konfliktpraxis vormoderner Synoden zwischen Religion und Politik,* Historische Zeitschrift. Supplement 67 (Berlin, 2015)

Davis, J. R., *Charlemagne's Practice of Empire* (Cambridge, 2015)

Davis, R. W. (ed.), *The Origins of Modern Freedom in the West* (Stanford, 1995)

Diem, A., 'Monks, kings and the transformation of sanctity: Jonas of Bobbio and the end of the holy man', *Speculum* 82 (2007) 521–59

Diem, A. and H. Müller, *'Vita, Regula, Sermo*: Eine unbekannte lateinische *Vita Pacomii* als Lehrtext für ungebildete Mönche und als Traktat über das Sprechen

Bibliography

(mit dem Text der *Vita Pacomii* im Anhang)', in R. Corradini, M. Diesenberger and M. Niederkorn (eds.), *Zwischen Niederschrift und Widerschrift, Forschungen zur Geschichte des Mittelalters* 18 (Vienna, 2010), pp. 223–72

Doignon, J., *Hilaire de Poitiers avant l'exile: Recherches sur la naissance, l'enseignement et l'épreuve d'une foi épiscopale en Gaule au milieu du IVe siècle* (Paris, 1971)

Dolan, A., '"You would do better to keep your mouth shut:" The significance of talk in sixth century Gaul', *Journal of the Western Society for French History* 40 (2012)

Dutton, P. E., *Charlemagne's Mustache and Other Cultural Clusters of a Dark Age* (New York; Basingstoke, 2004)

The Politics of Dreaming in the Carolingian Empire (London; Lincoln, 1994)

Dvornik, F., *Early Christian and Byzantine Political Philosophy: Origins and Background*, 2 vols (Washington. DC, 1966)

Engelberg-Pedersen, T., 'Plutarch to Prince Philopappus on how to tell a flatterer from a friend', in J. T. Fitzgerald (ed.), *Friendship, Flattery and Frankness of Speech: Studies on Friendship in the New Testament World*, Supplements to Novum Testamentum 82 (Leiden; New York; Cologne, 1996), pp. 61–79

Engels, L. J., *Fiducia dans la Vulgate: Le problème de traduction parrhesia–fiducia*, Graecitas et Latinitas Christianorum primaeva, Supplementa 1 (Nijmegen, 1964)

'Fiducia', in T. Klauser, E. Dassmann (eds.), *Reallexikon für Antike und Christentum* 7 (Stuttgart, 1969), pp. 839–77

Eynde, S. van den, '"A testimony to the non-believers, a blessing to the believers": The Passio Perpetuae and the construction of a Christian identity', in J. Leemans (ed.), *More Than a Memory: The Discourse of Martyrdom and the Construction of Christian Identity in the History of Christianity* (Leuven, 2005)

Fish, S., *There's No Such Thing as Free Speech: And It's a Good Thing Too* (Oxford, 1994)

Flierman, R. 'Religious Saxons: Paganism, infidelity and biblical punishment in the *Capitulatio de partibus Saxoniae*', R. Meens, D. van Espelo, J. Raaijmakers, I. van Renswoude et al. (eds.), *Religious Franks: Religion and Power in the Frankish Kingdoms. Studies in Honour of Mayke de Jong* (Manchester, 2016), pp. 181–201

Flower, R., *Emperors and Bishops in Late Roman Invective* (Cambridge, 2013)

Imperial Invectives against Constantius II: Athanasius of Alexandria, Hilary of Poitiers and Lucifer of Cagliari, Translated Texts for Historians 67 (Liverpool, 2016)

Fontaine, J., 'Hagiographie et politique de Sulpice Sévère à Venance Fortunat', *Revue d'Histoire de l'Église de France* 62 (1976) 113–40

Foucault, M., *Le Courage de la vérité: Le Gouvernement de soi et des autres II*, Course au Collège de France 1983–4 (Seuil, 2009)

Fearless Speech, ed. J. Parson (Los Angeles, 2001)

Fouracre, P., 'Merovingian history and Merovingian hagiography', *Past & Present* 127:1 (1990), 3–38

'The Origins of the Carolingian Attempt to Regulate the Cult of Saints', in J. Howard-Johnston, P. Hayward (eds.), *The Cult of Saints in Late Antiquity and the Early Middle Ages* (Oxford, 2000), pp. 143–65

Bibliography

'Why were so many bishops killed in Merovingian Francia?', in N. Fryde, D. Reitz (eds.), *Bishofsmord im Mittelalter – Murder of Bishops,* Veröffentlichungen des Max-Planck-Instituts für Geschichte 191 (Göttingen, 2002), pp. 13–35

Fouracre, P. and R. A. Gerberding, *Late Merovingian France: History and Hagiography 640–720* (Manchester, 1996)

Fowden, G., 'The pagan holy man in late antique society', *Journal of Hellenic Studies* 102 (1982) 33–59

Fransen, P.-I., 'Florilège pastoral tiré de Grégoire de Nazianze par Florus de Lyon', *Revue Bénédictine* 110 (2000), 86–94

Frederickson, D. E., 'ΠΑΡΡΗΣΙΑ in the Pauline Epistles', in J. T. Fitzgerald (ed.), *Friendship, Flattery and Frankness of Speech: Studies on Friendship in the New Testament World,* Supplements to Novum Testamentum 82 (Leiden; New York; Cologne, 1996), pp. 163–83

Ganz, D., *Corbie in the Carolingian Renaissance,* Beihefte der Francia 20 (Sigmaringen, 1990)

'The *Epitaphium Arsenii* and opposition to Louis the Pious', in P. Godman, R. Collins (eds.), *Charlemagne's Heir: New Perspectives on the Reign of Louis the Pious (814–840)* (Oxford, 1990), pp. 537–50

Garrison, M., 'An aspect of Alcuin: "Tuus Albinus" – peevish egotist? or *parrhesiast*?', in R. Corradini, M. Gillis, R. McKitterick, I. van Renswoude (eds.), *Ego Trouble: Authors and Their Identities in the Early Middle Ages,* Forschungen zur Geschichte des Mittelalters 15 (Vienna, 2010), pp.137–51

'Les correspondants d'Alcuin', in P. Depreux, B. Judic (eds.), *Alcuin de York à Tours: Écriture, pouvoir et résaux dans l'Europe du Haut Moyen Âge,* Annales de Bretagne et des Pays de l'Ouest 111:3 (Rennes, Tours, 2004), pp. 319–31

'Letter Collections', in M. Lapidge, J. Blair, S. Keynes (eds.), *The Blackwell Encyclopaedia of Anglo-Saxon England* (London, 1999), pp. 283–4

'Letters to a king and biblical exempla: The examples of Cathuulf and Clemens Peregrinus', *Early Medieval Europe* 7:3 (1998), 305–28

'*The social world of Alcuin:* Nicknames at York and at the Carolingian court', in L. A. J. R. Houwen, A. A. McDonald (eds.), *Alcuin of York,* Germania Latina 3 (Groningen, 1998), pp. 59–79

Gauthier, N., *L'évangélisation des Pays de la Moselle: La province romaine de Première Belgique entre Antiquité et Moyen-Age: IIIe – VIIIe siècles* (Paris, 1980)

Gemeinhardt, P. and J. Leemans, 'Christian martyrdom in late Antiquity: Some introductory perspectives', in P. Gemeinhardt, J. Leemans (eds.), *Christian Martyrdom in Late Antiquity (300–450 AD): History and Discourse, Tradition and Religious Identity,* Arbeiten zur Kirchengeschichte 116 (Berlin; Boston; 2012), pp. 1–11

George, J., 'Venantius Fortunatus: Panegyric in Merovingian Gaul', in M. Whitby (ed.), *The Propaganda of Power: The Role of Panegyric in Late Antiquity* (Leiden; Boston; Köln 1998), pp. 225–46

Glad, C. E. 'Philodemus on friendship and frank speech', in J. T. Fitzgerald (ed.), *Friendship, Flattery and Frankness of Speech: Studies on Friendship in the New Testament World,* Supplements to Novum Testamentum 82 (Leiden; New York; Cologne, 1996), pp. 39–60

Bibliography

Goetz, H.-W., 'La compétition entre catholiques et ariens en Gaule: Les entretiens religieux ("Religionsgespräche") de Grégoire de Tours', in: F. Bougard, R. Le Jan, T. Lienhard (eds.), *Agôn: La competition, Ve-XIIe siécle*, Haut Moyen Age 17 (Turnhout, 2012), pp. 183-98

Goffart, W., *Narrators of Barbarian History (AD 550–800): Jordanes, Gregory of Tours, Bede and Paul the Deacon* (Princeton, 1988)

Graver, M., *Cicero on the Emotions: Tusculan Disputations 3 and 4* (Chicago; London, 2002).

Gray, P. T. R. and M. W. Herren, 'Columbanus and the Three Chapters controversy – A new approach', *Journal of Theological Studies* n. s. 45 (1994) 160-70

Gregory, B. S., *Salvation at Stake: Christian Martyrdom in Early Modern Europe* (Cambridge, MA; London, 1999)

Grig, L., *Making Martyrs in Late Antiquity* (London, 2004)

Hafner, A., *Untersuchungen zur Überlieferungsgeschichte der Rhetorik ad Herennium*, Europäische Hochschulschriften 15, Klassische Sprachen und Literaturen 45 (Bern; Frankfurt am Main; New York; Paris, 1989)

Hahn, J., *Der Philosoph und die Gesellschaft: Selbstverständnis, öffentliches Auftreten und populäre Erwartungen in der hohen Kaiserzeit*, Heidelberger Althistorische Beiträge und Epigraphische Studien 7 (Stuttgart, 1989)

Halsall, G., 'Nero and Herod? The death of Chilperic and Gregory's writing of history', in K. Mitchell and I. Wood (eds.), *The World of Gregory of Tours*, Cultures, Beliefs and Traditions 8 (Leiden, 2002), pp. 337-50

Hanson, R. P. C., *The Search for the Christian Doctrine of God: The Arian Controversy (318–381)* (Edinburgh, 1988)

Harder, C. *Pseudoisidor und das Papsttum: Funktion und Bedeutung des apostolischen Stuhls in den pseudoisidorischen Fälschungen* (Cologne; Wiemar; Vienna, 2014)

Hargreaves, R., *The First Freedom: A History of Free Speech* (Stroud, 2002)

Harker, A., *Loyalty and Dissidence in Roman Egypt: The Case of the Acta Alexandrinorum* (Cambridge, 2008)

Hatlie, P., 'The politics of salvation: Theodore of Stoudios on martyrdom (*martyrion*) and speaking out (*parrhesia*)', *Dumbarton Oaks Papers* 50 (1996), 263-87

Heather, P., 'Themistius: A political philosopher', in M. Whitby (ed.), *The Propaganda of Power: The Role of Panegyric in Late Antiquity*, Mnemosyne, Supplementum 183 (Leiden, 1998), pp. 125-50

Heidecker, K. J., *The Divorce of Lothar II: Christian Marriage and Political Power in the Carolingian World* (Ithaca, NY; London, 2010)

Heil, U., 'The Homoians in Gaul', in G. M. Berndt, R. Steinacher (eds.), *Arianism: Roman Heresy and Barbarian Creed* (Farnham; Burlington, 2014), pp. 271-96

Heinzelmann, M., *Gregory of Tours: History and Society in the Sixth Century*, trans. C. Carroll (Cambridge, 2001)

Hen, Y., *Roman Barbarians: The Royal Court and Culture in the Early Medieval West* (New York, 2007)

'The uses of the Bible and the perception of kingship in Merovingian Gaul', *Early Medieval Europe* 7 (1998), 277-89

Bibliography

Henten, J. W. van, *The Maccabean Martyrs as Saviours of the Jewish People: A Study of 2 and 4 Maccabees*, Supplements to the Journal for the Study of Judaism 57 (Leiden; New York; Cologne, 1997)

Heydemann, G., 'Zur Gestaltung der Rolle Brunhildes in merowingischer Historiographie', in R. Corradini, R. Meens, C. Pössel, P. Schaw (eds.), *Texts and Identities in the Early Middle Ages*, Forschungen zur Geschichte des Mittelalters 13 (Vienna, 2006), pp. 73–85.

Hoffmann, H., 'Zur Mittelalterlichen Brieftechnik', in K. Repgen, S. Skalweit (eds.), *Spiegel der Geschichte: Festgabe für Max Braubach* (Münster, 1964), pp. 141–70

Hülsewiesche, R., 'Redefreiheit', *Archiv für Begriffsgeschichte* 44 (2002) 103–45

Humfress, C., *Orthodoxy and the Courts in Late Antiquity* (Oxford, 2007)

Humphries, M., 'Rufinus's Eusebius: Translation, continuation and edition in the Latin *Ecclesiastical History*', *Journal of Early Christian Studies* 16:2 (2008), 143–64

'Savage humour: Christian anti-panegyric in Hilary of Poitiers' Against Constantius', in M. Whitby (ed.), *The Propaganda of Power: The Role of Panegyric in Late Antiquity, Mnemosyne*, Supplementum 183 (Leiden, 1998), pp. 201–23

Hunink, V., 'St Cyprian, a Christian and Roman gentleman', in H. Bakker, P. van Geest, H. van Loon (eds.), *Cyprian of Carthage: Studies in his Life, Language and Thought* (Leuven, 2010), pp. 29–42

Hunter, D. G., 'Fourth-century Latin Writers: Hilary, Victornus, Ambrosiaster, Ambrose', in F. Young, L. Ayres, A. Louth (eds.), *The Cambridge History of Early Christian Literature* (Cambridge, 2004), pp. 302–17.

Hürten, H., '*Libertas* in der Patristik – *Libertas episcopalis* im Früh-mittelalter', *Archiv für Kulturgeschichte* 45 (1963) 1–14

Jacob, W., *Die handschriftliche Überlieferung der sogenannten* Historia tripartita *des Epiphanius-Cassiodor*, ed. R. Hanslik, Texte und Untersuchungen zur Geschichte der altchristlichen Literatur 59 (Berlin, 1954)

Jaeger, H., 'Parrhesia et fiducia: Etude spirituelle des mots', *Studia patristica* 1, 1 (Berlin, 1957) 221–39

Jaeger, W., *Early Christianity and Greek Paideia* (Cambridge, MA, 1965)

Paideia: The Ideals of Greek Culture, 3 vols, trans. G. Highet (Oxford, 1945)

Janson, T., *Latin Prose Prefaces: Studies in Literary Conventions*, Studia Latina Stockholmiensia 13 (Stockholm, 1964)

Jasper, D. and H. Fuhrmann, *Papal Letters in the Early Middle Ages*, History of Medieval Canon Law 2 (Washington, DC, 2001)

Johnston, E., 'Exiles from the edge? The Irish contexts of *peregrinatio*', in R. Flechner, S. Meeder (eds.), *The Irish in Early Medieval Europe: Identity, Culture and Religion* (London, 2016), pp. 37–52

Jong, M. B. de, '*Admonitio* and criticism of the ruler at the court of Louis the Pious', in F. Bougard, R. Le Jan, R. McKitterick (eds.), *La culture du haut Moyen Âge: Une question d'élites?*, Collection Haut Moyen Âge 7 (Brepols, 2009), pp. 315–38

'Becoming Jeremiah: Paschasius Radbertus on Wala, himself and others', in R. Corradini, M. Gillis, R. McKitterick, I. van Renswoude (eds.), *Ego*

Bibliography

  Trouble: Authors and Their Identities in the Early Middle Ages, Forschungen zur Geschichte des Mittelalters 15 (Vienna, 2010), pp. 244–62
 'Bride shows revisited: Praise, slander and exegesis in the reign of the Empress Judith', in L. Brubaker, J. M. H. Smith (eds.), *Gender in the Early Medieval World: East and West, 300–900* (Cambridge, 2004), pp. 257–77
  Epitaph for an Era (Cambridge, 2019)
 'Jeremiah, Job, Terence and Paschasius Radbertus: Political Rhetoric and Biblical Authority in the *Epitaphium Arsenii*, in J. L. Nelson and D. Kempf (eds.), *Reading the Bible in the Middle Ages* (London, 2015), pp. 57–76
  Paschasius Radbertus and Pseudo-Isidore: The evidence of the *Epitaphium Arsenii*, in V. L. Garver, O. M. Phelan (eds.), *Rome and Religion in the Medieval World: Studies in Honor of Thomas F. X. Noble* (Farnham, 2014), pp. 149–78
  The Penitential State: Authority and Atonement in the Reign of Louis the Pious (Cambridge, 2009)
 'The Resources of the Past: Paschasius Radbertus and his *Epitaphium Arsenii*, in S. Dusil, G. Schwedler, R. Schwitter (eds.), *Exzerpieren, Kompilieren, Tradieren: Transformationen des Wissens zwischen Spätantike und Frühmittelalter,* Millennium Studien 64 (Berlin; Boston, 2017), pp. 131–51
Jussen, B and G. Rohmann, 'Historical semantics in medieval studies: New means and approaches', *Contributions to the History of Concepts* 10:2 (2015), 1–6
Kempshall, M., *Rhetoric and the Writing of History, 400–1500* (Manchester, 2011)
 'The virtues of rhetoric: Alcuin's *Disputatio de rhetorica et de virtutibus*', *Anglo-Saxon England* 37 (2008) 7–30
Kennedy, G. A., *Classical Rhetoric and Its Christian and Secular Tradition from Ancient to Modern Times,* new edn (London, 1999)
 'Forms and functions of Latin speech', in G. M. Masters (ed.), *Medieval and Renaissance Studies* 10 (Chapel Hill, 1984), pp. 45–73
Keskiaho, J., *Dreams and Visions in the Early Middle Ages: The Reception and Use of Patristic Ideas, 400–900,* Cambridge Studies in Medieval Life and Thought, Fourth Series 99 (Cambridge, 2015)
Klassen, W., '*Parrhesia* in the Johannine Corpus', in J. T. Fitzgerald (ed.), *Friendship, Flattery and Frankness of Speech: Studies on Friendship in the New Testament World,* Supplements to Novum Testamentum 82 (Leiden; New York; Cologne, 1996), pp. 227–54
Klein, R., 'Die Kaiserbriefe des Ambrosius: Zur Problematik ihrer Veröffentlichung', *Athenaeum* n. s. 48 (1970) 335–71
Knibbs, E., 'Ebo of Reims, Pseudo-Isidore, and the date of the False Decretals', *Speculum* 92:1 (2017), 144–83
 'Pseudo-Isidore on the Field of Lies: "Divinis praeceptis" (JE †2579) as an Authentic Decretal', *Bulletin of Medieval Canon Law,* n. s. 29 (2011), 1–34
Kolb, F., 'Der Bussakt von Mailand: Zum Verhältnis von Staat und Kirche in der Spätantike', in H. Boockmann. K. Jürgensen and G. Stottenberg (eds.), *Geschichte und Gegenwart: Festschrift für K. D. Erdmann* (Neumünster, 1980), pp. 41–74
Koster, S., *Die Invektive in der griechischen und römischen Literatur,* Beiträge zur klassischen Philologie 99 (Meisenheim am Glan, 1980)

Bibliography

Kramer, R., 'Order in the church: Understanding councils and performing *ordines* in the Carolingian world', *Early Medieval Europe* 25:1 (2017), 54–69
  Rethinking Authority in the Carolingian Empire: Ideals and Expectations during the Reign of Louis the Pious (813–828) (Amsterdam, 2019)
Kreiner, J., *The Social Life of Hagiography in the Merovingian Kingdom*, Cambridge Studies in Medieval Life and Thought, Fourth Series 96 (Cambridge, 2014)
Laistner, M. L. W., 'The value and influence of Cassiodorus' *Ecclesiastical History*', *The Harvard Theological Review* 41 (1948), 51–67
Lamoureux, J. C., 'Episcopal courts in late Antiquity', *Journal of Early Christian Studies* 3 (1995), 143–67
Lanham, C. D., 'Freshman composition in the early Middle Ages: Epistolography and rhetoric before the *ars dictaminis*', *Viator: Medieval and Renaissance Studies* 23 (1992), 115–34
  'Salutatio' Formulas in Latin Letters to 1200: Syntax, Style and Theory, Münchener Beiträge zur Mediävistik und Renaissance-Forschung 22 (Munich, 1975)
Lanham, C. D., (ed.), *Latin Grammar and Rhetoric: From Classical Theory to Medieval Practice*, (London, 2002)
Lanham, R. A., *Handlist of Rhetorical Terms* (New Haven, 1983)
Lausberg, H., *Handbook of Literary rhetoric: A foundation for Literary Study*, ed. D. E. Orton, R. D. Anderson (Leiden; Boston; Cologne, 1998)
Leemans, J. (ed.), *More than a Memory: The Discourse of Martyrdom and the Construction of Christian Identity in the History of Christianity* (Leuven, 2005)
Leyser, C., *Authority and Asceticism from Augustine to Gregory the Great* (Oxford, 1980)
  'Let me speak, let me speak': Vulnerability and authority in Gregory's homilies on Ezekiel' in *Gregorio Magno e il suo tempo II: Questioni letterarie e dottrinali*, Studia Ephemeridis Augustinianum 34 (Rome, 1991) 169–82
Lössl, J., 'An early Christian identity crisis triggered by changes in the discourse of martyrdom', in J. Leemans (ed.), *More than a Memory: The Discourse of Martyrdom and the Construction of Christian Identity in the History of Christianity* (Leuven, 2005), pp. 97–119
Malherbe, A. J., 'Medical imagery in the pastoral epistles', in W. E. March (ed.), *Texts and Testaments: Critical Essays on the Bible and the Early Church Fathers* (San Antonio, 1980), pp. 19–35
Markus, R. A., *The End of Ancient Christianity*, new edn (Cambridge, 1998)
  Gregory the Great and His World (Cambridge, 1997)
Martyn, J. R. C., 'Pope Gregory the Great and the Irish', *Journal of the Australian Early Medieval Association* 1 (2005), 65–83
Mayr-Harting, H., 'Two abbots in politics: Wala of Corbie and Bernardus of Clairvaux', *Transactions of the Royal Historical Society*, Fifth Series 40 (1990), 217–37
McKitterick, R., *Charlemagne: The Formation of a European Identity* (Cambridge, 2008)
  The Frankish Church and the Carolingian Reforms, 789–895, Studies in History (London, 1977)
  History and Memory in the Carolingian World (Cambridge, 2004)
McLynn, N. B., *Ambrose of Milan: Church and Court in a Christian Capital. Transformation of the Classical Heritage* (Berkeley, 1994)

Bibliography

'A self-made holy man: The case of Gregory Nazianzen', *Journal of Early Christian Studies* 6:3 (1998), 463–83

McNamara, J. A., J. E. Halborg and E. G. Whatley, *Sainted Women of the Dark Ages* (Durham; London, 1992)

Meens, R., 'Politics, mirrors of princes and the Bible: Sins, kings and the well-being of the realm', *Early Medieval Europe* 7:3 (1998) 345–57

'The Sanctity of the Basilica of St. Martin: Gregory of Tours and the Practice of Sanctity in the Merovingian Period', in R. Corradini, R. Meens, C. Pössel, P. Shaw (eds.), *Texts and Identities in the Early Middle Ages, Forschungen zur Geschichte des Mittelalter* 13 (Vienna, 2006), pp. 345–57

Mein, A., 'Ezechiel as a priest in exile', in J. C. de Moor (ed.), *The Elusive Prophet: The Prophet as a Historical Person, Literary Character and Anonymous Artist,* Oudtestamentische Studiën 45, (Leiden; Boston; Cologne, 2001), pp. 199–213

Modéran, Y., 'L'Afrique reconquise et les Trois Chapitres', in C. Chazelle, C. Cubitt (eds.), *The Crisis of the Oikoumene: The Three Chapters and the Failed Quest for Unity in the Sixth-Century Mediterranean,* Studies in the Early Middle Ages 14 (Turnhout, 2007), pp. 39–82

Mohrmann, C., 'Episkopos-Speculator', in C. Mohrmann (ed.), *Études sur le latin des chrétiens* 4 (Rome, 1977), pp. 232–52

Momigliano, A., 'Parrhesia', in *A Patristic Greek Lexicon,* ed. G. W. H. Lampe (Oxford, 1961), pp. 1044–6

'Freedom of speech in Antiquity', in P. P. Wiener (ed.), *Dictionary of the History of Ideas: Studies of Selected Pivotal Ideas* (New York, 1973), pp. 252–63

Moorhead, J., *Justinian* (London, 1994)

Morgan, T., *Roman Faith and Christian Faith: Pistis and Fides in the Early Roman Empire and Early Churches* (Oxford, 2015)

Murphy, J. J., *Latin Rhetoric and Education in the Middle Ages and Renaissance,* Variorum Collected Studies Series (Aldershot, 2005)

Medieval Rhetoric: A Select Bibliography (Toronto, 1989)

'Quintilian's influence on the teaching of speaking and writing in the Middle Ages and Renaissance', in J. J. Murphy, *Latin Rhetoric and Education in the Middle Ages,* Variorum Collected Studies Series (Aldershot, 2005), pp. 153–83

Rhetoric in the Middle Ages: A History of Rhetorical Theory from Saint Augustine to the Renaissance (Berkeley; Los Angeles; London, 1974)

Murray, A. C., 'The composition of the Histories of Gregory of Tours and its bearing on the political narrative', in A. C. Murray (ed.), *A Companion to Gregory of Tours,* Brill's Companions to the Christian Tradition 63 (Leiden, 2015), pp. 63–101

Musurillo, H., *The Acts of the Christian Martyrs,* Oxford Early Christian Texts (Oxford, 1972)

Acts of the Pagan Martyrs, Greek Texts and Commentaries, new edn (New York, 1979)

Nelson, J. L., 'Aachen as a place of power', in M. de Jong and F. Theuws (eds.), *Topographies of Power in Early Medieval Europe* (Leiden, 2001), pp. 217–41

Bibliography

'Charlemagne and the bishops', in R. Meens, D. van Espelo, J. Raaijmakers, I. van Renswoude (eds.), *Religious Franks: Religion and Power in the Frankish Kingdoms: Studies in Honour of Mayke de Jong* (Manchester, 2016), pp. 337–55

'History-writing at the courts of Louis the Pious and Charles the Bald', in A. Scharer, G. Scheibelreiter (eds.), *Historiographie im frühen Mittelalter*, Veröffentlichungen des Instituts für Österreichischen Geschichtsforschung 32 (Vienna; Munich, 1994), pp. 435–42

'The *libera vox* of Theodulf of Orléans' in C. J. Chandler, S. A. Stofferahn (eds.), *Discovery and Distinction in the Early Middle Ages: Studies in Honor of John Contreni* (Kalamazoo, 2013), pp. 288–306

Opposition to Charlemagne. Annual Lecture, German Historical Institute London (London, 2009)

'Queens as Jezebels: Brunhild and Baltild in Merovingian History', in J. L. Nelson, *Politics and Ritual in Early Medieval Europe* (London; Ronceverte, 1986), pp. 1–48

Nie, G. de, *Views from a Many-Windowed Tower: Studies of Imagination in the Works of Gregory of Tours* (Amsterdam, 1987)

Noble, T. F. X., 'Kings, clergy and dogma: The settlement of disputes in the Carolingian world', in S. Baxter, C. E. Karkov, J. L. Nelson (eds.), *Early Medieval Studies in Memory of Patrick Wormald* (Farnham, 2009), pp. 237–52

'Secular sanctity: Forging an ethos for the Carolingian nobility', in P. Wormald, J. L. Nelson (eds.), *Lay Intellectuals in the Carolingian World* (Cambridge, 2007) 8–36

Norris, R. A., 'Apocryphal Writings and the Acts of the Martyrs', in F. Young, L. Ayres, A. Louth (eds.), *The Cambridge History of Early Christian Literature* (Cambridge, 2004), pp. 28–37

O'Hara, A., *Jonas of Bobbio and the Legacy of Columbanus: Sanctity and Community in the Seventh Century*, Oxford Studies in Late Antiquity (Oxford, 2018)

Opelt, I., 'Formen der Polemik im Pamphlet *De mortibus persecutorum*', *Jahrbuch für Antike und Christentum* 16 (1973), pp. 98–105

Die Polemik in der christlichen lateinischen Literatur von Tertullian bis Augustin (Heidelberg, 1980)

Palanque, J.-R., *Saint Ambroise et l'empire romain: Contribution à l'histoire des rapports de l'église et de l'état à la fin du quatrième siècle* (Paris, 1933)

Parkin-Speer, D., 'Freedom of speech in sixteenth-century English rhetoric', *Sixteenth Century Journal* 12 (1981) 65–72

Patzold, S., *Episcopus: Wissen über Bischöfe im Frankreich des späten 8. bis frühen 10. Jahrhunderts* (Ostfildern, 2009)

'Redéfinir l'office épiscopal: Les évêques francs face à la crise des années 820–830', in F. Bougard, L. Feller, R. Le Jan (eds.), *Les élites au haut Moyen Âge: Crises et renouvellements* (Turnhout, 2009), pp. 337–59

Peterson, E., 'Zur Bedeutungsgeschichte von *parrhesia*', in W. Koepp (ed.), *Reinhold-Seeberg-Festschrift I zur Theorie des Christentums* (Leipzig, 1929), pp. 283–97.

Pezé, W., 'Amalaire et la communauté Juive de Lyon: À propos de l'antijudaïsme lyonnais à l'époque carolingienne', *Francia* 40 (2013), 1–25

Bibliography

Le virus de l'erreur: La controverse carolingienne sur la double prédestination, Collection Haut Moyen Âge 26 (Turnhout, 2017)

Pirard, M. and B. Kindt, *Concordance of the Greek Version of the Ascetical Homilies of Isaac of Nineveh* (Louvain-la-Neuve, 2015)

Pohl, W., 'Heresy in Secundus and Paul the Deacon', in C. Chazelle and C. Cubitt (eds.), *The Crisis of the Oikoumene: The Three Chapters and the Failed Quest for Unity in the Sixth-Century Mediterranean*, Studies in the Early Middle Ages 14 (Turnhout, 2007), pp. 243–64

Pohlsander, H. A., 'A call to repentance: Bishop Nicetius of Trier to the Emperor Justinian', *Byzantion* 70:2 (2000) 456–73

Poster, C., 'A conversation halved: Epistolary theory in Greco-Roman antiquity', in L. Mitchell, C. Poster (eds.), *Letter-Writing Manuals and Instruction from Antiquity to the Present*, Studies in Rhetoric and Communication (Columbia, 2008), pp. 21–51

Raaflaub, K. A., 'Aristocracy and freedom of speech in the Greco-Roman world', in I. Sluiter and R. M. Rosen (eds.), *Free Speech in Classical Antiquity* (Leiden; Boston, 2004), pp. 41–61

Raaijmakers, J., 'I, Claudius: Self-styling in early medieval debate', *Early Medieval Europe* 25:4 (2017), 70–84.

Rädler-Bohn, E.M.E., 'Re-dating Alcuin's *De dialectica*: Or, did Alcuin teach at Lorsch', *Anglo-Saxon England* 45 (2016), 71–104

Ramsey, S., 'A reevaluation of Alcuin's *Disputatio de rhetorica et de virtutibus* as consular persuasion: The context of the late eighth century revisited', *Advances in the History of Rhetoric*, 19:3 (2016), 324–43

Rapp, C., *Holy Bishops in Late Antiquity: The Nature of Christian Leadership in an Age of Transition* (Berkeley; Los Angeles; London, 2005)

Rees, R., 'Authorizing freedom of speech under Theodosius', in D.W. P. Burgersdijk, A. J. Ross (eds.), *Imagining Emperors in the Later Roman Empire*, Cultural Interactions in the Mediterranean 1 (Leiden, 2018), pp. 289–309

Reimitz, H., *History, Frankish Identity and the Framing of Western Ethnicity, 550–850* (Cambridge, 2015)

Renswoude, I. van, 'The art of disputation: Dialogue, dialectic and debate', *Early Medieval Europe* 25:1 (2017), 38–53.

'Crass insults: Ad hominem attacks and rhetorical conventions', in U. Heil (ed.), *Das Christentum im frühen Europa: Diskurse – Tendenzen – Entscheidungen*, Millennium-Studien 75 (Berlin, 2019) pp. 171–194.

Renswoude, I. van and E. Steinová, 'The annotated Gottschalk: Symbolic annotation and control of heterodoxy in the Carolingian age', in P. Chambert-Protat, J. Delmulle, W. Pezé, J. Thompson (eds.), *La controverse carolingienne sur la prédestination: Histoire, textes, manuscrits*, Collection Haut Moyen Âge 32 (Turnhout, 2019), pp. 249–78

Reydellet, M., 'La diffusion des Origines d'Isidore de Séville au haut Moyen Âge', *Mélanges d'archéologie et d'histoire de l'école Française de Rome* 78 (1966), 383–437

La royauté dans la littérature latine de Sidoine Apollinaire à Isidore de Séville, Bibliothèque des Écoles françaises d'Athènes et de Rome 243 (Rome, 1981)

Reynolds, L. D., *Texts and Transmission: A Survey of the Latin Classics* (Oxford, 1983)

Bibliography

Rhee, H., *Early Christian Literature: Christ and Culture in the Second and Third Centuries* (London; New York, 2005)

Riché, P., *Education and Culture in the Barbarian West from the Sixth to the Eighth Century*, trans. J. J. Contreni (Columbia, 1976)

Roberts, M., 'The last epic of Antiquity: Generic continuity and innovation in the *Vita Sancti Martini* of Venantius Fortunatus', *Transactions of the American Philological Association* 131 (2001), 257–85

'Venantius Fortunatus and Gregory of Tours: Poetry and Patronage', in A. C. Murray (ed.), *A Companion to Gregory of Tours*, Brill's Companions to the Christian Tradition 63 (Leiden, 2015), pp. 35–59

Robbins, V. K., *Exploring the Texture of Texts: A Guide to Socio-Rhetorical Interpretation* (Valley Forge, 1996)

'Socio-rhetorical interpretation', in D. E. Aune (ed.), *The Blackwell Companion to the New Testament* (Chicester, 2010), pp. 192–219

Rose, E., *Ritual Memory: The Apocryphal Acts and Liturgical Commemoration in the Early Medieval West (500–1215)*, (Leiden; Boston, 2009)

Roskam, G., 'The figure of Socrates in *Acta Martyrum*', in J. Leemans (ed.), *Martyrdom and Persecution in Late Antique Christianity: Festschrift Boudewijn Dehandschutter*, Bibliotheca Ephemeridum Theologicarum Lovaniensium 260 (Leuven, 2010), pp. 241–56

Rouwhorst, G., 'The emergence of the cult of the Maccabean martyrs in late antique Christianity', in J. Leemans (ed.), *More than a Memory: The Discourse of Martyrdom and the Construction of Christian Identity in the History of Christianity* (Leuven, 2005), pp. 81–96

Rubellin, M., *Église et société chrétienne d'Agobard à Valdès* (Lyon, 2003)

Scherer, C., *Der Pontifikat Gregors IV (827–844): Vorstellungen und Wahrnehmungen päpstlichen Handelns im 9. Jahrhundert,* Päpste und Papsttum 42 (Stuttgart, 2013)

Scarpat, G., *Parrhesia: Storia del termine e delle sue tradizioni in latino* (Brescia, 1964)

Schäublin, C., 'The contribution of rhetoric to Christian hermeneutics', in C. Kannengiesser (ed.), *Handbook of Patristic Exegesis: The Bible in Ancient Christianity* (Leiden; Boston, 2006), pp. 149–63

Schieffer, R., 'Von Mailand nach Canossa: Ein Beitrag zur Geschichte der christlichen Herrscherbuβe von Theodosius der Groβe bis zu Heinrich IV', *Deutsches Archiv für Erforschung des Mittelalters* 28 (1972), 333–70

Schmude, M. P., 'Licentia', in G. Ueding (ed.), *Historisches Wörterbuch der Rhetorik* 5 (Tübingen, 2001), pp. 253–8

Simon, G., 'Untersuchungen zur Topik der Widmungsbriefe mittelalterlicher Geschichtsschreiber bis zum Ende des 12. Jahrhunderts', *Archiv für Diplomatik, Schriftgeschichte, Siegel- und Wappenkunde* 4 (1958), 52–119 and 5/6 (1959/60), 73–153

Sluiter, I. and R. M. Rosen (eds.), *Free Speech in Classical Antiquity* (Leiden; Boston, 2004)

Smit, P.-B. and E. van Urk (eds.), *Parrhesia: Ancient and Modern Perspectives on Freedom of Speech,* Studies in Theology and Religion 25 (Leiden, 2018)

Sotinel, C., 'The Three Chapters and the transformations of Italy', in C. Chazelle and C. Cubitt (eds.), *The Crisis of the Oikoumene: The Three Chapters and the Failed*

Bibliography

Quest for Unity in the Sixth-Century Mediterranean, Studies in the Early Middle Ages 14 (Turnhout, 2007), pp. 85–120.

Stancliffe, C., 'Jonas's *Life of Columbanus* and his disciples', in J. Carey, M. Herbert and P. Ó. Riain (eds.), *Studies in Irish Hagiography: Saints and Scholars* (Dublin, 2001), pp. 189–220

'Red, white and blue martyrdom', in D. Whitelock, R. McKitterick, D. N. Dumville (eds.), *Ireland in Early Medieval Europe: Studies in Memory of Kathleen Hughes* (Cambridge, 1982), pp. 21–46

St. Martin and his Hagiographer: History and Miracle (Oxford, 1983)

Starr, J. and T. Engberg-Pederson (eds.), *Early Christian Paraenesis in Context* (Berlin, 2005)

Steckel, S. 'Between censorship and patronage: Interaction between bishops and scholars in Carolingian book dedications', in S. Danielson, E. Gatti (eds.), *Envisioning the Bishop: Images and the Episcopacy in the Middle Ages,* Medieval Church Studies 29 (Turnhout 2014), pp. 103–26

Steidle, P. B., '*Parrhesia-praesumptio* in der Klosterregel St. Benedikts', *Zeugnis des Geistes: Beiheft zum 23e Jahrgang der Benediktinischen Monatschrift* (Beuron, 1947), pp. 44–61.

Sterk, A., *Renouncing the World Yet Leading the Church: The Monk–Bishop in Late Antiquity* (Cambridge, MA; London, 2004)

Stone, R., 'Kings are different: Carolingian mirrors for princes and lay morality', in F. Lachaud and L. Scordia (eds.), *Le Prince au miroir de la littérature politique de l'Antiquité aux Lumières* (Rouen, 2007), pp. 69–86

Stone, R. and C. West, *The Divorce of King Lothar and Queen Theutberga: Hincmar of Rheims's De divortio,* Manchester Medieval Sources (Manchester, 2016)

Story, J., 'Cathwulf, kingship and the royal abbey of Saint-Denis', *Speculum* 74:1 (1999), 1–21

Suchan, M., *Mahnen und Regieren: Die Metapher des Hirten im früheren Mittelalter,* Millennium-Studien 56 (Berlin, 2015)

Szakolczai, Á., *The Genesis of Modernity,* Routledge Studies in Social and Political Thought (London; New York, 2003)

Thiselton, A., *Thiselton on Hermeneutics: The Collected Works and New Essays of Anthony Thiselton* (Aldershot; Burlington, 2006)

Tierney, B., 'Freedom and the medieval church', in R. W. Davis (ed.), *The Origins of Modern Freedom in the West* (Stanford, 1995), pp. 64–100

Uhalde, K., 'Proof and reproof: The judicial component of episcopal confrontation', *Early Medieval Europe* 8:1 (1999), 1–11

Unnik, W. C. van, 'The Christian's freedom of speech in the New Testament', in *Sparsa Collecta: The Collected Essays of W. C. van Unnik,* Vol. 2, Supplements to Novum Testamentum 30 (Leiden, 1980), pp. 269–89

Vanderspoel, J., *Themistius and the Imperial Court: Oratory, Civic Duty and Paideia from Constantius to Theodosius* (Ann Arbor, 1995)

Vielberg, M., *Der Mönchsbischof von Tours im 'Martinellus': Zur Form des hagiographischen Dossiers und seines spätantiken Leitbilds,* Untersuchungen zur antiken Literatur und Geschichte 79 (Berlin; New York, 2006)

Untertanentopik: zur Darstellung der Führungsschichten in der kaiserzeitlichen Geschichtsschreibung, Zetemata, Monographien zur klassischen Altertumswissenschaft 95 (Munich, 1996)

Bibliography

Vocino, G., 'Bishops in the mirror: From self-representation to episcopal model. The case of the eloquent bishops Ambrose of Milan and Gregory the Great', in R. Meens, D. van Espelo, J. Raaijmakers, I. van Renswoude (eds.), *Religious Franks: Religion and Power in the Frankish Kingdoms. Studies in Honour of Mayke de Jong* (Manchester, 2016), pp. 331–49

Ward, G., 'Lessons in leadership: Constantine and Theodosius in Frechulf of Lisieux's *Histories*', in C. Gantner, R. McKitterick and S. Meeder (eds.), *The Resources of the Past in Early Medieval Europe* (Cambridge, 2015), pp. 68–85

Ward, J. O., *Ciceronian Rhetoric in Treatise, Scholion and Commentary*, Typologie des sources du Moyen Âge occidental 58 (Turnhout, 1995)
  'The Medieval and Early Renaissance study of Cicero's *De Inventione* and the *Rhetorica ad Herennium*: Commentaries and contexts', in V. Cox and J. O. Ward (eds.), *The Rhetoric of Cicero in Its Medieval and Early Renaissance Commentary Tradition*, Brill's Companions to the Christian Tradition 2 (Leiden; Boston, 2006), pp. 267–88

Weber, M., *The Sociology of Religion*, trans. E. Fischoff (London, 1965)

Weiler, B. 'Clerical *admonitio*: Letters of advice to kings and episcopal self-fashioning, c. 1000–1200', *History* 102:352 (2017), 553–737

Williams, D. H., 'A reassessment of the early career and exile of Hilary of Poitiers', *Journal of Ecclesiastical History* 42:2 (1991), 202–17

Wilmart, A., *Codices reginenses Latini*, 2 vols (Vatican, 1937–45)

Winter, S. C., '*Parrhesia* in acts' in J. T. Fitzgerald (ed.), *Friendship, Flattery and Frankness of Speech: Studies on Friendship in the New Testament World*, Supplements to Novum Testamentum 82 (Leiden; New York; Cologne, 1996), pp. 185–202

Winterbottom, M., 'Ad Herennium', 'Quintilian', in L. D. Reynolds (ed.), *Texts and Transmission: A Survey of the Latin Classics* (Oxford, 1983), pp. 98–100 and 332–4

Wirszubski, C., *Libertas as a Political Idea at Rome During the Late Republic and the Early Principate* (Cambridge, 1968)

Wood, I. N., *Gregory of Tours* (Oxford, 1994)
  'Letters and letter-collections from Antiquity to the early Middle Ages: The prose-works of Avitus of Vienne', in M. A. Meyer (ed.), *The Culture of Christendom: Essays in Medieval History and Commemoration of Dennis L. T. Bethell* (London, 1993), pp. 29–43
  The Missionary Life: Saints and the Evangelisation of Europe (400–1050) (London, 2001)
  'The secret histories of Gregory of Tours', *Revue Belge de Philologie et d'Histoire* 71 (1993) 253–70
  'The *Vita Columbani* and Merovingian hagiography', *Peritia* 1 (1998), 63–80

Wright, N., 'Columbanus's *epistulae*', in M. Lapidge (ed.), *Columbanus: Studies on the Latin Writings*, Studies in Celtic History (Woodbridge, 1997), pp. 29–92

Zechiel-Eckes, K., 'Ein Blick in Pseudo-Isidors Werkstatt: Studien zum Entstehungsprozess der falschen Dekretalen. Mit einen exemplarischen editor-ischen Anhang', *Francia* 28:1 (2001), 37–90
  Florus von Lyon als Kirchenpolitiker und Publizist: Studien zur Persönlichkeit eines karolingischen 'Intellektuellen' am Beispiel der Auseinandersetzung mit Amalarius (835–838) und des Prädestinationsstreits (851–855), Quellen und Forschungen zum Recht im Mittelalter 8 (Stuttgart, 1999)

Zelzer, M., '*Plinius Christianus*: Ambrosius als Epistolograph', *Studia patristica* 23 (1989) 203–8.

Bibliography

UNPUBLISHED MATERIAL

Creece, M. A., *Letters to the Emperor: Epistolarity and Power Relations from Cicero to Symmachus* (PhD thesis, St Andrews, 2006)

Langenwalter, A. B., *Agobard of Lyon: An Exploration of Carolingian Jewish–Christian Relations* (PhD thesis, University of Toronto, 2009)

Lyons, E. Z., *Hellenic Philosophers as Ambassadors to the Roman Empire: Performance, Parrhesia, and Power* (dissertation, University of Michigan, 2011)

Renswoude, I. van, *Licence to Speak: The Rhetoric of Free Speech in Late Antiquity and the Early Middle Ages* (PhD thesis, Utrecht University, 2011)

Scholten, D., *The History of a Historia: Manuscript Transmission of the* Historia Ecclesiastica Tripartita *by Epiphanius-Cassiodorus* (MA Thesis, Utrecht University, 2010)

INDEX

Aaron, priest, 105, 217
Acta Alexandrinorum, 24–25
Acts of the Apostles, 9, 25, 30, 33, 39, 51, 60
Adalhard of Corbie, abbot, 187, 193, 198–201, 202, 204, 211, 212, 214, 215–216, 219
admonitio, 95, 183, 190, 192–194, 204, 222, 247
admonition, 5, 7, 12, 43, 46, 58, 63, 74, 81, 93, 94, 95, 96, 97, 107, 108, 120–122, 124, 157, 169, 181, 182, 183, 190–194, 197, 200, 202, 207, 210, 224, 228, 241, 244
    letter of, 98, 99, 100, 159, 174, 181, 185, 187, 203, 204, 207, 210, 246
Ado of Vienne
    chronicle, 229
Aethelbald of Mercia, king, 183, 203
Aetius of Paris, archdeacon, 166
Agathon, desert father, 113, 114
Agilulf, king, 150
Agobard of Lyon, archbishop, 206–229, 230, 231, 235, 236, 237–238, 240, 245, 247
    Against the Law of Gundobad, 209
    Against the Teachings of Felix, 208, 209
    Liber apologeticus, 224–227, 228, 238
    letters of admonition, 222–224, 225, 227, 228
    On Injustices to Matfrid, 220
    On the Division of Imperial Rule, 223, 225, 233
    On the Insolence of the Jews, 220
    On the Privilege of the Apostolic See, 223, 225, 238
    On the Right Administration of Church Property, 211, 212
Agrippa, king, 10, 25
Airlie, Stuart, 206, 216
Alcuin, 190, 192, 193, 199, 203, 204, 205, 208
    letters of admonition, 186
    On Rhetoric and Virtues, 186, 217
Amalarius of Metz, bishop, 229

Ambrose of Milan, bishop, 72, 84, 87–108, 109, 118, 119, 124, 127, 128, 180, 194, 227, 242, 244, 245, 246
    Apologia David, 94, 95
    Callinicium letter, 90, 99–104, 106, 241
    Epistolae extra collectionem, 98, 103–104
    memory of, 129, 134, 175–178, 194–198, 202, 203, 204, 241, 246
    Thessalonica letter, 89, 91–99, 101, 102, 107, 108, 174, 241
Ammianus Marcellinus
    Res gestae, 65, 71, 77, 78, 165
Anthony, desert father, 114, 150, 200
Antichrist, 17, 41, 48, 49
Antiochus, king, 50, 54
Antiochus, monk, 114, 117
Antoninus Pius, emperor, 33
Aphraates, monk, 81–82
Apollonius, martyr, 29, 30
apologists, 27, 28, 29, 30, 33, 110
Apophthegmata patrum, 113
Apostolic Constitutions, 122–123
Arcadius, emperor, 68, 89, 92, 107
Ardo
    Life of Benedict, 189
Arn of Salzburg, bishop, 185, 191
Arsenius, desert father, 111, 201, 202, 203, 204
Athanasius of Alexandria, bishop, 42, 53, 54, 61, 84
    History of the Arians, 56
    Life of Anthony, 114, 150, 199–200
Athenagoras, 27, 30
audientia, 44
audientia episcopalis, 157
Augustine, bishop, 194
    City of God, 88, 90
    On Christian Doctrine, 123
Aunemund of Lyon, bishop, 136
Avitus of Vienne, bishop, 134, 158
Avitus, abbot of Micy, 167

Index

Babylas of Antioch, bishop, 117–119, 128
Benedict of Aniane, abbot, 189, 211
Bernard of Italy, king, 188, 214
Bernard of Vienne, bishop, 195, 218
Boniface IV, pope, 155, 159
Boniface, bishop, 182–183, 203, 220
   letter of admonition, 182–183, 209
Booker, Courtney, 124, 206, 233, 238
Brown, Peter, 11, 63, 64, 69, 70, 79, 88, 95, 157
Brunhild, queen, 150, 155–158, 165
Buc, Philippe, 176, 177, 178

Caesarius of Arles, 123
Caiaphas, high priest, 218, 233
Carloman I, mayor of the palace, 182
Carloman, king, 188
Cassandra, prophetess, 14
Cassian, 123
Cathwulf
   letter of admonition, 185, 192
Charlemagne, emperor, 183–186, 187, 189, 190, 192, 193, 196, 198, 199, 200, 207
Charles the Bald, emperor, 11, 195, 196, 197, 241
Chilperic I, king, 17, 161–162, 163, 165–173, 190
Chlodomer, king, 167
Chlodosinda, princess, 158
Chlotar I, king, 142
Cicero, 6, 7, 8, 10, 36, 71, 192
Clovis I, king, 148, 154, 158, 184
Collectio tripartita, 240
Columban, monk, 17, 149–154
Commodus, emperor, 1, 30, 248
Constans, emperor, 78, 199
constantia, 8, 9–10, 36–37, 38, 51, 59–60, 62, 148, 159, 193, 194, 201, 247
Constantine, emperor, 67, 69, 77, 84, 196, 199
Constantius II, emperor, 41–62, 68, 72, 73–76, 88, 89, 129, 142, 144, 199, 224, 227, 239
Copeland, Rita, 11
correctio, 169, 194, 198, 229, 247
   in rhetoric, 210
correction, 5, 8, 192, 194, 210, 228, 229
   mutual, 121, 169
   of texts, 209–210
   self-, 187
correptio, 95, 122, 169, 194
Council
   of Aachen (816), 208
   of Aachen (817), 211, 223
   of Aachen (829), 214
   of Ariminum (Rimini) (359), 43, 58
   of Arles (813), 191, 197
   of Attigny (822), 196, 211–214, 218
   of Berny-Rivière (580), 161

   of Compiègne (823), 214
   of Compiègne (833), 225, 227
   of Constantinople (359/60), 44, 45, 46, 48, 49, 55
   of Constantinople (381), 85
   of Diedenhofen (821), 211
   of Paris (361), 58, 61
   of Paris (577), 165
   of Reisbach (798), 191, 197
   of Rome (800/1), 193
   of Seleucia (359), 43, 44, 48, 58
   of Worms (829), 223
Cyprian of Carthage, bishop, 186, 194
   as martyr, 29

Dasius, martyr, 32
David, king, 95, 105, 122
De ordine palatii, 187–189, 191, 198, 215, 225
Decretum Gelasianum, 141, 195
Decretum Gratiani, 240
Desiderius of Vienne, bishop, 136
Desiderius, king, 184
Diem, Albrecht, 150, 178
Diogenes, philosopher, 118, 245
Domitian, emperor, 8
Dorotheus of Gaza
   Directions on the Spiritual Life, 114–115

Eberulf, chamberlain, 175–176
Ebo of Rheims, archbishop, 219, 228, 235
Einhard, abbot, 192, 205
   letter of admonition, 205
Elijah, prophet, 184, 192, 218, 226
Epistolae Austrasiacae, 135, 158
Esther, queen, 156
Eugenius, emperor, 98
Eulalia of Mérida, martyr, 39, 148
Eunapius of Sardis, 68, 78
   Lives of the Philosophers and Sophists, 67, 69, 71, 79, 80
Eusebius of Caesarea
   Ecclesiastical History, 23, 27, 30, 118, 164
Eutherius, chamberlain, 77–78
Ezekiel, prophet, 46, 62, 92–93, 101, 102, 122–125, 145, 167, 218, 241, 246

Facundus of Hermiane, bishop, 134, 178
familiarity, 9, 68, 69, 113–115, 116–117, 181, 188, 220
Felicitas, martyr, 35–36
Ferrandus of Carthage, deacon, 190
Festus, magistrate, 26
fides, 51, 59, 232, 241
   publica, 59, 60

Index

fiducia, 9–10, 51, 60, 62, 112, 113, 193, 194, 198, 247
Field of Lies, 230, 231, 236
Flavius Josephus, 9
Florus of Lyon, deacon, 229, 235, 240
   Collection of Sayings of Twelve Fathers, 239–240
Flower, Richard, 11, 50
Foucault, Michel, 109–110, 119, 125–126
Fouracre, Paul, 136, 148, 153
Fravitta, general, 68
Freculf of Lisieux, bishop
   Histories, 195, 197, 198
Fredegund, queen, 161, 170, 173

Garrison, Mary, 12, 153, 158, 193, 204
Genovefa, saint, 15, 17, 146, 203
Germanus of Paris, bishop, 155–158, 220
gossip, 161, 163, 174, 175, 222
Gratian, emperor, 88, 90, 98, 99, 202
Gregory IV, pope, 17, 230–242, 247
Gregory Nazianzen, bishop, 85, 120, 125, 240, 246
   Apologetica, 120, 123, 226
   autobiographical poem (*De vita sua*), 85
   On Silence, 120
   Speech to the Terrified Citizens of Nazianzus (*oratio 17*), 233–240
Gregory of Tours, bishop, 17, 135, 141, 148, 161–179, 190
   Histories, 162–179
   Life of Nicetius, 142–144, 145, 165
   Life of the Fathers, 142–145
Guntram, king, 155, 163, 171–173, 175–176, 178–179

Hadoard of Corbie, 193
Hadrian, emperor, 66
Halsall, Guy, 170–173
Heinzelmann, Martin, 171, 172
Helisachar, chancellor, 215–216, 219
Herefrid, priest, 183
Hermogenes of Corinth, 77, 78
Herod, king, 54, 171, 173
Herodian of Antioch
   History of the Empire, 1, 248
Hilary of Poitiers, bishop, 3, 12, 17, 41–62, 72, 86, 88, 89, 95, 109, 124, 128, 179, 224, 227, 242, 246
   Against Constantius, 48–58, 59, 61, 227, 239
   Commentaries on the Psalms, 59–60, 61
   memory of, 141–142, 149, 178
   Preface to Opus historicum, 58–59
   To Constantius, 44–48, 58, 60
Himarius, sophist, 77, 78

increpatio, 95, 194, 198, 247
invectives, 53–54, 56, 202, 238, 239–240
Iphicles, philosopher, 65
Isaac of Nineveh
   Mystical Treatises, 115–117, 128, 180
Isidore of Seville
   Etymologies, 186, 193, 247
Ithacius, Bishop of Ossanuba (Faro), 139–140

Jeremiah, prophet, 62, 105, 201–202, 216–217, 218, 237, 238, 246
John Chrysostom, bishop, 83, 84, 117, 127
   Discourse on Babylas, 117–120, 128
John the Baptist, 50, 54
Jonas of Bobbio
   Life of Columban, 149–150, 153
Jonas of Orleans
   Instruction for a King, 186
   On the Instruction of the Laity, 186, 195, 198
Jong, Mayke de, 11, 194, 202, 206, 222, 224, 236
Jovian, emperor, 72
Judith, empress, 225
Julian, emperor, 71, 77
Julius Rufinianus
   De figuris sententiarum et elocutionis, 2
Justin Martyr
   as apologist, 27, 30, 33
   as martyr, 30, 41
Justina, empress, 90
Justinian, emperor, 133–135, 144, 145, 150, 153, 157, 158, 195, 202

Kempshall, Matthew, 12, 202

Leidrad of Lyon, archbishop, 207–208, 211, 235
Leovigild, king, 147–148
Leudast, count, 162, 172
Leudegar of Autun, bishop, 17, 136–137, 148
Leyser, Conrad, viii, 120
Libanius, orator, 78, 83, 227
libere loqui, 36, 37, 151, 153, 159
libertas, 1, 6, 8, 10, 14, 15, 61, 122, 152, 153, 159, 193, 232, 240–242, 247
   apostolic, 50–51, 52, 57, 59, 62, 88, 128
   dicendi, 100, 128, 159, 193, 207, 244
   in rhetoric, 6
   of Christians, 38, 51–52, 59, 89, 134, 244
   of citizens, 5–6, 38, 52, 89, 100–102, 128, 244
   of martyrs, 145
   of mind, 61, 82, 144
   verbi, 233–234, 236, 239, 242, 248

Index

licentia, 6, 159, 247
  in rhetoric, 2, 6, 7–8, 193, 210, 247
  loquendi, 112
Life of Alcuin, 189
listening
  freely, 22, 136, 190
  willingly, 4, 45, 48, 66, 75, 83, 100, 104, 107, 108, 162, 172, 192, 196, 197, 210, 215, 216, 225, 230, 232
Lives of the Desert Fathers, 110, 159, 201, 202
Louis the Pious, emperor, 11, 17, 189, 196, 197, 198, 200, 230–233, 234, 236, 237, 238, 240
Lucifer of Cagliari, bishop, 42, 48, 53–54, 56, 61

Maccabean martyrs, 26, 32, 50, 52, 54
mala fama, 221, 228
manuscripts
  Bamberg, Staatsbibliothek, Msc. Patr. 7, 99
  Bamberg, Staatsbibliothek, Msc. Patr. 78, 235
  Bern, Burgerbibliothek 351, 193
  Copenhagen, Kongelige Bibliotek, fol. 22, 99
  Lyon, Bibliothèque Municipale 599, 235
  Milan, Biblioteca Ambrosiana J 71 sup, 99
  Paris, Bibliothèque nationale de France, lat. 1622, 226
  Paris, Bibliothèque nationale de France, lat. 13371, 239
  Paris, Bibliothèque nationale de France, lat. 2853, 206, 226, 237, 239
  St Petersburg, National Library of Russia, F. v.I. no. 1, 198
  St Petersburg, National Library of Russia, lat. Q. v 46, 235
  Vatican, Bibliotheca Apostolica Vaticana, Reg. lat. 141, 235, 238, 239–240
Marcellina, saint, 91, 98, 103, 104–107
Martin of Tours, bishop, 138–141, 146, 162, 164, 167–168, 172, 174, 176, 177, 178, 179
martyr acts (martyrdom narratives), 21–40, 43, 49, 51, 52, 53, 83, 110, 120, 123, 126, 141, 145, 146, 147, 148, 159
Martyrdom of Pionius and his Companions, 29, 34–35
Martyrdom of Polycarp, 21–22, 27, 28, 32
martyrs of Lyon, 30, 32
Masona of Mérida, bishop, 146–148
Matfrid of Orléans, count, 219, 220
Maximus of Ephesus, philosopher, 71
McLynn, Neil, 90
mirrors for princes, 75, 181, 183–187, 190–192, 195, 203, 204
Moses, prophet, 216
mumbling, 215, 216, 218

Nathan, prophet, 94, 95, 105
Nelson, Jinty, 11, 191, 204
Nero, emperor, 41, 49, 171, 173
Nicetius of Trier, bishop, 17, 142, 148, 177, 178, 179
  letter to Justinian, 133–135, 153, 158

On the Twelve Abuses of the World, 186
oratio libera, 6, 8, 159

Pachomius, desert father, 110
paideia, 25, 34, 35, 66–67, 77, 79, 89, 187
palace, image of, 60, 111, 116–117, 221
panegyric, 72, 73, 75, 101, 118, 119, 162
parrhesia
  as boldness, 9, 10, 22, 25, 26, 28, 36, 39, 50, 52, 53, 54, 64, 67–69, 79, 81, 83, 84, 87, 112, 114, 115, 119, 123, 128, 193, 200
  as familiarity, 9, 113–115, 116
  as pastoral frankness, 126
  as privileged access, 9, 67–69, 79, 83, 116, 128, 180
  as pure speech, 123–124, 246
  before God, 9, 31, 32, 68, 83, 88, 102, 115–117, 128, 180
  in rhetoric, 2, 6–9, 193–194, 207
  in the New Testament, 9–10
  listening with, 21, 22
  of apostles, 9, 10, 25, 26, 60, 125
  of bishops, 11, 83–86, 87, 88, 89, 92, 97, 108, 109, 117–123, 157, 198, 234, 236, 245–246
  of Christians, 39–40, 127–128, 246
  of citizens, 5, 128, 244, 249
  of holy men, 79–83, 88, 102
  of Jesus, 9, 10, 31, 39
  of Job, 117
  of martyrs, 35, 41, 43, 50, 51, 52–53, 54, 88, 109–110, 116, 119, 125, 126, 127, 128, 145, 147, 169, 199
  of monks and ascetics, 109–126, 200, 246
  of philosophers, 1, 5, 62, 63–77, 79, 88, 128, 245, 246
  of Socrates, 33, 34–35, 39, 70, 124
  open, plain and clear, 6, 9, 10, 30–32, 39
parrhesiast, 5, 14, 88, 108, 227, 245, 246
Passio of Leudegar, 136–137
Passio of Perpetua and Felicitas, 35–37
Paul, apostle, 25, 26, 30, 59, 60, 121
Paul of Mérida, deacon
  Lives of the Holy Fathers of Mérida, 146–148
Paulinus of Milan
  as secretary of Ambrose, 89, 98, 103
  Life of Ambrose, 177, 195

277

Index

Paulinus of Perigueux
Life of Martin, 140
penance, 105, 118, 119
   of Louis the Pious, 196–201, 206, 211, 225, 226, 228, 233, 237
   of Theodosius, 96–97, 107, 177, 196
Perpetua, martyr, 3, 14, 17, 35–37, 41
Philip the Arab, emperor, 118
Philo of Alexandria, 9, 116
Philostratus
Lives of the Sophists, 66, 78
Pionius, martyr, 17, 30, 34–35
Polycarp, martyr, 17, 21–22, 27, 32, 41
Pomerius, grammarian, 123
Praejectus of Clermont, bishop, 136, 137
praesumptio, 112, 151, 160, 234
Praetextatus of Rouen, bishop, 165–170, 172, 174
Priscillian of Avila, bishop, 139, 168
Priscus of Epirus, philosopher, 71
privileged access, 31, 44, 64, 67–69, 76, 79, 82, 83, 84, 90, 102, 107, 116, 128, 145, 180, 220
prophetic speech, 60, 93, 94–95, 103, 107, 108, 122, 124, 125, 202, 218–219, 222, 247
Proverbia Graecorum, 184
Prudentius
Crowns of Martyrdom, 39, 148
Pseudo-Isidorean decretals, 235–236

Quintianus of Rodez, bishop, 144
Quintilian
Institutes of Oratory, 2, 6, 8, 12, 47, 54, 193

Radbert of Corbie
Epitaph for Arsenius, 193, 201–203, 236
Life of Adalhard, 199–201
Rapp, Claudia, 11, 63, 85–86
Reimitz, Helmut, 164, 167
religious toleration, 63, 75, 89, 99
Remigius of Rheims, bishop, 154, 158, 184
repentance, 87, 94, 133, 156, 182, 201, 226
Rhetorica ad Herennium, 7–8, 13, 47, 193
Rufinus of Aquileia
   as translator, 23, 120, 164, 196, 234, 235, 236–237, 238, 240
   Ecclesiastical History, 23, 120, 164, 196
Rufinus, advisor of Theodosius, 68
Rufinus, rhetorician, 34
Rule of Basil of Caesarea (Asketikon), 121
Rule of Benedict, 112–113
rumour, 50, 69, 74, 99, 152, 154–157, 161, 163, 165, 166, 173–175, 181, 182, 191, 203, 212, 219–222, 225, 228
Rutilius Lupus
De figuris sententiarum, 7, 12, 47

Salvius of Albi, bishop, 170
Samuel, prophet, 190
Sayings of the Desert Fathers, 117
secrets, 77, 116, 117, 173–175, 180
Sedulius Scotus
   notebook (*Collectaneum*), 193, 195
   On Christian Rulers, 195, 196, 198
Seneca, 8, 10, 95
Sigebert I, king, 149, 155, 156, 164
Sigobrand of Paris, bishop, 136
silence, 41, 49, 50, 51, 102, 115, 123, 125, 166, 199, 201, 216, 218, 233, 241
   of ascetics, 119–122
   of desert fathers, 110–111
   of Jesus, 25, 26, 31, 112
   of monks, 111–113
silence (verb), 1, 35, 38, 94, 102, 108, 151, 152
slander, 34, 50, 152, 161, 172, 173, 222, 225, 228
Smaragdus, abbot
Royal Way, 186
Socrates, church historian, 63
   Ecclesiastical History, 79, 117
Socrates, philosopher, 33, 34–35, 37, 39, 70, 72, 124
Sopater, philosopher, 67, 69
Sozomen, church historian
   Ecclesiastical History, 63, 79, 80, 82, 83, 84, 87–88, 90, 97, 117, 195
speech impediment, 136–137, 216–217, 218
Stephen, proto-martyr, 33, 35, 37, 39
Sterk, Andrea, 80, 85–86
Suetonius
Lives of the Caesars, 6, 8
Sulpicius Severus
   Dialogues, 138–140, 167, 168, 202
   Life of Martin, 138, 140, 141, 146, 159
Sunna of Mérida, bishop, 147
Symmachus, senator, 101
Synesius of Cyrene, bishop, 68, 85, 92, 227

Tacitus, 6, 8, 126, 165
Tertullian, 27, 35, 194, 226
Tertullus, orator, 217
Themistius, court philosopher, 63, 64, 72–76, 78, 88, 89, 99, 180
   Panegyric to Constantius II, 72–75, 144
Theoderet
   Ecclesiastical History, 68, 80, 90, 117
Theodosius I, emperor, 17, 68, 72, 85, 87–108, 111, 118, 128, 174, 180, 201, 227, 244
   memory of, 129, 134, 176–178, 194–198, 201, 202, 204, 241–242, 245
Theodulf of Orleans, 186, 190, 193, 204, 205
Theudebert, king, 142, 158, 177

278

Index

Theuderic I, king, 142, 143
Theuderic II, king, 149
Trajan, emperor, 98
Tripartite History, 194–198, 201, 202–203, 204, 241

Valens, emperor, 63, 72, 75, 81, 82
Valentinian I, emperor, 65, 138, 146, 172
Valentinian II, emperor, 88, 90, 98, 101
Venantius Fortunatus
  Life of Hilary, 61, 141–142, 149, 178
  Life of Martin, 141
  Panegyric to Chilperic, 162

Verba seniorum
  attributed to Pelagius I, 111, 113
  attributed to Rufinus, 111
Vespasian, emperor, 6, 8
Vielberg, Meinolf, 15, 78, 167

Waifarus of Aquitaine, count, 184
Wala, abbot, 193, 201–202, 204, 214, 215–216, 219, 231
watchman, 92–93, 101, 122–125, 145, 166, 167, 241, 246
Wilmart, André, 238, 239
Wood, Ian, 158, 173–175, 185